A PLACE
CALLED
YELLOWSTONE

ALSO BY RANDALL K. WILSON

America's Public Lands:
From Yellowstone to Smokey Bear
and Beyond

A PLACE
CALLED
YELLOWSTONE

The Epic History of the
World's First National Park

Randall K. Wilson

COUNTERPOINT
CALIFORNIA

A PLACE CALLED YELLOWSTONE

First Counterpoint edition: 2024

Library of Congress Cataloging-in-Publication Data
Names: Wilson, Randall K., 1966- author.
Title: A place called Yellowstone : the epic history of the world's first national park / Randall K. Wilson.
Other titles: Epic history of the world's first national park
Description: First Counterpoint edition. | Berkeley, California : Counterpoint, 2024. | Includes bibliographical references and index.
Identifiers: LCCN 2024010184 | ISBN 9781640096653 (hardcover) | ISBN 9781640096660 (ebook)
Subjects: LCSH: Yellowstone National Park—History. | National parks and reserves—United States—History. | United States. National Park Service—History.
Classification: LCC F722 .W55 2024 | DDC 978.7/52—dc23/eng/20240301
LC record available at https://lccn.loc.gov/2024010184

Jacket design by Nicole Caputo
Jacket image © Dukas Presseagentur GmbH / Alamy
Book design by Laura Berry

COUNTERPOINT
Los Angeles and San Francisco, CA
www.counterpointpress.com

Printed in the United States of America

1 3 5 7 9 10 8 6 4 2

For Suzanne M. Horbury and Keith E. Wilson

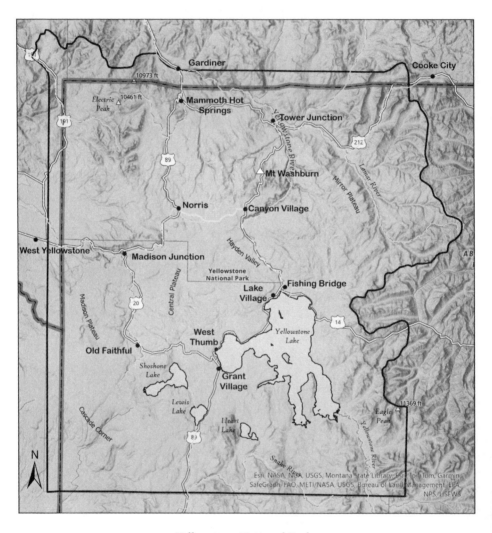

Yellowstone National Park

The Crow country is exactly in the right place. Everything good is to be found there.

— APSÁALOOKE (CROW) CHIEF EELÁPUASH,
IN A SPEECH TO THE ROCKY MOUNTAIN
FUR COMPANY, C. 1833[1]

The Yellowstone Park is something unique in the world as far as I know. Nowhere else in any civilized country is there to be found such a tract of veritable wonderland made accessible to all visitors.

—PRESIDENT THEODORE ROOSEVELT,
APRIL 24, 1903

Contents

PART FOUR: YELLOWSTONE IN THE MODERN WORLD

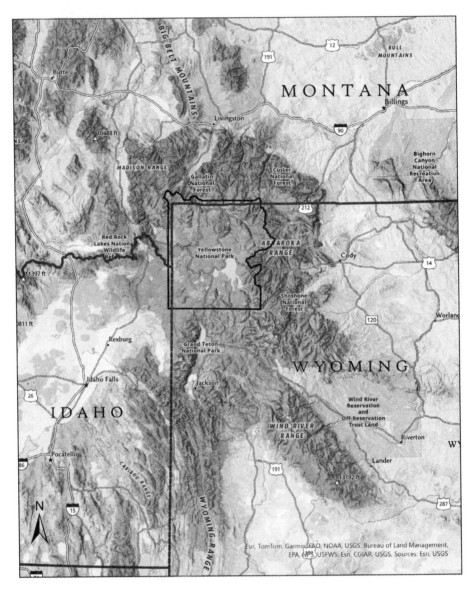

Yellowstone National Park and Beyond

Preface

DRIVING WEST THROUGH WYOMING ON INTERSTATE 80, SOME-where between Cheyenne and Rawlins, there's a moment when anyone heading toward Yellowstone National Park has the same realization: Yellowstone is far away. And not just a little bit. It is remarkably distant from just about everywhere and everyone else in the continental United States.

It wasn't always this way. For more than 11,000 years, Native Americans treated Yellowstone as a homeland, a place treasured for its abundant high-quality obsidian, seasonal hunting and gathering, and the spiritual and medicinal value of its geothermal features. Yellowstone wasn't on the fringes of society but at the center of it.

However, for Euro-American explorers and settlers arriving in the early to mid-1800s, Yellowstone's long winters and high elevation meant it was generally avoided, even unknown. Ecologically speaking, this was a net positive, protecting the area from the logging, mining, and settlement that scarred so many other landscapes. This relative isolation allowed Yellowstone to persist as both an Indigenous territory and wildlife refuge until the 1870s.

But this remoteness also meant that visiting the park has always required a rather long and difficult journey for American citizens, the vast majority of whom reside east of the Mississippi, south of Denver, or along the West Coast. Nonetheless, they have come; over 4 million people annually in recent years. And the numbers keep growing.

This book is about how such a faraway place evolved into a national icon and, in the process, fundamentally shaped the way Americans think about, value, and interact with nature. Just as the National Mall in Washington, D.C., serves as a touchstone for political discourse, Yellowstone has done the same for environmental conservation.

Encompassing a 2.2 million–acre chunk of northwestern Wyoming and spilling into narrow strips of both Idaho and Montana, Yellowstone National Park is named for the major river running through it. The Yellowstone River was originally called Roche Jaune by eighteenth-century French fur trappers. This moniker was derived from the Minnetaree (or Siouan Hidatsa) people, who referred to it as *Mi-tse-a-da-zi* ("Rock Yellow River"), a reference to the colored bluffs along the river's banks as it flows through eastern Montana to join with the Missouri. The Apsáalooke (Crow) people knew it as *E-chee-dick-karsh-ah-shay*, translating to "Elk River," likely due to its alignment with the seasonal migration route of the great elk herds of the Northern Rockies. Nonetheless, in 1798, English geographer and surveyor David Thompson, working for the North West Company of fur traders, adopted the name Yellow Stone from the French translation, which, in time, evolved into Yellowstone.[1]

Since its founding, the park has been called many other things: Wonderland, America's Serengeti, the Crown Jewel of the National Parks, and America's Best Idea. As the forerunner to the enormously popular national park system, Yellowstone remains one of the few entities capable of bridging ideological divides in the United States. But its history is also filled with exclusion and conflict, setting precedents for Native American land dispossession, land-rights disputes, and prolonged legal battles over wildlife. Its legacies are both celebratory and problematic. The story of Yellowstone is the story of the nation itself.

The following account spans the full arc of Yellowstone's history: starting from its geological foundations and role as an Indigenous homeland, through its exploration and discovery by Euro-Americans, to its establishment and development as a national park in the modern era. Along the way, it illuminates how this extraordinary landscape became one of the most famous and influential places on earth.

A place called Yellowstone.

Part One

FOUNDATIONS

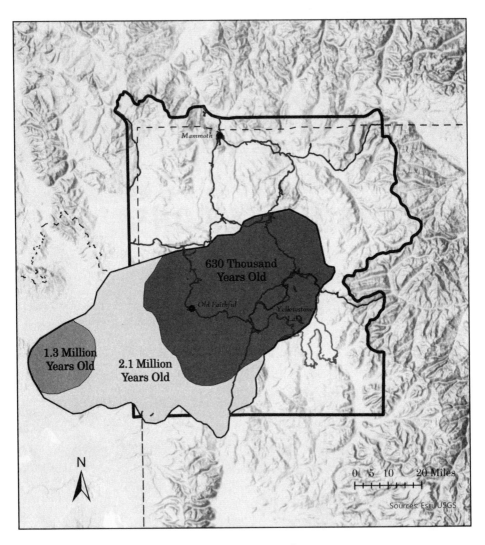

Major calderas in the Greater Yellowstone region

Indigenous Territories in the Greater
Yellowstone region, circa 1870

The Day the Earth Screamed

(1959 AND 2.1 MILLION YEARS AGO)

ON THE EVENING OF MONDAY, AUGUST 17, 1959, YELLOWSTONE National Park lay under a gorgeous star-filled sky. The late-summer moon shone especially bright, reflecting off the rivers, springs, and geysers.

In the recreational hall near Old Faithful Inn, tourists gathered for the annual beauty pageant for female park employees.[1] The gender roles of the 1950s were in full force: contestants started out in formal evening gowns before competing in talent, trivia, and even swimsuit rounds. The audience watched, eager to see who would be crowned 1959's Miss Yellowstone, or the runner-up, Miss Lake Hotel.[2]

Twenty-five miles north, at a lookout station situated high on Mount Holmes, a nineteen-year-old fire spotter scanned the forested landscape. At 10,335 feet, the peak was one of the highest points in the Gallatin Range, providing an expansive view of the western side of the park. With a final glance at the clear night sky, he prepared for bed.[3]

Just beyond the park boundary near the town of West Yellowstone, where the Madison River flows out of the Hebgen Lake dam, more than forty families were settling in for the night.[4] These included Irene and Parley "Pud" Bennett and their four children, visiting from Coeur d'Alene, Idaho, who set up camp just beyond Rock Creek Campground. Given the beautiful evening, they decided to sleep outside under the stars.

Down in the campground itself, Ray and Myrtle Painter, from Ogden, Utah, along with their three children, sixteen-year-old Carole and twelve-year-old blonde twins, Anne and Anita, parked their trailer into one of the last open spots by the river. Ray looked forward to a morning of fishing in one of the nation's best trout streams.

Around 11:30 p.m., with the kids finally asleep, Myrtle walked down to the river's edge to wash her hair. The serene night gave no indication of what was to about to happen.

In fact, the few warnings that did exist had been discarded as irrelevant long ago.

* * *

Almost a century earlier, in late August 1870, Lieutenant Gustavus Cheyney Doane of the U.S. Second Cavalry out of Fort Ellis, Montana Territory, leaned sharply forward in his saddle as his horse lurched its way up the slopes of what would be christened that same day as Mount Washburn. Doane was leading the military escort for the Washburn Expedition to Yellowstone. He was also the only member of the party with training in geological science. As he reached the summit and took in the full vista, he realized what this fantastical landscape represented.

That evening by the campfire, Doane made the following entry in his journal:

> The view from the summit is beyond all adequate description . . . Filling the whole field of vision, and with its boundaries in the verge of the horizon, lies the great volcanic basin of the Yellowstone. Nearly circular in form, from 50 to 75 miles in diameter . . . a single glance at the Interior slopes of the ranges shows that . . . the great basin has been formerly *one vast crater of a now extinct volcano.*[5]

Doane was not the first to notice this. In 1805, the first American governor of the Louisiana Territory sent a roughly drawn map on animal skin to President Thomas Jefferson that identified the presence of a "volcano" near the vicinity of the modern-day park. But Doane's report was the first published and credible account describing Yellowstone as a *caldera*: the colossal crater left behind after a massive volcanic eruption. His observations were confirmed a year later by

Dr. Ferdinand Hayden, the leader and namesake of the 1871 Yellowstone Expedition:

> The basin has been called by some travelers the vast crater of an ancient volcano . . . Indeed the geysers and hot springs of this region, at the present time, are nothing more than . . . the escape-pipes or vents for those internal forces which once were so active, but are now continually dying out.[6]

Though both men were generally correct, they each made one glaring error. The volcanic and other geologic forces lying beneath Yellowstone were anything but "extinct" or "dying out." On the contrary, they were—and continue to be—very much alive.

* * *

Back at the Old Faithful Recreation Hall, the audience applauded the newly announced Miss Yellowstone 1959. At 11:37 p.m., a sudden violent rumbling shuddered through the building. The beauty pageant came to an abrupt halt as the ground began to shake, timbers creaked, and wall hangings fell and shattered on the floor.

Some 500 panicked tourists rushed for the doors. Outside, Old Faithful and other geysers throughout the Lower Geyser Basin—some of them dormant for decades—began erupting all at once. At the Old Faithful Inn, water pipes broke and spurted. People in bathrobes climbed out of windows, and the stone chimney in the dining room collapsed to the floor. Visitors piled into cars and frantically tried to escape. But with rockslides closing the road to West Yellowstone, cars soon clogged the roads in all other directions, snaking toward the north and south park exits.

Up on Mount Holmes, the young fire spotter was thrown from his bed onto the hard wooden floor. He scrambled to his feet and rushed to look outside, straining to keep his balance. In the distance, he saw a massive plume of dust or smoke rising in the moonlight near Hebgen Lake. And in the lake itself, he could just make out what looked like a thin pencil line moving laterally across the dark waters.

Though he didn't realize it at the time, the plume was the airborne debris from a massive landslide, one caused by an earthquake in the Madison River Canyon that measured 7.3 on the Richter scale. And that thin line was the crest of a twenty-foot tidal wave.[7]

For campers in the canyon below, there was no time for observation, nor even panic. Without warning, the quiet evening was torn by a thunderous sound like 1,000 freight trains. The ground beneath trailers and tents rippled and shook. Just opposite the campground, a landslide came careening down the north face of the canyon, pulling 80 million tons of rocks, soil, and trees over 1,000 feet in a matter of seconds.[8] The slide was powerful enough to generate hurricane-strength winds in front of it. And when the debris slammed into the water, the force of it emptied the riverbed, sending thirty-foot waves in each direction.

Myrtle Painter sat by the riverside wetting her hair. Before she could comprehend what was happening, a rushing wall of wind and water picked her up and flung her down the rocky shore. Her daughter Carole, who was sleeping in the car with the family dog, woke moments before the vehicle was lifted, slammed into a tree, and flung spinning into the river. Water rushed in through the shattered windows. Carole managed to climb out of the sinking car and wade safely to shore. But her mother and the trailer containing the rest of her family were nowhere to be seen.

The same towering mass of wind and waves also hit the Bennett family. Irene was lifted and thrown across the river like a rag doll. Her husband tried desperately to hang on to a small pine moments before he and his children were swept away. Throughout the canyon and along the shores of Hebgen Lake, cars, trailers, and tents were thrown through the air, crushed by falling boulders and trees, or flung into the water.

And just as quickly, the violence stopped. For a few moments all was silent. Then, little by little, a small but growing chorus of voices began to cry for help.

* * *

In the aftermath, Irene Bennett regained consciousness and found herself battered and naked, pinned face down in the mud under a large tree. Shaking with cold, covered in blood and mud, she slowly dug her way out, praying for help and calling out for her children.

Meanwhile, Carole Painter walked the debris-littered riverbank searching for her family. In the distance, she spotted someone sitting on a twisted mound of boulders and vegetation. It was her mother. Myrtle could barely move. She had suffered a collapsed lung, a multitude of bruises and cuts, and a nearly severed arm. Carole helped her mother slowly climb up and away from the rising waters.

Seeing a lantern light on the hillside above her, Carole called out for help: "My mother's lost her arm. Don't leave us, please."[9]

In the darkness, she heard a woman's reassuring voice call back, "Maybe I can help."

It was a nurse from Billings, Montana, named Tootie Greene.

Up on the ridge, a massive tree had come crashing down on the Greene family's tent, but they all escaped without serious injury. Ray and Tootie Greene had pulled their nine-year-old son from the wreckage and rushed to their car, hoping to drive back to the road. But the debris stranded it in place. Instead, hearing cries for help down below, the couple lit a camping lantern and began gathering supplies to aid those in need. As a registered nurse, Tootie Greene quickly found herself at the center of the rescue effort.

Farther down the shoreline, the Painter family was reunited. Carole Painter found her twin sisters with only minor injuries near the remains of their trailer, which were sinking in the dark water. Even their father survived. As for the Bennett family, Irene was ultimately rescued by her eldest son, sixteen-year-old Phil, who had a badly broken leg. But the rest of the Bennett family—Irene's husband and three other children—were lost during the disaster.

* * *

The 7.3-magnitude Yellowstone earthquake was the largest ever recorded in the Rockies. It was detected over 700 miles away in cities like Denver and Seattle. Aftershocks continued for days. As late as 1964, a shock of magnitude 5.8 was designated as an aftershock from the initial quake.[10] But neither the great size nor intensity of the 1959 event would have been possible without Yellowstone's volcanic geology.

Yellowstone is not just any volcano. It is the largest and most powerful active volcanic center in North America and one of the two largest on the planet.[11] The oldest and largest eruption at Yellowstone took place 2.1 million years ago, during the Pleistocene epoch.[12] It was a time when mastodons, saber-tooth tigers, and massive 2,000-pound ground sloths roamed the landscape under shadows cast by the eighteen-foot wingspans of vulture-like *teratons* soaring high above.

That first eruption may have begun with the slightest of tremors: a subtle vibration flowing across the forest floor, shimmering up tree trunks, along branches, and out to the tip of each limb. And just as suddenly, stillness, the event detectable only by fine ripples across the otherwise-static waters of a nearby pond. But even this would have been enough to emit an ancient message to all wildlife who could sense it: *Flee!*

Over the next hours, days, or even years, the rumblings continued. Each time, they lasted a little longer, shook the ground with greater intensity than before. Until, one day, it happened. The countdown hit zero, and one of the largest, most powerful volcanos in the world exploded. The earth opened up, arched its spine, and unleashed a blood-curdling scream.

Deafening noise. Blinding, incinerating heat. A release of power beyond any scale of human experience. The eruption remade the continent: Erasing all life in its immediate path. Pulverizing, clogging, and burying the old topography. Blotting out the sun. Altering the climate.

The volcano literally resculpted the landscape, swallowing entire mountains. Scientists postulate that before this first mega-eruption, there were mountains standing where Yellowstone Lake resides today and the Teton Range extended northward beyond Jackson Lake. In fact, the entire area of modern-day Yellowstone National Park was once as mountainous as the surrounding Absaroka or Gallatin Ranges.

The most conservative estimate of this first Yellowstone mega-eruption is that it released about 600 cubic miles of debris. This is roughly 2,400 times the amount of debris from the 1980 eruption of Mount Saint Helens, which killed fifty-nine people and damaged much of eastern Washington State. The largest recorded eruption in human history, the 1815 Tambora eruption in Indonesia, triggered a global "volcanic winter" when it emitted thirty-six cubic miles of debris, less than 6 percent of Yellowstone's. Some scientists argue that the

Yellowstone blast *could* have been over three times larger still. If true, it would be the largest volcanic eruption known to science.[13]

The forces behind this mega-eruption also had other critical effects on the landscape. The "hot spot" that provided a pathway for molten magma to travel from deep inside the earth to the surface also allowed magma to accumulate beneath Yellowstone, creating a massive 300-mile-diameter bulge that pushed the entire Yellowstone Plateau upward nearly 1,700 feet. This abnormal rise in elevation not only produced Yellowstone's long winters (and ice cap during the last ice age) but also served to fracture and deepen existing geologic faults in the region. Consequently, the 1959 quake was much more severe than it otherwise would have been.[14]

Since that first super-eruption, there have been two more of comparable size, roughly 1.3 million years ago and 630,000 years ago. If this trend continues, with mega-eruptions taking place every 600,000 to 700,000 years, then Yellowstone is due for another major event. But whether it happens tomorrow, in 50,000 years, or never transpires, no one can say. What we do know is that Yellowstone's volcanic geology not only refashioned the landscape but also continues to power the geysers, hot springs, and mud pots that attract so many visitors to the park each year.

* * *

All told, twenty-eight people lost their lives to the 1959 earthquake, either during the night or afterward at the hospital, like Myrtle Painter, who succumbed to her injuries four days later.[15] News of the Yellowstone quake made many in the country acknowledge, for the first time, a fundamental truth: the park was more than just a vacation destination or national symbol. It was also home to a unique and powerful geology that, despite its dangers, also helped to explain thousands of years of human history in the region.

During the westward expansion of the United States in the nineteenth century, the high elevation and harsh winters of the Upper Yellowstone kept explorers, miners, and settlers at bay. Lewis and Clark, seeking a water route to the Pacific and passage across the Continental Divide, had little reason to wander into the Yellowstone region. By the 1840s, settlers on the Oregon Trail or miners seeking riches in the California goldfields found more favorable paths to the south. By keeping the area "off the map" for white pioneers, Yellowstone's volcanic geology allowed it to evolve into a safe haven for wildlife while those same species faced potential extinction elsewhere.

For Native Americans, Yellowstone's unique landscape had the opposite effect. For thousands of years, the area served as a territorial homeland, a vital stop in the annual migrations of Indigenous hunting and gathering societies. But before this could transpire, the half-mile-thick block of ice sitting atop the Upper Yellowstone Plateau needed to melt. And approximately 12,000 years ago, that's precisely what happened.

Homeland

(13,000 YEARS AGO TO AD 1800)

BENEATH A SMALL OUTCROPPING OF PINES ON THE EDGE OF A narrow ravine, a hunter stood concealed as snowmelt dripped steadily from the needles onto the damp, cool earth. Before him, a small herd of woolly mammoths approached, grazing at a leisurely pace. Slowly, the massive creatures entered the ravine and worked their way down to a meandering stream. In the rear of the group, an older mammoth struggled with a limp. The hunter waited as the creatures passed. Suddenly, he moved out from the tree cover, arched back his arm, and flung the atlatl. The deadly projectile plunged deep into the flesh of his target. On cue, the hunter's companions on the far side of the ravine launched their own weapons and charged forward with spears. The herd scattered in confusion and the injured mammoth fell to the ground. The hunt was a success.

Extracting his projectile from the carcass, the first hunter sat for a moment to rest. Then suddenly, he froze, sensing a new presence in the vicinity. Appearing one by one over the rise, a pack of six dire wolves confronted the hunters. The wolves, like the humans, had been tracking the mammoth herd over the past few days. Unable to make a kill of their own, they now turned their attention to the fresh carcass on the ground. Teeth bared and growling, the pack crept forward as the hunters reached once more for their spears. The battle was fierce, but when it was over two wolves lay dead. One man was down with severe wounds, but the rest of the hunters escaped with only minor

13

injuries. Most importantly, they had succeeded in defending their kill. The success of this hunt would help ensure survival of the clan through the months ahead.

Thirteen thousand years ago, tracking down prey on the grassy foothills of what is now Montana required stealth, strategy, and enormous skill. But hunters of the early Holocene also benefitted from a critical technological advance: projectile points made of obsidian, a form of volcanic glass that in the hands of expert artisans could produce a blade sharper than surgical steel.[1] Typically two to four inches long and one or two inches wide, with a telltale thin plate at the base, the points were bound to a bone rod foreshaft that could be hurled with a throwing staff known as an atlatl or attached to a long spear. Obsidian could also be fashioned into knives, which the hunters now used to begin field-dressing the fallen mammoth.

Over the following days, other clan members arrived to help process the meat, hides, and bones of the fallen animals and to care for the injured hunter. In time, they loaded their travois—sleds pulled by dogs or humans—and began the long journey to the fall encampment. When the hunters arrived at the main camp, the mood was solemn. A one-year-old boy had died. His position in the clan is unknown, but the massive burial included hundreds of weapons and tools, suggesting that he may have been the son of a chieftain or spiritual leader. A thick layer of red ochre dust was placed over the body and the artifacts before the grave was sealed with earth and stone.[2] To date, the burial is unique. Nowhere else in North America have researchers found tools from this time period along with human remains. This singular quality, along with the large number of artifacts, have led archeologists to wonder if the boy's passing signified something more—possibly a spiritual omen, or a sign that the time had come for a new migration. Or perhaps it was simply a response to an intense loss from a tight-knit community.

* * *

In 1968, workers discovered the burial site on private ranch land owned by the Anzick family, located near the town of Wilsall, Montana, about thirty miles north of Livingston. Consequently, archeologists commonly refer to the child as the "Anzick boy," though he is also known as the "Clovis boy." Radiocarbon dating placed the boy's death at roughly 10,700 years ago, though more recent analyses using tree-ring data pushed it back to nearly 13,000 years ago.[3] A DNA analysis completed in 2014 showed that the Anzick boy is related to Indigenous people from Siberia and that he is an ancestor to essentially all Native Americans in the Western Hemisphere.[4]

The projectile points and other material artifacts found in the burial represent what scientists call the Clovis culture, a name for people using common forms of stone tools from roughly 12,000 to 10,500 years ago. Named after a site near Clovis, New Mexico, where the materials were first discovered in 1929, Clovis artifacts have since been found at sites from Mexico to Canada. Organic matter on projectile points indicate that Clovis peoples hunted woolly mammoths, ancient bison, horses, canids (possibly dogs or wolves), single-humped camels, and other now-extinct megafauna, along with smaller game. As hunter-gatherers, they also collected edible and medicinal plants and mined obsidian and quartz to produce meticulously crafted stone weapons and tools.

The peoples who used Clovis artifacts first arrived in North America during the Late Pleistocene era, often referred to as the last ice age. At that time, the expansion of glaciers and ice sheets in the preceding millennia had lowered the sea level enough to create a land bridge across the Bering Strait, offering a potential route for human migration from Siberia to North America (though people may have also traveled by boat). Over the next 1,000 years, the earth's climate began to warm and the glaciers receded, causing the sea level to rise once more. In Yellowstone, the half-mile-thick ice cap eventually melted away, providing access to the area comprising modern-day Yellowstone National Park.

The Anzick child and his family, along with their descendants, not only represent some of the earliest inhabitants of North America but were likely the first to see and claim Yellowstone as a homeland. After all, the burial site is located within eighty miles of the national park border and less than twenty-five miles from the Yellowstone River. The Colby site, another Clovis-era locale, lies roughly one hundred miles east of Yellowstone and contains the bones of seven woolly mammoths.

Archeologists surmise that as hunter-gatherers, Clovis peoples traveled widely throughout the northern Great Plains and Rocky Mountains, including into Yellowstone, as they traded, searched for minerals, and followed the seasonal migrations of wild game.

In 2007 and again in 2013, archeologist Douglas MacDonald and his team found Clovis projectile points in two locations within park boundaries: on the south shore of Yellowstone Lake and along the Yellowstone River near the town of Gardiner, Montana.[5] These findings place Clovis peoples within the modern-day park at least 11,000 years ago.

These ancestral Native Americans would have been the first to walk the shores of Yellowstone Lake and the first to see the Grand Canyon of the Yellowstone. They were the first to marvel at the eruptions of Old Faithful, the polished white terraces of Mammoth Hot Springs, and the vivid colors of Grand Prismatic Spring. For this reason, some refer to the Anzick boy and his clan as the "first family of Yellowstone."[6]

* * *

For at least the past 11,000 years until the era of U.S. westward settlement in the mid-1800s, the Native American presence in Yellowstone was not only continuous but ever expanding.

Current archeological finds suggest that during the earliest period, from roughly 10,000 BCE to 7,500 BCE, visits to the Upper Yellowstone were relatively infrequent. As the climate continued to warm and glaciers receded, rivers ran high with spring snowmelt, but winters would have remained long, making lower-elevation areas more desirable for encampments most of the year. Such locales offered not only a milder climate but ready access to ancient bison, mammoths, and other Late Pleistocene megafauna.[7]

Then, beginning around 7,500 BCE and lasting through the mid-nineteenth century, ancestral Native Americans established a pattern of increasing habitation. So-called Cody Culture artifacts, named for an archeological site discovered near Cody, Wyoming, indicate that early peoples using new styles of stone tools and weapons made regular use of the shores along Yellowstone Lake, which contains some of the best evidence of continual Native American habitation in Yellowstone. Here, scientists have unearthed a multitude of archeological sites with artifacts ranging from 7000 BCE to AD 1800. Near Fishing Bridge, for example, archeologists discovered a 6,000-year-old fire hearth. Sites near Arnica Creek in West Thumb and on the Flat Mountain Arm of the lake have been dated to 4,000 and 2,000 years old, respectively.[8] All sites show evidence of tool-making. Native Americans also frequented volcanic mineral deposits at various sites, including Obsidian Cliff, just off today's Grand Loop Road between Mammoth and the Norris Geyser Basin. This high-quality rock was used and traded across North America.

Another park location with a long record of continual use and habitation is the so-called Mummy Cave site, located less than twelve miles from the eastern park entrance. In 1962, researchers discovered a human burial dated to AD 724. Digging further, they went on to find material artifacts covering thirty-eight different cultural periods ranging from roughly 9,280 to 700 years ago.[9]

While a number of objects found at the Mummy Cave site suggest a connection to the Shoshone people, archeologists caution that the further one goes back in time, the more difficult it is to link specific current-era Native American nations with particular artifacts. This holds true for sites throughout Yellowstone and reflects the fact that so many of the surviving objects more than 1,500 years old—like projectile points and stone tools—were shared across different human populations on the continent.[10] More distinctive forms of material culture, such as pottery or organic material like clothing, baskets, or even human remains, are less likely to be found due to the acidity of Yellowstone's soils, which tend to erode organic matter relatively quickly.

Nonetheless, other kinds of evidence—oral histories, cultural traditions, and even documented eyewitness accounts by early European trappers and explorers—confirm that no less than twenty-seven different tribal nations view Yellowstone as part of their ancient homeland. Some of these Indigenous peoples were physically present in the region during Euro-American westward expansion in the early 1800s, while others, such as the Kiowa, had long since migrated to the southeast.

* * *

While Yellowstone National Park is often presented as "untouched wilderness," it was inhabited for thousands of years. According to the linguist William Clark (no relation to the explorer) in the early 1880s, Crow leader Iron Bull drew a circle on the ground and described his nation's historical ties to the Yellowstone River country this way:

> "This is the earth the Great Spirit made [for] them. The Pie-gans [Blackfeet] he put them here," indicating a point in the line of the circle he made, "then the Great Spirit made the Sioux, the Snakes [Shoshone], Flat-heads [Salish] and many others and located them all around the earth. The Great Spirit put us right in the middle of the earth, because we are the best people in the world."[11]

Similar origin stories are present in the oral traditions of numerous other Indigenous cultures in North America. Together, they confirm the enduring and powerful cultural attachment of Native Americans to Yellowstone.

Their continued presence can also be observed in the well-worn network of ancient trails leading to and through the park. From the northeast came the Apsáalooke (Crow) Nation and from the southeast, the Eastern Shoshone. From the north came the Piikani (Blackfeet) Nation, and just west of the Rockies, the Salish (mistakenly referred to as Flatheads by early European traders), Qlispé (Pend d'Oreille), and Kutenai, all of whom would regularly come into the Upper Yellowstone region to hunt and trade. From farther east came the Northern Cheyenne, Nakota (Assiniboine), and the Oceti Sakowin nations: Dakota and Lakota Sioux.

From the west and southwest came the Nimíipuu (Nez Perce), Liksiyu (Cayuse), Schitsu'umsh (Coeur d'Alene), Lemhi Shoshone, and the Bana'kwut (Bannock) nations. Frequently entering Yellowstone via Targhee Pass, these groups might follow the long-established Bannock Trail through the modern-day park to reach buffalo hunting grounds to the north or east. Even tribes such as the Kiowa, living far away on the southern Great Plains by the 1870s, maintain oral histories that trace their point of origin to the geothermal landscapes of the Upper Yellowstone.[12]

In addition to these seasonal residents, one tribe of Mountain Shoshone, the Tukudika (also called Sheep Eater Shoshone), actually lived year-round in the Yellowstone Park area. This group traveled on foot, used dogs to carry packs and pull travois, and relied on bighorn sheep as a staple of their diet (hence their anglicized name). As skilled artisans, the Tukudika traded obsidian projectile points and cutting tools, *steate* (soapstone) bowls, and other items with various Indigenous peoples that passed through the region.

In modern society, we tend to think of habitation in terms of year-round settlement in one location. But hunter-gathering societies have always been mobile, making annual migrations across traditional territories, following seasonal changes in vegetation and the movements of wild game. Habitation that occurs across an entire region rather than a specific locale is habitation nonetheless.

* * *

Yellowstone's journey from ancestral homeland to the world's first national park—and, eventually, a national icon—would be anything but straightforward. As the term implies, a national park is an institution born of a modern nation-state. The first precondition, therefore, was a political entity able to claim sovereignty over the land in question. This requirement was met in part in 1776 with the founding of the United States and confirmed in 1788 with the adoption of the U.S. Constitution, which included a Property Clause establishing federal authority over all lands and territories belonging to the United States. And it was finalized with the country's westward expansion: a combination of land purchases, military conquests, and a long series of treaties (negotiated, broken, and rewritten numerous times) that resulted in the United States laying claim to the land that would one day become known as Yellowstone.

Yellowstone's transformation also required the rise of a broad-based conservation movement and the official "discovery" and designation of the park as a place worthy of protection. A culturally and politically viable conservation movement would take much longer to emerge and would not gain significant public attention until the mid- to late nineteenth century. Notably, success in promoting the idea of public parks also relied on the emergence of a new breed of upper-class sport hunter, one with enough power to stimulate political action.

But it was Yellowstone's exploration and discovery that took the longest. Given the 11,000 years of human habitation in the area, this fact may be surprising. Nonetheless, official discovery by Euro-Americans would not be achieved until well after the end of the Civil War, in a process spanning over half a century, progressing in fits and starts. The task was complicated by early-nineteenth-century social norms, which dictated that formal exploration and discovery of any place of importance required individuals with specific social standing and racial privilege. Native American accounts, though by far the most informed and credible, would not suffice.

The official process of discovery began thirty years after American independence and some three years after the Louisiana Purchase, in the waning days of the Lewis and Clark Expedition. And it began with one man, somewhere along the banks of the Missouri River in modern-day North Dakota.

Part Two

EXPLORATION AND DISCOVERY

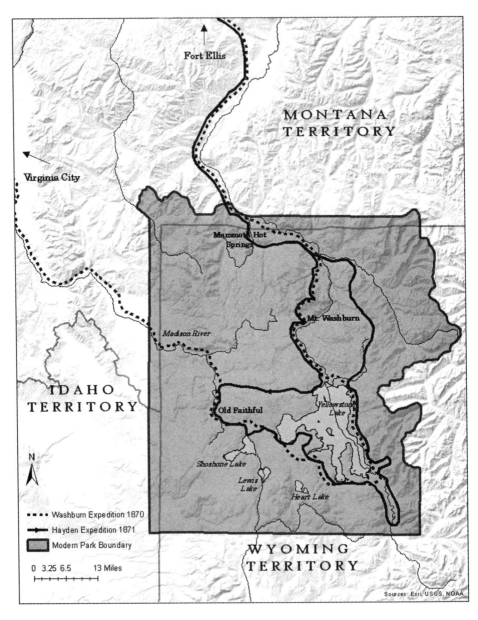

Major Routes of Exploration, 1870–1871
(Washburn and Hayden)

First Sight

(1806–1814)

NAKED, EXHAUSTED, AND SHIVERING FROM THE ICY WATERS of the Madison River, John Colter lay hidden beneath the piled mass of branches and mud of an old beaver lodge. Peering between logs, Colter kept watch for his pursuers, a band of Piegan Blackfeet warriors who had captured him hours before as he checked traps for beaver just northwest of modern-day Yellowstone National Park.

Colter drew a deep breath to settle his nerves. The late-August sun was beginning to fade behind the western Rockies. As the adrenaline subsided, Colter became more aware of the pain pulsing from his bruised and bloodied feet. If he could survive until nightfall, then maybe, under cover of darkness, there was a chance for survival. He adjusted his position and settled in to wait.

* * *

At thirty-three, Colter had already accomplished more than most people do in a lifetime. As a former member of the Lewis and Clark Expedition, he was one of the very first American citizens to see the Rocky Mountains, cross the Continental Divide, and complete the overland journey to the Pacific. It had been only five years since he was recruited by William Clark as one of "nine young men from Kentucky" to serve among the thirty-three permanent members of the fabled Corps of Discovery. Private Colter suffered some early missteps, resulting in disciplinary action for drunkenness. But he had been chosen for his hunting and tracking skills and would go on to serve the rest of his tour of duty with distinction.

Three years after departure, in 1806, the expedition reached the final leg of its homeward journey. While resting at the Hidatsa and Mandan villages nestled along the banks of the Missouri in modern-day North Dakota, Colter approached his commanders with an unexpected request. Having met two independent trappers seeking a guide upriver, Colter asked permission to leave the corps to join the men and seek his fortune in the fur trade.

Lewis and Clark granted his request and continued on to Saint Louis, while Colter turned west once more. Within a few short weeks, the three trappers had a falling out and went their separate ways. No longer pursuing beaver pelts, Colter instead did something extraordinary: he spent the next eight months traveling alone as he explored the headwaters of the Yellowstone and Bighorn Rivers. The journey took him deep into the Yellowstone Plateau, making John Colter the first American citizen ever to witness the boiling springs, bubbling mud pots, and monumental geysers of Yellowstone's landscape.

* * *

Historians have long debated the precise timing and route of Colter's Yellowstone trek. Because he never left behind a written record of his travels, we are left with secondhand accounts that offer only tantalizing hints.

For more than a century, the dominant view has been that Colter conducted his sojourn sometime between 1807 and 1808 and that he was not only the first Euro-American to see Yellowstone but also the first to visit Jackson Hole and witness the magnificent Teton Range. However, in recent years, historians Ronald Anglin and Larry Morris have offered a compelling alternative interpretation. Given the seasonal constraints on winter travel and the particular contexts of his later journeys, they argue that Colter's trip took place between 1806 and 1807 and likely began near Pryor Gap, which lies south of modern-day Billings, Montana.[1] From there, he traveled to the Clarks Fork of the Yellowstone, tracing it upstream to its headwaters before crossing over what is known today as Colter Pass, near Cooke City.

He then followed the Soda Creek drainage into what would eventually become Yellowstone National Park. From there, he traveled downstream along the Lamar River to its confluence with the Yellowstone. Fording the river at the old Bannock Trail crossing near Tower Falls, he continued along the western bank, crossing over Dunraven Pass before rejoining the river through the Hayden Valley to Yellowstone Lake. Skirting the lake to the west, he witnessed the geysers and hot springs at West Thumb and then tracked the Yellowstone headwaters up to Two Ocean Plateau.

From this point, Colter likely continued south to Brooks Lake before following the Wind River downstream to a site near modern-day Dubois, Wyoming, where he may have spent the winter at a Crow encampment. In the late spring of 1807, he resumed his travels northward along the Shoshone River toward modern-day Cody. He crossed the waterway near a place later called Colter's Hell, a section of river where once-active hot springs and steam vents filled the air with a particularly pungent and sulphureous aroma. After traversing Heart Mountain, Colter rejoined the Clarks Fork, which returned him to Pryor Gap and presented the chance to retrace his steps back to the Missouri River.

* * *

With his overland exploration of Yellowstone complete, Colter decided it was finally time to return to civilization. In Saint Louis, he could see his young son, share his new geographical knowledge with William Clark, and collect his Corps of Discovery back pay from Meriwether Lewis, who now served as the territorial governor of Louisiana. Colter's western trapping days were behind him. It was time to turn the page, start a new life.

And so, as the spring of 1807 gave way to summer, Colter found himself paddling once more down the Missouri River. But upon reaching the mouth of the Platte, near the present-day border of Nebraska and Iowa, he encountered a party of some forty to fifty white men heading upstream on keelboats. Led by entrepreneur Manuel Lisa, soon-to-be founder of the Missouri Fur Company, the group intended to build a series of trading forts along the Missouri and Yellowstone

Rivers. More importantly for Colter, the party included several of his former companions from the Corps of Discovery, including George Drouillard and John Potts. With an offer from Lisa to join the expedition, Colter abandoned his homeward journey and decided to give fur trapping another try. Perhaps this time he would succeed in making his fortune.

At the confluence of the Yellowstone and Bighorn Rivers, Lisa ordered his men to construct Fort Raymond. In December 1807, he dispatched several trappers, including Colter, to invite nearby tribal nations to trade. Traveling alone and covering some 500 miles, Colter made contact with a number of Crow and Salish encampments, eventually persuading about 800 people to accompany him back to the fort. In the spring of 1808, as the group passed through the Three Forks area, they were attacked by a much larger party of Piegan Blackfeet warriors. During the battle, Colter suffered a leg injury. Unable to stand, he nonetheless made effective use of his sharpshooting skills from the ground, earning him respect and praise from his tribal companions. Though the fight resulted in heavy casualties on both sides, the Crow and Salish ultimately prevailed in driving off the Blackfeet and traveled on with Colter to Fort Raymond.[2]

While waiting for his leg to heal back at the fort, Colter met with Potts and began making plans for a new trapping venture. Both men knew just the place where beaver populations would be particularly abundant: northwest of modern-day Yellowstone National Park, near the Three Forks of the Missouri. Despite Colter's recent hostilities with the Blackfeet in that very same area, and against his better judgment, he agreed to depart with Potts in the late summer of 1808. Perhaps this time it would be different.

* * *

It is somewhat surprising that two seasoned hunters like John Colter and John Potts—both veterans of the Lewis and Clark Expedition—were caught so completely off guard by such a large contingent of horsemen. As the two men sat floating in their canoes on a branch of the Jefferson River, checking and preparing traps, Colter heard the rumblings of approaching intruders and urged Potts to take cover. But

Potts ignored him, insisting it was merely a herd of bison. Within moments, the men were surrounded by a Blackfeet hunting party numbering in the hundreds.

Arrows drawn, the leaders of the party motioned for Colter and Potts to come ashore. There was little choice but to comply, though both men knew it likely meant a slow and tortuous death. Colter paddled obediently to the riverbank, where he was immediately disarmed and stripped naked. Colter called out to his friend to join him, but Potts hesitated. Weighing the options, he apparently decided that a quick death was more desirable than whatever was about to happen to Colter. In the meantime, an impatient warrior let loose an arrow, catching Potts in the hip and knocking him back into his canoe. Struggling upright, Potts put his rifle to his shoulder and fired, killing a man standing on the bank. In seconds, amid shouts of anger, a flight of arrows pummeled Potts's body. Rushing into the water, the Blackfeet converged on Potts's canoe. They dragged his struggling body to the shore, where they proceeded to hack him apart with knives and tomahawks.

Colter watched with a mix of fear and disgust as the warriors flung portions of his friend's innards into his face. Once they finished with Potts, several angry men turned their knives on Colter, but others intervened to hold them back. As Colter stood there naked, anxious, and vulnerable, he noticed a group of elders in deep discussion. He could not speak the Blackfeet language but knew they were deciding his fate. Moments later, one of the chiefs walked over to address him.

Pointing toward the open prairie, the man said in the Crow tongue, "Go. Go away."

Although Colter understood the words, he was surprised by the command. He took a few uncertain steps and looked back at the elder, who urged him to move quickly. Colter began to walk faster, but the old man kept gesturing to speed up. Still hesitant, Colter kept his pace to a brisk walk, fearing that to run might result in a shot in the back.

When he'd ventured approximately eighty yards, Colter looked back to find a group of warriors taking off their blankets and leggings and arming themselves with spears. Finally, he understood. He was about to be hunted. Perhaps it was a fitting end for a white trapper who had come into Blackfeet country uninvited to illegally hunt for pelts. What's more, he had added insult to injury by trading goods and firearms with the Blackfeet's primary enemy, the Crow. As he took off in a sudden sprint, Colter heard a chorus of cries rise up from the main party. The group of warriors charged after him. The race was on.

* * *

A seasoned outdoorsman and hunter still in his early thirties, Colter was very much in his physical prime. Thomas James, a trapper who met Colter as part of Lisa's 1809 expedition, described him as standing "five feet ten inches" and exuding an "open, ingenious and pleasant countenance of the Daniel Boone stamp." According to James, "Nature had formed him, like Boone, for hardy endurance of fatigue, privations and perils."[3] These were the very qualities that had earned his invitation to join Lewis and Clark. His time with the corps not only honed his survival skills and strengthened his endurance but also provided valuable knowledge of the terrain. If he could somehow elude capture, he might just find his way back to safety.

Adrenaline pumping, Colter literally ran for his life. Moving with the speed that only fear can muster, he dodged and swerved through the Montana prairielands as cactus needles and rocks punctured his unprotected feet. Colter hoped to reach the Madison River, which lay some five miles south-southeast. He glanced over his shoulder. It seemed like he was pulling away from his pursuers, who were now spread out and falling back. If he could make it to the water, perhaps he had a chance.

But as he sighted the river, Colter's energy gave out. With legs suddenly like leaden weights, he slowed to catch his breath and a nosebleed erupted, pouring blood down his face. He looked back once more and saw that he had left all pursuers behind, save one. And the man was closing in rapidly.

Colter knew he couldn't outrun the hunter. He called out in the Crow language, hoping the words might make his attacker reconsider or, at the very least, pause. Instead, the determined warrior charged forward, lifting his spear for a killing throw at roughly twenty yards.

Colter struggled on for few more steps before he abruptly stopped, raised his arms, and swung around to face his adversary, hoping to dodge the oncoming spear. Possibly surprised by Colter's sudden halt and bloodied face, or perhaps due to his own exhaustion, the warrior stumbled as he attempted to launch his weapon. The spear point lodged into the ground and the pole broke off under the weight of the man's falling body. Without thinking, Colter grabbed the spearhead and stabbed his attacker in the chest, pinning him to the ground.

Colter extracted the bloody weapon and ran for the river with renewed strength. A few minutes later, he could hear angry cries in the distance as the other pursuers found their dead companion. Passing through a stand of cottonwoods, Colter plunged into the icy water. On the far bank was an old beaver lodge. Diving beneath the logs, Colter found the entrance and proceeded to pull himself out of the cold water to hide within the small enclosure beneath the mound of mud and branches.

* * *

Colter's pursuers soon arrived at the river. For some two hours, he could hear them shouting to one another as they searched up and down along the banks. Suddenly, the piled branches above Colter's head creaked and sagged under someone's weight. Heart racing, Colter held his breath, certain that at any moment he would be found. After a few agonizing minutes, the warrior wandered off. Eventually all of the voices faded away and darkness descended.

In time, Colter decided it was finally safe to leave his refuge. He slipped into the dark waters of the Madison, made his way to shore, and began the 200-plus-mile trek back to Fort Raymond. To avoid further encounters with the Blackfeet, he decided to leave their territory. Though it added another 125 miles to his journey, Colter swung southeast, following the Gallatin River, and entered once more into modern-day Yellowstone National Park. Arriving this time from the northeast corner, he followed the Yellowstone River upstream to the Bannock Crossing at Tower Falls, before retracing in reverse the route he had taken two years earlier.

Traveling only by night, bushwhacking over the Gallatin Range to avoid the more commonly used passes, without clothing or supplies and only a broken spearhead for protection, Colter journeyed some

350 miles in just eleven days. When he arrived back at the fort, the men didn't recognize him at first. But after Colter identified himself and shared his harrowing tale, the story of Colter's Run would eventually take its place in the folklore of the early West.

* * *

In the two years after his famous "run," Colter returned twice more to the Three Forks area, once to collect the traps he'd left behind, and once to guide a relatively large party of trappers led by Major Andrew Henry and Pierre Menard for the Missouri Fur Company. But each excursion followed the same script: initial success trapping beaver followed by hostilities with the Blackfeet, ending with a desperate escape through the northern reaches of the modern-day park. On his final trek, after numerous skirmishes that left five of his companions either dead or captured, Colter decided enough was enough.

On April 22, 1810, he informed Major Henry of his decision. Colter packed up his meager supplies and, with two other men, promptly left the western mountains, never to return. About a month later, after a 2,500-mile journey, he approached the frontier town of Saint Louis.

* * *

On or about the morning of May 21, 1810, forty-two-year-old John Bradbury stood on the limestone bluff marking the termination of Market Street in Saint Louis. His vantage point offered a sweeping view of the Mississippi River. But as he looked upstream toward the confluence with the Missouri, he could just make out a single canoe emerging from the mist.

Born in England and trained as a botanist, Bradbury was a distinguished scientist and writer working on behalf of the Liverpool Botanic Garden. On advice from former president Thomas Jefferson, Bradbury traveled to Saint Louis to accompany John Jacob Astor's American Fur Company expedition to the West with the intention of documenting new North American plant species. But on this morning, he watched with interest as the lone paddler came into view. Bradbury saw a rugged man with the look of a trapper, wearing animal-skin clothing in a lightly packed canoe. With one last stroke of the oar, the man glided to the bank and stepped wearily from his boat.

Four years after the return of Lewis and Clark, John Colter, the last member of the Corps of Discovery, had finally returned home.

* * *

In the days following his arrival, Colter learned that William Clark was out of town and that Territorial Governor Meriwether Lewis had died some six months earlier by apparent suicide. This news would later force Colter to initiate legal proceedings against Lewis's estate in order to receive his long-overdue back pay. In the meantime, he gave a personal interview to Bradbury, who would publish a colorful account of Colter's Run in a book about the botanist's travels in the United States.[4] Bradbury's 1817 work would later influence Washington Irving's famous portrayal of Colter in *The Adventures of Captain Bonneville*. Published in 1837, Irving's popular book immortalized Colter's escape from the Blackfeet and firmly established the trapper's legendary status in early American folklore. But interestingly, neither work made mention of his trip through Yellowstone's mysterious landscape.

A few weeks later, in July 1810, William Clark returned to Saint Louis and Colter had the opportunity to share his knowledge of Yellowstone with his old captain. Clark, who was now brigadier general of the Louisiana Territorial Militia and a U.S. agent for Indian Affairs, was eager to finally complete the Corps of Discovery's map and publish their journals. Although the expedition's primary task was to find a water route to the Pacific, as chief cartographer, Clark also yearned to discover the source of the continent's major rivers, possibly resolving current theories that the two great American river systems, the Missouri/Mississippi and the Columbia, shared a single source in the northern Rockies. But time limitations during the expedition prevented Clark from exploring the upper reaches of the Yellowstone or Bighorn Rivers to find out. On their return from the Pacific, the Corps of Discovery split into smaller groups to cover more of the Upper Missouri river basin. During a camp made near the site of modern-day Livingston, Montana, Clark may have expressed his desire to explore the Yellowstone headwaters before he reluctantly moved on to rejoin Lewis downstream at a pre-appointed time.

Historians Anglin and Morris suggest that this was Colter's primary motivation for his Yellowstone trek in 1806 and 1807. If true, it explains much about both the timing and the route. Neither the hunt for furs (Colter's original goal in 1806) or the search for Crow encampments to invite to Lisa's trading fort (his mission in 1807 and 1808) would explain a journey through Yellowstone's high country. Instead, perhaps Colter wanted to do a favor for his old commander, the man who gave him a chance to join the Corps of Discovery and then supported his request to strike out on his own as a trapper. This would also explain why Colter's Yellowstone wanderings never made it into his documented interviews with Thomas James in 1809 or John Bradbury in 1810. We may never know his motivation, timing, or precise route, but we do know that Colter and Clark met multiple times in Saint Louis in 1810 and that Colter gave input that helped fill in the empty spaces on Clark's map, including Yellowstone.

Unfortunately, Colter would die before ever seeing his Yellowstone findings or other exploits in print. During the War of 1812, he enlisted in the U.S. Mounted Rangers under the command of his lifelong friend, Captain Nathan Boone (son of the fabled Daniel), but lasted only a little over two months before falling gravely ill and passing away. Despite his short life, he became a storied figure in western history. As a hunter, trapper, and explorer, Colter served as the prototype of the iconic American mountain man, lending his name to a host of landscape features across the northern Rockies. But arguably his single most important contribution to American history was his journey through Yellowstone. Colter's descriptions provided the basis of the first published account of the region in the journals and maps of the Lewis and Clark Expedition, released in 1814.

* * *

William Clark's final map of the Upper Yellowstone region offered an impressive record of a place he never saw with his own eyes. Although it contained errors of scale and directionality and a few outright mistakes (including placing the Rio Grande near Jackson Hole), the map provided a fairly accurate delineation of the Yellowstone River and its tributaries up to Yellowstone Lake, which Clark labeled Lake Eustis. Beyond that, Clark traced the river's headwaters to Two Ocean Pass and included depictions of other Missouri tributaries that pass through or near the Yellowstone Plateau, including the Clarks Fork, the Bighorn, and the Shoshone Rivers.

It is true that other written accounts of Yellowstone predated Lewis and Clark's.[5] In a letter to President Thomas Jefferson dated October 22, 1805, General James Wilkinson, the first governor of the vast and newly acquired Louisiana Territory, described several local "items of interest" for the president's amusement. They included a roughly drawn map he characterized as "a Savage delineation on a Buffalo Pelt, of the Missouri and its South Western Branches" that "expose[d] the location of several important Objects, & may point the way to a useful enquiry—among other things a little incredible, a volcano is distinctly described on Yellow Stone River." In fact, the crafty Wilkinson[7] had already arranged for such an "enquiry," outfitting an expedition to the area as evidenced in a letter to the secretary of war in September 1805.[8] But there is no further word on whether Wilkinson's expedition actually took place.

In contrast, Lewis and Clark's journals and map represented a published confirmation of at least some of Yellowstone's wonders by two of the most well-known and respected governmental authorities of their day, albeit in muted fashion. The only reference to Yellowstone's geothermal features on Clark's map is his written notation "Hot Spring Brimstone," which occurs on the map near the Yellowstone River along a linear feature labeled "Colter's Route 1807." The journals also contain a short addendum that Clark included after returning to Saint Louis:

> At the head of this river the nativs [sic] give an account that there is frequently herd [sic] a loud noise, like Thunder, which makes the earth Tremble, they State that they seldom go there because their children Cannot sleep—and Conceive it possessed of spirits, who were averse that men Should be near them.[9]

While this journal entry may refer to a river other than Yellowstone, the fact that Clark's final Corps of Discovery map contains no demarcation of geyser basins or any of the large geysers themselves outside of West Thumb suggests that Colter never witnessed them.[10]

The 1814 publication of Lewis and Clark's map and journals raises some additional questions. Given the widespread fame of the Lewis and Clark Expedition at the time, how is it that this document did not lead to calls for a more formal exploration of Yellowstone? One would think that even these small notations would have garnered some public interest. Nonetheless, Yellowstone's transformation from historical footnote to national icon—from "first sight" to formal discovery—remained decades away. The long delay had much to do with larger geopolitical events, and even more to do with who was accorded the privilege of "discovery."

Building the Myth

(1822–1853)

ON FEBRUARY 13, 1822, A PUBLIC NOTICE APPEARED ON THE second page of the *Missouri Gazette and Public Advertiser.*

TO
ENTERPRISING YOUNG MEN

The subscriber wishes to engage ONE HUNDRED MEN, to ascend the river Missouri to its source, there to be employed for one, two or three years. –For particulars, enquire of Major Andrew Henry, near the Lead Mines, in the County of Washington, (who will ascend with, and command the party) or to the subscriber at Saint Louis.

—Wm. H. Ashley

A brigadier general in the Missouri Territorial Militia during the War of 1812, William Ashley now served as the new state's first lieutenant governor.[1] His political ambitions were growing, and, in need of funding, he sensed opportunity in the fur trade. To lead the expedition, Ashley partnered with Major Andrew Henry. Henry was an experienced trapper who had traveled up the Missouri with Manuel Lisa and John Colter in 1807 and led the expedition during Colter's final trek to the Three Forks area in 1810.

Several of those that signed on as part of "Ashley's Hundred" would become legendary figures in early American western history, including Jedediah Smith, David Jackson (of Jackson Hole fame) and Hugh Glass.[2] The party also included a man who, over the next four decades, would do more than anyone else to build the myth of Yellowstone in the American psyche: a lanky, fresh-faced seventeen-year-old named Jim Bridger.[3]

* * *

In the four short years between John Colter's return to Saint Louis and the publication of the Corps of Discovery's journals, a great deal changed in the United States. Beginning in June 1812, the country found itself once more engaged in full-out war with Great Britain. Though the British saw the conflict as little more than a defensive skirmish, for Americans the stakes were higher. After two years of fighting, which saw several failed American invasions of Canada and the British capture and subsequent burning of the White House and U.S. Capitol, it's no wonder Clark's cartographic notations about Yellowstone garnered little public attention. The crises triggered by the War of 1812 (lasting until February 1815[4]) pulled the nation's focus eastward and brought a temporary close to American explorations in the West.

Moreover, when the smoke finally cleared from the conflict with Britain, the resumption of federally sponsored expeditions did little to inspire new interest in the American West. The Atkinson Expedition of 1819—also known as the Yellowstone Expedition—sought to establish a series of forts along the Missouri River to the mouth of the Yellowstone, but poor planning meant they got no further than Fort Lisa, near modern-day Omaha.

The following year, an expedition led by Major Stephen Long and Captain John Bell followed the Platte River across the Great Plains to Colorado's Front Range. Upon reaching the mountains, where Major Long saw but did not climb the peak named after him, the party traveled south before returning along the Arkansas River across modern-day Oklahoma. Ill prepared for the dry conditions on the high plains, the Long-Bell Expedition barely escaped starvation by eating their own horses. Echoing the sentiments expressed by Zebulon Pike after his 1806–1807 expedition, Major Long recommended that the Great Plains be renamed the Great American Desert, unsuitable for farming or settlement.[5]

After that, the federal government largely turned its back on the American West. For the next two decades, from the 1820s through the early 1840s, the only Euro-Americans making their way into the northern Rockies—and hence, into Yellowstone—were trappers working for the major American and British fur companies.

* * *

In the early 1800s, Britain's Hudson's Bay Company represented one of the largest and most successful commercial ventures in the world. Established in 1670, the legendary trapping syndicate had maintained a continuous presence in North America for over 150 years. In contrast, the U.S. fur industry didn't emerge until 1808, with Manuel Lisa's Missouri Fur Company. Headquartered in Saint Louis, Lisa's business included William Clark as company agent and counted among its investors Major Andrew Henry, Reuben Lewis (brother of Meriwether), and Jean Pierre Chouteau (son of Saint Louis's cofounder, René Auguste Chouteau).

At about the same time, entrepreneur John Jacob Astor formed the American Fur Company in New York City. Astor, who by the time of his death would be the wealthiest man in the United States, began as a retailer of furs purchased from French Canadian and British companies. He soon realized, however, that he could make greater profits with his own supply chains. Though Astor focused initially on the Pacific Northwest, he envisioned a commercial empire that would not only span the continent but reach overseas to China and Europe. In 1810, he sponsored an expedition to the Pacific coast. His "Astorians" trapped their way across the northern Rockies to Oregon, where they established Fort Astoria in 1811. Astor hoped the fort would control the fur trade along the Columbia River while also providing a base for sailing to Asian markets.[6]

However, both American companies suffered considerably under the British during the War of 1812. It took a decade for Astor to reestablish his American Fur Company and for the Missouri Fur Company to reemerge under new ownership. Hoping to take advantage of this situation, other American entrepreneurs entered the market, most notably William Ashley.

Ashley's Rocky Mountain Fur Company was essentially a regional company focused on the northern Rockies. But what really set him apart was his business model. While the major fur companies required exclusive multiyear contracts from trappers in their employ, Ashley relied on a system of "free" or independent employees. After working for one to three years, trappers could buy supplies and sell furs to Ashley's firm as they saw fit. In addition, beginning in 1824 and lasting for sixteen seasons, the Rocky Mountain Fur Company initiated the famous rendezvous system. These annual gatherings held at various sites deep in the mountains allowed trappers to sell and resupply without having to haul their goods all the way to eastern trading posts or cities. This arrangement reduced the cost of maintaining forts for the company and allowed trappers to stay in the field year-round.

Consequently, as mountain men spread out through the northern Rockies in search of beaver pelts, a number of them, including Jim Bridger and Osborne Russell, eventually found their way to the geyser basins of the Upper Yellowstone. For the next two decades, it was through their voices—expressed in company reports, diary entries, and campfire tales—that news of Yellowstone spread to the "outside world."

* * *

Of course, such modes of sharing information explain much about Yellowstone's anonymity during this period. First off, many of the early fur trappers left no written account of their exploits, either because they were illiterate—as was the case with Jim Bridger—or because they never survived to tell the tale. Life as a trapper was exceedingly hard and it was not uncommon to meet an early and violent death from extreme weather, wild animals, or Indigenous war parties. Jim Bridger himself carried a three-inch arrowhead in his hip for over two years as a result of one such run-in.[7] And the bloody near-death experiences of Jedediah Smith and Hugh Glass after their respective encounters with grizzly bears became the stuff of legend (and Hollywood movies like *The Revenant*).

Secondly, even when trappers did bother to keep written records, their words rarely garnered public attention. One of the earliest known exceptions to this rule was an anonymous letter printed in the *Philadelphia Gazette and Daily Advertiser* in 1827. The author, later identified as Daniel T. Potts, was one of General Ashley's original recruits and wrote the letter to his brother on July 8 of that year. Potts detailed not only the exciting and difficult life of a trapper—fighting desperately for his life in battles with the Blackfeet—but also the boiling springs and geysers surrounding Yellowstone Lake:

> The Yellow-stone has a large fresh water Lake near its head . . . on the south shores of this lake is a number of hot and boiling springs some of water and others of most beautiful fine clay and resembles that of a mush pot and throws its particles to the immense height of from twenty to thirty feet in height.[8]

Written documentation by mountain men generally took one of two forms: reports compiled for fur companies or personal journal entries.[9] In the latter category, few surpassed the articulate observations of Osborne Russell, an American trapper who visited the Upper Yellowstone at least five times in the 1830s, before moving west to become a judge in Oregon. Russell offered poetic descriptions of the lands he traversed, including a romantic portrait of Yellowstone's Lamar Valley in 1835:

> There is something in the wild romantic scenery of this valley . . . the impressions made upon my mind while gazing from a high eminence on the surrounding landscape one evening as the sun was gently gliding behind the western mountain and casting its gigantic shadows across the vale were such as time can never efface from my memory.[10]

Nonetheless, direct written accounts remained scarce. Those that did exist were hidden from the public until their rediscovery by family members or historians many decades later. A far more common practice, and, in fact, the primary means through which fur trappers spread knowledge, was through oral tradition. For mountain men, recounting tales around the campfire provided both information and entertainment. And exaggerated retellings kept the stories fresh and listeners engaged. In time, such practices gave rise to the tradition of tall tales in American folklore, where figures like Paul Bunyan and Pecos Bill regularly crossed over into fiction as they performed obviously fantastic feats such as digging the Grand Canyon with an axe or riding a tornado like a wild bronco.

But here was the rub. Despite the entertainment value of these tales, doubts about their veracity represented perhaps the greatest obstacle to spreading knowledge of Yellowstone to the wider public. For no one was this contradiction more true than for the most famous mountain man of the era, Jim Bridger.

* * *

Bridger was born in 1804 in Richmond, Virginia. At the age of eight, he moved west with his family to Saint Louis.[11] Within five years, both parents and a sibling died of disease, making orphans of adolescent Jim and his younger sister. An aunt moved in to care for the children, allowing Jim to apprentice with a local blacksmith. Between long days with the hammer and anvil, Jim spent early mornings hunting to put food on the table. After five years of apprenticeship, the teenaged Bridger possessed skills highly valued by fur traders. His ability to make or repair horseshoes, beaver traps, wagon wheels, and other mechanical devices—including rifles—made him a prized recruit despite his young age. For Bridger, joining Ashley's expedition in 1822 launched the start of a renowned career.

In the early days of the expedition, Bridger's young mind was like a sponge. The lessons came hard and fast. Within the first few months, he survived attacks from the Blackfeet and Arikaras, learned the ins and outs of the peltry trade, helped construct Major Henry's new fort near Manuel Lisa's crumbling post at the confluence of the Yellowstone and Bighorn Rivers, and endured his first winter in the northwest.[12] At night, he gleaned knowledge of the western lands from older trappers and, of course, listened intently to their tall tales over the campfire.

By twenty, Bridger was already making his mark as an explorer. In

1824, around a campfire on the Bear River, some older trappers made bets on where the river actually flowed. They sent off young Bridger to find out. Building himself a bullboat—a bison hide stretched over a willow frame—Bridger floated downriver some twenty-five miles to where it emptied into a massive inland sea. He took a drink and immediately gagged on the salty water. Upon his return, the trappers thought he must have found an inland extension of the Pacific Ocean. But Bridger had, in fact, become the first Euro-American to see the Great Salt Lake.[13]

The 1830s saw Bridger in his prime, becoming co-owner of the Rocky Mountain Fur Company and cutting a striking figure. Bridger's friend, Major General Grenville Dodge, described him as "over six feet tall, spare, straight as an arrow, agile, rawboned and of powerful frame, eyes gray, hair brown and abundant . . . expression mild, manners agreeable. He was hospitable and generous, and was always trusted and respected."[14]

Somewhere along the line, Bridger picked up the moniker "Old Gabe." Mountain men typically went by nicknames, and legend says Bridger received his from the hymnal-toting Jedediah Smith, who reckoned Bridger reminded him of the angel Gabriel.

Bridger served as a living link between cultures. Fluent in the Crow and Blackfoot languages and also adept at sign language, he was married three times to Indigenous women, each of whom ultimately died in childbirth, including Little Fawn (or Mary), daughter of Chief Washakie of the Wind River Shoshone.[15] Known as Blanket Chief among the Crow and Shoshone—possibly due to a blanket made for him by his first wife, Cora—Bridger's trustworthy reputation among many Native Americans gave him access to additional knowledge of the western landscape that helped him succeed. Later in life, it also facilitated his role as a cultural intermediary during treaty negotiations between the U.S. government and various tribal nations.

Many mountain men of the day had similar skills. But what truly distinguished Bridger was his brilliant cartographical mind. Having once passed through a country, he could recall in detail each turn of the trail, every subtle shift in topography, and the most important directional beacons. A pathfinder in the truest sense, Bridger's knowledge of the northern Rockies was unmatched among Euro-American trappers of the period.

According to a contemporary who traveled with Bridger, "the whole West and all the passes and labyrinths of the Rocky Mountains were mapped out in his mind. He had such a sense of locality and direction that he used to say 'he could smell his way where he could not see it.'"[16]

But one place in the western landscape had a particular hold on Bridger's mind. Back in 1824, or possibly 1825, Bridger trekked through the Upper Yellowstone for the first time. Over his lifetime, he would visit eight or nine times more, including twice with his friend Kit Carson, in 1834 and 1850 respectively. He witnessed all of the major sites, from the Mammoth Hot Springs to Two Ocean Pass. He saw the Upper and Lower Geyser Basins, the massive springs along the Firehole River, the sights at Yellowstone Lake, and the Grand Canyon of the Yellowstone. From the 1820s through the 1860s, no American citizen was better acquainted with Yellowstone than Jim Bridger.

* * *

If Osborne Russell was the most inspired diarist among the early trappers passing through Yellowstone, Jim Bridger was undoubtedly the most influential in spreading word of the landscape. His telling differed depending on the audience. When it came to guiding trappers, settlers, or army units, he prioritized geographic accuracy. None could equal his precision; those who doubted him quickly came to regret it. But at the end of the workday, around a campfire or in a tavern, Bridger's creative mind and sense of humor came to the fore, spinning yarns that stretched the truth to the point of absurdity. And if the audience contained "greenhorns" or "pilgrims"—newly arrived pioneers, missionaries, army recruits, or wealthy sport hunters—his imagination knew no limits.

For Bridger's friends, and most seasoned westerners, these realms were separate and distinct. But to the uninitiated in his audience, the difference between tall tale and cartographical fact was inextricably blurred. He delivered his most outrageous statements in a solemn and earnest tone. And much of the landscape itself seemed literally incredible.

When Bridger spoke of actual sights—Yellowstone rivers defying gravity by flowing straight up to the sky; of catching a fish in one pool, then swinging the rod over to an adjacent pool to cook it; or of watching trout swim over mountains—what was an uninitiated greenhorn to think? Such tales might be followed by accounts of a lake filled with millions of beavers "nearly impossible to kill because of their superior cuteness." Or stories of a mountain made of glass (or, sometimes, diamonds, depending on Bridger's mood). All of it sounded like fantastical nonsense. Captain Eugene Ware, who befriended Bridger while stationed with him at Fort Laramie in the 1860s, documented Bridger's story about Yellowstone's mountain of glass:

> Bridger said, "Up there is one of the strangest mountains that I ever did see. It is a diamond mountain, shaped something like a cone. I saw it in the sun for two days before I got to it, and then at night I camped right near it. I hadn't more than got my horse lariated out . . . when I saw a camp-fire and some Injuns right through the mountain on the other side. So I didn't build any fire, but I could see them just as plain as if there hadn't been anything but air. In the morning I noticed the Injuns were gone, and I thought I would like to see the other side of the mountain. So, I rode around to the other side and it took me half a day."
>
> Ware asked, "Might not that have been a mountain of salt?"
>
> "Oh, no," replied Bridger. "I went up and knocked off a corner of it, a piece of rock as big as my arm, a big, long piece of diamond, and brought it out, and afterwards gave it to a man, and he said it was a diamond alright."[17]

Adding to the confusion was that each story contained a kernel of truth. One could presumably interpret geysers as rivers flowing "up to the sky." Yellowstone's Obsidian Cliff might look like reflected glass or gems in the moonlight, as Yellowstone's second superintendent Philetus Norris noted in his 1877 report. The Firehole River does in fact flow with hot steaming water in places, ushered in from nearby hot springs. And the thin crusted surface in Yellowstone's various geyser basins might readily allow animals or people to potentially fall through to the "nether regions" below (as park warning signs still attest today).

Watching trout swim over mountains was similarly plausible at Two Ocean Plateau, located up above Yellowstone Lake, where a single stream served as headwaters for both the Columbia River (via the Snake) and the Missouri/Mississippi Rivers (via the Yellowstone). By meandering through a level meadow where it then split, with one side flowing to the Pacific Ocean and the other to the Atlantic, the river offered opportunity for intermountain travel. Osborne Russell confirmed this phenomenon in the 1830s, watching "twelve-inch trout" swimming back and forth at the fork, technically crossing over the Continental Divide.

Most written evidence of Bridger's stories comes from those who could discern the difference between tall tales and Bridger's expert knowledge of the West. These were military men, typically trained as scientists and surveyors, who often trusted Bridger with their lives as he guided them through hostile or unknown country. But even they were worried about the effect his stories might have on Bridger's reputation. As Captain Ware noted in the 1860s:

> [Bridger] wasn't an egotistical liar that we so often find . . . [But] one of the difficulties with him was that he would occasionally tell some wonderful story to a pilgrim, and would try to interest the new-comer with a lot of statements which were ludicrous, sometimes greatly exaggerated, and sometimes imaginary.[18]

While Bridger's stories did much to build the myth of Yellowstone as a fantastical—and potentially fictional—landscape, for those with a scientific interest in the American West, the trapper was a profound source of geographic knowledge. In fact, if one looks beyond the stories, Bridger represented the best hope of "discovering" Yellowstone and bringing it to the attention of the American public.

* * *

By the late 1830s, the American fur industry had slid into an irreversible decline, the result of a diminished supply of beaver and changing market demands in Europe for silks and other goods. In 1840, the final rendezvous took place along the Green River. While some trappers transitioned to bison hunting, most sought other ways to ply their geographic knowledge. The arrival of the first pioneer settlers on the western plains provided one such opportunity.

In 1842 and again in 1843, Lieutenant John C. Fremont completed two successful western survey expeditions.[19] The publication of Fremont's reports generated a wave of public interest in pioneer migration over what would soon be known as the Oregon Trail.

Some 1,000 settlers made the trek to the Pacific coast in 1843. Over the next decade, the number of western migrants soared to unprecedented heights as the nation expanded by millions of acres. Three events catalyzed this territorial growth: the 1845 annexation of Texas, the 1846 signing of the Oregon Compromise with Great Britain, and the 1848 conclusion of the war with Mexico.[20] Together, these actions nearly doubled the land area of the continental United States. Suddenly, in the eyes of Euro-American settlers, vast new domains lay open to homesteading and resource extraction. Meanwhile, the discovery of gold in California brought hundreds of thousands more rushing across the continent, seeking their fortune in the western mining camps.

Faced with a growing flood of settlers and prospectors, some former trappers set up trading posts, while others served as guides leading pioneers to Oregon, miners to California, or wealthy aristocrats on sport-hunting ventures. Still others hired on as scouts for the U.S. Army. Bridger, perhaps unsurprisingly, engaged in all three with remarkable success.

In 1843, Bridger and an old trapping friend, Louis Vasquez, opened the Fort Bridger trading post along the Oregon Trail in the southwest corner of modern-day Wyoming. A modest affair, consisting initially of a single log cabin, the post served both white settlers and Native Americans alike. Due to its strategic position, Bridger's fort became an ideal resupply point for wagon trains and prospectors heading west across the Great Salt Lake Desert to Utah, or along the trails to Oregon or California.

Business boomed as thousands passed through Fort Bridger, including members of the ill-fated Donner Party in 1846 and, the following year, a man named Brigham Young and his Mormon followers in search of a "promised land" near the shores of the Great Salt Lake. Bridger met privately with Young and offered advice to him and his "Council of Twelve" on the region, including the best route to take. He offered to serve as their guide but did not make it back in time from a previously planned trading venture.

Despite his new role as trader and guide, Bridger continued to spread the word about Yellowstone. In 1849 and 1850, while serving as scout for Captain Stansbury's Topographical Survey of Utah, Bridger met Lieutenant J. W. Gunnison, who recorded the following:

> He gives a picture, most romantic and enticing of the headwaters of the Yellow Stone. A lake sixty miles long, cold and pellucid, lies embosomed amid high precipitous mountains . . . Geysers spout up seventy feet high, with a terrific hissing noise, at regular intervals and collect in the pool below. The river issues from this lake, and for fifteen miles roars through the perpendicular canyon at the outlet. In this section are the Great Springs, so hot that meat is readily cooked in them, and as they descend on the successive terraces, afford at length delightful baths.[21]

Aside from the exaggerated length of Yellowstone Lake (unless the writer was describing circumference; the lake is roughly twenty miles by fourteen miles), the landscape descriptions are remarkably accurate, from the height and sounds of the geysers to the account of the terraces at Mammoth Hot Springs (referred to here as the "Great Springs").

In 1851, Bridger again shared his cartographic knowledge of Yellowstone, this time during the Fort Laramie Treaty Council. Brokered by the U.S. government, the council was an attempt to settle boundary disputes among tribal nations on the northern plains, allow safe passage for white settlers on the Oregon Trail, and permit the United States to build a series of forts in Native American territory. Notably, the treaty would also recognize the northwest half of modern-day Yellowstone National Park as part of the Crow nation and the southeast portion as Shoshone territory (using the Yellowstone River as boundary).

Bridger attended the council as an interpreter. While there, he met an old friend, a Flemish Jesuit priest named Father Pierre-Jean De Smet. Serving as a missionary to the Blackfeet Nation, De Smet was hired by federal officials to map out the new tribal boundaries determined by the treaty. But during the meeting, he also drafted a map of the Upper Yellowstone region based on Bridger's descriptions.

According to historian Aubrey Haines, if one looks past the absence of proper scale, De Smet's map provides an accurate demarcation of all of the major waterways, geological features, and geothermal areas in the modern-day park.[22] It delineated Two Ocean Pass, Yellowstone Lake (in oval form), notations for the major geyser basins, the Grand Canyon of the Yellowstone, and the Lamar River valley, as well as references to a "Sulpher Mtn." (likely Mammoth Hot Springs). In short, it far surpassed any other cartographic representation of the region then in existence.

In his accompanying letter, De Smet underscored the potential value of Yellowstone:

> I think that the most extraordinary spot . . . is in the very heart of the Rocky Mountains . . . between the sources of the Madison and Yellowstone . . . Bituminous, sulphurous and boiling springs are very numerous in it . . . Gas, vapor and smoke are continually escaping by a thousand openings, from the base to the summit of the volcanic pile; the noise at times resembles the steam let off by a boat . . . Near Gardiner river . . . there is a mountain of Sulphur.

De Smet concluded by acknowledging his debt to Bridger, describing him as being "familiar with every one of these mountains, having passed thirty years of his life near them."[23]

On numerous occasions, Bridger also took people directly into Yellowstone as a guide. In 1846, on a trading expedition to the Crow and Sioux nations, Bridger led a party from his trading post to Yellowstone, making sure to show them the sights. He conducted a similar trip with a group that included Kit Carson in 1850. Both that visit and the 1846 trek included tours of Yellowstone Lake and the Upper and Lower

Falls in the Grand Canyon of the Yellowstone. According to Captain Eugene Topping, who documented the event, members of Bridger's group "saw the geysers of the lower basin and named the river that drains them the Fire Hole." Topping went on to note that "the report of this party made quite a stir in St. Louis."[24]

In other words, an account of Bridger's 1850 Yellowstone trip was made public in some fashion to residents of Saint Louis, but it was not enough to warrant formal confirmation of Yellowstone's unique landscape. Bridger seems to have been tantalizingly close to ushering in the actual "discovery," at least as far as the American public was concerned. If he could simply guide the right person with enough authority and influence, the deed would be done and Bridger might receive at least some of the credit. Most likely, that "right person" would need to be the leader of a federally sanctioned exploration of the region. However, at this point in American history, with the focus on westward settlement and mining discoveries, there was little reason to venture into the winter stronghold of the Upper Yellowstone. It would be another nine years before the national government finally decided to take a look.

Standing on the Edge

(1853–1860)

IN JULY 1856, JIM BRIDGER RETURNED FROM LEADING A PRI-
vate hunting party into Fort Union, a trading post situated near
the mouth of the Yellowstone on the Missouri River. There he met
U.S. Army lieutenant Gouverneur Kemble Warren, who was preparing
for an expedition up the Yellowstone River. Warren's trek was actually the first of two federal topographical surveys dispatched into the
Yellowstone country to discern potential wagon routes to the western
mining camps and points farther west. While Warren's survey would
focus on the lower Yellowstone up to the Powder River, a second expedition, slated for 1859–1860 and led by Captain William Raynolds,
would explore the upper region. In need of a guide for both surveys, the
lieutenant offered the job to Bridger.

This was an attractive proposal. The past few years had been a time
of personal upheaval for Bridger. In 1853, he lost his trading post to
an attack by Mormon militia. The raid, though sudden, was not entirely unexpected. For years, Bridger had enjoyed good relations with
Brigham Young, but the growth of Mormon settlements in the Salt
Lake Valley antagonized Paiute and Shoshone residents, and Bridger's
friendliness toward Native Americans drew suspicion from Mormon
leaders. In the 1850s, tensions increased as national concerns grew
over the practice of polygamy in Mormon settlements and rumors that
Young sought to establish an independent theocratic nation in Utah.

For Young, the capture of Fort Bridger may have been a preemptive strategic maneuver in preparation for a future confrontation with the U.S. military. In 1857 and 1858, President Buchanan did send troops into Salt Lake City to ensure the peaceful replacement of Young with a new territorial governor, but the so-called Utah War was a nonevent. With no military confrontations and no casualties—except a Mormon attack on a westbound wagon train—Buchanan pardoned all involved. Fort Bridger, however, remained under lease as an army barracks for the next thirty-two years.

Though Bridger avoided capture during the attack, he would never regain his trading post. Instead, he established a homestead for his wife and daughter in the town of Little Santa Fe, Missouri, just south of Kansas City. Now working exclusively as an army scout and guide for pioneers, miners, and hunters heading west, Bridger accepted Warren's offer and began preparing to return once more to Yellowstone.

* * *

Warren, who would later gain national fame on Little Round Top at the Battle of Gettysburg, was in the process of drafting the first comprehensive topographical map of the western United States. His interest in Bridger, therefore, went beyond the immediate needs of the expedition. As the party ascended the Yellowstone River, Warren pressed Bridger for information about the remaining blank spaces on his map. Bridger not only complied but proceeded to enthrall his companions with tales of Yellowstone's amazing landscape over the evening campfires. Among those most entranced by Bridger's stories was a twenty-eight-year-old naturalist by the name of Dr. Ferdinand V. Hayden.[1]

Hayden, like Bridger, would serve on staff for both the 1856–1857 and 1859–1860 expeditions. In terms of personality, however, he was in many ways the polar opposite of the old trapper. A highly ambitious man, Hayden had the strategic sense to befriend those in positions of influence but also a tendency to repel rivals and peers alike with his self-centered, single-minded striving. Though he wielded a keen intellect, Hayden was often blinded by his zealous pursuit of praise. He'd been abandoned as a young child when his parents' marriage dissolved and was raised by an uncle. After attending Oberlin College, he eventually earned a medical degree from Albany Medical College, but

Hayden's true passion lay in the natural sciences, especially geology and paleontology.

Though still in his late twenties at the time of the Warren expedition, Hayden had already established himself as a competent field scientist. In 1853, he embarked on his first collecting expedition to the White River Badlands of modern-day South Dakota with his colleague, Fielding Meek. The following year, he ascended the Upper Missouri on a sprawling journey that went as far as the confluence of the Yellowstone and Bighorn Rivers and included trips to the Black Hills. Specimens he brought back represented some of the first dinosaur fossils discovered in the West and led to his election to the Academy of Natural Sciences in Philadelphia.

During this latter survey, Hayden earned a unique nickname from the Sioux, who referred to him as the "man-who-picks-up-stones-running." In each of his prior surveys, Hayden worked deep in Indian Country without a military escort, accompanied only by a handful of guides and packers who helped him haul his growing collection of specimens from place to place. The story goes that one day, as Hayden searched alone for specimens, he was surprised by a group of Sioux warriors. He tried to flee but was soon caught. Grabbing the heavy bags from Hayden's shoulders, the warriors dumped out the contents. As rocks and broken shells tumbled to the ground, the Sioux exchanged glances. They handed Hayden his bags and simply walked away. In human cultures across the world, mental illness (real or imagined) is often cause for compassion rather than hostility. There is no known confirmation of the story, which first appeared in an 1856 newspaper account, but Hayden cited it as the reason why he was generally left to his own devices in territory otherwise prone to attacks.[2]

In any event, the 1856–1857 Warren expedition proved extremely successful in scientific terms. For Hayden, the significance of the specimens he brought back—the rocks, animal skins, insects, seashells, and fossils—heightened his professional reputation. A colleague noted that Hayden had "discovered more than half the [large vertebrate] species brought from the Upper Missouri country, including all explorers back to the time of Major Long."[3]

As for Lieutenant Warren, on his return to Washington, he finally completed his map of the West. After years of compiling information from existing surveys, his own observations, and knowledge gleaned from mountain men like Bridger, Warren drafted a full picture of the region. Published in 1859, Warren's was the first comprehensive cartographic treatment of the western half of the United States. Despite the input from Bridger, it still contained a few "blank spaces," including in the Upper Yellowstone. The task of shedding light on this terra incognita, including its purported wonders, would fall to the second Yellowstone River expedition: the survey led by Captain William F. Raynolds.

* * *

The Raynolds Expedition of 1859–1860 was the first federal topographical survey explicitly focused on the Upper Yellowstone region. More specifically, Raynolds was to lead an "exploration of the region of country through which flow the principal tributaries of the Yellowstone river, and of the mountains in which they, and the Gallatin and Madison forks of the Missouri, have their source." However, like the Warren survey, Raynolds's mission included additional objectives outlined in his official orders—to describe the area's Indigenous presence, agricultural and mineral resources, climate and topography, and "the facilities or obstacles which the latter present to the construction of rail or common roads, either to meet the wants of military operations or those of emigration through, or settlement in, the country."[4]

Beyond these expectations, the army also required the captain to fulfill diplomatic agreements with the Sioux and Crow nations by dispersing blankets and other "annuities" according to the 1851 Treaty of Fort Laramie. Finally, Raynolds was ordered to observe a pending solar eclipse near the Canadian border in mid-July. But for the scientists on staff, the most exciting aspect of the expedition was the opportunity to explore the mysterious area surrounding the Upper Yellowstone.

With Jim Bridger serving as guide, federal military sponsorship, and a team of the nation's top scientists, Raynolds was poised to make his mark on Yellowstone history. If ever there was a chance to put the rumors of this mythical landscape to rest and to declare Yellowstone officially "discovered," this was it.

A meticulous, rather prudish, and deeply religious man, Raynolds was in many ways an odd choice for the assignment. Although he had some experience as a field scientist for the Northeast Boundary Survey and as a cartographer during the Mexican War, his most notable work involved supervising the construction and repair of lighthouses along the eastern seaboard.[5] In short, Raynolds was better suited to a desk job than a challenging field command.

Raynolds's journal account of the mission denotes increasing levels of frustration with a litany of issues including the weather, the landscape, its Indigenous inhabitants, and even his own men. Given orders to assess the Native Americans he encountered, Raynolds was quick to levy patronizing judgements. He found the Sioux to be "ignorant . . . savages" devoid of dignity. And after an initial fascination with the highly ornamented clothing, face paint, and hairstyles of the Crow leaders, he came to a similar conclusion, complaining of their "moral deficiencies."

Of course, he found plenty of "moral deficiencies" among his own men as well. Trained as a surveyor and engineer, Raynolds never fought in combat and at times struggled to maintain the respect of his army regulars. While his men likely appreciated Raynolds's insistence on resting each week to observe the Sabbath, they also resented his self-organized church services, for which attendance was strongly encouraged.

From the outset, Raynolds clashed with his headstrong young naturalist. For Hayden, the loss of a valuable day collecting specimens each Sunday was a sin in and of itself, not to mention a colossal waste of precious time in the field. Raynolds, meanwhile, found Hayden's lack of military discipline exasperating. The scientist's tendency to leave the expedition unannounced to go collecting, sometimes for days, only to return and fill Raynolds's supply wagons with rocks and fossils for the Smithsonian Institution, tied the captain into knots. Eventually, Hayden realized that he risked turning a potentially influential superior into an adversary and took steps to appease Raynolds, even attending the occasional Sunday service. Nonetheless, tensions remained.

Yet from time to time, Raynolds also displayed strength of character, including a sincere concern for the spiritual welfare of his men.

And his deep commitment to honesty afforded him the rare ability to admit fault when his decisions went awry. He also reserved a high level of admiration for his army scout. Though Bridger was only fifty-five at the time, Raynolds referred to him as the "Old Man of the Mountains." Perhaps this was due to the effects of a lifetime spent outdoors, which added years to Bridger's bronzed and wrinkled face. Or perhaps it was merely a sign of the captain's respect for Bridger's legendary status. While Raynolds seemed to complain about every other member of his party, Bridger received only praise.

For his part, the affable Bridger seemed to get along with everyone, including Captain Raynolds, despite his many quirks. Just before departure, the mountain man had returned to Little Santa Fe for a brief family visit only to learn that his wife, Mary, had died in childbirth. It was the third time Bridger had lost a spouse and child. It is quite possible that Bridger looked on the Yellowstone expedition as a chance to revive himself. His wife's people, the Wind River Shoshone, believed Yellowstone contained sacred sites, places where the spiritual and material worlds intermeshed in powerful ways.

* * *

The party left Saint Louis in May 1859 and advanced up the Missouri River by steamer to Fort Pierre in modern-day South Dakota. Raynolds's first stop required him to address a party of Sioux leaders to confirm the terms of the 1851 treaty. This he did in a condescending manner as he begrudgingly handed out blankets, firearms, and other supplies pursuant to the agreement. At the same time, he demanded safe passage of his party through Sioux lands, although the treaty clearly stated that whites would never enter Sioux territory. Assuring the chiefs that his expedition was only passing through and not interested in taking Sioux land, the meeting adjourned with uneasy feelings all around.

From Fort Pierre, Bridger guided the party overland north and west to the confluence of the Yellowstone and Powder Rivers. Entering Crow territory, Raynolds again met with tribal leaders to confirm friendly relations with the United States and safe passage for the expedition. The captain also hired former trapper Robert Meldrum as a second guide, to allow the party to split into two groups and survey a larger area.

In late October, the expedition arrived at the mouth of Deer Creek on the Platte River, a spot near modern-day Casper, Wyoming. Taking over some abandoned cabins near the U.S. Indian Agency, Raynolds decided to set up camp for the winter.

As the party waited out the cold snowy months, most everyone suffered a bit of cabin fever. Hayden still managed to undertake four different collecting excursions, but his resentment for Raynolds continued to grow. Careful not to criticize his captain openly, Hayden kept his views to himself and his confidants. In a letter to one of his benefactors, Spencer Baird of the Smithsonian Institution, Hayden wrote, "Capt. R. is an old <u>fogie</u> and can't quite appreciate my large views about the importance of various branches of science." In another, he summed up what was blatantly apparent to all of his fellow expedition members. "I am not happy on this trip. My Christian Captain is in trouble with someone all the time. About all he cares for is to get back with his wife. I do not think I shall ever go out again unless Warren were to go."[6] The comment, however, glosses over the fact that Hayden also complained relentlessly about Lieutenant Warren during the 1856–1857 expedition.

As accurate as Hayden's stinging indictment of Raynolds may have been, the captain made similarly unflattering, yet truthful, observations of Hayden. Writing to his commanding officer, General Humphreys, during those same winter months, Raynolds observed,

> [Hayden] seems to live only for the world and worldly fame, and I tried my best to argue in favor of living for a higher and better end. He admits readily but does not feel. I fear his whole aim is this world's rewards. God grant he may see his error.[7]

Of course, living in close proximity to one's colleagues for extended periods can bring simple truths to the fore. Various aspects of one's character become amplified, and none more so than those which irritate. Both Raynolds's moralism and Hayden's obsession with fame and glory would do much to determine the futures of both men. But these shortcomings were not the only qualities that defined the pair. Raynolds's capacity for sincerity and Hayden's scientific brilliance would also play a significant role in the events to come.

* * *

The winter of 1859–1860 was abnormally long and cold, producing an exceptionally heavy snowfall in the northern Rockies. Consequently, the party could not resume traveling until May 10 and, even then, could only do so by pushing through fields thick with snow. Two weeks later, the men finally arrived in the Wind River Valley. In order to cover more ground, Raynolds divided the expedition into two groups with a plan to rendezvous at the Three Forks of the Missouri on June 30. Once reconvened, the parties would then proceed to the Canadian border to observe the solar eclipse due to appear in mid-July.

Raynolds ordered the first group, led by Lieutenant Henry Maynadier and guided by scout Robert Meldrum, to follow the Powder River to the north, before turning west to trace the edge of the modern-day national park boundary across southern Montana. Raynolds's group, in contrast, intended to pass directly into the Upper Yellowstone region from the southeast via the Wind River. In so doing, Raynolds intended to officially document and "discover" Yellowstone's mythic geothermic features before continuing on to Three Forks.

When Bridger heard this plan, he protested that it was impossible. The snow was still too deep, especially on the high mountain passes between the Wind River and Upper Yellowstone. Instead, he argued that they should pursue another route to the west that would likely require two crosses over the Continental Divide.

Raynolds paused. For whatever reason—anxiety at the prospect of finally discovering Yellowstone, or the need to prove to his men that he was still the one in charge—Raynolds chose this moment to exert his authority and ignore the old scout's advice.

For his part, Bridger appears to have held his tongue. He may have been coming down with an illness and too weak to debate the matter. Perhaps he was still mourning his wife's death or had simply grown tired of Raynolds's attitude. It is true that making history sometimes requires bold and foolhardy action. But such action can also lead to monumental failure. If Raynolds wanted to reject the counsel of the Old Man of the Mountains and pay the price, Bridger would not stand in his way.

It took only a few days for Raynolds to regret his decision. As the expedition tried to push their way up a steep mountainside, they became bogged down in massive snowdrifts. On May 30, the party found themselves blocked by a sheer mountain barrier. With his men exhausted and Bridger now fighting a fever, Raynolds let the party rest while he and Hayden pushed on to a high point to assess the situation. The sight was not promising. Raynolds wrote, "Directly across our route lies a basaltic ridge rising not less than 5,000 feet above us, its walls apparently vertical with no visible pass."[8]

Severely disappointed, Raynolds ordered the party to turn back and trust that Bridger would find an alternative route to the west. To his credit, Raynolds took responsibility for the unfortunate turn of events, admitting, "Bridger had said from the outset that this would be impossible, and that it would be necessary to cross over to the head-waters of the Columbia, and back again to the Yellowstone." In his final written report, he described his meeting with Bridger when he arrived back at camp:

> Bridger remarked triumphantly and forcibly to me upon reaching this spot, "I told you you could not go through. A bird can't fly over that without taking a supply of grub along." I had no reply to offer, and mentally conceded the accuracy of the information of "the old man of the mountains."[9]

Instead, Bridger guided the party south and west through deep snow over Union Pass near Union Peak, both of which Raynolds named. From there they moved into the Gros Ventre Valley. Amid the difficult conditions, Raynolds grew increasingly anxious over whether they would complete the mission. In his journal he noted "a spirit of insubordination and discontent . . . manifest among the men." Nonetheless, though it lay hidden under two feet of snow, Bridger succeeded in finding the old trappers' trail that led them to Two Ocean Pass. The next day, Raynolds, Bridger, Hayden, and six others embarked on a reconnaissance mission to discern if the full party could make the journey. After hours of plunging, slogging, and scrambling their way through deep snowdrifts, the men stood at the summit of Two Ocean Pass and looked down on the headwaters of the Yellowstone. But their victory was short-lived. According to Raynolds,

> To the north . . . the view seemed almost boundless and nothing was in sight but pines and snow . . . My fondly cherished schemes of this nature were all dissipated, however, by the prospect before us, as a venture into that country would result in the certain loss of our animals, if not of the whole party."[10]

His decision made, Raynolds gave up on Yellowstone and resigned himself to reaching the meeting with Lieutenant Maynadier by June 30. Bridger charted a new course, taking them southwest through Jackson Hole and over Teton Pass, before turning north to follow the Madison River up to Three Forks.

As the party descended into Jackson Hole, Raynolds's eyes fell for the first time on the magnificent spires of the Grand Tetons. The sight pulled his mind, and his report, ever so briefly into a romantic sense of wonder. "Far off . . . stretched across the valley," Raynolds wrote, "[stands] a ragged cliff of brilliant red, above whose center [shines] with even greater brilliancy the snow-covered peaks of the Great Teton, dazzling in the clear atmosphere, with the reflected rays of the newly-risen sun."[11]

These poetic articulations hint at what might have been if Raynolds had witnessed the amazing geothermal features of Yellowstone. However, on the northward march to Three Forks, there was still one last chance to make history. As the party camped at Henry's Lake, Hayden embarked on another of his short surveys. Taking along topographer J. D. Hutton and two other men, Hayden rode approximately five miles east to Targhee Pass, where the small party found an elevated vantage point providing views of a valley that stretched away to the east. Unsure of where it led—whether to the fabled Yellowstone or to some other river valley—the four men reluctantly turned back to rejoin the party. On their arrival, Hayden described what he had seen to Bridger, who explained it was likely the Burnt Hole (or Madison River) Valley. Raynolds recorded the event in his journal:

> They found the summit distant only about five miles from our route . . . From it they could see a second pass upon the other side of the valley, which Bridger states to lead to the Gallatin. He also says that between that point and the Yellowstone there are no mountains to be crossed.[12]

One wonders what discussions ensued around the campfire that evening. With the expedition essentially standing on the edge of the western entrance to Yellowstone, with a relatively easy—if snow-filled—pathway to the geyser basins, did anyone make the case for changing course? Raynolds's journal is surprisingly silent on this matter. All we know is that the expedition pressed on the next morning, heading north to the meeting with Maynadier. But why? Was being on time for the meeting at Three Forks (for which, ironically, Maynadier was several days late), or witnessing the solar eclipse in mid-July (which Raynolds ended up missing anyway) really more important than Yellowstone's "discovery"? Was it a matter of misaligned priorities, or had Raynolds simply lost enthusiasm? Did Bridger, who presumably knew how close they were, actually recommend a detour? Or had he, by now, given up on Raynolds?

And what did Hayden think of all of this? After his discussion with Bridger, he had to realize how close he was to reaching his goal. Was it an opportunity squandered or an opportunity saved? By putting off the discovery, Raynolds was giving someone else a chance to step in and claim the honor, maybe even Hayden himself. Perhaps the adage was true: good things come to those who wait.

For Raynolds's part, he appeared content to let the moment pass and return home. As he concluded in his final report,

> The valley of the upper Yellowstone . . . is, as yet, a terra incognita. My expedition passed entirely around, but could not penetrate it . . . Although it was June, the immense body of

snow baffled all our exertions . . . Had our attempt to enter this district been made a month later in the season, the snow would have mainly disappeared, and there would have been no insurmountable obstacles to overcome. I cannot doubt, therefore, that at no very distant day the mysteries of this region will be fully revealed . . . I regard the valley of the upper Yellowstone as the most interesting unexplored district in our widely expanded country.[13]

Consequently, members of the Raynolds Expedition, like so many others before them, had to be content with Jim Bridger's stories of bubbling springs, spouting geysers, and mountains of glass, rather than see the sights for themselves.

In less than a year's time, the broader currents of national history would intervene once more, keeping Yellowstone off the map and out of mind for the majority of the American public as the nation plunged into civil war.

Chasing Glory

(1862–1869)

AS THE CIVIL WAR RAGED, THE FEDERAL GOVERNMENT NO longer supported scientific expeditions to the American West, but its interest in the region's gold, silver, and other resources never waned. Fearful of the growing number of confederate sympathizers moving into western mining camps, Congress took a number of strategic actions to secure these lands for the Union cause. Federal land grants to railroad companies supported the construction of transcontinental lines that would tie western territories to the North. Passage of the 1862 Homestead Act offered 160-acre farmsteads at heavily subsidized prices to prospective settlers. Yet another strategy involved the use of federal funds to protect westbound wagon trains.

Congress hoped the influx of settlers would provide the basis for new western towns, cities, and territories, and eventually new states, with Union sympathies. In time, these new residents would also provide the impetus for renewed explorations into places like the Upper Yellowstone.

* * *

In January 1862, Congress appropriated $25,000 "for the Protection of Overland Emigrants to California, Oregon and Washington Territory."[1] A portion of these funds supported a wagon train traveling from Saint Paul to Fort Benton, then on to the new mining camps in modern-day Idaho led by twenty-six-year-old Captain Jim Fisk.[2] Fisk was charged to "enlist and equip a body of fifty men to protect emigrants on the northern route" against things like accidents, attacks, and starvation.[3]

Less than ten days after arriving in Saint Paul, the young captain assembled a full crew of migrants and armed escorts ready for the journey. Given the speed at which Fisk accomplished this task, it is fair to ask just how he pulled it off. The short answer is by bending the rules. Rather than hire a separate military escort, Fisk enlisted the settlers as their own protectors. An offer to provide weapons, wagons, and even wages to westbound migrants was an easy sell to those planning to go anyway. To fill the roles of guide, teamsters, and cooks, Fisk turned to recommendations from influential Minnesotans. In this way, he had the good fortune of hiring Pierre Bottineau as guide, the same man who guided the original military survey of the intended route. In a similar fashion, Fisk hired as "Second Assistant and Commissary" a twenty-nine-year-old bank clerk named Nathaniel Pitt Langford.

The son of a banker from Oneida, New York, Langford had recently moved to Saint Paul to work at his brother-in-law's financial firm. Though Langford lacked military, scientific, or western field experience of any kind, Fisk readily assigned him a leadership position at the request of Langford's other influential brother-in-law, attorney James Wickes Taylor.[4] A leader in Minnesotan politics and a special agent for the U.S. Treasury Department, Taylor was also a former associate of Samuel P. Chase, who currently served as President Lincoln's secretary of the treasury (and would later become chief justice of the U.S. Supreme Court). In the years to come, Taylor would open many doors for Langford, including some— like this one—that would eventually lead him to Yellowstone.

On June 16, the Fisk party pulled out of Saint Paul. By the time they reached Fort Abercrombie on the Minnesota-Dakota border, their number totaled 53 wagons with 117 men and 13 women, 168 oxen, 14 teams of horses and 8 mules.[5] As the journey resumed, they encountered the typical trials of a westward migration: difficult weather, rationed food, and long days in the saddle. But ultimately, they arrived across the northern plains without major mishap.

However, as the wagon train entered the northern Rockies, the settlers received word of a new gold strike near Grasshopper Creek, located about one hundred miles northwest of Yellowstone. The discovery produced a ramshackle town called Bannack seemingly overnight. Sensing opportunity, a few migrants decided to end their westward journey to seek riches in the new mining camp. Among those that stopped was second-assistant Nathaniel Langford.

* * *

By the spring of 1863, Bannack had grown to over 1,000 residents. But boom towns, by their nature, don't last long. As more and more people flooded into Bannack, economic opportunities grew thin, sending prospectors elsewhere in search of the next big strike. In May, one such group found gold about seventy-five miles away in a place called Alder Gulch. Even richer than the Bannack strike, the new discovery spawned a town originally christened Varina by confederate sympathizers in honor of Jefferson Davis's wife, before the local miners' court judge renamed it Virginia City.[6] In a matter of months, it replaced Bannack as the region's economic and political center.

Around the same time, another group of prospectors decided to try their luck to the south, exploring the headwaters of the Snake River in modern-day Yellowstone National Park. Led by a miner named Charles Ream and a self-effacing civil engineer and army veteran known as "Colonel" Walter De Lacy, some forty men soon encountered a series of hot springs and old geyser cones.[7] At the confluence with the Shoshone River, they split into two groups. De Lacy led one group north to Shoshone Lake, where they traced the eastern shoreline before following a stream, which today bears De Lacy's name, and proceeded into Yellowstone's Lower Geyser Basin. The second group followed Charles Ream to Lewis Lake, before crossing over to Shoshone Lake to trace its western shore. Ream's party then found the Firehole River and followed it downstream through the Upper and Lower Geyser Basins. Afterward, Ream followed the Madison out of the Yellowstone area, while De Lacy continued north to the Gallatin River before turning west to Virginia City.

Neither De Lacy nor Ream found gold, but that did not discourage further mining exploration in the Upper Yellowstone. From 1863 through the mid-1870s, numerous prospecting expeditions passed through the area, but none resulted in significant mineral strikes.[8] They did, however, leave participants with stories of Yellowstone's hot springs and geysers. But just like the trappers before them, miners had a reputation for exaggeration. This was especially true regarding potential discoveries of gold, but it also applied to tales of the landscapes. As a result, prospectors' efforts to tell the world what they had seen were often greeted with skepticism.

De Lacy, however, would prove an exception. Rather than simply talk about what he'd seen, the colonel used his training in engineering to draft a map of the southwestern portion of modern-day Yellowstone. Though it covered only a small portion of the park, the document marked the first formal cartographic record of Yellowstone's geothermal landscape—one based not on secondhand accounts, such as those supplied by Jim Bridger, but on direct observation.

* * *

Meanwhile, back in Bannack, Nathaniel Langford was rising to a position of prominence. Well-spoken and persuasive, ruggedly handsome with a thick beard, high forehead, and penetrating gaze, Langford exuded the arrogance of power common among ambitious Euro-American men in the late-nineteenth-century American West. Unlike the mountain men, many of whom learned to respect Native American knowledge and military might, Langford's generation (and those that followed) often dismissed them out of hand. Arriving in the West after the early Indian Wars of the 1840s and 1850s, Langford did not see Indigenous peoples as a potent threat, nor did he value their culture. By the 1860s, U.S. military campaigns in the Great Lakes region had made way for white settlement by pushing tribal nations westward onto the northern plains. For Langford and others of his ilk, this was a sign of things to come. When it came to manifest destiny, he was a true believer.

More than aspiring to economic wealth, Langford wanted to be a part of this history. When he first arrived in Saint Paul in the 1850s, Langford used his family ties to join the Masons and quickly rose through the ranks. Once in Bannack, he wasted little time in founding the first masonic lodge in what eventually would become Montana Territory.[9] Within a year, residents elected Langford president of the local Union League, a branch of the semi-secret men's organization established throughout the West to lend support to the Union cause during the Civil War.[10] By the summer of 1863, Langford established a sawmill and met Sam Hauser, a civil engineer whose prospecting efforts had paid off well enough to bankroll the construction of a new smelting plant. Within months, Hauser and Langford joined forces to establish the First National Bank of Virginia City.

By December of that year, Langford joined a local contingent sent to Washington, D.C., to convince the federal government that Montana should become a new U.S. territory. The group argued that territorial status would ensure that the enormous mineral wealth of the Montana goldfields would remain firmly in Union control. In Washington, Langford took part in meetings with U.S. senators, testified at congressional hearings, and, reportedly, joined a group of Montana dignitaries for an audience with President Lincoln himself.

Upon his return to Virginia City, Langford accepted a leadership position on the town's Vigilante Committee, a largely unaccountable organization that dealt out lethal "justice" to whomever they saw fit (at least until more formal legal institutions could be established).[11] But this was only the beginning. The year 1864 would prove to be pivotal, not only for Langford but for the American West writ large.

On May 26, Congress passed a law establishing Montana Territory. It also approved a charter for the Northern Pacific Railroad Company and, in the process, provided a railroad land grant of approximately 60 million acres—the largest in U.S. history—to help cover the cost of construction.[12] On June 30, President Lincoln signed a law granting the Yosemite Valley to the state of California for the purposes of preservation. Though few realized it at the time, in less than a decade, this precedent-setting legislation would provide a roadmap for protecting Yellowstone. But for now, other issues took center stage.

As the summer progressed, growing numbers of migrants arrived in Montana. Having led a group of settlers over what would later be called the Bozeman Trail, miner John Bozeman concluded that there were better ways to earn money than panning for gold. In August 1864, in a valley located roughly sixty miles northeast of Virginia City, he and several partners platted out the town of Bozeman City. Situated in an area ideal for crops and livestock, Bozeman hoped the town would serve as a trading center for migrants. Two months later, approximately one hundred miles north, in a place called Last Chance Gulch, another gold strike occurred. In a matter of weeks, the mining camp gave rise to a new town called Helena.

As for Langford, November brought news of his presidential appointment as federal tax collector and bank examiner for Montana Territory. And in December, during its inaugural session, the Montana Territorial Legislature granted Langford a charter for a new commercial venture: the Bozeman City and Fort Laramie Wagon Road and Telegraph Company.[13] This enterprise would offer a direct link for settlers from the Oregon Trail to the Montana gold mines via the Bozeman Trail with a combined wagon and ferry service. Langford's ascent to power appeared complete.

In search of a guide to lead customers over his new toll road, at some point in late 1864 or early 1865, Langford met with Jim Bridger in Virginia City. According to Langford, the old trapper agreed to the arrangement,[14] but during the conversation, talk turned to other matters, including stories of a strange landscape on the Upper Yellowstone.

It is likely that Langford had already heard rumors of Yellowstone from miners in Bannack. But writing in his memoirs years later, Langford noted that Bridger's account caught his full attention. The precision of the mountain man's descriptions, especially of the geysers, rang true for Langford. They were not the exaggerated fables so often associated with the Old Man of the Mountains. As Langford recalled,

> [Bridger] said that he had seen a column of water as large as his body, spout as high as the flag pole in Virginia City, which was about sixty feet high. The more I pondered upon this statement, the more I was impressed with the probability of its truth . . . but I did not think that his imagination was sufficiently fertile to originate the story of the existence of a spouting geyser, unless he had really seen one, and I therefore was inclined to give credence to his statement, and to believe that such a wonder really did exist.[15]

We don't know if Langford asked Bridger to guide him to Yellowstone. But Langford writes that after meeting Bridger he was "determined" to see the place for himself. The seed of an idea had been planted. Within a year, Langford took steps to organize an exploratory expedition to the area. Just as Bridger had filled the minds of Captain Raynolds, Ferdinand Hayden, and countless others with dreams of a mythical landscape, he had inspired Langford to see Yellowstone too.

* * *

The events leading Langford to Yellowstone had much to do with the assertion of Indigenous power over the northern Great Plains. Although Robert E. Lee's surrender to General Ulysses S. Grant in April 1865 marked the beginning of the end of America's civil war, the area northeast of the Bighorn Mountains in modern-day Wyoming, known as the Powder River Country, was devolving into a new war zone.

Ceded to the Crow Nation in the 1851 Treaty of Fort Laramie, the territory was now controlled by the Oglala Lakota Sioux, who expanded westward in search of bison. In addition, the area now hosted thousands of Northern Arapahoe and Cheyenne who had fled north in the aftermath of the Sand Creek Massacre in Colorado Territory.

However, the Bozeman Trail—the very same trail Langford hoped to use for his toll-road business and which offered the most direct route from Fort Laramie to the Montana goldfields—crossed directly through the area. The Lakota Sioux, Arapahoe, and Cheyenne had no interest in allowing such trespasses into their territory and launched attacks on migrant caravans and military units attempting to pass through.

In response, the U.S. military initiated the Powder River Expedition, a campaign (lasting from July to October 1865) to construct a series of forts as protective weigh stations along the Bozeman Trail. Jim Bridger, who served as the chief army scout at Fort Laramie at the time, advised against this strategy. He went so far as to blaze an alternative trail, later known as the Bridger Trail, that stayed west of the Bighorn Mountains and thereby avoided Sioux lands altogether. But the army moved ahead and constructed Fort Reno, Fort Kearney, and Fort C. F. Smith along the Powder River.

Though the U.S. Army enjoyed superior resources and weaponry, they were no match for the guerilla tactics used by Native American warriors. Led by Oglala Sioux leader Red Cloud, between 1866 and 1867, tribal forces attacked settler and military wagon trains with increasing frequency. The low point for the army took place in December 1886, when young Captain William Fetterman defied orders and led his troops into an ambush. With the death of his entire company of eighty-one soldiers, the so-called Fetterman Fight (or Battle of the Hundred Slain) would stand as the worst defeat of the U.S. military on the Great Plains until the Battle of Little Bighorn ten years later.

By 1867, Jim Bridger was sixty-three years old. Frustrated with the ill-conceived military campaign and feeling the aches and pains of aging, he resigned from the U.S. Army for the last time and retired to live with his daughter on his farm in Little Santa Fe. Bridger would never again return to the Rocky Mountains or to Yellowstone, though his influence would linger for generations.

Meanwhile, with little change on the ground and pressure from the transcontinental railroad companies to reach a peace deal with the tribes, in late 1867 the federal government capitulated. The 1868 Treaty of Fort Laramie (and corresponding Treaty of Fort Bridger) established the Great Sioux Reservation, consisting of all of South Dakota Territory west of the Missouri River. It also ensured Indigenous hunting rights on all public domain land extending west to the Yellowstone River. Notably, this expanded Sioux domain came at the expense of the Crow and Shoshone nations, who lost millions of acres, including lands comprising present-day Yellowstone. Moreover, the U.S. Army agreed to give up the forts along the Powder River and to abandon the Bozeman Trail.[16] Within a day of the army's departure, the Lakota Sioux, Arapahoe, and Cheyenne arrived on the scene, setting fire to the three forts.

As the wooden structures went up in smoke, so did Langford's plans for a toll road, ferry, and telegraph business. Instead, he began looking for other opportunities, including a possible exploration of the Upper Yellowstone.

* * *

At about the same time as the Powder River Expedition, another set of conflicts arose with Native Americans further north. Growth of the new mining towns in Montana convinced the federal government it was time to reduce the territory held by the Blackfeet Nation. In October 1865, a group of dignitaries from Helena set out for Fort Benton to negotiate a new treaty. The group included the acting Montana Territory governor, Thomas Meagher; former trapper and guide Malcolm Clarke; and a young, bookish, recently arrived lawyer named Cornelius Hedges. But as they approached Great Falls, the party got caught in a violent snowstorm, forcing them to find shelter at Saint Peter's Jesuit Mission.

For two days, the group waited out the storm as guests of the Jesuit brothers, their evening hours filled with lively conversation. As a world traveler and veteran of the Irish fight for independence, Governor Meagher had lived one of the most exciting lives of his generation. He held court with the zeal of an Irish bard, weaving epic tales of battles against the English, his daring escape from a Tasmanian prison, his sojourn through South America, and the heroic feats of the Irish Brigade that he led during the U.S. Civil War.

But the travelers, including Meagher himself, were even more captivated with the stories told by Father Francis X. Kuppens, an energetic young protégé of Jim Bridger's friend, Father De Smet. From both De Smet and the Blackfeet he befriended, Kuppens learned of the Upper Yellowstone's sights and, in 1865, convinced some young Blackfeet warriors to take him on their spring hunt so that he might see them for himself. They showed him the Grand Canyon of the Yellowstone, the geysers in the Firehole Basin, and other amazing features, all of which he relayed to his guests. According to Kuppens,

> None of the visitors had ever heard of the wonderful place. Gen. Meagher said if things were as described the government ought to reserve the territory for a national park. All the visitors agreed that efforts should be made to explore the region and that a report of it should be sent to the government."[17]

It must be noted that Kuppens didn't record his account until 1897, a full fifteen years after the establishment of Yellowstone National Park and some thirty years after the supposed events took place. It is difficult to know if this encounter is in fact the pivotal meeting that established the idea of creating a national park or not. But an article by Cornelius Hedges corroborated the meeting and the potential inspiration it provided for a Montana-led trek to Yellowstone.[18]

* * *

Despite Governor Meagher's call for action, plans for a Yellowstone expedition were continually put on hold. The first delays were triggered by a rumored rise in hostilities among the Blackfeet and Lakota Sioux, including attacks on Saint Peter's Jesuit Mission and the death of John Bozeman (though circumstances suggest Bozeman may have been killed by a jealous white man rather than angry Blackfeet).[19] In the summer of 1867, following the pattern set by the Powder River campaign, the U.S. Army constructed two new forts: Fort Shaw, located eighty miles north of Helena, and Fort Ellis, lying east of Bozeman.

With the forts completed, Governor Meagher, Nathaniel Langford, and Truman Everts, who worked with Langford in the tax office, published an announcement in the *Montana Post* for a Yellowstone exploration scheduled for early fall. But roughly two weeks before departure, plans were scrapped following the news of Governor Meagher's death.[20]

Though the death was officially deemed an accident—the presumably tipsy governor had supposedly flipped over the rails of a riverboat at Fort Benton—some contended it was murder. Langford offered a $1,000 reward to recover the body, but it was never found. Consequently, most territorial dignitaries, including Langford and Everts, decided to stay in Helena to keep tabs on the political fallout. Only a small contingent of "Montana Territorial Volunteers" chose to move ahead with the Yellowstone trip. But the expedition, led by Captain Charley Curtiss and Dr. James Dunlevy, got only as far as Mammoth Hot Springs before returning home with (unfulfilled) plans to develop a borax mine.[21]

Over the next two years, several more attempts were made to organize an expedition. The 1869 appointment of retired general and Indiana congressman Henry Washburn as surveyor general of Montana Territory provided a new focal point for planning. Numerous officials, including Langford, Everts, Hedges, and cartographer Walter De Lacy, who now worked in Washburn's office, once again made preparations for a summer departure. And once again, a notice of intent was published in the local paper for a monthlong expedition "composed of soldiers and citizens . . . Among the places of note which they will visit, are the Falls, Coulter's Hell and Lake, and the Mysterious Mounds. The expedition is regarded as a very important one, and the result of their explorations will be looked forward to with unusual interest."[22]

Clearly unabashed at the idea of "explorers" pre-identifying the sights they planned to "discover," the announcement underscores the entitlement of political elites when it came to acts of discovery. Ironically, despite the determination of the announcement, the last-minute withdrawal of U.S. Cavalry support due to continued hostilities with the Blackfeet pulled the plug on the excursion.[23]

Nonetheless, in September 1869, three volunteers decided to go anyway. The group included two Quakers turned miners, David Folsom and Charles Cook, and a former sailor and freighter named William Peterson.

* * *

All three men had long experience in the Montana mining towns and were self-sufficient hunters and woodsmen. Trained as a surveyor, Folsom had come out to the Bannack goldfields in 1862 with Nathaniel Langford. He and Cook had worked in the rough-and-tumble mining camps ever since. And Peterson had sailed around the world on merchant vessels and worked for years as a packer.

Supplied with three horses, two pack animals, and an updated copy of De Lacy's map, the three men made their way southeast from Bozeman into the Yellowstone River Valley. They stopped at Bottler's Ranch, which brothers Frederick and Phillip had established the year before near Emigrant Gulch. With their large barn filled with the drying hides of mule deer, elk, and bison, the homestead actually focused more on hunting wild game than raising livestock. Nonetheless, Bottler's offered a natural waystation for travelers into Yellowstone.

Continuing on, Folsom, Cook, and Peterson followed the Yellowstone River upstream through Yankee Jim Canyon to the mouth of the Gardiner River. Deciding to continue along the Yellowstone rather than divert to the Gardiner River, the group missed Mammoth Hot Springs. Instead, they joined the well-trodden Bannock Trail, a major

Indigenous thoroughfare that cut through the modern-day park. After crossing to the eastern bank of the Yellowstone, they explored the area around Tower Falls.

Already knowing that upriver presented the difficult prospect of traversing the Grand Canyon of the Yellowstone, they decided to detour eastward along the Lamar River before circling back around what would later be known as Mount Washburn. This route allowed them to rejoin the Yellowstone River at a point near or just above the falls. They arrived at the edge of the canyon to a jaw-dropping view between modern-day Artist Point and Sublime Point, where Folsom wrote, "language is inadequate to convey a just conception of the awful grandeur and sublimity of this masterpiece of nature's handiwork."[24]

Jaws back in place, they continued south into Hayden Valley. As they camped that evening, the three men felt the powerful explosions of Mud Volcano ripple through the earth as they tried to sleep. The next morning, they arrived at Yellowstone Lake. They crossed to the western shore at the river's outlet near Fishing Bridge and followed the lake's northern edge to West Thumb. Here they spent two days exploring. Folsom described the lake as an

> inland sea, its crystal waves dancing and sparkling in the sunlight as if laughing with joy for their wild freedom. It is a scene of transcendent beauty which has been viewed by but few white men and we felt glad to have looked upon it before its primeval solitude should be broken by the crowds of pleasure seekers which at no distant day will throng its shores.[25]

From West Thumb, they traveled due west, passing by Shoshone Lake before crossing the Continental Divide and descending into the Lower Geyser Basin. Following in De Lacy's footsteps from his 1863 trek, they reached the Great Fountain Geyser just as it was erupting: "The setting sun shining into the spray and steam drifting towards the mountains gave it the appearance of burnished gold, a wonderful sight." The party then followed the Madison River westward out of the park area, arriving back in Helena on October 11.

* * *

While the journey had been challenging, Folsom and Cook soon found that publicizing their findings was the more difficult task. Just like the trappers and miners before them, Folsom and Cook did not have enough credibility to convince eastern publishers that their tales were true. Both the *New York Tribune* and *Harper's Magazine* refused them. Only one lesser-known periodical, the *Western Monthly Magazine*, agreed to take a chance on their story. Published in July 1870 under Cook's name (though largely derived from Folsom's diary), the piece garnered scant public attention.

Meanwhile, Nathaniel Langford and his business partner, Sam Hauser, invited Folsom to give a public talk on his findings in Helena. After agreeing, Folsom's nerves gave out once he saw the room full of strangers. He refused to take the stage and instead gave a private briefing to Langford and Hauser, convincing Langford of the need to plan his own trip the following summer.[26]

That winter, Folsom took a job as a surveyor for the territorial government, where he shared his adventures—and his journal—with the newly appointed surveyor general, Henry Washburn, and cartographer Walter De Lacy. Folsom apparently suggested to Washburn at this time that the Yellowstone area be protected for public use. Meanwhile, he helped De Lacy revise and update his map of the area.

In May 1870, during a trip through Helena, General Phillip Sheridan learned of the Yellowstone excursion and requested a meeting with Folsom, Cook, and Peterson. According to Sheridan's memoirs, he was impressed enough to authorize a small military escort for a "superficial exploration" of Yellowstone for the summer of 1870. Depending on the outcome, he noted that it might justify a much larger "engineer-led" expedition the following year to "scientifically examine and report upon this strange country."[27]

For Langford, the news of General Sheridan's meeting with Folsom was a jolt to action. With word spreading about the latest excursion, Langford realized time was short. In a matter of months, *someone* would formally "discover" Yellowstone. If it was going to be Langford, he needed to act fast.

Thirty-Seven Days

(1870)

LATE IN THE AFTERNOON ON SEPTEMBER 8, 1870, UNDER A crystal-blue sky, the nineteen-person Washburn Expedition rode horseback through a thick stand of lodgepole pines lining the southern edge of Yellowstone Lake.[1] Frequently dismounting to traverse fallen logs and muddy wetlands, the men floundered as tree branches tore their packs, horses balked, and tempers flared. Before long, the group splintered in search of easier passage, intending to regroup on the other side.

One man, fifty-four-year-old Truman Everts, soon found himself riding alone. A middle-aged bureaucrat with no wilderness experience to speak of, Everts was now beyond both earshot and eyesight of his companions. Undeterred, he pushed forward, thinking he'd discovered an ideal route. As he struggled through dense brush, he came upon a lost packhorse. He tried but was unable to keep hold of the animal's lead rope and watched in dismay as it ran off. Nonetheless, he figured the horse would find its way back to the main party eventually, as would Everts himself by the end of the day. He continued on.

As the afternoon waned, slanted rays of sunlight cut through the pine needle canopy, briefly lighting up the forest in one last brilliant display before giving way to dusk. And as darkness fell, so too did Everts's spirits.

Where was everyone?

He called out repeatedly. But no one answered. In the silence, Everts felt the first twinge of worry well up in the pit of his stomach.

Although an official member of an exploratory expedition, Everts was anything but a self-reliant woodsman. On the contrary, he had spent most of his life as a paper-pushing accountant. Having just served six years as a tax assessor for Montana Territory—and now between jobs[2]—Everts's skill set was decidedly unsuited to wilderness survival. Like several other members of the expedition, his participation was more a function of his standing in Montana politics than his ability to cope in the outdoors.

Small in stature, bespectacled, and a bit soft around the edges, Everts nonetheless held strong opinions about the world and his place in it—which, by the way, lay somewhere near the top, thank you very much. In the coming weeks, this attitude would lead Everts into a litany of difficult, if not perilous, situations. It would also provide him with the dogged determination needed to survive.

But for now, with darkness descending and no sign of his companions—and without a coat, blanket, or supplies—Everts decided to make a solitary camp for the night. One night alone wouldn't be so bad. He still had matches for making a fire, his horse for company, and a gun for protection. Things would be fine in the morning.

Finding a spot under some trees, he gathered pine boughs for bedding and settled in. But before sheer exhaustion took over, Everts had one last thought: How had he ever concluded that it was a good idea for a severely nearsighted, middle-aged bureaucrat to accompany an exploratory expedition into the wilds of the Upper Yellowstone? Right now, he could be sleeping, warm and safe, in his own bed. What, pray tell, had he been thinking?

* * *

The Washburn Expedition (more awkwardly known by scholars as the Washburn-Langford-Doane Expedition, to give the major figures their historical due) represented the culmination of roughly five years of strategic planning by Nathaniel Langford and his associates. Their self-appointed mission was nothing less than to confirm or deny, once and for all, the fantastical reports of wonders located near the headwaters of the Yellowstone River.

As Langford was well aware, it was rather late in the game for an expedition to Yellowstone focused on "discovery." News of its geothermal features had been circulating for close to seven decades among the trappers and prospectors who frequented lands west of the Mississippi. And of course, Yellowstone was hardly a revelation to Indigenous peoples who had inhabited the area for millennia. But the apparent lack of furs and mineral wealth, the intense winters, and recent hostilities with Native Americans disrupted plans for formal exploration. Despite Folsom's recent expedition, the American public remained largely unaware of Yellowstone's sensational landscape.[3]

But finally, the time was right. For Langford, the chance to "discover" Yellowstone aligned with his self-image as an explorer and nation-builder. Beyond that, he had come to believe that this special place might yield him some sorely needed economic and political benefits.

The past two years had been a rough ride for Langford. After his toll-road business fell through in 1868, he was relieved to receive a second term as tax collector for Montana Territory. But when he learned that President Andrew Johnson planned to nominate him as the next territorial governor, Langford promptly resigned his tax-office post, only to find the Senate refusing to confirm him. With Johnson now a lame-duck president—and generally reviled in Washington over Reconstruction issues in the South—Congress had little interest in doing his bidding.[4] It didn't matter that Langford was a lifelong Republican, previously appointed by President Lincoln. He still found himself unemployed.

Langford began making other plans. From Washington, he went to New York City to meet with officials from the Northern Pacific Railroad, a new transcontinental line seeking to link Lake Superior to Portland, Oregon. Langford then stopped in Saint Paul to accompany his brother-in-law, Minnesota governor William Marshall, on a survey of the railroad's planned route.

In June 1870, Langford returned to the East to meet with financier Jay Cooke at his home in Philadelphia. Known as "the man who financed the Civil War," Cooke now backed the Northern Pacific

Railroad. Hoping to raise capital through bond sales, Cooke and Langford likely discussed how an expedition extolling the sights of Yellowstone might attract potential investors, benefitting both the railroad and Montana Territory.[5] Details of the meeting are unknown, but Langford appears to have enjoyed financial support from the Northern Pacific from this point onward.

On his way back to Montana, Langford met with Major General Winfield Hancock in Saint Paul to arrange military protection for the expedition. He reached Helena on July 27 and, by mid-August, had assembled nine committed participants, along with two packers, two African American cooks, a dog named Booby, and a contingent of six U.S. cavalrymen led by Lieutenant Gustavus Cheyney Doane.

The party assembled at Fort Ellis armed with copies of Folsom's journal and De Lacy's revised map. Like the 1869 trek, the Washburn Expedition had less to do with actual discovery than verification. Members already knew with a rather high degree of certainty the route, time-table, and areas they planned to explore within the so-called terra incognita. But unlike previous visitors, dating back to Jim Bridger and John Colter, they carried with them a measure of power and prestige that they hoped would make a difference in publicizing their findings.

And with that, on the morning of August 22, 1870, the Washburn Expedition set out to "discover" Yellowstone.

* * *

The titular leader of the expedition, thirty-eight-year-old retired Union general Henry Washburn, had served with distinction during the Civil War and later served two terms as a congressman from Indiana. During the fighting at Vicksburg, however, he developed a chronic case of consumption, which forced him to retire from national politics while still relatively young.[6] In search of a less-stressful occupation in a drier climate, he plied his Washington connections to secure the post of surveyor general of Montana Territory.

In addition to Washburn, two other men shared leadership responsibilities. Langford, also thirty-eight, wielded a great deal of influence for his standing in Montana politics (including his recent near miss as governor) but also for arranging most of the logistical and financial support for the expedition. The other informal leader, thirty-year-old Lieutenant Doane, served as commander of the military escort. Charged with keeping the party safe, the highly ambitious lieutenant dreamed of fame as an explorer like his childhood hero, John Fremont.[7] Trained as a geologist, Doane was determined to keep a meticulous scientific account of the expedition's findings for his official report.

The six other "official" members of the expedition—Freemasons all and ranging in age from thirty-one to forty years—included lawyer Cornelius Hedges; engineer, entrepreneur, and future Montana governor Samuel Hauser; merchant and hunter Warren Gillette; shopkeeper Benjamin Stickney; and miner and speculator Jake Smith. The final two members were Truman Everts and his young, politically connected assistant, Walter Trumbull. At twenty-four years of age, Trumbull's inclusion reflected the influence of his father, the powerful Illinois senator and abolitionist Lyman Trumbull.

On the fourth day out from Fort Ellis, after stopping at Bottler's Ranch, the expedition made camp at the confluence of the Gardiner and Yellowstone Rivers. Like the Folsom Expedition before it, the Washburn Party decided to cross the Gardiner in favor of following the Yellowstone, thereby missing Mammoth Hot Springs.

Upon reaching Tower Falls (which Samuel Hauser measured and named), General Washburn decided to take David Folsom's advice and explore a path on the west side of the Yellowstone River to avoid the long detour made during the 1869 expedition. He rode his horse up to an overlook that offered a distant view of Yellowstone Lake. Upon his return to camp, the group decided to christen the peak Mount Washburn in the general's honor. The next day, the entire party made the ascent, allowing Lieutenant Doane to record his epiphany on the volcanic origins of the Yellowstone Plateau.

In the following days, the group proceeded up the Grand Canyon of the Yellowstone, taking measures of the falls and handing out place names left and right: Cascade Creek, Crystal Falls, Silver Thread, Alum Creek. They crossed today's Hayden Valley holding to its western edge, which allowed the men to witness Mud Geyser and the belching Mud Volcano, before crossing back to the east side of the Yellowstone River. On September 3, they arrived at Yellowstone Lake.

Somewhere along the way, Lieutenant Doane suffered a puncture wound on his thumb, which had become severely inflamed. Thus far, the expedition had been fortunate enough to avoid injury. Truman Everts had come down with a short fever, but otherwise, all remained in good health. Nonetheless, in the wild country without medical treatment, even a seemingly minor injury could result in a fatal bacterial infection. The growing agony emanating from Doane's thumb suggested serious potential harm. Langford agreed to act as surgeon but denied Doane's request for chloroform, fearing it posed an even greater health risk.

> [Doane] swallowed his disappointment, and turned his thumb over on the cartridge box, with the nail down. Hedges and Bean were on hand to steady the arm, and before one could say "Jack Robinson" I had insert the point of my penknife, thrusting down to the bone, and had ripped it out the end of the thumb. Doane gave one shriek as the released corruption flew out in all directions upon surgeon and assistants, and then with a broad smile on his face he exclaimed, "That was elegant!"[8]

Langford applied a poultice made of bread and water to the injury, and Doane slept for the next thirty-six hours. When the Lieutenant was ready to resume travel, Langford and Washburn choose a new route circumnavigating Yellowstone Lake. The group set out on September 5 but struggled to find a path. Langford and Doane climbed up a mountainside for reconnaissance, allowing Langford to map out the southward stretching "arms" and the western "thumb" of the lake. This action led Washburn to name two nearby peaks for the men.[9]

But despite this new geographic information, the going was rough. For the next two days, the party slogged through heavy brush on the southern edge of the lake before tilting north across the Continental Divide. Exhausted, they made camp on September 9 in a small clearing near Surprise Creek. In the jumbled haste of setting up camp, it took some time before anyone noticed that someone was missing.

Where was Truman Everts?

* * *

The next day, waking up with the sun amid early morning frost, sore, hungry, and chilled to the bone, Truman Everts pondered the very same question.

After the long night alone, Everts hoped the morning would bring a quick ending to his solo adventure. Gathering his things, he mounted his horse and began anew, attempting to find the shore of Yellowstone Lake and reunite with the main party. But within the crowded stands of timber, he soon lost his sense of direction. Given his poor eyesight, Everts found it necessary to dismount repeatedly to scout the ground for possible tracks or signs of a trail. Each time he did so, his horse stood still, patiently awaiting Everts's return to the saddle.

Until he didn't, at which point Everts's situation quickly deteriorated. Everts later recounted: "While surveying the ground my horse took fright, and I turned around in time to see him disappearing at full speed among the trees. That was the last I ever saw of him."

Everts spent the rest of the day trying to track down the animal to no avail. He then decided to post several written notices in case his companions might find them. Everts was now truly alone. The loss of his horse also meant the loss of his gun and saddlebags, which contained matches. With only two small knives, an opera glass, and the clothes on his back, the full weight of Everts's predicament settled heavily on his shoulders.

As the sun descended, he faced the prospect of a second night alone in the wilderness, but this time without a campfire. And this time, sleep didn't come easy. Every rustling leaf or creaking branch brought horrific visions of man-eating wolves or bears. Shivering in the cold and wracked by pangs of hunger, Everts huddled under a tree and waited impatiently for the morning light.

The next day, Everts awoke exhausted and weak. He checked his posted notices but found no trace of his companions. Still determined to rejoin them at Yellowstone Lake, he got turned around and headed in the opposite direction, ultimately finding his way to modern-day Heart Lake.

Near the shores of this waterbody (which Everts named Bessie Lake in honor of his daughter), he noticed a plant with distinctive light-green spiky leaves. Pulling the plant up by the roots, Everts found it resembled a radish or turnip and ventured an exploratory nibble. Eureka! It wasn't half bad.

The plant known as *elk thistle* (*Cirsium foliosum*), later renamed *Everts's thistle*, turned out to contain edible roots. This critical discovery provided a pleasant-enough food source that helped him avoid starvation. After filling his belly, a relieved Everts stretched out under a tree and settled down for a nap in the warm afternoon sun.

But this respite was short-lived.

After some hours, Everts was jolted awake by the shrill human-like screech of a mountain lion. Letting loose with a howl of his own, he moved with speed fueled by mortal fright. Everts grasped the branches of the tree above his head and pulled himself up, scrambling as high as he dared. Moments later, the predator appeared below him, a massive cat moving slowly round and round the base of the tree.

Everts felt the beast sizing him up as it tried to decide on the best way to launch itself into the tree and devour his short, somewhat-meaty frame. The creature's low, snarling growls periodically gave way to nerve-racking screams, sending the hysterical bureaucrat lurching to the far side of the tree, shaking in fear.

At first, Everts responded to each roar with a fear-laden shriek of his own, throwing branches down on the beast and shaking the tree in an attempt to scare it off. But these efforts seemed to have no effect. As darkness descended, Everts tried a different tactic: silence and stillness. After several more hours of pacing, "growling and snuffing," the big cat finally gave up and leapt away into the forest. In his relief—and rapid loss of adrenaline—the exhausted Everts half climbed, half fell out of the tree, dropping to the ground with a thud. Despite his fears that the predator might return, he was soon asleep right back in his original spot.

The next day, Everts awoke late, with the sun already high in the sky. But as he looked up, he saw dark clouds quickly rolling in. Soon, Everts felt the sting of pelting hail followed by snow. Seeking shelter under a nearby spruce, Everts passed the next two days resting and eating thistles. Once he even supplemented his diet by catching and consuming raw a small songbird that inadvertently sought shelter under the same tree. During a break in the storm, Everts ventured out and discovered some hot springs on the far shore of the lake. Relocating his primitive camp closer to the springs, he found he could use the steam and heated ground to warm himself and even cook his thistle roots in the boiling water.

All told, Everts remained near Heart Lake for about seven days. At one point, while sleeping, he rolled over and broke through the crust near one of the springs, burning his hip in the steam. Another time, he managed to lose his "two small knives." But when the storm finally passed, he had an epiphany: perhaps he could make a fire using the magnifying properties of his opera glass? After several attempts, smoky tendrils burst into a tiny orange flame! Soon he was warming himself next to a cheery campfire.

His spirits raised, Everts attempted more ambitious tasks: fashioning a pair of slippers from his torn boot leather, making a rudimentary fishing hook and line from a pin and string (though ultimately useless in catching fish), and crafting a knife of sorts out of his belt buckle, which he then used to make pouches to carry thistle roots.

However, despite these improvements, Everts's stay at Heart Lake may have done more harm than good. A short hike up the mountainside (today's Mount Sheridan) would have pointed Everts to Yellowstone Lake and his friends. Instead, he remained relatively hidden, reducing the odds that he would ever be found.

* * *

Back at the Washburn camp, on the first night of Truman Everts's absence, none of the expedition members registered much concern. Periodically firing gunshots into the air and keeping a signal fire blazing all night, they fully expected to see him ride into camp in the morning.

But the next day, when Everts failed to appear, the men made more concerted efforts. Walter Trumbull and Warren Gillette retraced their path back to the previous day's campsite. Along the way, they left bags of provisions and blazed trail markers on trees. Meanwhile, Langford and Hauser climbed a ridge high above Yellowstone Lake and lit a massive signal fire, one that eventually transformed into a full-scale forest fire.

When none of these tactics worked, the group decided to move to a better campsite on the West Thumb of Yellowstone Lake, from which they could launch a more systematic search. On September 12, the third day of Everts's disappearance, the men paired up and set off in different directions to find their lost comrade. Langford and General Washburn actually came within half a mile of Heart Lake. But because Langford's horse broke through the crust of a hot spring and burned its leg, they were forced to turn back empty-handed.[10]

The next day, the same hailstorm that hit Everts engulfed the Washburn camp. For the next two days, most of the men stayed in their tents except for Lieutenant Doane. During his snowy ride, he stumbled across the multicolored springs of West Thumb Geyser Basin. After making careful notes in his journal, he returned to camp to share his discovery.

On September 16, the skies cleared, but there was still no sign of Everts, who had now been missing for an entire week. Despite the addition of trout and occasional wild game to their food supply, the expedition's rations were running low. They had planned for thirty days of travel and now twenty-five had elapsed. Not knowing how long it would take them to find their way home, General Washburn reluctantly called off the search.

Their companion was most likely dead. For the good of the expedition, it was time to move on.

All but one consented to this course of action. Warren Gillette, the best woodsman of the group, volunteered to stay behind and continue the search as long as someone accompanied him. After consulting with Lieutenant Doane, General Washburn agreed to allow two soldiers to stay and help. Gillette's motivations were likely amplified by the fact that he was courting Everts's daughter, Bessie. It just wouldn't do to leave his potential father-in-law behind.

The next morning, with ten days of rations in hand, the three searchers bade farewell to the main party. Led by General Washburn, the expedition set a course due west toward the Madison River basin.

* * *

The same day he was given up for dead, Truman Everts came to a decision of his own.

As pleasant as it all was, he could no longer stay at Heart Lake. Winter's arrival meant certain death. Everts's only hope lay in finding a way out on his own. Packing a supply of thistle roots, Everts struck out once more for Yellowstone Lake, hoping to find his friends' trail.

But as he traversed the dense forest, he once again became disoriented. Unable to find the lake and failing to make a fire before an overcast sky blocked the use of his opera glass, Everts spent a cold night on a "bleak hillside." In the morning, discouraged, he backtracked to Heart Lake to recover his confidence before trying again.

As luck would have it, William Gillette and the two soldiers arrived on the shores of Heart Lake on the very day Everts departed on his latest failed bid to find Yellowstone Lake. The search party apparently scouted the shore for campfire smoke and, not seeing any, left the area. Had the timing been different or had they walked the entire perimeter, they might have found Everts's campsite or even the man himself. Instead, Gillette and his comrades reluctantly gave up their search and headed for home a few days later.

Oblivious to this near miss, Everts rested two days at his old camp before setting out again. And this time he finally succeeded. Through dumb luck, Everts found not only the shores of Yellowstone Lake but also the Washburn campsite near West Thumb. Though disappointed at the absence of food caches or messages from his companions (they had actually left behind both but had placed them closer to where Everts initially disappeared), he lit a campfire and fell asleep cheered by the thought that he might follow their tracks home. However, his optimism was soon replaced by scorching pain as he awoke in the night to find he had rolled into his own fire.

A few nights later, he went one better. As he lay sleeping, a sudden loud roar exploded in his ears. Wide-eyed, he looked for a hungry mountain lion but saw instead that his campfire had transformed into a massive forest fire. Surrounded by a wall of flames, Everts crawled to safety, sustaining burns to his hands, hair, and face. Nonetheless, he later recalled feeling excited by the devastation he had caused:

I never before saw anything so terribly beautiful! It was marvelous to witness the flash-like rapidity with which the flames would mount the loftiest trees. The roaring, cracking, crashing, and snapping of falling limbs and burning foliage was deafening. On, on, on traveled the destructive element, until it seemed as if the whole forest was enveloped in flame.[11]

Over the next four weeks, Everts endured a journey filled with mishaps and self-inflicted injuries, amplified by a lack of food and increasingly harsh weather. At one point, he broke his glasses, further blurring his already-poor eyesight. Another time, he found catchable minnows in a creek, which he greedily devoured, only to find his stomach could not keep them down.

On top of these physical trials, Everts's memoir recounts powerful bouts of mental anxiety and fear tempered with equally forceful moments of unflagging determination to survive. Already pushing the limits of his body and mind, Everts's Yellowstone journey soon stretched him even further toward the outer margins of sanity. As he later wrote,

Weakened by a long fast, and the unsatisfying nature of the only food I could procure . . . my mind . . . was in a condition to receive impressions akin to insanity. I was constantly traveling in dream-land, and indulging in strange reveries such as I had never known before. I seemed to possess a sort of duality of being, which, while constantly reminding me of the necessities of my condition, fed my imagination with vagaries of the most extravagant character.[12]

Everts began to hallucinate with increasing frequency, seeing and conversing with an apparition of an old acquaintance. Significantly, this "friend" advised him against trying to cross the Madison Mountains and encouraged him to return to Yellowstone Lake, advice Everts eventually followed. And as time wore on, he was joined by an entire menagerie of ghostly companions representing various parts of his own body: arms, legs, stomach, and so on. Each spirit-like body part had its own voice, personality, and demands, providing the sick man with a feeling of companionship.

Ultimately, Everts found his way to the Yellowstone River and followed it downstream in an attempt to retrace the inbound route of the Washburn Expedition. He scrambled his way to the Grand Canyon of the Yellowstone, then proceeded on to Tower Falls.

All around him, he could see bountiful sources of food—deer, elk, geese, squirrels, trout—but he had no means of catching anything. Instead, he came across a gull's wing and crushed the bone to make a broth, devoted unsuccessful hours to chasing grasshoppers or toads, and inadvertently set more nighttime forest fires. Miraculously, he avoided further encounters with predators, which would have made short work of Everts in his weakened state—or, for that matter, in his prime.

By October 16, after surviving more than five weeks in the wilderness and traversing some fifty miles, Everts now resembled a wounded, dying animal. Babbling incoherently, with his joints locking up, blurred eyesight, and frostbitten feet and toes, he slowly crawled on hands and knees onto the Blacktail Deer Plateau.

For better or worse, Everts's odyssey was coming to an end.

* * *

Meanwhile, the Washburn Expedition entered the final and most important leg of its journey. The day after leaving Yellowstone Lake, the party came upon the Firehole River and proceeded downstream. As they entered the Upper Geyser Basin, the party witnessed the majestic eruption of what would become one of the world's most famous sights: Old Faithful Geyser.

In their excitement, the party hastily set up camp in a small grove of pines near the Beehive Geyser, then spread out to hunt for more. By the end of the day, they had given names to some of the most famous geysers in the park: Old Faithful, Beehive, Castle, Giant, Giantess, and Grotto.

But by 9:00 a.m. the next day—less than twenty-four hours after their arrival—they left the Upper Geyser Basin and continued down the Firehole River. Their path took them past "an enormous bluestone spring," known today as Grand Prismatic, and the blown-out crater of Excelsior Geyser, from whence gushed massive amounts of boiling water into the river below.

That night they made camp at the confluence of the Firehole and

Gibbon Rivers, where Langford later claimed that the idea of creating the world's first national park was first conceived. In the morning, they continued down the Madison River and exited the modern-day national park boundaries. Turning north, they continued on toward Virginia City, which they reached on September 23. The next day, Lieutenant Doane and his soldiers left for Fort Ellis, and by September 27, the rest of the group arrived in Helena.

Five days later, Gillette also arrived in town empty-handed. The *Helena Herald* wrote, "we feel fully satisfied that everything has been done for the recovery of Mr. Everts that humanity can suggest, and to Mr. Gillette is due the highest credit and gratitude of all our citizens."[13]

Unfortunately for Gillette, it was not enough "credit and gratitude" to sway the affections of Bessie Everts. With his advances rebuffed, Gillette would resign himself to bachelorhood until the end of his days.[14]

* * *

On October 6, in one final gesture of hope, Cornelius Hedges's law partner, Judge R. Lawrence, posted a reward of $600 for Everts's safe return. The offer was immediately taken up by two mountaineers, George Pritchett and John Baronett. The second man, who would come to be known as "Yellowstone Jack," was an experienced miner, hunter, and guide. Hoping to trace the Washburn route before the first fall snows, the men set out at once with two Crow scouts. In ten days, they traveled south from Bozeman, past Bottler's Ranch, and beyond the confluence of the Gardiner and Yellowstone Rivers and arrived at the Bannock Trail. On October 16, near a place called the Cut, a narrow opening between the Blacktail Deer Plateau and Crescent Hill, Baronett's dog spotted what appeared to be a small bear crawling along the mountainside.

> My first impulse was to shoot . . . When I got near to it I found it was not a bear, and for my life could not tell what it was. It did not look like an animal that I had ever seen and it was certainly not a human being . . . I went up close to the object; it was making a low groaning noise, crawling along upon its

knees and elbows, and trying to drag itself up the mountain. Then it suddenly occurred to me that it was the object of my search.[15]

By all accounts, Everts was a mess, his life hanging by a thread. Weighing approximately ninety pounds (Everts claimed fifty), his clothes were in shreds, his exposed skin blackened or covered in un-healed burns, his feet frostbitten and bare. Given that sleet was begin-ning to fall, Everts was likely hours away from death.

Everts's rescuers gathered him up and took him to their campsite before transferring him to a miner's cabin on Turkey Pen Creek, just east of modern-day Gardiner. Baronett cared for the sick man while Pritchard went to Bozeman for help.

For the next few days, things were touch and go for Everts. His monthlong diet of fibrous thistles had blocked his digestive tract. But amazingly, Everts's luck held out. An old hunter passing by happened to have a supply of oil on hand rendered from bear fat. A pint of the greasy elixir succeeded in restoring Everts's system, and, from that point on, he made a slow yet steady recovery.

On November 4, Everts arrived in Helena. A week later, though he still walked with a cane, he felt strong enough to attend a celebra-tory banquet. The Washburn Expedition—including Everts's personal trial—was finally over.

* * *

With the expedition complete, the wonders of Yellowstone were offi-cially "discovered." But what this really meant was that the expedition's written accounts became the first to be validated in national publica-tions. The prestige of its members silenced most doubters and ensured the dissemination of their findings on a national scale.

Within days of their return, General Washburn, Cornelius Hedges, Warren Gillette, Walter Trumbull, and Nathaniel Langford all wrote short pieces for the *Helena Herald* and other newspapers. Most pre-dicted that Yellowstone would attract throngs of future visitors. Sev-eral argued for the transfer of the area from Wyoming to Montana

Territory. And one piece, by Hedges, hinted at the idea of protecting the land, to "secure its future appropriation to the public use," but without offering clarification on just what he meant.

Washburn's account received high praise and was picked up by Denver's *Rocky Mountain News* and *The New York Times*. But the most influential works were authored by Langford, Everts, and Doane. The Lieutenant's report to the U.S. Army offered the most accurate scientific descriptions of Yellowstone's geologic features. It also confirmed the region's volcanic origin and was praised for skillfully oscillating between scientific observation and romantic prose. General Sherman arranged for its publication, and soon, like John Wesley Powell's account of his adventure down the Colorado River, Doane's Yellowstone report gained a wide public audience.

Langford, meanwhile, penned a lengthy two-part essay entitled "The Wonders of Yellowstone" for the newly launched magazine *Scribner's Monthly*.[16] Notably, the articles included several landscape drawings by painter Thomas Moran based on Langford's descriptions.

In addition to Langford's account (in the May–June 1871 issue), *Scribner's* also published Truman Everts's story, "Thirty-Seven Days of Peril."[17] Everts's dramatic tale of survival fascinated the general public. Though heavily edited to show Everts in the best possible light, the piece did not shy away from describing his trial by fire, including the dangers he faced as a result of his own missteps.

But if the essay brought Everts personal fame, it did even more for Yellowstone. It helped build the idea of the landscape as a place of untamed and sometimes terrifying wilderness, but also one that was "safe" to visit. Public audiences, especially eastern readers, could relate to Everts. If an inexperienced, middle-aged bureaucrat could overcome the area's wild travails, then perhaps they could too. This enhanced the appeal of Yellowstone as a potentially exciting destination, a place where nature was at once wild and controlled.

In other words, a park.

In fact, Everts's piece ends with a prediction that people would soon flock to Yellowstone to see it for themselves. Echoing Captain Raynolds's journal entry from ten years before, Everts claimed that "the time is not far distant when the wonders of the Yellowstone will be made accessible to all lovers of sublimity, grandeur and novelty in natural scenery."[18]

But even before the publication of these accounts, there were those who saw the need for one more "final" exploration. As prestigious as the Washburn party was, a group of *territorial* dignitaries was no substitute for *nationally* known figures in the pantheon of discovery.

In short, there was still one last opportunity for someone to have the final word on Yellowstone. And there was one man who knew with utter certainty that he, and he alone, was ideally suited to the task. He was the one who had listened for hours to Jim Bridger's stories during the long winters of 1856 and 1859; the one who stood atop Targhee Pass before submitting to his captain's orders to turn back; and the one who now served as the head of the U.S. Geological and Geographic Survey of the Territories.

His name? Dr. Ferdinand V. Hayden.

Final Discovery

(1871)

ON THE EVENING OF JANUARY 19, 1871, NATHANIEL LANG-
ford entered the ornate Lincoln Hall in Washington, D.C., to deliver a
public address entitled "Recent Explorations on the Yellowstone." The
talk was the first of a planned twenty-four-lecture tour financed by Jay
Cooke for the Northern Pacific Railroad.[1]

Only three months after toasting the return of the Washburn
Expedition, the fellowship was dispersing far and wide. The general,
his condition worsened by a cold contracted in the latter stages of the
expedition, was about to lose his battle with tuberculosis. He would
pass away the following week at the age of thirty-eight. Meanwhile,
Truman Everts was preparing for a move back East, where his national
fame and public favor would soon dissipate.[2] The others resumed the
professions they'd had prior to the expedition: Lieutenant Doane back
at Fort Ellis and Cornelius Hedges and Sam Hauser in Helena, where
Hauser's mining and railroad businesses would eventually land him in
the governor's office.

As for Langford, soon after writing his Yellowstone articles for
Scribner's, he developed a lengthy 13,000-word oral presentation as
part of a publicity campaign for the Northern Pacific. Hoping to attract
investors and drum up political support for the new transcontinental
line, Langford did his best to present Yellowstone as a "must-see" destination for American tourists.

But that night in Lincoln Hall, despite a glowing introduction from speaker of the house, James Blaine of Maine, Langford felt ill at ease. Clearing his throat, he sensed a rather intense gaze emanating from a gentleman seated near the back of the room. With dark-brown hair combed back to reveal a large forehead, languid eyes, and an Abe Lincoln–style beard, the man exuded confidence and consequence. Langford may not have recognized Dr. Ferdinand Hayden at first, but over the next eighteen months, the two men would become forever entwined in events leading to a watershed moment in conservation history: the creation of the world's first national park.

* * *

Historians have long debated just what Hayden gleaned from Langford's presentation that evening. Some have argued that Hayden didn't conceive the notion of exploring Yellowstone until hearing Langford's speech. Others, including Langford himself, went a step further, suggesting that the idea to create a national park was first articulated to the public in these lectures. Such assertions imply that Hayden somehow "stole" something from Langford, but there is no evidence to support either claim.[3]

In all likelihood, Hayden found most of the presentation old news. Already well acquainted with Jim Bridger's stories, Hayden had come tantalizingly close to "discovering" Yellowstone some ten years earlier on the Raynolds Expedition, long before Langford or Washburn had even heard of the place.

And unlike Langford, Hayden's real interest in Yellowstone had less to do with geysers and more with the chance to map out the common source of two of North America's greatest rivers: the Missouri and Columbia.[4] In short, it would be wrong to say that Hayden co-opted the idea of an expedition that night. As one Hayden biographer notes, the geologist likely developed his summer plans in early December, well before Langford's January lecture.[5]

What we can say with greater certainty is that by attending Langford's talk, Hayden observed the degree to which Yellowstone was garnering attention, not only from the general public but from railroad companies and, most importantly, members of Congress. Speaker Blaine's introductory remarks underscored this point. Numerous politicians, including Judge William Kelly of Pennsylvania and Henry Dawes of Massachusetts, had long supported the transcontinental railroads. Now, they were taking a clear interest in Yellowstone.

Unfortunately for Langford, his lecture tour was soon cut short. After the talk in Washington, he gave a second presentation on January 21 at Cooper Union Hall in New York City. Shortly thereafter, he fell ill with an upper-respiratory ailment, forcing him to retreat to his family home in Oneida to recuperate. Langford gave his talk only once more—at Jay Cooke's estate in Philadelphia—before calling it quits and heading back to Montana.

But while Langford put his plans on hold, Hayden moved full steam ahead, intensifying his congressional lobbying efforts for summer research funding. On March 3, with passage of the Sundry Civil Act of 1871, he secured a $40,000 budget for his annual Geological Survey of the U.S. Territories.[6] According to the legislation, Hayden's survey would examine the sources of the Missouri and Yellowstone Rivers. In addition, Hayden planned to chart a route for a potential rail line from Utah to Yellowstone Lake via Two Ocean Pass. As part of this expanded itinerary, Hayden accepted contributions in kind from various railroad companies, including free transportation for his men and supplies on the Union Pacific and Central Pacific Railways.

By mid-May, Hayden established a base camp near Ogden, Utah, where expedition members began to assemble. In contrast to the Washburn party, Hayden's included an array of scientific specialists, including mineralogist Dr. Albert Peale, botanists Dr. George Allen and Robert Adams, topographers Anton Schönborn and A. J. Smith, entomologist Cyrus Thomas, meteorologist J. W. Beam, zoologist Edward Carrington, and physician Dr. Charles Turnbull.

Aware of the power of visual images to garner wide public attention,[7] Hayden arranged for artist Henry Elliott to join the group, along with several individuals skilled in the relatively new practice of landscape photography. The latter included William Henry Jackson (who had worked with Hayden previously) and two assistant photographers, George Dixon and Joshua Crissman.

The expedition also included six "political" members: young relatives or protégés of influential politicians, including Representative

Henry Dawes's son, Chester, and Illinois senator "Black Jack" Logan's son, William. Identified as "general assistants" in the survey's manifest, their real purpose was to appease Hayden's congressional patrons. Finally, another twenty men served as cooks, packers, hunters, and guides. Organizing the entire entourage was Hayden's talented long-time administrative assistant, thirty-year-old James Stevenson.

On June 11, they packed their wagons and headed north to Fort Hall in Idaho Territory before continuing on to Virginia City. Along the way, Hayden received word from Jay Cooke asking if landscape painter Thomas Moran might join them to record visual images for the Northern Pacific and *Scribner's Monthly*. Hayden agreed, and on June 30, Moran caught up with the group. A few days later, the entourage arrived at Fort Ellis to join their military escort.

Led by a decorated veteran of the Civil War, Captain George Tyler, the detachment of soldiers brought the total number of participants to eighty-three men. In size and scope, Hayden's survey dwarfed the Washburn Expedition in every possible way, including the range and level of scientific expertise, political influence, and artistic ability.

But just when it seemed that everything was in order, Hayden encountered one last snafu. Upon arrival at Fort Ellis,[8] he learned that General Sheridan had made good on his earlier promise to outfit an independent military-led scientific expedition to Yellowstone. Commanded by Captain John Barlow, chief of the Army Engineers for the Division of the Missouri, and assisted by Captain David Heap, the eleven-man team had orders to collect geological and topographical data on the region.

Though federally funded and escorted by the U.S. Cavalry, the Hayden Survey was still an endeavor run predominantly by civilian scientists. At least initially, Barlow's presence dealt a serious blow to Hayden's ego. But in short order, he adjusted. After all, Barlow was a rather introverted career military scientist, lacking Hayden's prestige in academia and his political connections in Washington. Moreover, his introductory letter to Hayden was respectful, requesting, on behalf of General Sheridan, permission to join his expedition. He intended to work *with* Hayden, not supplant him. In fact, over the coming weeks, even though the two groups would often take different routes and travel at different speeds (moving a day or two apart), Hayden would frequently collaborate with Barlow to their mutual benefit.

* * *

On July 15, 1871, the Hayden Survey left Fort Ellis, with Barlow following a day behind. As with earlier expeditions, they headed southeast to the Yellowstone River and followed it due south until stopping at Bottler's Ranch. Leaving their wagons with the Bottlers, the party transferred their gear to pack horses and continued on through Yankee Jim Canyon. But at the confluence of the Gardiner River (known to them as Warm Creek or Hot Springs Creek), Hayden decided to turn away from the Yellowstone and climb up toward Mammoth Hot Springs, one of the few sights missed by both the Folsom and Washburn parties.

Like earlier expeditions, the Hayden Survey quickly learned that just about everywhere they went in Yellowstone, someone else had gotten there first. This simple truth was evidenced not by archeological finds or human-made alterations in the landscape but by the physical presence of individuals standing there with grinning faces to greet them as they arrived.

Mammoth Hot Springs (called White Mountain Hot Springs by Hayden)[9] was a case in point. Upon arrival, Hayden found an encampment referred to by its inhabitants as "Chestnutville," a spa of sorts run by the owner of a shady "gentleman's club" in Bozeman City called "Chestnut's Folly."[10] Nearby they found Jim McCartney's bathhouse, located on a 320-acre homestead claim near a seemingly extinct geyser cone that Hayden named the Liberty Cap. McCartney hoped to build a two-story hotel in the coming weeks. And he was not alone. Another homesteader, Matthew McGuirk, planned to do the same along the Gardiner River. These early entrepreneurs sought to promote the "curative waters" as a remedy for ailments ranging from arthritis to syphilis. According to Hayden, business was already booming:

> Around these springs are gathered at this time, a number of invalids, with cutaneous diseases, and they were most emphatic in their favorable impressions in regard to the sanitary

effects. The most remarkable effect seems to be on persons af-
flicted with syphilitic diseases of long standing.[11]

The clientele with these assorted illnesses appeared to be residents
from Bozeman City, prospectors on their way to the Clarks Fork mines,
and soldiers from Fort Ellis, all of whom, it seemed, had patronized
Chestnut's Folly or similar establishments in the recent past.

Unabashed at the scene, Hayden and Barlow set about the business of scientific exploration: gathering topographical data; collecting
mineral and biological specimens; and assessing the springs' temperatures, sizes, depths, and chemical compositions. William Jackson took
photographs, and Moran put his watercolors to work. In his journals,
Hayden proclaimed the area "one of the most remarkable groups of hot
springs in the world."

> The snowy whiteness of the deposit at once suggested the name
> of White Mountain Hot Springs. It had the appearance of a fro-
> zen cascade . . . Before us was a hill 200 feet high composed of
> the calcareous deposit of the hot springs with a system of step-
> like terraces . . . The steep sides of the hill were ornamented with
> a series of semicircular basins, with margins varying in height
> from a few inches to six or eight feet, and so beautifully scalloped
> and adorned with a kind of bead-work that the beholder stands
> amazed at this marvel of nature's handiwork. Add to this a snow-
> white ground, with every variety of shade, of scarlet, green, and
> yellow, as brilliant as the brightest of our aniline dyes.[12]

Leaving Mammoth, the survey group headed south to climb
a "round, dome-like mountain" that rose some 2,000 feet above the
springs (possibly Bunsen Peak). The summit offered views in all directions, including a somewhat dim outline of the Tetons. The parties
then returned to the Yellowstone River and camped near Lost Creek.

* * *

Jack Baronett (still in the process of becoming Yellowstone Jack)
never did receive the $600 reward for rescuing Truman Everts. When

Baronett and his partner came to collect, the judge who offered the money refused to pay, insisting that since Everts had survived, he should deliver the sum himself. But when asked, Everts snubbed his rescuer, arguing that he never needed saving anyway. In an interview he gave decades later, Baronett lamented that he should have left Everts to rot.[13]

Nonetheless, Baronett did benefit from the rescue in a roundabout way. During the search, he learned of the gold strikes near the future site of Cooke City. Having toiled for years in various mining camps, he realized that a toll bridge on the Yellowstone serving would-be prospectors might be a profitable enterprise. Consequently, he built a ninety-foot log bridge across the Yellowstone near the fork of the Lamar River. Suitable for pack animals and horses, Baronett charged two bits per animal per crossing, which most miners—and Captain Barlow—happily paid to avoid the potential dangers of the Bannock Crossing several miles upstream.

While Barlow explored Junction Butte on the eastern bank, Hayden stayed west of the river to examine Tower Falls. After naming the nearby canyon Devil's Den, Hayden's group continued southward along a well-worn Native American trail that took them to the summit of Mount Washburn.

Standing at the peak, Hayden peered through the smoky haze of a recent wildfire. Despite the muddled view, he perceived the geologic truth of Yellowstone's landscape with utter clarity:

> We may say, in brief, that the entire basin of the Yellowstone is volcanic . . . [At] a period not very remote in the geological past, this whole country was a scene of wonderful volcanic activity. I regard the hot springs so abundant all over the valley as the last stages of this grand scene. Hot springs, geysers, etc., are so intimately connected with what we usually term volcanoes that their origin and action admit of the same explanation.[14]

Hayden's pronouncement reaffirmed Doane's earlier observation that Yellowstone was in fact volcanic in origin. This point would carry enormous weight in later debates about the potential of the area as a national park. But for now, Hayden descended Mount Washburn and proceeded due south to the next enthralling feature on their itinerary: the upper and lower waterfalls of the Yellowstone River.

Like others before him, Hayden struggled to find words to describe the scene:

> No language can do justice to the wonderful grandeur and beauty of the cañon below the Lower Falls: the very nearly vertical walls, slightly sloping down to the water's edge on either side, so that from the summit the river appears like a thread of silver foaming over its rocky bottom, the variegated colors of the sides, yellow, red, brown, white, all intermixed and shading into each other; the Gothic columns of every form standing out from the sides of the walls with greater variety and more striking colors than ever adorned a work of human art.[15]

Hayden went on to record that "Mr. Thomas Moran, a celebrated artist, and noted for his skill as a colorist, exclaimed with a kind of regretful enthusiasm that these beautiful tints were beyond the reach of human art."[16] Nonetheless, as William Jackson took the first-ever photographs of the falls, Moran pulled out his watercolors. Once back home in his studio, Moran's field sketches would provide the basis for one of the most famous and influential early depictions of Yellowstone ever seen by the American public.

From the falls, the survey followed the river until they entered an immense grass-laden valley later named for Hayden himself. In his notes, the geologist simply identified it as the former bed of an ancient lake. After stopping briefly to explore Mud Volcano, on July 28, the expedition made camp near the mouth of the Yellowstone River at Yellowstone Lake. Here they constructed a twelve-foot "tarred-canvas skin" boat, which they christened the *Anna* in honor of Congressman Henry Dawes's daughter. James Stevenson and Henry Elliott undertook the maiden voyage, sailing over to Dot Island, before proceeding to take soundings in the lake. Meanwhile, Hayden, Barlow, and a small entourage traveled to the Firehole River to examine the geyser basins while others explored West Thumb.

On his initial descent into the Lower Geyser Basin on the morning of August 3, Hayden likened the valley to "some manufacturing city like Pittsburgh, as seen from a high point, except that instead of the black coal smoke, there are here the white delicate clouds of steam."[17] The party examined numerous geothermal features until they were stopped in their tracks in the Midway Geyser Basin by Grand Prismatic Spring. According to Hayden,

> the marvelous beauty of the strikingly vivid coloring far surpasses anything of the kind we have seen in this land of wondrous beauty: every possible shade of color, from the vivid scarlet to a bright rose, and every shade of yellow to delicate cream, mingled with vivid green from minute vegetation.[18]

Continuing on to the Upper Geyser Basin on August 5, Hayden and Barlow set up camp on either side of the Firehole. Within minutes of their arrival, a "tremendous rumbling" shocked the party. Sighting a massive tower of rising steam, the men rushed over in time to witness a column of water six feet in diameter erupt to a height of over 200 feet. They named it the Grand.

Over the next few days, Hayden was lucky enough to witness many of the greatest hits of the basin: eruptions of the Giant, the Fan, the Grotto, and, of course, Old Faithful. Regarding this most famous of geysers, Hayden recorded that due to its "regularity, and its position overlooking the valley . . . [it] was called by Messers. Langford and Doane 'Old Faithful.'"[19]

They explored the Giantess and Castle geyser cones and named the Punchbowl and the Dental Cup. And on their last day in the basin, while eating breakfast, they watched, amazed, as a standing cone three feet tall and five feet in diameter suddenly erupted. None had assumed the feature was actually a geyser. They agreed to call it the Beehive.

The geothermal springs seemed to hold the greatest allure for Hayden. The "prismatic colors" left a powerful impression, perhaps akin to the religious awakening Captain Raynolds had wished for him all those years ago. "In the actual presence of such marvelous beauty," Hayden proclaimed, "life becomes a privilege and a blessing."[20]

On August 6, they returned to Yellowstone Lake near West Thumb. There they found Lieutenant Doane in camp with orders to relieve Captain Tyler and send the bulk of the army escort back to Fort Ellis. Thomas Moran decided to depart with Tyler, leaving six cavalrymen under Doane's command.

Doane had hoped to lead Hayden's military escort from the start but had been called as a witness for a military trial in Saint Paul. The lieutenant still had ambitions of becoming a famous explorer like John Wesley Powell or John Fremont,[21] but the accolades received for his 1870 Yellowstone report failed to translate into a promotion. In fact, after the Washburn Expedition, Doane gained notoriety for something worse: his role in the Marias Massacre, a botched attack against a friendly band of Piegan Blackfeet who were under the protection of the U.S. government. The merciless slaughter of over 200 women, children, and tribal elders triggered a public backlash, including calls for reforming federal policy toward Native Americans. Now returned from Saint Paul, Doane hoped participation on Hayden's Survey might renew his prospects for career advancement.

After meeting with Doane, Hayden decided to circumnavigate Yellowstone Lake. Barlow stayed with Hayden's party as far as Flat Mountain Arm, before splitting off on his own to follow Beaver Creek to Heart Lake. In the process, Barlow renamed what the Washburn party had christened the Red, Brown, and Yellow Mountains as Mount Sheridan. From there, Barlow traced the headwaters of the Snake River.

Hayden, meanwhile, continued around the lake until he reached the Upper Yellowstone River, which he then followed to Bridger Lake. Guided now by Lieutenant Doane, Hayden hoped to explore Bridger's Two Ocean Pass, not only as a potential rail route but to fulfill the long-held dream of finding the common source of the Columbia and Missouri/Yellowstone Rivers. But the party failed to find it. After visiting Bridger Lake, which Hayden later dismissed as a mere puddle, Doane—like Truman Everts before him—promptly lost his sense of direction. After hours of fruitless wandering and growing frustration, Hayden finally admitted defeat and ordered a return to Yellowstone Lake. Failure to locate the pass was a bitter pill to swallow, but

Hayden was eventually placated by the other findings he would report back to Congress.

Upon reaching the shores of Yellowstone Lake, the expedition made camp near Steamboat Point and waited for Barlow. On the night of August 19, both parties recorded the rumblings of an earthquake, and the next day, Barlow appeared. On August 22, the expeditions began their return journey, retracing their initial path with some slight modifications: Hayden followed Pelican Creek to Mirror Lake, and Barlow detoured through the Sour Creek drainage before reconvening in the Lamar Valley. After crossing Baronett's Bridge, they returned to Bottler's Ranch to retrieve their wagons. Hayden's party arrived at Fort Ellis on August 30 and Barlow two days later. From there, Hayden made arrangements to transport his collected specimens to Washington, D.C., while Captains Barlow and Heap, with their own scientific data, headed to Chicago and Saint Paul, respectfully.

All that was left now was to catalog the data and write up the reports, and Yellowstone would be finally and formally "discovered."

* * *

Or so it seemed.

It's worth considering why historians tend to talk about the Hayden Survey in the singular, rather than the Hayden and Barlow *Surveys* in the plural. It may simply reflect that Hayden's was the larger and better-funded endeavor. Along with his ambition and political connections, it is perhaps not surprising that he would garner most of the limelight. But it is also undoubtedly explained by the loss of Barlow's samples and specimens to the Great Chicago Fire. On October 8, 1871, shortly after Barlow's return to the regional War Department office, Mrs. O'Leary's cow kicked over a lantern and ignited a conflagration that would consume over three square miles of the city, including Barlow's Yellowstone data. Only the maps, safely transported to Saint Paul by Captain Heap, survived.

Hayden, as it turns out, suffered his own losses. On the return journey from Yellowstone, Schönborn, the topographer, planned to stop in Omaha to sort out his field notes before joining Hayden in Washington. An affable man with a known weakness for alcohol, it appears that instead of working, Schönborn spent most of his days in Omaha drinking too much. One afternoon, he returned to his hotel room, sat down on the bed, and slit his throat with a razor. The hotel manager found Schönborn's lifeless body sprawled on the bed along with a train ticket for departure the next day to the nation's capital.

News of the suicide shocked Hayden to the core. Beyond the loss of a dear friend, he now faced the problem of transforming Schönborn's scribbled notations into comprehensible information. In the end, he relied heavily on Barlow's cartographic data to complete the survey's maps. All final reports, however, bore Hayden's name alone.

At the end of the day, like the other expeditions that came before, Hayden's "discoveries" were places previously known and, in some cases, even inhabited. Still, Hayden's Survey added much to the formal knowledge of Yellowstone. He returned with loads of new mineral and biological specimens (less Barlow's burnt offerings to the Chicago fire), improved geological measurements, and data enabling the first map of Yellowstone that was aligned to a spatial coordinate system.

But perhaps the two greatest contributions of the Hayden Survey included the visual records of Yellowstone—expressed in Jackson's photographs, Elliott's drawings, and Moran's watercolors—and the political and scientific prestige attached to Hayden's official reports.

While the discoveries of the Washburn Expedition carried weight, it was Hayden's voice that resonated with the full heft of the national government, the scientific community, and the economic interests of corporate America. Consequently, *his* reports offered the final confirmation of the geothermal wonders. *His* maps provided the final word on place names. *His* measurements were deemed the most accurate. Ultimately, Hayden's recommendations would exert enormous influence in debates about the future of this place called Yellowstone.

* * *

At the end of October, Hayden made his triumphant return to Washington, D.C. Walking beneath the elm trees lining the National Mall, he moved with purpose, boots crunching down on the gravel path as he approached the imposing red-brick structure of the Smithsonian Castle.

In his office, Hayden found a pile of letters awaiting his attention:

congratulatory notes from colleagues, confirmations of the receipt of field specimens from Yellowstone, an invitation to publish an account of his travels in *Scribner's Monthly*. Flipping through the stack, suddenly, he froze. Setting the other letters aside, he sat down to open an envelope dated October 27, on stationery embossed with "Jay Cooke and Co., Banker and Financial Agents of the Northern Pacific Railroad." The note came from A. B. Nettleton, secretary to Jay Cooke, and it posed an intriguing question:

> Judge Kelley has made a suggestion that strikes me as being an excellent one, viz.: Let Congress pass a bill reserving the Great Geyser Basin as a public park forever—just as it has reserved that far inferior wonder the Yosemite valley and big trees. If you approve this would such a recommendation be appropriate in your official report?[22]

Judge "Pig Iron" Kelley was actually Congressman William Kelley of Pennsylvania, longtime supporter of the transcontinental railroads. While Hayden's interest in Yellowstone centered on its prospects for geological science, those with a financial stake in the railroads saw it as a different opportunity. There was a reason Jay Cooke helped sponsor the Montana-led exploration of Yellowstone in 1870, a reason he ordered his congressional lobbyists to support Hayden's Survey in 1871. And now, there was a reason that his secretary was suggesting Hayden promote the public-park idea to Congress. Though it likely had little to do with the burgeoning Romantic movement for the protection of nature, it could indirectly serve those ends. If park status stopped homestead and mining claims, it would not only conserve the natural landscape, but keep it open for future scientific exploration. What it might mean in the long run for those living in the region, or for the nation as a whole, was anybody's guess.

Still, for Hayden, there was only one possible response to a query from such an influential benefactor. Taking up his pen, he dashed off his answer and set to work.

The World's First National Park

(1872–1877)

ON DECEMBER 18, 1871, SENATOR SAMUEL POMEROY, REPUB-
lican of Kansas, rose from his seat to take the floor of the U.S. Senate
Chamber.

> I ask leave to introduce a bill to set apart a certain tract of land
> lying near the headwaters of the Yellowstone as a public park.
> It has been ascertained within the last year or two that there
> are very valuable reservations at the headwaters of the Yellow-
> stone . . . There are valuable hot springs [and] geysers. Profes-
> sor Hayden has made a very elaborate report on the subject.[1]

By unanimous consent, the Senate agreed to introduce the bill
known as S. 392. Following standard protocol, after being read aloud
twice and ordered for printing, the bill was referred to the Committee on Public Lands, a committee chaired, unsurprisingly, by Senator
Pomeroy.

Later that same day, newly elected delegate of Montana Territory,
William Clagett, introduced an identical bill (H.R. 764) in the House
of Representatives. Within weeks of Hayden's return to Washington,
Congress moved with an unusual sense of urgency and purpose on the
Yellowstone question: drafting, sponsoring, and introducing legislation
that would eventually create something new in American history. But
why? Where did all of this energy and political motivation come from?

* * *

To modern eyes, the decision to establish a system of national parks seems obvious. The writer Wallace Stegner famously pronounced national parks as America's "best idea."[2] They serve as one of the rare government institutions that enjoy support across social and economic divides. The export of this idea is one of the nation's celebrated contributions to the world. But in December 1871, few if any could foresee that future.

Added to the question of political momentum, one must also consider the source of the national park idea itself. Yellowstone relied on some important precedents. Going back to the colonial era, there are multiple examples of federal efforts to remove land from settlement for strategic purposes, most typically timber stands for shipbuilding and valuable mineral deposits.[3] In 1832, Congress set aside Arkansas Hot Springs to resolve disputes over competing land claims. Then, in 1864, for the first time in history, the federal government protected land for conservation purposes when President Lincoln signed the Yosemite Grant. This action ceded Yosemite Valley to California as a state park, but the arrangement ultimately failed due to mismanagement.[4] Significantly, none of these early actions sought to establish a *national* park like Yellowstone.

For close to one hundred years, the most common answer to the question about the origins of the national park idea came from Nathaniel Langford, as described in his account of the Washburn Expedition. Picture the scene: After their first (and only) day in the geyser basins, the party made camp near the confluence of the Gibbon and Firehole Rivers where they come together to form the Madison (known today as Madison Junction). During the evening campfire, Cornelius Hedges proposed that the area should be protected in perpetuity as a national park. The others agreed and supposedly committed themselves to promoting the idea from that day forward.

Langford's story gained legitimacy and lasting influence when it was treated as fact by Hiram Chittenden, who authored the first reputable history of Yellowstone National Park in 1895.[5] Later, Langford himself confirmed the story in his own memoirs of the trip, published in 1905.[6] Though released thirty-five years after the events took place, Langford's book is supposedly a direct reproduction of journal entries made during the expedition. His original diary was never found, but Langford's account served as the gold standard for decades, even leading Yellowstone park staff to organize annual reenactments of the campfire episode for visitors. This practice lasted until 1964, when park historian Aubrey Haines finally debunked the tale.[7]

It turns out that no written evidence exists to corroborate the campfire story. As historians Lee Whittlesey and Paul Schullery confirmed, no member of the Washburn Party mentioned the event in their original journals.[8] What we do find in articles written by Hedges, Everts, and Langford are predictions that people will someday wish to visit Yellowstone. In Hedges's case, there is also a plea to transfer Yellowstone from Wyoming to Montana Territory so it can be put to "public use," but his meaning is unclear.

Of course, Langford was not the only one to make such a claim. Langford's friend, David Folsom, in the 1894 publication of his memoirs, argued that he originated the national park idea during his 1869 expedition and shared it with General Washburn before the 1870 trip.[9] Langford, who penned the foreword in Folsom's book, did not dispute this but gently suggested the idea arose more generally from the three expeditions led by Folsom, Washburn, and Hayden respectively. So too, Father Xavier Kuppens asserted that Montana governor Meagher first developed the idea during his visit to the Jesuit mission in 1865.[10] Other claims came from Hayden[11] and Montana delegate Clagett.[12] But, like Langford's assertion, all of these came well after the fact, and none were supported with documented evidence.

So if the call for establishing Yellowstone as a national park did not originate with the late-nineteenth-century explorers, how then can we explain the flurry of congressional action in December 1871? American Romanticism provides one possible answer. The American variant took place a bit later than European Romanticism, but it shared a concern with the social, moral, and environmental ills caused by the Industrial Revolution. In the United States, artists and writers such as George Catlin, Ralph Waldo Emerson, Sarah Fenimore Cooper, and Henry David Thoreau advocated for protecting nature against the cold economic calculus of modern society. Wild nature offered humans a path to moral and spiritual well-being and deserved respect for its own sake. But such sentiments never expanded beyond a minority opinion in the

1870s, when the dominant view of nature insisted that it be valued primarily as an economic resource. Consequently, they fail to explain the political pragmatism needed to push legislative action on Yellowstone.

The truth is both more complex and far less romantic. The paper trail is thin, but it is definitive. It begins with Nettleton's memo to Hayden from the offices of Jay Cooke and Company. From there, the influence rippled out—first to Washington, D.C., mobilizing the railroad's many allies in Congress; then on to *Scribner's* headquarters in New York City; to the Minnesota governor's mansion in Saint Paul; and, eventually, all the way to Helena, Montana.

The driving force behind the creation of the world's first national park was the Northern Pacific Railroad and, by extension, the political delegation from Montana Territory. Both entities had much to gain from park creation. The railroad hoped to attract investors and new customers while Montana hoped to expand its territory, encourage settlement, and spur economic growth. As one of the most powerful industries in nineteenth-century America, the railroads had all the political muscle needed to put the wheels of Congress into motion.

* * *

Within days of Hayden's reply to Nettleton in October 1871, the extraordinary influence of the railroad industry was on full display. As lobbyists threw their full weight behind the Yellowstone measure, politicians fell in line and legislative machinations spun into high gear.

Senator Samuel Pomeroy was an interesting choice to lead the charge. Born in Massachusetts, Pomeroy worked as a school teacher and, later, a congressman, before leading a group of settlers to Kansas Territory in 1854. After a stint as mayor of Lawrence, he became one of the state's first senators when Kansas achieved statehood in 1861. Now a balding, full-bearded fifty-five-year-old with a pleasant demeanor, Pomeroy was a Radical Republican, which is to say, an ardent abolitionist. Unlike most of his peers, he also championed universal suffrage, sponsoring a failed constitutional amendment to that end in 1868. But Pomeroy's ideological positions likely had little to do with his role in introducing the Yellowstone bill. Presumably, he was selected because he chaired the Senate Committee on Public Lands and maintained strong ties to the railroad industry, having served as past president of the Atchison, Topeka, and Santa Fe Railroad.

That said, given his New England background, one wonders if Pomeroy was not also influenced by the Romantic writers and poets from his home state. Or, during his years in Kansas, if he encountered a certain "Old Man of the Mountains," who happened to be living out the last years of his life just fifteen miles south of Kansas City, in the town of Little Santa Fe.

The bill's sponsor in the House was Montana Territory's newly elected delegate to Congress, William Clagett. He took his marching orders from Langford and other territorial leaders, most of whom saw their economic and political fortunes firmly anchored to the Northern Pacific Railroad. Although territorial delegates could not vote, Clagett could sponsor and introduce legislation, serving as an obedient conduit for a bill drafted by others.

The authorship of the bill itself is unknown. No early drafts survived, nor are there ancillary documents that might shed light on who actually put pen to paper. The fact that Senator Pomeroy was the first to introduce the legislation in Congress and was present during the passage of the Yosemite Grant back in 1864 suggests that, at the very least, he played some role in the writing, but there is no way to confirm it.

In wording and tone, it is clear that the 1872 Yellowstone bill was based in part on the 1864 Yosemite legislation, which helps to explain its rapid preparation. As Aubrey Haines points out, the rationales for environmental protection are quite similar between the two, the major difference being that Yosemite was proposed as a state park rather than a national park.[13] This distinction is, of course, what makes Yellowstone exceptional as the first-ever national park in the United States and the world.

Editorials in the *Bozeman Avant Courier* provide evidence that the Montana delegation offered strong support for protecting Yellowstone. But they wanted the transfer of land from Wyoming to Montana as a state park, following the Yosemite model.[14] They rightly argued that Montana's citizens had organized the Yellowstone expeditions of 1869 and 1870, had done the most to publicize the area, and that the urban centers of Bozeman and Virginia City—such as they were—allowed visitors the most direct access to the park.

But there were serious concerns about taking such action. First of all, Yosemite was a *state* park, not a *territorial* one. There was no precedent for creating such an entity. Second, the boundary of the proposed Yellowstone Park stretched across three different territories, with the largest portion by far lying within the bounds of Wyoming. The political calculus in Washington quickly ruled out a wholesale transfer of so much land from one territory to another. The only path forward that would still allow Montana some influence was a compromise: make Yellowstone a *national* park. This way, stewardship would transfer to the federal government, ensuring Montana at least some voice in the future of the park while avoiding potential interterritorial rivalries.

With the matter settled, the final version of the bill was dispatched to Senator Pomeroy and Delegate Clagett for introduction to Congress. In the days following, Hayden, Langford, and their allies launched a full-scale lobbying campaign.

* * *

To sway Congress, Hayden organized an elaborate display in the Capitol rotunda consisting of geological specimens and a sampling of Elliott's drawings, Moran's watercolor sketches, and Jackson's photographs (Moran's masterpiece, the massive oil painting of Yellowstone Falls, was not completed until months after the vote). Each member of Congress also received copies of Langford's *Scribner's* article and Doane's 1870 expedition report. Hayden authored an essay of his own in *Scribner's* February issue of 1872. The piece arrived too late for the Senate vote but was made available for deliberations in the House. Most importantly, at the request of Representative Dawes and Interior Secretary Delano, Hayden offered separate written testimony in support of the bill.

Inside the House and Senate chambers, the ensuing congressional debates said much about the motivation and rationale for establishing Yellowstone National Park. First, proponents argued that protecting Yellowstone would be a source of national pride. Establishing the world's first national park would give the young nation a response to the rich cultural history of Europe. The United States may not yet have distinguished traditions in the arts, sciences, or literature, but it did contain natural wonders that equaled or even surpassed those found in Europe. As noted in a House committee report based on Hayden's testimony,

> In a few years this region will be a place of resort for all classes of people from all portions of the world. The geysers of Iceland, which have been objects of interest for the scientific men and travelers of the entire world, sink into insignificance in comparison with the hot springs of the Yellowstone . . . As a place of resort for invalids, it will not be excelled by any portion of the world.[15]

Protecting Yellowstone amounted to an act of national maturity. It would demonstrate societal wisdom by putting a stop to those who would "take possession of these remarkable curiosities . . . so as to charge visitors a fee as is now done at Niagara Falls for the sight of that which ought to be as free as the air or water."[16] Underscoring this point, park supporters declared a need to act with urgency to protect it:

> If this bill fails to become a law in this session, the vandals who are now waiting to enter into this wonder-land will, in a single season, despoil, beyond recovery, these remarkable curiosities, which have required all the cunning skill of nature thousands of years to prepare.[17]

A second set of arguments centered on financial concerns. Since the land lay within the public domain and to date was free of squatters or homesteaders (at least to their knowledge), no funding was needed for land purchases. The costs of constructing roads and facilities for visitors could be covered with leases to vendors overseen by the secretary of the interior. Consequently, the bill contained no appropriations for park management, and advocates promised to withhold requests for federal funding for the first five years.

Third and perhaps most importantly, park supporters argued that Yellowstone itself held no economic value. As Senator Pomeroy stated during the Senate floor debate, "There are no arable lands; no agricultural lands there. It is the highest elevation from which our springs descend and . . . it cannot interfere with any settlement for legitimate agricultural purposes."[18] The House committee report was even more emphatic, citing the severity of the winters, the altitude, and the lack of valuable mines or minerals in the volcanic mountains.[19]

Such statements were profoundly strategic, designed to appease the dominant view of nature in nineteenth-century American society, namely that it should be valued, first and foremost, in economic terms. The idea of nature-as-commodity also represented the greatest hurdle to park creation at the time. All realized that the Yellowstone bill would likely fail if the lands in question were deemed suitable for settlement or mining. But if Yellowstone could be shown as economically worthless, there was no harm in setting it aside for public recreation.

Of course, those backing the bill *did* see economic value in Yellowstone, just not in the conventional sense. Rather than logging, mining, or homesteading, they envisioned a new kind of economic opportunity: nature tourism. The entire reason the Northern Pacific and the Montana delegation pushed for park creation had to do with economic incentives. But interestingly, perhaps for strategic reasons, neither the railroad executives nor their allies in Congress felt the need to make this point explicit during congressional debates.

And it worked. The only dissenting voice in the Senate debate came from Cornelius Cole of California, who questioned the need to set the land aside if it had no value for settlement anyway. He was answered by Illinois senator Lyman Trumbull, whose son, Walter, had been a member of the Washburn Expedition. Trumbull replied that the law could easily be repealed later if it turned out to be "in anybody's way."[20] In the House, Representative John Taffe of Nebraska questioned whether the park would "interfere with the Sioux reservation" established in 1868. Though the Upper Yellowstone lay outside the bounds of Sioux territory, Representative Dawes answered that regardless of geography, "all treaties made by this body are simple matters of legislation." Moreover, "Indians can no more live there [in Yellowstone] than they can upon the precipitous sides of the Yosemite Valley."[21] This telling response repeated several influential myths of the time, namely that Indigenous peoples had no legitimate land claims (since treaties could be rewritten so easily) and that they could not (and therefore, did not) live in Yellowstone anyway. Both claims were demonstrably false, but they effectively ended the floor debate.

On January 30, 1872, the measure passed in the Senate. It took another month for the bill to work its way through the House of Representatives, during which time, Hayden's article in *Scribner's* came out, imploring Congress to protect Yellowstone as a "great public park for all time to come."[22] On February 27, there were attempts to send the bill to several House committees for further review. But the powerful Henry Dawes successfully made the case for an immediate vote. The measure passed with 115 ayes, 60 nays, and 60 abstentions.

On March 1, 1872, approximately four short months after the return of the Hayden Expedition, President Ulysses S. Grant signed the bill into law, making Yellowstone the world's first national park.

* * *

The Yellowstone Act set aside over 2.2 million acres of land from sale or settlement as a "public park or pleasuring ground." In so doing, it marked a turning point in American conservation history: for the first time, a portion of the public domain was designated as a place for environmental protection for the benefit of all American citizens.

At the same time, it established another powerful legacy: that conservation could spring not from the adoption of an environmental ethic but from political pragmatism driven by economic interests. In decades to come, this conceptual foundation would produce long-running tensions in efforts to develop more conservation-oriented management priorities in our national parks. In American society, the impulse to commercialize nature—to use it to make a buck—has always stood side by side with the desire to protect nature for its own sake. Future debates on issues ranging from wildlife protection to visitor access would all trace their roots back to this fundamental truth: Yellowstone, as a first step in the rise of American conservation values, did not supplant commercial resource use; rather, it embodied both objectives in an uneasy tandem.

* * *

The act assigned managerial authority to the secretary of the interior, with the charge to preserve "from injury or spoliation . . . all timber, mineral deposits, natural curiosities, or wonders within . . . [and to] provide against the wanton destruction of the fish and game."[23] This was all well and good, but without making "wanton destruction" an actual crime with legal penalties, and without budgetary appropriations to hire managers, there was no way to carry out the mandate. As might be expected, this also made hiring the first superintendent a tough sell.

Initially, park proponents favored Truman Everts for the role. Still basking in the glow of national fame from his "Thirty-Seven Days of Peril" article, Everts was unwilling to take a job without salary. Moreover, his support of Horace Greeley's Liberal Republicans made him politically unpalatable. Eventually, Nathaniel Langford accepted the position with the understanding that he would continue his new job as federal bank examiner for the Pacific states and western territories.

In practical terms, the situation was destined for failure. As should have been predicted, Langford spent most of his time traveling across the West conducting bank assessments for the Treasury Department. Without a salary, a staff, or accommodation in the park, Langford rarely visited, appearing only twice during his five-year term.

The first of these visits occurred shortly after his appointment, when Ferdinand Hayden returned to Yellowstone to conduct a second survey in the summer of 1872. With a budget almost twice the size of the previous year's, Hayden split the party into two groups: a northern division, led by himself, and a southern division, led by his able assistant James Stevenson. The purpose, as before, was to gather scientific and topographical data in the park and surrounding region, and also to scout potential wagon or rail routes. As superintendent, Langford accompanied the southern division, which included a detour to Jackson Hole, where he and Stevenson claimed to be the first Euro-Americans to summit Grand Teton peak.

After the trip, Langford submitted his first and only annual report to the interior secretary. In it, he recommended a road system establishing the rough outline of today's figure-eight pattern, itself loosely based on the expedition routes of 1869–1872. In addition, he called for government funding for road building and repeated his call for the transfer of Wyoming's portion of Yellowstone Park to Montana Territory.

While criticized for his absence from the park, given the legal and financial situation, there was little Langford could do. To his credit, he drafted the first rules of conduct for visitors and reviewed petitions for park hotel and concession leases. The regulations Langford proposed to the interior secretary would sound familiar to national park managers today. They included no timber cutting without permission; no commercial hunting, trapping, or fishing; no fires unless necessary (and always fully extinguished).[24] But of course, as he noted, without actual legal penalties for infringement or on-the-ground enforcement, the rules carried little weight.

Park leases, however, were a different story and quickly became the reason things began to unravel for Langford. As he was still in the pocket of the Northern Pacific Railroad, Langford rejected all petitions that came across his desk, waiting instead for the railroad to complete its line and build their own Yellowstone hotel and transportation businesses. This balancing act became increasingly difficult after the Panic of 1873, when the railroad (and Jay Cooke) went bankrupt and, in the process, pulled the national economy down with it. With the Northern Pacific terminus stuck in Bismarck, North Dakota, there was little hope that the railway would arrive in Yellowstone anytime soon.

Nonetheless, Langford held the company line, growing increasingly unpopular among local business owners who clamored for park access. It's telling that Langford's second visit to Yellowstone in 1874 was to evict a squatter, Matthew McGuirk, from his bathhouse claim on the Gardiner River (though interestingly, Langford took no action concerning McCartney's hotel and bathhouse in Mammoth Hot Springs or Jack Baronett's toll bridge).

In the meantime, Langford made repeated, if unsuccessful, requests to Washington for park funding and took to calling himself "National Park Langford"—a play on his first two initials, *N* for Nathaniel and *P* for Pitt.

* * *

Despite this unsettled state of affairs, visitors began to arrive in Yellowstone, some 300 people the first year and about 500 annually through the mid-1870s. There were three types of tourists: local residents who could fend for themselves in the wild country, well-to-do aristocrats who could afford the expense of a full entourage, and members of military expeditions.

Among the wealthy visitors of the period, one individual stands out. The Fourth Earl of Dunraven, an Irish noble, traveled through the park in 1874 and again in 1877. Guided by the flamboyant Texas Jack Omohundro, former partner of Buffalo Bill Cody, the Earl took in the geothermal sights but spent most of his time hunting bison, elk, and other big game animals. The Earl was notable not just for his early visits—and his infamous attempt to purchase Estes Park in Colorado as a personal hunting ground—but also for the book he published in 1876 about his Yellowstone adventures.[25] His writing played a major role in building the park's reputation as an international attraction, a contribution that led to the naming of Dunraven Pass near Mount Washburn in his honor.

The military expeditions, typically referred to as "inspections" or "reconnaissance missions," were actually nothing more than hunting and fishing trips for the army's top brass. Two such trips in 1875 are noteworthy for the reports they produced on park conditions.

The Belknap Party, led by Secretary of War William Belknap, included on staff Colonel William Strong, who would go on to publish a book about the trip in 1876. Because Lieutenant Doane of the Washburn Expedition served as guide, Strong was able to document a "before and after" perspective on the abundance of wild game between 1870 and 1875. Whereas pronghorn, bighorn sheep, bison, and elk were plentiful in 1870, they were rarely seen five years later due to overhunting. Strong's powerfully worded conclusion presented a damning indictment of Langford:

> It is an outrage and a crying shame that this indiscriminate slaughter of the large game of our country should be permitted. The act of Congress setting aside the National Park expressly instructs the Secretary of the Interior to provide against the wanton destruction of the game and fish found within the limits of the Park . . . No attempt has yet been made, however, to enforce the act in the Park, and unless some active measures are soon

taken . . . there will be none left to protect . . . How is it that the Commissioner of the Park allows this unlawful killing?[26]

A second expedition that summer was led by Corps of Engineers officer Captain William Ludlow. Once again, the trip produced an influential report, but it was also notable for the participation of a young naturalist by the name of George Bird Grinnell. His introduction to Yellowstone would change his life and launch a decades-long commitment to protect the park through his role as editor of *Forest and Stream* magazine. Meanwhile, Ludlow's 1876 report detailed not only the scarcity of big game due to poaching but also vandalism and wildfires caused by careless tourists. Noting the lack of managerial protection, Ludlow recommended turning park management over to the War Department so that soldiers could protect the game, build roads and bridges, and keep visitors in line.[27]

Amid the flow of nonmilitary visitors to Yellowstone in 1875, a lone traveler from the East Coast arrived in late August. Dressed in buckskins and looking the part of an old-time trapper, he was in fact a scientific collector for the Smithsonian Institution in Washington, D.C., named Philetus Norris. Ironically, an editorial in the Bozeman newspaper claimed that Norris's purchase of a hundred boxes in town for collecting "specimens" marked him as a criminal. "Must this robbing the Park of its treasures be kept up continuously and especially by vandals from the East? Where is Langford?"[28]

A rugged pioneer who founded towns in Ohio and Michigan, edited a newspaper, and now worked as a museum collector, Norris was a man with an excess of energy and a need for action. Five years earlier, he had ventured to Yellowstone to explore the area, only to turn back when his guide, Frank Bottler, became injured, prompting Norris to visit California instead. Now, on his return to the park, he noticed the degradation taking place. A longtime friend of mountaineers Jack Baronett and George Huston, Norris learned that the Bottler brothers had killed as many as 2,000 elk that summer alone, taking only the tongues and the hides and leaving the rest to rot. On his return to Washington, Norris sent letters to the interior secretary complaining of the poor conditions in the park and offering his own services as superintendent.

As for Langford, the writing was on the wall. In response to Washington's continued denial of his funding requests, he stopped communicating with the Department of the Interior and made no further visits to the park. Meanwhile, he faced growing criticism over his unwillingness to grant leases for concessions and the ongoing deterioration of park conditions due to poaching and vandalism. Of course, the latter problem was largely out of his control. Nonetheless, by early 1877, with the Rutherford Hayes administration now in power, the new secretary of the interior, Carl Shurz, sent a letter to Norris appointing him as the new superintendent.

It took a while for Langford to receive word of the decision, but when it came, he shrugged it off. Not pleasant news, but not unexpected. While he had welcomed the prestige of the post, in practice it had become an exercise in frustration. Langford spent another eight years traveling through the western states as a federal bank examiner before retiring to Saint Paul in 1885. There he would spend the rest of his life writing his memoirs and carefully building his image as a pioneer, vigilante, territorial statesman, and, most significantly, the "founding father of Yellowstone."

* * *

On April 19, 1877, the same day he received notice of his Yellowstone appointment, Norris fired off a letter of his own to James McCartney, owner of McCartney's "Hotel and Bathhouse" at Mammoth Hot Springs, asking him to serve as assistant superintendent until Norris's arrival in midsummer.

Born in Palmyra, New York, in 1821, Norris left home as a teen to work in the western fur trade. He never made his fortune but managed to befriend some of the old-time mountain men, including Jack Baronett, whom he would later rejoin in Yellowstone. Norris was a charismatic figure, bounding with energy and a can-do spirit. In 1838 at the age of nineteen, he founded the town of Pioneer, Ohio, where he got married and ran a steam mill. During the Civil War, he fought for the Union and worked as a spy behind enemy lines. After the war, he received a federal appointment as a land trustee in Michigan, where he founded the self-named town of Norris (today a suburb of Detroit). In Norris, he also established a newspaper (the *Suburban*), recruited the railroad to pass through town, maintained a toll road, and worked in real estate. In addition to all of this, he obtained employment as a collector for the Smithsonian Institution, a position that allowed him periodic travel through the West, including his trips to Yellowstone in 1870 and 1875.

By the end of April, Norris departed Washington, D.C., for his home in Michigan, where he wrote an editorial in the *Suburban* announcing his appointment as Yellowstone superintendent and printed off cloth flyers listing visitor rules, which he planned to distribute around the park. He then continued his westward journey, first by rail, then by riverboat, and, finally, on horse and wagon. But as Norris neared the Clarks Fork mines, he learned that General William Sherman, commander of the U.S. Army, intended to tour the park. Norris immediately set off to meet the general's party, which had gathered at Bottler's Ranch.

While preparing for his trip, General Sherman received word of hostilities between a band of Nez Perce and U.S. Calvary detachments in an area just west of the park. For the general, such news was no cause for alarm. On the contrary, he felt quite safe as he believed the tribes were superstitious and fearful of Yellowstone's geysers and hot springs. A common sentiment of the time, it was yet another belief about Indigenous peoples that happened to be absolutely false.

Shortly after arriving at Bottler's Ranch, Norris proceeded to guide the small party, which included the general's son, two other officers, three packers, and a four-soldier escort. On August 7, near Tower Falls, Norris's stirrup snapped, throwing him from his horse. With injuries to his neck and back, Norris hobbled back to Mammoth to recuperate as General Sherman's entourage continued into the park.

Part Three

YELLOWSTONE FOR WHAT AND FOR WHOM?

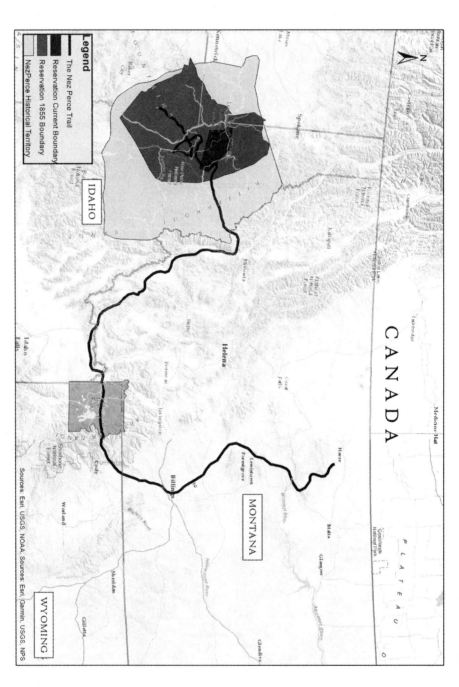

The Nez Perce Trail

Legend

The Nez Perce Trail
Reservation Current Boundary
Reservation 1855 Boundary
NezPerce Historical Territory

IDAHO

MONTANA

WYOMING

CANADA

Sources: Esri, USGS, NOAA, Sources: Esri, Garmin, USGS, NPS

The Nez Perce War

(1877–1879)

ON THE EVENING OF AUGUST 23, 1877, EMMA CARPENTER Cowan and eight companions sat around a large campfire in the Lower Geyser Basin in Yellowstone National Park. Sitting next to her husband, George, Emma was joined by her brother, Frank, her thirteen-year-old sister, Ida, a cook, and four neighbors from back home.

The crackling, spitting "pop" of sap-filled pine branches threw sparks into the starry night. Enjoying the warmth of the blaze against the descending coolness of the mountain air, Emma and her friends sang songs, told stories, and acted out silly skits. Relaxed and contented, Emma watched the firelight play across the smiling, laughing faces of her companions. What better way to celebrate the final evening of an idyllic weeks-long vacation to "Wonderland"?[1]

* * *

Hailing from the town of Radersburg, Montana Territory—about sixty miles north of Bozeman—the Cowans had decided to visit Yellowstone at Frank's urging. He'd invited his family and a few neighbors from Helena to be among the park's first tourists. For Emma and George, it was a chance to celebrate their second wedding anniversary and lift Emma's spirits after a recent miscarriage.

This would be twenty-four-year-old Emma's second visit to Yellowstone. Her first was on a family visit in 1873, only one year after the park's creation. Though it had been open for five years now,

121

Yellowstone remained unmanaged, with only rudimentary roads and lodging. Visitors were few. The major limiting factor for both tourists and services was the park's location.

In the mid-1870s, a journey to Yellowstone could only be described as long, arduous, and expensive. From the South, rail lines took passengers only as far as Corrine, Utah, a little town just north of Ogden. Upon arrival, travelers faced a 438-mile rough, dusty ride by stagecoach or horseback to Virginia City or Bozeman. But the trip was far from over. Bozeman required another seventy-three-mile journey to Mammoth, and Virginia City lay over ninety miles from the Lower Geyser Basin.

The northern route took much longer but offered more comforts. In 1872, the Northern Pacific line reached Bismarck, North Dakota. From there, travelers took a two-week, 800-mile riverboat ride up the Missouri River to Fort Benton, followed by a 250-mile stage journey to Bozeman or a 390-mile ride to Virginia City.[2]

That same year, a wagon toll road was cut from Bozeman through Yankee Jim Canyon. Built by A. Bart Henderson, the plan was to extend the road to Mammoth Hot Springs and eventually to Yellowstone Lake. Unable to secure a federal charter for his road, in 1874, Henderson sold the canyon segment to a man named Yankee Jim, who gave the canyon its name and ran the toll road until 1910.

Starting in 1874, tourists also had the option of hiring stage transportation on Zack Root's Express from Bozeman to Mammoth, where they could stay at McCartney's one-story log Hotel and Bathhouse. McCartney provided room and board, but the room required sleeping on a hard-packed dirt floor in your own blankets. The Earl of Dunraven called it the last bastion of civilization because it was the last place a person could buy whiskey before entering the Yellowstone wilderness. At Mammoth, visitors could also rent horses and buy guided tours from old mountaineers, such as George Huston and Ed Hibbard.

Not to be outdone, the citizens of Virginia City paid Gilman Sawtell $2,000 to build their own roughed-out stage road linking their city to the Lower Geyser Basin by way of Targhee Pass. They christened it the Virginia City and National Park Free Wagon Road. No tolls, but it required travelers to supply their own transportation and lodging.

While only the well-to-do could afford the time and expense of the long journey from the States, the rest of Yellowstone's early visitors tended to be members of military expeditions or local residents who could provide for themselves. Though considered wealthy by local standards (George was a lawyer), the Cowan Party lay firmly within this last category.

* * *

On August 6, the group departed Radersburg and headed south to the Virginia City Free Road. Outfitted with four saddle horses, a supply wagon, and a double-seated carriage, they worked their way down to Henry's Lake, camping as they went. About one week later, they crossed Targhee Pass and entered Yellowstone Park through today's West Yellowstone entrance, making camp at the future site of Riverside Station.

For the next couple weeks, the party enjoyed sun-drenched days among the wonders of Yellowstone. Setting up a "home camp" at the terminus of the wagon road in the Lower Geyser Basin, they supplemented their supplies with freshly caught "speckled" and cutthroat trout. Trails took them via horseback to the bubbling mud pots, geysers, and translucent hot springs.

After they pitched tents to spend a few nights near Castle Geyser, Emma witnessed a nighttime eruption that covered the camp with spray and emitted an "unearthly" roar. She later noted, "I was sure the earth would be rent asunder and we would be swallowed up." Meanwhile, Frank and several others branched off to visit the falls of the Grand Canyon of the Yellowstone and the crystalline blue waters of Yellowstone Lake. During this time, Emma wrote, the Cowan Party never saw another soul.

In the 1870s, the idea of wild nature as unpeopled was gaining currency in American society. With Native Americans increasingly confined to reservations, their absence on other parts of the public domain was treated as a given. In the case of Yellowstone, such views were born of faulty but oft-repeated assumptions dating back to the journals of Lewis and Clark. Time and again, Euro-American settlers, politicians, and military officers like General Sherman asserted that Indigenous peoples feared the hot springs and geysers of Yellowstone and therefore avoided them at all costs.

But as the Cowan Party would soon learn, failure to see or recognize Indigenous people on the landscape did not equate to their absence. It did not erase their long history of habitation nor the important cultural connections they continued to maintain with Yellowstone.

* * *

Eventually, the Cowans reconvened at their main camp, where they were surprised by a small group of horsemen.[3] Though armed and wearing cavalry uniforms, the soldiers were not on patrol but part of General Sherman's touring party. The soldiers told them about recent fighting with the Nez Perce in Big Hole Basin, located west of the park, but said not to worry.

Emma later recalled, "The scout who was with the General's party assured us we would be perfectly safe if we would remain in the [Geyser] Basin, as the Indians would never come into the Park. I observed, however, that his party preferred being elsewhere, as they left the Basin that same night."[4]

Unsettled by this news, the Cowans resolved to return home on the morning of the twenty-fourth. However, for the last night's campfire, they decided to cheer themselves up with a bit of frivolity. "Naturally we felt somewhat depressed and worried over the news received," Emma wrote. "My brother Frank and Al Oldham, in order to enliven us somewhat, sang songs, told jokes, and finally dressed up as brigands with pistols, knives and guns strapped on them."[5] As the night wore on, the party grew increasingly jovial as guitar, fiddles, and laughing voices made "the woods ring with their nonsense and merriment." But in the darkness, just beyond the light of the fire, the Cowans entertained a much larger audience.

* * *

Numbering some 700 men, women, and children, Nimíipuu (or Nez Perce[6]) who observed the Cowans that night were on a journey of their own. Rather than tourism, the tribe came to Yellowstone seeking freedom, which they hoped might be found in western Montana among their longtime allies in the Crow Nation. For the Nez Perce, this was a journey for survival against terrifying odds.

Their flight had begun roughly two months earlier, when the Wallowa Valley Nez Perce refused to leave their ancestral homeland in northeastern Oregon for relocation to the Lapwai Reservation in Idaho Territory.[7]

The Nez Perce had previously been on friendly terms with the United States. Ever since their first encounter with Lewis and Clark, the Nez Perce consistently provided aid to American explorers, trappers, and settlers; served as scouts for the U.S. Cavalry; and gave up much of their traditional territory for white settlement. Many tribal members even converted to Christianity. The Nez Perce Treaty of 1855 demarcated a reservation of 7.5 million acres, which encompassed only about half of their 16 million–acre ancestral lands.

Then, in an all-too-familiar turn of events, prospectors discovered gold in the Wallowa region. This led the federal government to draft a new treaty in 1863 that radically reduced the reservation to 770,000 acres (about 10 percent of its former size) and opened the valley to white settlement.

But there was one problem. The original inhabitants of the valley, the Wallowa Nez Perce, never signed the 1863 treaty. This marked a divide between the Christianized Nez Perce bands that did sign and the traditionalist bands that did not. Meanwhile, white miners and homesteaders moved rapidly into the newly "opened" lands of the Wallowa.

In 1873, recognizing the validity of Nez Perce claims, President Ulysses S. Grant issued an executive order that divided lands in the valley between the Wallowa Nez Perce and white settlers. However, in 1875, Grant gave in to pressure from Oregon politicians and revoked the order, thereby dissolving the Wallowa reservation and creating conditions ripe for a showdown.

Over the next three years, the Wallowa Nez Perce chiefs, including Hin-mah-too-yah-lat-kekt (Joseph), Peopeo Kiskiok Hihih (White Bird), and Allalimya Takanin (Looking Glass), tried unsuccessfully to negotiate a new agreement to regain control of their ancestral homeland. In the meantime, they lived in the valley as reluctant neighbors with white settlers, knowing that at any time the situation might turn explosive.

* * *

The spark that lit the fuse was provided on a June morning in 1876, when a man named Alexander Findley walked out to his pasture and noticed some of his horses missing.

Findley took matters into his own hands when he and several companions found and killed a Nez Perce man named Wihautyah, whom they claimed had stolen the horses. Though this was hardly the first instance of violence against the Nez Perce by whites, the recent fighting in Little Bighorn between General Custer and the Sioux lent added weight to this particular incident. White settlers were on edge.

The Nez Perce leaders agreed to allow U.S. authorities to address the murder through the court system. The evidence was weighted heavily against Findley even before the missing horses turned up on their own. Everyone expected a guilty verdict. Instead, in October 1876, the court tossed out all charges, citing lack of evidence and stating that Findley acted in self-defense. In response, settlers began arming themselves for the expected retaliation by the Nez Perce.

As tensions mounted, General Oliver Howard, commander of U.S. military forces in the region, convened a group to resolve the matter. The commission concluded that the Nez Perce must be forced to comply at all costs. After several more months of unsuccessful negotiations, the government tried to purchase the Wallowa Valley from the Nez Perce. When this failed, in May 1877, Howard issued a thirty-day moratorium requiring the Nez Perce to move to the Lapwai Reservation or declare war. Deciding to submit rather than risk open warfare, in early June the chiefs assembled the five Wallowa bands in preparation for the move.

With only two days before the deadline, an angry young tribal member named Wahlitits decided to exact revenge on the white man that had killed his father in a separate incident. When he couldn't find the man, he and several others attacked and killed another white settler also known for his cruelty. Apparently, this settler once shot a Nez Perce woman merely because her horse trespassed on his land. The killing by Wahlitits triggered a spree of Nez Perce raids, resulting in eighteen deaths among white settlers in the valley.

In response, General Howard prepared for war.

* * *

In his first move, the general dispatched some one hundred soldiers to confront the Wallowa Nez Perce at their camp in White Bird Canyon.[8] At this point, tribal leaders still hoped for a peaceful solution to the standoff. After all, the U.S. troops included Christianized Nez Perce from the Lapwai Reservation serving as scouts and interpreters. Perhaps the Wallowa could renew negotiations by working with these friends and former neighbors.

On June 17, 1877, cavalry troops approached the canyon as six Nez Perce warriors waited holding a white flag. Moments later, a few nervous soldiers hastily fired their carbines, triggering an all-out cavalry charge. This first battle proved an overwhelming victory for the Nez Perce, who killed about one third of the cavalry troops while suffering no casualties of their own and only three wounded.

After this fight, there would be five more encounters between the Nez Perce and U.S. soldiers as roughly 700 to 800 Nez Perce, burdened with household supplies and approximately 2,000 head of livestock, embarked on a 1,600-mile journey. For over three months, they would elude more than 2,000 U.S. troops in an odyssey that would culminate in a bloody battle just forty miles shy of their destination across the Canadian border. Before then, however, the Nez Perce and their pursuers would pass straight through the nation's first national park.

* * *

The second battle, taking place near Clearwater in Idaho Territory on July 11, resulted in an indecisive skirmish with few casualties on either side. Escaping over Lolo Pass into Montana Territory, the Nez Perce outran General Howard and thought they were safe among friendly whites. But on August 9 in Big Hole Basin, Colonel John Gibbon and 161 men out of Fort Shaw ambushed the Nez Perce in a predawn raid. Alerted by telegraph from Howard, Gibbon was able to intercept the unsuspecting Nez Perce.

Ordering his men to take no prisoners, Gibbon's soldiers shot indiscriminately into tepees and killed between seventy and ninety people, the vast majority of them women and children, some of whom were later found burned to death or with cracked or smashed skulls from rifle butts. A group of Nez Perce warriors organized a counterattack, allowing the rest of their people to escape.

Suffering twenty-nine dead and forty wounded, Gibbon's troops were unable to pursue the Nez Perce and retreated to Fort Shaw. But soon, Howard's forces from Oregon arrived to carry on the chase.

After fleeing the battle, the Nez Perce decided to cut through Yellowstone in an attempt to reach their allies in the Crow Nation. Three days later, as darkness fell, exhausted and deeply saddened by their losses at Big Hole, the Nez Perce moved into the Lower Geyser Basin. Advance scouts spotted the flames of the Cowan Party in the distance. As the Nez Perce quietly made camp for the night, several wandered over to watch and listen to the strange goings-on at the white folks' campfire.

* * *

At daybreak on August 24, Emma awoke abruptly in the cool morning air. Disoriented and unsure what had stirred her from sleep, her heart skipped as she detected the "guttural tones of unfamiliar voices" speaking a strange language just outside the tent.

Suddenly, she recalled the words of General Sherman's cavalry scout describing the fighting against the Nez Perce in Big Hole Basin, followed by his false promise of safety as long as the tourists stayed inside the park.

What a foolish notion.

Sitting up in her blankets, Emma peered through the canvas flaps to see several Nez Perce standing by the morning campfire, attempting to have a conversation with A. J. Arnold and another member of the Cowan party. Her fears confirmed, Emma woke her husband, George. They dressed in a hurry and exited the tent. With an awkward nod to their visitors, the Cowans rallied the rest of the party to break camp, pack up the wagons, and make an expedited departure.

By this time, there was a steady flow of Nez Perce streaming into the Cowan campsite. Slowly, Emma began to grasp the enormity of the situation. Peering through a thin stand of pines, the full expanse of the main Nez Perce encampment spread out before her: hundreds of people breaking camp amid a small forest of makeshift tepees. And in the distance, literally thousands of horses.[9]

While the Cowans packed, several band members, including a warrior named Red Scout, requested food. As a man began handing over bags of flour and sugar from the supply wagon, he caught the eye of George Cowan, who rushed over with revolver in hand and angrily ordered the Nez Perce away. The men complied, but their furrowed brows suggested the matter was far from over. Emma later concluded that George's domineering attitude was probably not a wise choice. As she later recounted, "the Indians naturally resented it and I think this materially lessened [George's] chances of escape."[10]

The Cowan party soon moved out, heading westward down the wagon road to exit the park. But moments later, a group of mounted Nez Perce halted them at gunpoint, ordering them to turn around and follow the main column for a meeting with the chiefs along the East Fork of the Firehole River (later named Cowan Creek). When the trail became too narrow, the Nez Perce disassembled and ransacked the wagons, relieving them of all goods that could be carried on horseback. Those to whom George had denied provisions earlier now took their full measure but without an ounce of gratitude toward the hardheaded leader of the tourists.

At the confluence of modern-day Cowan Creek and Nez Perce Creek, they stopped to meet with a number of tribal elders, including Chiefs Joseph, White Bird, and Looking Glass and another leader who, according to Emma, went by the name of Poker Joe, although he was also known as Lean Elk or Hototo in the Nez Perce language.

Acting as an interpreter, Hototo told the Cowans that if they were willing to trade their horses and saddles for some exhausted Nez Perce mounts, they would be free to go. While disgruntled at losing their wagons, gear, and now their horses, the Cowans also realized the deal was their best and perhaps only chance for escape. Without hesitation, they agreed.

Hototo warned them to ride quickly and avoid the main trail, as the chiefs anticipated difficulty controlling some of the younger warriors. Many were still grief-stricken, angry, and seeking revenge for the massacre of their children and other loved ones at Big Hole.

Now astride tired ponies, the Cowans began working their way back down the trail once more. But after only a half mile or so, a group of warriors rode up behind them and told them that the chiefs had changed their minds and wanted to see them again. Reluctantly turning their mounts around, the Cowans rode in an uneasy silence surrounded by their captors.

Suddenly, gun shots exploded as two men came running down the trail toward them. Emma learned later that they were scouting to make sure the main group of Nez Perce would be unaware of the violence about to take place. Turning to her husband, Emma saw him get off his horse and collapse to the ground. According to Emma,

> Shots followed and Indian yells, and all was confusion . . . In less time that it takes me to tell it, I was off my horse and by my husband's side, where he lay against a fallen pine tree. I heard my sister's screams and called to her. She came and crouched by me, as I knelt by his side. I saw he was wounded in the leg above the knee, and by the way the blood spurted out I feared an artery had been severed . . .
>
> Every gun of the whole party of Indians was leveled on us three. I shall never forget the picture, which left an impress that years cannot efface. The holes in those gun barrels looked as big as saucers.[11]

Seeing a warrior with "an immense Navy pistol" aiming at her husband, Emma threw her body in the way to shield him, but rough hands pulled her back as she watched Red Scout step up. He placed the barrel against George's head and pulled the trigger.

> My husband's head fell back, and a red stream trickled down his face from beneath his hat. The warm sunshine, the smell of blood, the horror of it all, a faint remembrance of seeing rocks

thrown at his head, my sister's screams, a sick faint feeling, and all was blank.[12]

* * *

During the melee, two members of the Cowan Party escaped into the woods. Shortly thereafter, Hototo arrived on the scene, sent by the chiefs on suspicion of trouble. Together with Red Scout, who now regretted his defiance of the chiefs' orders, Hototo convinced the warriors to stand down, ensuring safety for Emma and the other remaining members of the Cowan Party.

Returning to the main Nez Perce camp, Emma and Ida were reunited with Frank and also met John Shively, an old prospector captured earlier who was serving as temporary guide for the Nez Perce. Upon meeting Chief Joseph, Emma was struck by his dignified manner and "somber stillness." Though distraught at her husband's death, Emma later remarked that she was treated well by the Nez Perce, who offered her food, blankets, and even a baby to hold in an attempt to ease her pain. At night she and Ida slept near the campfire on buffalo robes, surrounded by Nez Perce women as a sign of protection.

The next day, Emma, Frank, and Ida, along with a captured U.S. soldier (whom they later learned was a deserter from Fort Ellis), were set free once again.[13] This time, Hototo accompanied the group for several miles down the trail to ensure their safety. Before departing, he instructed them, "Ride all night. All day. No sleep."

This time, the Cowans succeeded in escaping. After passing Yellowstone Falls and Tower Creek, they stumbled upon a detachment of cavalry soldiers near the Yellowstone River, who escorted them to safety at Mammoth Hot Springs.

While at Mammoth, Emma learned of another group of tourists in the park at the time of her visit, including eleven young men from Helena, who had also experienced violent run-ins with the Nez Perce. Most escaped unharmed, but two members of that group would later die. She also met some rather notable visitors, including the colorful Earl of Dunraven with his small party led by guide "Texas Jack" Omohundro.

Though distressed at the idea of her husband's body lying exposed in the wilderness, "perhaps dragged and torn by wild beasts," there was no way to safely return for a proper burial. Emma resigned herself to the fact that there was nothing more she could do. She, Frank, and Ida left with the earl's party for Bozeman.

As they neared Fort Ellis, Emma spotted a dust cloud on the horizon. Soon they were passed by Lieutenant Doane and several Crow scouts leading a detachment of cavalry troops south in a bid to head off the Nez Perce at Mammoth Hot Springs. Frank joined the soldiers hoping for a chance to look for George's body, while Emma continued on to Radersburg.

One week after arriving home, Emma received a knock at the door. On the front porch, she found two neighbors holding the extra edition of the *Helena Daily Independent*. The headline made her heart leap:

COWAN ALIVE
WITH GENERAL HOWARD'S COMMAND[14]

Somehow, George had survived after all! Emma rushed back inside and began packing for a return journey to Yellowstone.

* * *

Miraculously, the gunshots to George's leg and head were not fatal. Possibly due to damp gunpowder, the bullet from the point-blank blast never penetrated his skull.[15] When he awoke from the concussion caused by his head wound, George found a stick, which he used to gingerly pull himself to a standing position. Once stable, he looked up to see a lone Nez Perce warrior on horseback staring at him. The man dismounted, lifted his rifle, and shot George a third time, hitting him as he turned through the left hip and out the abdomen.

Once again, George collapsed; this time falling face-first to the ground. Assured that the deed was finally done, the warrior remounted and galloped off to rejoin the main party. Meanwhile George lay in the meadow, bleeding freely from the new wound in his stomach and the freshly broken nose caused by the fall.

But George Cowan proved difficult to kill.

In addition to being a lawyer, George was a veteran of the Civil

War and a number of battles against Native Americans in northern Montana. No stranger to physical hardship, his stubborn resolve would soon become his most valuable asset.

Once again, he slowly regained consciousness. For the next four days and nights, he crawled and dragged himself ten miles back down the trail. Without food, fire, or bandages, George tore his clothes with his teeth to bind his wounds. When he finally reached the Cowan's old campsite in the Lower Geyser Basin, George found some old coffee grounds and a few matchsticks that had been left behind. And it was there, on August 30, that army scouts pursuing the Nez Perce under General Howard's command found him.

But George's difficulties were far from over. The scouts, wishing to stay on the trail of the Nez Perce, decided to keep moving. They knew General Howard's main company would find George the next day. Before they left him, they shared what provisions they could spare and lit a campfire to keep the injured man warm. But during the night, the wind picked up, transforming the small fire into a raging blaze that quickly spread to the surrounding trees.

A startled George awoke choking, surrounded by thick smoke and blinding heat. He crawled to safety and made yet another narrow escape but suffered burns on his hands and knees in the process.

Nonetheless, he survived to greet General Howard's men the next morning.

About ten days later, with the help of the soldiers and A. J. Arnold, who had also been rescued by Howard's troops, George arrived in Mammoth Hot Springs. An army surgeon removed the bullet from his head and treated his other wounds. Eventually, both men made their way to Bottler's Ranch, where George finally reunited with Emma.

Despite their encounter with the Nez Perce, both Cowans recovered and went on to live long and full lives. George had the mushroomed bullet from his head wound made into a fob for his pocket watch. And in the coming decades, the couple would record the events in their memoirs and return to the park several more times. All in all, Emma concluded that their adventures in Yellowstone resulted in a happy ending.

The same could not be said for the Nez Perce.

* * *

After the Cowans' departure, the main column of Nez Perce turned southeast toward Yellowstone Lake, where they stayed for several days while a handful of warriors raided another tourist camp. In total, the Nez Perce spent about two weeks in the park. Some early commentators suggested this proved the erroneous notion that the Nez Perce were lost because they—like other Native Americans—always avoided Yellowstone due to superstitions about the geysers. Bolstering this argument was the fact that the Nez Perce captured a white prospector, John Shively, on the day they entered the park to serve as a guide.

The truth is that the Nez Perce were well acquainted with Yellowstone. According to the firsthand account left by Yellow Wolf, a member of the Wallowa Nez Perce and survivor of the war, the traditional hunting route through Yellowstone would have been to take the Bannock Trail from the Madison River to the Yellowstone River, then cut north toward Mammoth Hot Springs to the buffalo plains of modern-day Montana.[16] Alternatively, they might have continued on the trail due east to the Clarks Fork Valley.[17]

But on this trip, their goal was to meet with the Crow Nation, which lay north and east of Yellowstone. They also knew the cavalry was in close pursuit and would likely try to seal off all usual exits from the park. This meant the Nez Perce needed to find a new or unexpected route, while at the same time eluding their pursuers. As it turns out, this was a wise decision.

* * *

Just as he had done at Big Hole, General Howard used the telegraph to stay one step ahead of the Nez Perce. In response to Howard's request for aid, General Sherman dispatched troops to seal off each of Yellowstone's main exits in a bid to trap the Nez Perce within the park. He sent Lieutenant Doane down from Fort Ellis to guard Mammoth Hot Springs and arranged for Colonel Samuel Sturgis and 360 men to guard the Clarks Fork exit to the east. Meanwhile, Major Hart, along with 250 cavalry and 100 scouts, guarded the Shoshone River exit, and Colonel Wesley Merritt's 500 soldiers blocked the southern route via the Wind River.

For his part, General Howard and his 600 soldiers continued in direct pursuit, coming into the park through the western entrance along the Madison River before turning north and east toward modern-day Cooke City. Slowed by having to pull ten supply wagons over rough terrain and exhausted by the long trek from Oregon, Howard could not keep pace with the Nez Perce. Instead he relied on advanced reports from Lieutenant Fisher, who led forty Bannock scouts in an attempt to stay close on the heels of the Nez Perce.

On August 31, a small force of Nez Perce raiders attempted to burn Baronett's Bridge over the Yellowstone before attacking Mammoth Hot Springs and the Henderson Ranch, located about one mile north of modern-day Gardiner. The warriors were likely scouting the viability of the northern exit, but after clashing with Doane's troops, tribal leaders decided that they needed an alternate route.[18]

Not wishing to pass near the mining camps of modern-day Cooke City, the Nez Perce were left with three options: to cut southeast following the Shoshone River toward Cody, continue on the main trail to the Clarks Fork Valley, or find an alternative and more direct path eastward over the Absaroka Mountains.

Meanwhile, under advice from his scouts, Colonel Sturgis concluded that the mountainous route to the Clarks Fork River would prove too difficult for the Nez Perce. Leaving his position, Sturgis marched his troops southward toward the Shoshone River. Observing this movement, the Nez Perce decided to risk a steep and narrow trail directly through the Absaroka Mountains, bringing them directly into the Clarks Fork River valley. Before Sturgis realized his mistake, the Nez Perce had escaped from Yellowstone and were making a run northward across the plains.

But the victory was short-lived. Upon making contact with the Crow Nation, the Nez Perce learned that they would not find safety with their allies.[19] Fearing retaliation from the U.S. Army, the Crow wanted no part of the conflict. On the contrary, a number of Crow warriors had already joined up with U.S. troops as scouts against the Nez Perce, riding with Lieutenant Doane and Colonel Sturgis.

On September 13, just west of Billings, Montana, the Nez Perce repelled an attack by Colonel Sturgis's troops. The next day a war party of over 200 Crow and Bannock riders launched an assault of their own on the Nez Perce. While casualties were low, the Nez Perce lost several hundred horses to the Crow,[20] devastating their resources and dealing a damaging psychological blow. Their longtime friends had become enemies.

Despite these setbacks, the Nez Perce again outdistanced the U.S. troops led by General Howard and Colonel Sturgis. On September 29, about forty miles from the Canadian border, the exhausted Nez Perce made camp on the banks of Snake Creek just north of the Bear Paw Mountains. Correctly believing that they were several days ahead of Howard, the Nez Perce took a much-needed rest.

Unfortunately, less than twelve miles away, Colonel Nelsen Miles and 400 soldiers, including thirty Cheyenne scouts, also made camp. Once again, a telegraph message from General Sherman had alerted Miles, who led his troops on a desperate 160-mile forced march to try to cut off the Nez Perce before they reached the border.

At approximately 4:00 a.m. on September 30, Army scouts located the Nez Perce camp and Colonel Miles ordered the attack. In addition to a frontal assault, the troops launched a flanking maneuver to cut off the Nez Perce from their horses. Without access to the herd, there was no chance for a large-scale escape. While a scattered number of women and children eluded the soldiers by making a run to the north, the majority of the Nez Perce were forced to make a stand.

After five days of fighting, the battle ended in stalemate. Miles could not defeat the Nez Perce, but neither could the Nez Perce flee to freedom as they had done so many times before. Without their horses, the Nez Perce were caught in a standoff that was turning into a siege.

On October 4, General Howard arrived, bringing crucial supplies and reinforcements to Colonel Miles. That night, Chief White Bird and somewhere between 150 and 250 Nez Perce chanced a daring escape to the north, successfully slipping through enemy lines to reach the Canadian border. However, the next morning, tribal leaders realized that without ammunition and food, the roughly 450 Nez Perce that remained had no choice but to end the fighting. Chief Joseph rode down to the U.S. camp and surrendered his rifle to Colonel Miles.

At some point during the negotiations, an army translator recorded

Chief Joseph's words as he delivered one of the most famous statements in American history:[21]

> I am tired of fighting. Our chiefs are killed . . . The old men are all killed . . . It is cold and we have no blankets . . . I want time to look for my children and see how many of them I can find. Maybe I shall find them among the dead . . . Hear me, my chiefs, I am tired; my heart is sick and sad. From where the sun now stands, I will fight no more forever.

As part of the surrender agreement, Colonel Miles promised to let them return to the Lapwai Reservation in Idaho. But soon after, he was overruled by General Sherman, who sent the Nez Perce instead to a series of military forts (i.e., prisons) before they ultimately arrived in Oklahoma Territory. For eight years, Chief Joseph and Yellow Bull lobbied for the tribe's return to Idaho as they watched many members die of sickness and grief on the unfamiliar plains. Finally, in 1885, 118 tribal members were allowed to return to the Lapwai Reservation. The remaining 150, including Chief Joseph, were still deemed too dangerous by the U.S. government and transferred to the Colville Reservation in eastern Washington, where Joseph died in 1904.

* * *

The fate of the Nez Perce is reminiscent of the profound historic tragedies suffered by Indigenous peoples throughout North America. The fact that this story played out, at least in part, within the country's first national park is particularly disorienting. At first glance, there is something surreal about tourists in Yellowstone being caught up in the western Indian Wars. It represents a collision of two things that for many people occupy very different moments in American history.

After all, national park tourism feels like a very modern thing, an activity that millions of people engage in every year and celebrate as a public right. In contrast, the deliberate subjugation of Indigenous peoples by U.S. military forces might seem to belong to a more distant past. However, Emma Cowan's encounter with Chief Joseph and the Nez Perce in Yellowstone forcefully underscores the shared history of these two phenomena. In fact, the Nez Perce War would carry far-reaching implications not only for Yellowstone but for the future of the entire national park system.

Though Emma's account was written some twenty-five years after the fact, the newspapers of the day carried the incident widely and in real time. Headlines read like scenes from an action movie.

WONDERLAND.
SCENES OF BLOODSHED.
TWO NARROW ESCAPES FROM THE CLUTCHES OF
THE RED DEVILS![22]

THE INDIAN WAR!
LATEST FROM HOWARD
A HARD BATTLE ON THE YELLOWSTONE
STURGIS IN PURSUIT[23]

GEO. COWAN KILLED IN HIS WIFE'S ARMS[24]

On the national scale, a significant portion of the public actually sympathized with the plight of the Nez Perce, especially after Chief Joseph's speech was published. But regionally, news of the Cowan incident, in combination with the Battle of Little Bighorn the year before, fanned flames of resentment toward Native Americans.

While park promoters wanted publicity, this was the wrong kind. Worried that potential visitors might be put off by fears of violence, they adopted a two-pronged—and highly contradictory—strategy. On one hand, park superintendent Norris, the railroad industry, and territorial and local officials worked fervently behind the scenes to ban Indigenous people from the park, both the resident Tukudika (Sheep Eater Shoshone) and the many others from nearby tribal nations who visited on a seasonal basis. On the other hand, for tourist consumption, some park promoters cultivated the myth that native peoples always avoided Yellowstone because they were frightened of the geothermal features and the land's "evil spirits." Ergo tourists had nothing to fear.

As we know, the Indigenous presence in Yellowstone stretches back 11,000 years or more. Up through the 1870s, it was used continuously as a territorial homeland, as evidenced by an abundance of archeological artifacts and ethnographic data. Dozens of tribes made regular use of the park area for mining, hunting, plant gathering, and cultural or ceremonial activities. Even today, twenty-seven different tribal nations consult with Yellowstone officials on pertinent cultural-resource management issues.

So why did so many white visitors to Yellowstone ascribe to this belief? It may have arisen as a misguided attempt to explain why Native Americans were rarely seen in the park by white visitors. In reality, Indigenous people likely chose to avoid the places crowded by tourists in order to lessen the chance of conflicts and improve the odds of a successful hunt.

Nonetheless, in his first annual report to the secretary of the interior, Superintendent Norris characterized the events of 1877 as a one-off:

> The lamentable Indian raid, burning of houses, bridges, and massacre of innocent tourists within the park, soon after my leaving there, is as anomalous as unexpected; the first, and probably the last of the kind, as it is wholly aside from all Indian routes, and only chosen in the desperation of retreat by the Nez Perce, who have acquired sufficient civilization and Christianity to at least overpower their pagan superstitious fear of earthly fire-hole basins and brimstone pits.
>
> Owing to the isolation of the Park, deep amid snowy mountains, and the superstitious awe of the roaring cataracts, sulphur pools, and spouting geysers over the surrounding pagan Indians, they seldom visit it, and only a few harmless Sheepeater hermits, armed with bows and arrows, ever resided there, and even they now vanished . . .[25]

But the very next year, in the summer of 1878, it *did* happen again. And then once more in 1879.

* * *

The so-called Bannock War of 1878 broke out over concerns by Bana'kwut (Bannock) tribal members in Idaho that traditional food-gathering areas on the Camas Prairies, just outside the Fort Hall Reservation, were being overrun by livestock from white ranchers. Already suffering from food shortages on the reservation, the loss of access to these staple resources triggered an uprising of several hundred Bannock warriors, joined by a number of Northern Paiutes and Umatillas.

Led by Chief Buffalo Horn, a former scout for the U.S. military during the Nez Perce War, the collective moved across Idaho and Oregon, raiding and clashing with white settlers and cavalry troops. As the leaders were killed or captured, the group splintered into small bands until, in August 1878, only a small group of sixty to eighty Bannocks remained. They moved eastward into Yellowstone National Park, attempting to follow their traditional trail to freedom on the buffalo plains. But, like the Nez Perce, their flight ended by an attack from Colonel Nelson Miles just outside the park near Bennett Creek on September 4, 1878.[26]

Then, in 1879, the Sheep Eater conflict (incredulously, also labeled a "war" by the U.S. government, likely to justify taking violent action) consisted of only a small band of family groups, totaling between forty and eighty Sheep Eater Shoshone from central Idaho. Falsely accused of some local murders, they took flight into the modern-day Frank Church-River of No Return Wilderness. The fighting never crossed into Yellowstone, nor did it ever involve the Tukudika (Sheep Eaters) who resided in the park. Still, the fact that Yellowstone Sheep Eaters shared the same name as the accused raised suspicions that they might rise up too.

In response to all of this, Superintendent Norris took action against the perceived "Indian menace." In 1878, using the first-ever congressional budget appropriations for the park, Norris constructed a rough-cut road south from Mammoth Hot Springs to the Lower Geyser Basin in order to facilitate troop movements against future incursions from the West. He also requested a small military outpost near the western park entrance and funds to build a fortified blockhouse at Mammoth Hot Springs to use as park headquarters. Construction for both commenced in 1879.

That same year, on the heels of the so-called "Sheep Eater War,"

Norris got permission to order the removal of the resident Tukudika from Yellowstone. Most went to the Wind River Reservation at the invitation of Chief Washakie of the Eastern Shoshone, while others moved to the Fort Hall Reservation in Idaho.

In 1882, the federal government brokered a land cession from the Crow Nation that reduced their reservation holdings even further and removed any claim they once had to lands along the northern boundary of Yellowstone National Park. Meanwhile, Norris made annual visits to the surrounding reservations to elicit unofficial promises from the federal Indian agents that the tribes would stay out of the park. And with that, a precedent was set for removing Native Americans—along with any other preexisting residents deemed unwanted—from lands included in many of our national parks.

Historian Mark Spence has documented the process of dispossession in parks ranging from Yosemite to the Grand Canyon; from Glacier to the Everglades; and from Mesa Verde to the Badlands.[27] Most commonly, those removed were Native Americans, but in some cases, other racial minorities or poor whites were evicted, as in Shenandoah and Great Smoky Mountains National Parks.[28] With some notable exceptions, mostly in Alaska but also in parks established in recent decades, the history of our national parks has been the protection of places largely devoid of human inhabitants, giving rise to notions of wilderness as "unpeopled" landscapes. Such things are yet another powerful legacy of Yellowstone.

Selling Yellowstone

(1878–1883)

ON MONDAY, JANUARY 15, 1882, THE NEW YORK TIMES TUCKED
a brief news item into a column on the bottom of the front page:

A RAILROAD TO YELLOWSTONE PARK

A syndicate has been formed of wealthy gentlemen more or
less intimately connected with the Northern Pacific, to build
a branch tourists' line from some point on the line, probably
Bozeman, Montana, to the heart of the Yellowstone National
Park, and erect there a large hotel for the accommodation of
visitors . . . The syndicate has exclusive hotel privileges for the
park and will invest $150,000 in a hotel of 500 rooms, to be
ready for occupancy when the road is open.[1]

This "syndicate" would eventually evolve into the Yellowstone Improvement Company, a corporate entity financed and controlled by
Wall Street investors and Northern Pacific Railway executives. Though
garnering little attention at the time, the article was the first and most
direct sign that in Yellowstone, everything was about to change.

*　*　*

Meanwhile, over 2,000 miles west of New York City, park superintendent Philetus Norris was wintering in Mammoth Hot Springs with
a skeleton crew. Unlike his predecessor, Nathaniel Langford, Norris

142

gave the job of protecting the park his full attention. He established Yellowstone's first road network, constructed the first park headquarters, hired the first gamekeeper, and initiated the keeping of scientific records—exceptional accomplishments given his limited time and resources.

But Norris was a complex man. Ten years older than Langford, Norris shared the Montana pioneer's romanticized vision of westward settlement. While Langford celebrated his time as a "vigilante" and the economic gains of railroad, mining, and resource development, Norris looked back to an earlier time, idolizing the era of mountain men like John Colter and Jim Bridger. Respected by the early white settlers in the region, Norris was equally at home with men of science like Ferdinand Hayden. Through his Smithsonian connections, Norris set the tone for future park managers to collect scientific data as part of the job. To this end, he kept the first records of geyser eruptions, wildfire occurrences, and weather. He also oversaw the initial survey of park boundaries, suggesting a realignment of the northern and western lines so that the park lay wholly within a single territory (Wyoming), which would allow for a new county-level jurisdiction for criminal prosecutions of those breaking Yellowstone's rules. To compensate for the lost land, he proposed an expansion of the park's eastern boundary. None of these recommendations were acted on, but they demonstrate Norris's initiative.

On the other hand, Norris played a prominent role in removing and banning Indigenous people from the park, a problematic legacy that would fuel public debates and affect the entire national park system for decades to come.

Of course, at the time, few Euro-Americans questioned such actions. More challenging for Norris was maintaining his self-image as a mountaineer and reining in his desire for self-promotion. Dressing the part in full buckskins, moccasins, and feathered hat, Norris opened himself up to ridicule from visitors who thought he looked out-of-date. And his constant efforts to attach his name to sites throughout the park invited further criticism. Historian Aubrey Haines wrote that one journalist touring Yellowstone concluded that he was in fact touring "Norris Park."[2] Another visitor elaborated:

[The Superintendent] has honored the park by bestowing his lordly name upon numerous attractions . . . Mount Norris, Norris Geyser Basin, Norris Fork of the Gibbon, Norris cut off, Norris Obsidian-glass Road, Norris Plateau, Norris Geyser, Norris Museum, Norris Paint-Pot, Norris Falls, Norris Pile Spring.[3]

For others, the greater sin was Norris's teetotaler stance toward alcohol. He never succeeded in banning the sale of liquor in the park, but his efforts put him at odds with potential local allies, including proprietor James McCartney, whom he tried to evict from the park numerous times (finally succeeding in 1881). Whether it be Yellowstone tourists, miners heading to the Clarks Fork mines, or soldiers from Fort Ellis, most if not all strongly preferred having a "watering hole" inside the park.

Finally, some critics took issue with Norris's commitment to "get the job done" come hell or high water. While in some ways this trait allowed Norris to achieve ambitious construction goals on a shoestring budget, it did not always sit well with those who actually experienced the spine-crunching ride over his rough-cut wagon roads.

Central to the success of Norris's planned improvements was the fact that Congress finally approved the first-ever park appropriations. Made available in July 1878, the $10,000 budget provided $1,500 for Norris's annual salary, with the rest earmarked for purchasing building materials and hiring several assistant supervisors along with a crew of laborers. In 1880, the annual budget increased to $15,000.

Heavily influenced by the Nez Perce and Bannock Wars, Norris's first project consisted of building a road connecting Mammoth Hot Springs to the Lower Geyser Basin to allow for troops to move between the park's northern and western entrances. After taking on Clarence Stephens as assistant superintendent, Norris hired twenty "mountaineer laborers" to construct sixty miles of rudimentary roadway in thirty days. With ridiculously steep grades and tree stumps cut just low enough to allow a standard wagon axel to pass over, calling it a road may have been a bit generous. But given the intense mountain topography and lack of proper engineering tools, the road was still an asset.

In subsequent years, rather than upgrading his earlier work, Norris chose to extend the network of roads as far as possible, stretching east through the Hayden Valley and beyond to Yellowstone Lake. In 1879, he also commenced construction on a new park headquarters in Mammoth. Norris's blockhouse stood on Capitol Hill (across from the Mammoth Terraces) and served administrative, residential, and defensive purposes, crowned with a turret that allowed rifle fire in all directions.[4] In total, by the end of his fifth and final season in 1881, Norris constructed about 120 miles of new wagon roads and marked out one hundred miles of trails, complete with signage for visitors. Though later regraded, rebuilt, and, in some cases, rerouted by the U.S. Army Corps of Engineers, Norris's general road pattern, which aligned with the one promoted by Langford, served as the template for the modern figure-eight road system that exists today.

Through it all, Norris dutifully wrote detailed annual reports to the secretary of the interior. As he built roads, he kept an eye out for archeological artifacts, sending these and geothermal specimens to the Smithsonian for display. He initiated the idea of a game reserve in the Lamar Valley to protect the remaining bison herds against poachers. To this end, in July 1880, he hired Harry Yount, a seasoned mountain man, to build a cabin and winter in the park as Yellowstone's first gamekeeper. Yount served for just one year, reporting that the job was too much for one person alone. Instead, a police force was needed, not only to protect wildlife but to enforce park rules for visitors. Norris concurred and included the recommendation in his reports. But this idea, like so many others, went unheeded.

More damaging to Norris's reputation—at least in Washington— was his unflinching refusal to sell out to wealthy investors. Whereas Langford allied himself with the Northern Pacific Railroad, Norris stubbornly, and perhaps naively, resisted the growing pressure for corporate control over Yellowstone. To be sure, he desperately wanted the park opened and developed for visitors. This is why he helped Baronett rebuild and improve his toll bridge after the Nez Perce War and gave ready approval for "Uncle John" Yancey and George Marshall to build log cabin hotels near modern-day Roosevelt Lodge and the Firehole River respectively. In 1881, he also invited F. Jay Haynes into the park. As the official photographer for the Northern Pacific, Haynes met Norris in Bismarck in 1877. With Norris's support, Haynes set up a seasonal photography studio and residence in Mammoth, thereby launching an eighty-seven-year presence in Yellowstone for Haynes and his descendants.

But despite Norris's quest for an orderly distribution of park leases for hotels and concessions, he failed to see the political and economic storm clouds on the horizon—ones tethered to the ever-expanding railroads, which everyday inched closer and closer to Yellowstone.

* * *

In 1879, as the Northern Pacific Railway finally emerged from bankruptcy, it did so under the leadership of a man who would soon share his name with a main-line city: Frederick Billings. With Billings now at the helm, construction on the transcontinental line renewed in earnest, charging west from Bismarck toward Miles City (named for the general who captured Chief Joseph). Meanwhile, from the railroad's Pacific Coast terminus in Tacoma, Washington, construction crews worked feverishly, laying track eastward toward Montana.

Despite his success in bringing the dormant company back to life, in 1881, after less than two years, Billings lost his job in a hostile takeover by another railroad baron, Henry Villard. As owner of the Oregon Steamship Company and the Oregon and California Railroad, Villard held a monopoly over all major rail and river traffic in the Pacific Northwest. The only potential rival in the region was the Northern Pacific. Rather than compete, Villard decided to buy it out. And over the next two years, he pushed hard to complete the transcontinental line, including a branch connection into Yellowstone.

But Villard was not the only one with this idea. During the years when the Northern Pacific lay dormant in economic limbo, the Union Pacific Railroad slowly but steadily continued to lay track northward from Ogden, Utah. Purchased by financier Jay Gould during the Panic of 1873, the Union Pacific sought to offer service all the way to Virginia City and from there into Yellowstone via the western entrance in the Madison River Valley. And, for much of the 1870s, it appeared that Gould's Union Pacific would beat the Northern Pacific to the park.

As the two major railroads drew ever closer, tensions increased in the local populace over which would win out as the major gateway for tourists. The economic stakes were high. Business leaders in Bozeman saw their fortunes tied to the Northern Pacific, while those in Virginia City and points south supported the Union Pacific. And because any move by Yellowstone's superintendent might be interpreted as an attempt to favor one competitor over another, Norris found himself in an unwinnable situation.

The approaching railroads were like the jaws of a mighty beast, slowly but inevitably clamping down on the park. And for Norris, smack in the middle of it all, there was nowhere to run.

* * *

Norris's demise as Yellowstone superintendent began in his second season, when he received word that a survey party[5] from the Union Pacific's Utah and Northern branch line was scouting a route from Virginia City to the Lower Geyser Basin. Norris took a meeting with the surveyors and helped them identify a route, which he mentioned in his annual report. Although railroad officials soon abandoned the plan, news of Norris's involvement incurred the wrath of newspaper editors and business leaders in Bozeman who now viewed him as hostile to their interests.

Norris suffered a second setback over the issue of mail service. Back in July of 1874, a weekly seasonal mail route was authorized between Bozeman and Mammoth Hot Springs. But for reasons unknown to Norris, the route was abandoned in favor of a new one that would connect Bozeman to Fort Brown (renamed Fort Washakie in 1878, located near modern-day Lander, Wyoming) by cutting through Yellowstone itself. Representatives from the Gilman and Salisbury Stage Line, the same line that held the contract to bring Union Pacific passengers from the end of the line to Virginia City or Bozeman, won the contract. The proposed route was, at the time, completely untenable as there were no stage roads running north to south through the park. And immediately after winning the bid, Gilman and Salisbury suggested an alternative route running between Virginia City and Mammoth via the Madison River Valley, cutting out Bozeman altogether.

Trusting Gilman and Salisbury, Norris supported the unfolding arrangements and helped to scout out a new wagon road for the mail service into the west park entrance. But, unbeknownst to Norris, the U.S. Postal Service decision to reroute the mail in the first place was part of a fraudulent scheme. The so-called "star service route" scam involved the U.S. Postal Department approving a new mail route. Then, a conspiring contractor would win the contract with a ridiculously low bid. Afterward, the contractor would "discover" that there were "unknown costs" involved and request ever greater amounts of federal money to complete the route, with financial kickbacks going to high-ranking federal officials. *The New York Times* estimated that over $6 million of public money was spent on such schemes in the first six months of 1879.[6] In the case of the Virginia City–Yellowstone route, costs reached $20,000, with approximately one quarter going to Assistant Postmaster General Thomas Brady.[7]

When all of this came to light, the Bozeman newspapers launched a scorching campaign to remove Norris as park superintendent. Citing his compliance with the scam, they labeled Norris incompetent and untrustworthy. Once Norris learned the truth, he withdrew his support from Gilman and Salisbury, thus alienating himself not only from Bozeman but now also from Virginia City interests, Union Pacific investors, and others complicit with the mail scam in the federal government.

The third and final blow fell with the 1882 announcement of the Northern Pacific Railway's syndicate. As reported in *The New York Times*, the company intended to construct and control rail service, hotels, and other major concessions within Yellowstone. Already on record as a critic of a corporate takeover of the park, Norris had written to the secretary of the interior condemning the idea in 1880.[8] His position thus clearly stated, the railroad interests labeled him a problem in need of removal. Despite a letter of support from General Sheridan, the die was cast. Norris's days were numbered.

Within a matter of weeks of the *Times* article, Norris received word of his termination from Interior Secretary Kirkwood, effective March 31, 1882. The next day, the secretary appointed sixty-two-year-old Patrick H. Conger, a Civil War veteran; former deputy U.S. marshal in

Dubuque, Iowa; and Indian agent for the Sioux Reservation in Yankton, Dakota Territory, as Yellowstone's new superintendent.

Ironically, Nathaniel Langford lost his position as superintendent, at least in part, for his unflinching allegiance to corporate interests. Now, Norris was fired for doing just the opposite.

* * *

On May 22, 1882, Conger reached Yellowstone by way of the Union Pacific's Utah and Northern branch line to Virginia City, then by stage to the Lower Geyser Basin. After spending the night at George Marshall's cabin, he rode horseback on Norris's rough road to Mammoth, arriving late in the evening, where he received a hospitable welcome from Norris's former assistant and now acting superintendent, Clarence Stephens.

Conger differed profoundly from his two predecessors. His selection by Interior Secretary Kirkwood, a former governor of Iowa, was recommended by Iowa senator William Allison, who knew Conger in Dubuque when they both served as Republican delegates for President Lincoln in the 1860s.[9] As a political appointee, Conger had no experience as a frontiersmen, builder, or entrepreneur. He arrived in Yellowstone knowing no more about the park than any other first-time tourist. But this mattered little to the political and economic power brokers, who simply wanted a man who would do their bidding without asking questions.

To Conger's surprise, Stephens informed him of his own pending departure. Either out of faithfulness to Norris or perhaps disgust at the way his old boss had been treated, Stephens had submitted his resignation back in mid-May. In early June, his replacement arrived. Like Conger, George L. Henderson was an Iowa Republican but with even stronger political connections through his brother, Iowa congressman and future speaker of the house David Henderson. The fifty-four-year-old Henderson was widowed and brought with him his adult son, Walter, and four daughters, Barbara, Jennie, Helen, and Mary, who ranged in age from twelve to twenty-one. In July, Barbara was appointed postmistress at Mammoth, launching a decades-long involvement by the Henderson family in Yellowstone's post office and other park concessions.[10]

Conger's term began smoothly enough. After hiring a work crew, including Assistant Captain Eugene S. Topping, Conger focused on improving Norris's road system: removing stumps, reducing grades, inserting culverts for drainage, and adding a bridge over the Gardiner River. At least initially, he worked well with Assistant Superintendent Henderson, who lived in the blockhouse with his children that first summer and later moved into one of McCartney's abandoned log cabins.

Like Norris, Conger supported the expansion of small leaseholders, including Uncle John Yancey's "hotel and saloon" in Pleasant Valley, which opened in summer 1882 to serve miners traveling to the Clarks Fork mines. Farther along that route, near the future site of the Lamar Buffalo Ranch, George Jackson and Buckskin Jim Cutler received permission to set up another waystation, and even farther along, William "Billy" Jump did the same in Harry Yount's old gamekeeper's cabin near Soda Butte. Meanwhile, George Marshall continued to operate his lodge in the Lower Geyser Basin.

Outside the park, other changes were underway. On April 11, 1882, Congress amended the treaty with the Crow Nation, eliminating their traditional land claims to the northern tier of Yellowstone Park, including the area encompassing the Clarks Fork mining district. The boundary change served to legitimize the formerly illegal mining activities and, in so doing, attracted the attention of new investors, including Jay Cooke. Meanwhile, the Northern Pacific Railway continued construction, moving steadily eastward across the southern tier of Montana Territory.

In late fall 1882, as Conger settled in to write his first annual report, he highlighted the road improvements and announced the construction of a new "summer headquarters" in the Lower Geyser Basin. He also noted the usual recurring problems with vandalism, wildfires, and poaching but was otherwise happy to report that no major scandals or traumatic events had occurred under his watch. In terms of notable visitors, Conger recorded that General Phillip Sheridan passed through the park in September with a large military contingent. He also mentioned that he settled financial accounts with merchants in Bozeman and Virginia City. His report complete, Conger bade farewell to Henderson, who planned to winter in the park, and departed for his home in Iowa.[11]

* * *

At least according to his written account, Conger's first season as superintendent passed quietly enough. But it turns out that Conger left out several key events. Prominent among these was the arrival of the corporate syndicate mentioned in *The New York Times* back in January.

From midsummer through the early fall of 1882, the syndicate evolved into a powerful economic entity. Led by Henry Douglas and Carroll Hobart, who also served as construction superintendent for the Northern Pacific branch line into Yellowstone, the company worked with new Interior Secretary Henry Teller to secure a lease agreement for hotels, telegraph, transportation service, and other concessions throughout Yellowstone Park.[12]

Following protocol, the Interior Department sent the application to Superintendent Conger for review. But by the time Conger's reply was received in Washington, the point was moot. It didn't matter that Conger voiced concern over the amount of land and rights given to the corporate entity—the assistant interior secretary overseeing Yellowstone, Merritt Joslyn, had already signed the contract. Though not in its final form since the actual building sites had yet to be "specified or surveyed," for all practical purposes, the preliminary contract ensured final approval.[13]

But even while negotiations were ongoing, Hobart was already in the park selecting building sites, digging foundations, erecting a sawmill, and cutting timber. By early fall, most of this work was complete. Meanwhile, Northern Pacific work crews cut a road running south from the new townsite of Livingston (named after railway executive Johnston Livingston) into the Yellowstone Valley, where it connected to the old Bozeman-Mammoth toll road. On September 19, the company, which already included a powerful board of directors comprised of railroad executives, senators, and lawyers, contracted with infamous Wall Street investor "Uncle Rufus" Hatch to provide the bulk of the necessary startup capital.

By October, Northern Pacific accountants were fanning out ahead of railway survey crews, buying up the needed land from ranchers and homesteaders to construct the branch track to Mammoth. About the time Conger reached his home in Iowa in November 1882, the tracks of the main transcontinental Northern Pacific line reached Livingston. Six weeks later, in mid-January 1883, the first train car would arrive. Shortly thereafter, on January 18, the syndicate led by Hobart, Douglas, and Hatch adopted the title of Yellowstone National Park Improvement Company.[14] Hobart became vice president and general manager, while Hatch served as the majority shareholder.

In hindsight, it seems that all of this construction activity deserved some mention in the Yellowstone superintendent's annual report. Perhaps the fact that the work was technically illegal had something to do with its absence. Or that Secretary Teller, a staunch supporter of the railroad industry, was waist-deep in the matter but didn't want to risk the political fallout of exposure. Some have suggested that the reason Assistant Secretary Joslyn signed the contract instead of Teller was to provide political cover for the latter's involvement.[15] But did Conger's silence on this matter mean that he, like Langford before him, was also in cahoots with the Northern Pacific?

It turns out Conger *did* address these issues, but rather than include them in his annual report, he discussed them in a separate private letter to Secretary Teller. In it, Conger complained bitterly about Hobart's actions and attitude: indiscriminately cutting trees and killing game, initiating construction without permission, and all the while treating Conger with contempt.[16] Like Norris, it appears that Conger put the interests of Yellowstone above an opportunity for easy economic and political gain. But this did him no favors. Because Teller was already entrenched with Hobart, Conger's letter likely sealed his fate.

But tellingly, the actions of the Yellowstone Improvement Company were not the only "undocumented" events of 1882 significant to the future of the park. In terms of Yellowstone's long-term conservation legacy, perhaps the most important event that summer was the visit by General Sheridan.

* * *

At first glance, the most remarkable aspect of Sheridan's trip was his unprecedented route into the park. With 150 men and some 300 horses and mules, Sheridan approached Yellowstone from Jackson Hole and, in so doing, marked out a new trail from the Snake River to West Thumb on Yellowstone Lake.[17] Known as the Sheridan Trail, the path was made a roadway in 1895.

But this was just the first legacy of Sheridan's visit. Guided by Yellowstone Jack Baronett, the party toured the geyser basins, taking careful note of the reduced big game due to poaching and the rampant vandalism caused by tourists. Wildfires were another problem, one to which Sheridan's own group contributed by inadvertently igniting a blaze that claimed over 15,000 acres.[18] But the greatest significance of Sheridan's trip took place on the return journey.

During their exit from the park, Sheridan's party passed through the Clarks Fork mining camps in the northeast corner. The group then continued north until they came upon construction crews working on the Northern Pacific Railway line near Billings. The construction superintendent, possibly Carroll Hobart, offered a tour of the new townsite. In the course of discussion, he took the liberty of proudly outlining plans for a new corporation poised to take full control of Yellowstone's lodging, transportation, and concession operations in the coming months. The general found this news extremely troubling but kept his thoughts to himself.

That changed when Sheridan returned to Washington. In his report for the War Department, published in fall 1882, the general made several recommendations. The first entailed a proposal to expand Yellowstone's boundaries forty miles to the east and roughly ten miles south so that the park might better encompass the full seasonal habit of large game, namely bison, elk, and bighorn sheep. Arguing that the mountainous areas in this expanded region of roughly 3,344 square miles held little settlement value, he noted that the action would cost the government next to nothing but would radically improve wildlife-protection efforts.

Second, he offered to deploy—upon request—U.S. Army troops to Yellowstone to protect wildlife and enforce park rules. Echoing Colonel Ludlow's recommendation from 1875 and Harry Yount and

Superintendent Norris's later calls for a park "police force," Sheridan observed that the personnel and resources provided by the Interior Department were insufficient to stop poaching, vandalism, and wildfires. If the Interior Department agreed, Sheridan claimed that he could station troops in the park within a matter of days at no additional cost to the government.

Third, and finally, Sheridan lamented current plans for selling out the park to commercial interests:

> On arriving at the railroad I regretted exceedingly to learn that the National Park had been rented out to private parties . . . The improvements in the park should be national, the control of it in the hands of an officer of the government, and small appropriations be made and expended each year for the improvement of roads and trails. It has been now placed in the hands of private parties for money making purposes, from which claims and conditions will arise that may be hard for the government and the courts to shake off.[19]

Sheridan's words on this last point are decidedly understated. He does not detail the monopolistic terms of the pending contract, nor does he name names, though it is likely that he learned both from his encounter with the Northern Pacific official in Billings. Nonetheless, his report made a plea to "all sportsmen of this country, and to the different sporting clubs" to take action.[20] And a number of like-minded individuals heeded the call.

As a group, these individuals would form a diverse coalition of park protectors with a common interest in Yellowstone and the nascent idea of environmental conservation. Agreeing with Sheridan's recommendations for expanding and protecting the park, these entities were similarly appalled by the Yellowstone Improvement Company's attempt to monopolize park concessions. Operating in different spheres of American society—congressional politics, national media, and the federal government—this eclectic mix of men (and they were all men) worked together to promote the first explicitly environmental conservation legislation in American history.

* * *

Fifty-two-year-old George Vest made an unexpected conservationist ally. Born in Kentucky, Vest was migrating to California in 1853 when he stopped in Missouri and decided to stay. Working first as a lawyer, he later entered politics as a representative in the Missouri statehouse. During the Civil War he joined the Confederacy, serving in both the Confederate House and Senate. After the war, he returned to private law practice in Missouri, famously delivering the "man's best friend" eulogy in a trial over the killing of a hunting dog. Soon after, Vest won election to Congress as a Democratic senator from Missouri. Small of stature with a rounded face, a thinning head of silver hair, a thick mustache, and a heavy Kentuckian accent, he staunchly supported the "lost cause" of the Confederacy until his death. Despite that fact, he also became a close friend and trusted confidant of General Sheridan, the same man who played a leading role in bringing about the defeat of the South and who presaged Sherman's scorched-earth campaign in Georgia by doing the same in the Shenandoah Valley. Nonetheless, the two men remained trusted allies in the fight to protect Yellowstone until the general's death in 1888.

George Grinnell's connection to Sheridan was more straightforward. Born to a wealthy family in Brooklyn (his father served as stockbroker to Commodore Cornelius Vanderbilt) and raised on the former estate of John James Audubon in Manhattan, Grinnell grew up influenced by the conservation ideals espoused by the famous naturalist and his widow, Lucy.[21] But Grinnell's interest in Yellowstone and the fate of America's dwindling bison herds was born of firsthand experience. On his first trip out West in 1870, as a twenty-year-old college student, Grinnell watched in wonder as his train ground to a halt amid a massive undulating sea of bison that took over three hours to cross the tracks. Two years later, he was afforded the opportunity to accompany over 4,000 Pawnee on one of the final traditional buffalo hunts in western Kansas.

Grinnell first met Sheridan in 1874 in Chicago, where they hit it off immediately. Both were in town preparing for General George Armstrong Custer's first expedition into the Black Hills, for which Grinnell served as naturalist. That trip led to a dubious discovery of gold in Lakota country and a return expedition that would end with Custer's defeat to Sitting Bull and Crazy Horse at Little Bighorn.

But for Grinnell, who opted out of Custer's fateful return trip, the 1874 expedition gave him the chance to befriend Army Corps Engineer Captain William Ludlow. A year later, in 1875, Ludlow invited Grinnell to serve as naturalist for an exploration of Yellowstone, where both men documented the impacts of poaching and vandalism in the park. The following year, while working on his doctoral degree at Yale, Grinnell began writing the natural history page for *Forest and Stream* magazine, one of the nation's first conservation-oriented publications. In January 1881, Grinnell became its editor. For the rest of his life, he would use this platform to call for the protection of nature in all its forms, and, in particular, Yellowstone.

* * *

The initial salvo in the fight for Yellowstone came from Senator Vest, who sponsored two resolutions in the U.S. Senate. The first, which passed on December 7, 1882, called for an investigation into park concessions. Specifically, it required the interior secretary to "transmit to the Senate copies of any contracts entered into by the Interior Department in regard to leasing the Yellowstone National Park."[22] The second resolution, passed on December 12, called for a legislative review of park management. Meanwhile, Grinnell drew public attention to the issue by publishing excerpts of the reports penned by Captain Ludlow in 1875 and General Sheridan in 1882. Both items ran in the December 14 issue of *Forest and Stream*.[23]

When Secretary Teller turned over the contracts to the Senate, Vest ordered them printed as official government documents, and the full scope of the Yellowstone Improvement Company's monopolistic intentions came to light.[24] Meanwhile, in the January 4, 1883, issue of *Forest and Stream*, Grinnell described the details in an editorial entitled "The Park Grab."

Grinnell's editorial explained that the Yellowstone Improvement Company sought monopoly control over all hotels, general stores, stagecoach transportation, telegraph, tour, and boating services throughout the park. What's more, they would enjoy "free use" of park timber for fuel and construction purposes, waters to supply hotels and other buildings, arable land for crops, and pasture for domestic cattle. The contract awarded ten-year leases of roughly 640 acres each on seven tracts, for a total of over 4,400 acres at an annual cost of two dollars per acre. The fee, according to Grinnell, was a "pitiful sum" compared to the "enormously valuable privileges" received. In closing, he exclaimed, "There certainly was never a more audacious and hare-faced plot to rob the people, nor one which apparently encountered so little opposition."[25]

Meanwhile, Vest busied himself with drafting new legislation for park protection. On January 5, 1883, he reported a bill (S. 2317) to amend the original Yellowstone Park Act along the lines suggested by General Sheridan. The bill expanded park boundaries, allowed the stationing of U.S. troops for park protection, granted force of law to park rules and regulations with defined penalties for violations, and placed Yellowstone under the criminal jurisdiction of Gallatin County, Montana Territory, for criminal prosecution. It also tightened the leasing arrangements, prohibiting the granting of monopoly control to any party and ensuring rights of public access to all sites in the park. Additionally, it increased the park annual budget, raising the superintendent's salary to $2,000 per year and allowing for the hire of ten assistants. And finally, it allowed the secretary of war to assign a Corps of Engineers officer to oversee road surveys and construction.[26]

Grinnell lobbied hard for the bill in the pages of *Forest and Stream*. The lead article in each issue in January 1883 made the case to protect Yellowstone against the monopolizing scheme of the Yellowstone Improvement Company. In the January 11 issue, Grinnell exposed how the company, without a signed lease, had commenced construction on the massive hotel at Mammoth. He also reported that the company was killing Yellowstone's wild game to feed its workers at the very time that wildlife populations in the park suffered from poaching. In fact, the syndicate had contracted with local hunters to supply some 20,000 pounds of meat rather than pay the cost of bringing food into the park.[27] The following week, Grinnell authored a piece entitled "The People's Park," in which he urged congressional action:

We hope most earnestly that the bill introduced by Senator Vest may receive speedy attention and become a law of the land. It cares for the interest of the people, and protects them from all monopolistic land-grabbing schemers. In caring for the people, it cares for the game and the fish, and thus deserves the most cordial support of every citizen.[28]

Although supported by several influential members of Congress who had championed the Yellowstone Act in 1872, including Henry Dawes (now a senator), Vest's new park bill died before it ever came to the floor for a vote. Over the past eleven years, the broad coalition that had enabled passage of the 1872 Yellowstone Act had dissolved. In particular, the powerful railroad lobby—largely responsible for the creation of Yellowstone National Park—now withheld support for any new protective measures.

Despite rhetoric to the contrary, the railroad industry's motives for supporting park creation were always economic gain. Now those motives were clearly exposed. Reaping the rewards of their political and economic investment meant giving free rein to the Northern Pacific's informal subsidiary, the Yellowstone Improvement Company. For the railroad companies and their allies in Congress, cashing in on Yellowstone was the plan all along.

Nonetheless, the public awareness generated by Grinnell, Vest, and Sheridan was having an effect. During negotiations over the park bill, Vest sent a letter directly to Interior Secretary Teller. In response, on January 15, 1883, the secretary issued new Yellowstone regulations, including a full ban on hunting within park boundaries. No longer could wildlife (so listed) be killed for recreation or as food. In addition, fishing was restricted to line and hook, and all timber cutting was forbidden "except upon special permission from the Department of Interior."[29]

While advocates welcomed this as a step in the right direction, the new rules were not enough. Undeterred, Senator Vest tried another legislative strategy: inserting Yellowstone protections as amendments to a must-pass appropriations bill. This time, he found success. Though it did not include all of the reforms called for in the defeated bill, the

Sundry Civil Act of 1883 increased park appropriations from $15,000 to $40,000, directing $2,000 toward the salary of a park superintendent and $900 for each of ten assistants. It restricted the size of park leases to no more than ten acres and required them to be located no closer than one-quarter mile to any geyser or Yellowstone Falls. It allowed for the assignment of an army engineering officer to guide the survey and construction of roads and bridges and, finally, allowed the secretary of war to appoint army troops in the park at the request of the interior secretary.[30]

On March 9, the Yellowstone Improvement Company officially signed a ten-year lease with the Department of the Interior, legitimizing the construction activities that had been underway since the previous fall. Though the size of their expected lease shrank from over 4,000 acres to ten, the company got around this hurdle by slicing up its allotments into seven portions distributed across the main tourist sites in the park.

At Mammoth Hot Springs, construction of the National Hotel continued at a fevered pace. Designed by architect L. F. Buffington to accommodate 800 guests in some 400 rooms, the hotel was built on a grand scale and geared toward an elite clientele. Painted green with a red roof, the four-story building stretched approximately 414 by 54 feet, with wings extending behind in an "E-shaped" design.[31] The grand lobby contained separate waiting rooms for ladies and gentlemen, a parlor, newsstand, barbershop, and bar, while a cavernous dining hall filled an entire wing. All guest rooms were located on upper floors.

Elsewhere in the park, the Yellowstone Improvement Company made plans to operate tent hotels. Located in the Norris Geyser Basin, Grand Canyon, and Upper Geyser Basin near Old Faithful, the tents served as a temporary solution until more permanent structures could be built.[32] For transportation and guiding services to and through the park, Hobart contracted with George Wakefield and Charles Hoffman for the exclusive right to carry passengers from the end of the Northern Pacific branch line to Mammoth and points beyond for twelve cents per mile.[33] For the Northern Pacific, after a ten-year delay, Yellowstone was finally open for business. Time would tell if their investment in the park idea would pay off.

* * *

By the opening of the 1883 summer season, approximately 150 rooms in the National Hotel were completed and ready for use. Though construction continued, the hotel could house between 300 and 500 guests depending on lodging arrangements, which often included guests sharing rooms, and even beds, with strangers.

In contrast to the lack of bed space, the furnishings in the hotel were more reflective of Hobart and Hatch's five-star aspirations. Approximately $60,000, or one-third of the construction budget, was spent on furniture in public spaces, including silverware, dining sets, and a massive kitchen with capacity for fifteen cooks working under two highly paid French chefs and a German baker. The main parlor was embellished with a Steinway pianoforte, while the lobby sported a series of vermillion spittoons and a stuffed mountain lion. As a finishing touch, all public areas were adorned with electric arc lights.

Despite these frills, early visitors noted the inflated prices and poor service. Aside from the unpleasant shock of bunking with strangers, guests had to deal with thin walls, inconsistent plumbing, and the constant presence of workmen, hammers, paint fumes, and sawdust.[34]

For Superintendent Conger, who returned to Mammoth in March 1883, the situation was similarly challenging. Much had changed in the park since last season, and not necessarily for the better. Though he had funding to hire ten new assistants, unfortunately for Conger, they were all selected by Interior Secretary Teller. Aside from the problem that their mandated pay of $900 did not cover housing, food, or necessary equipment (like a horse), the much larger issue was the fact that all were political appointees. As the sons and nephews of powerful East Coast elites, the privileged young men who arrived for duty lacked knowledge, experience, and motivation. While a handful gave the job an honest effort, most viewed it merely as a paycheck. And because they all answered directly to the interior secretary, none felt the need to recognize Conger's authority. One observer characterized them as "a herd of irresponsible imbeciles."[35] Consequently, the superintendent found himself increasingly at odds with his own staff, including George Henderson, who developed an especially antagonistic attitude toward Conger. And if this wasn't enough, the failure of Congress to provide criminal penalties for breaking park rules meant that the new assistants still lacked any power of enforcement, even if they were so inclined.

Moreover, despite the fact that the park budget had increased to $40,000, most of the new money was off-limits to Conger. Congress earmarked a full $29,000 for road construction under the control of an Army Corps of Engineers officer. On July 6, 1883, the war secretary assigned Lieutenant Dan Kingman to this role.[36] Eventually, the lieutenant would make substantial contributions to the park road system. But his late-summer arrival in Yellowstone meant there was little time to make use of the funds. About the same time, the U.S. Geological Survey dispatched geologist Arnold Hague to conduct topological surveys of Yellowstone, a task he would pursue for the rest of his career. In time, Hague became not only one of the park's staunchest defenders— alongside Sheridan, Grinnell, and Senator Vest—but the leading expert on Yellowstone's place names.[37]

As for Conger, he found himself in the challenging position of carrying out Secretary Teller's instructions to honor the lease arrangement with the Yellowstone Improvement Company, while simultaneously pushing back against Hobart's efforts to misuse park land and resources for his own gain. It was a no-win situation. Guests resented Conger's attempts to prohibit them from contracting with less expensive independent tour guides or transportation operators inside the park, essentially forcing them to do business with Hobart. Meanwhile, Hobart resented Conger's efforts to document the questionable actions of the company.

Despite all of these challenges, toward the end of the summer season, three major events took place that marked 1883 as a banner year for Yellowstone. The first was a visit by President Chester Arthur. As part of a series of excursions taken to improve his health, President Arthur arrived on August 23, becoming the first sitting president to visit the park. His party included the secretary of war, Robert Lincoln (son of Abraham); Senator George Vest; and Governor John Crosby of Montana Territory. Guided by Yellowstone Jack Baronett and documented by photographer F. Jay Haynes, the party entered the park from Jackson Hole. After a week touring the geyser basins and other sights, the president's party spent their last night in Mammoth, where they stayed in their own tents rather than in the new National Hotel. Nonetheless, on invitation from Rufus Hatch, President Arthur agreed to join him for drinks at the hotel with a select number of guests before departing the next day on a private train car—the Edwin Forest—running on the newly completed Northern Pacific branch line.

The second event, and the reason for Rufus Hatch's presence in the park at that time, was to celebrate the official opening of the National Hotel and completion of the Northern Pacific's new Yellowstone branch line, which now extended to the new town of Cinnabar.[38] Though still eight miles shy of Mammoth Hot Springs, the railroad's difficulties in purchasing land that granted right-of-way meant it would be several more years before tracks finally reached the town of Gardiner. Nonetheless, coinciding with the president's visit, Hatch hosted over seventy-five dignitaries and a fleet of journalists from the United States and Europe on an extravagant tour. Guests included "lords, earls, counts and barons" as well as correspondents from the *Telegraph* of London, *Figaro* of Paris, *Imperial Gazette* of Vienna, and *Allgemeine Zeitung* of Munich.[39] From the United States, the most significant personage in this category was former Chicago mayor and then-owner of the *Chicago Tribune*, Joseph Medill.

The third major event in Yellowstone that season was by far the most extravagant. Hosted by railroad magnate Henry Villard, 300 guests from around the world enjoyed an all-expenses-paid thirty-day tour to celebrate the completion of the nation's newest transcontinental railroad. On September 8, 1883, guests arrived in Gold Creek in western Montana to witness the ceremonial driving of the golden spike by former president Grant, before embarking on a tour of Yellowstone Park. Once again, guests included politicians (including Interior Secretary Teller), wealthy businessmen, and European nobility. With Villard's approval, the Northern Pacific spent $500 on each guest and roughly $200,000 on the entire affair. It was a rare moment in which Villard's ego temporarily displaced his otherwise shrewd business sense. But the bill would come due.

* * *

As summer faded into fall, the costs and benefits of the 1883 season were tallied. Each of the three major events resulted in voluminous and far-reaching publicity for Yellowstone. Publications across the nation ran F. Jay Haynes's photographs of President Arthur and his entourage. And despite some criticism of the quality of service, roadways, and accommodations, newspaper correspondents from the United States and Europe portrayed the park in a generally favorable light. As intended by Villard and Hatch, the message was clear: Yellowstone National Park was open for business.

On the other side of the ledger, at least for Villard and Hatch, the picture was less rosy. The two capitalists had overplayed their hand. Villard's extravagant spending of company money forced him to relinquish control of the Northern Pacific. In a matter of weeks, company shareholders would remove him as president.

Similar misfortune, albeit on a smaller scale, came to call on Rufus Hatch. After spending approximately $35,000 of his own cash on his Yellowstone spree, Hatch discovered that his personal investments took a huge hit in the stock market. He blamed the mismanagement on the distraction of playing host in Yellowstone, but that did nothing to change the result.

As for Superintendent Conger, before the close of this rather difficult season, he endured one more bit of unwelcome news. As tensions escalated between him and Hobart, Hobart convinced Secretary Teller to dispatch Special Agent W. Scott Smith of the Interior Department's General Land Office to investigate the state of affairs in the park. Undoubtedly biased by complaints that came from Hobart, Assistant Superintendent Henderson, and other resentful park assistants, Smith delivered a scathing review of Conger's performance to Teller in October. Conger was charged with a laundry list of unethical behavior, from unfairly attacking his own assistants to renting out government property for personal profit. As one might expect, the report recommended Conger's immediate removal.

When Conger learned of the report, he blamed Henderson and launched an impassioned defense in a private discussion with Secretary Teller.[40] But like Norris before him, Conger found himself isolated. His true opponent was not Henderson but Hobart, a man who wielded the political power of the Northern Pacific Railroad. Consequently, in Conger's formal report for 1883, knowing his boss would want it so, he spoke glowingly of the new National Hotel and other operations run by the Yellowstone Improvement Company, even though privately he held Hobart and his cronies in contempt. Despite these acts of submission, Conger knew in his heart that it was the beginning of the end. And, though Hobart didn't yet know it, the demise of the Yellowstone Improvement Company would soon follow.

* * *

Meanwhile, as the winter of 1883 took hold, somewhere out on the northern plains, the deep booming echoes of a Sharps rifle marked the ending of a much more significant era. With the sound of gunfire still ringing in the frigid air, the last members of the great northern bison herd dropped to the ground, leaving only scattered remnants of a species that had once numbered in the tens of millions. Now, except in rare havens like Yellowstone, this defining element of the North American landscape slipped quietly into oblivion.

Sending in the Cavalry

(1884–1886)

IN THE DEAD OF WINTER 1884, RUMORS BEGAN TO CIRCULATE in the towns of Bozeman, Virginia City, and Livingston that all was not well with the Yellowstone Improvement Company. Merchants who had done business with Carroll Hobart were still waiting to be paid. Even up in Mammoth, builders working on the still-unfinished National Hotel hadn't received wages since July.

Hobart, Hatch, and Douglas blamed the problem on a shortened first summer season, the "hostile" 1883 appropriations bill that shrank their leasable acres, and stock market woes—anything but their own mismanagement. They predicted better days ahead, but in the meantime, despite gouging customers with inflated prices, Hatch estimated the company fell into the red by some $85,000.[1]

Then, in the last week of February, the construction workers ran out of patience. They took control of the National Hotel and staged a sit-in strike. Armed and provisioned for the long haul, the workers refused to budge on threat of torching the building until Hobart handed over wages due.

The situation worsened as infighting erupted between Hatch, Hobart, and Douglas.[2] Canny Rufus Hatch struck first. In early March, he filed for bankruptcy in New Jersey, where the Yellowstone Improvement Company was originally chartered. A federal judge granted bankruptcy protection and declared A. L. Love, a Livingston businessman and Hatch's collaborator, as receiver—an arrangement that gave

Love (which really meant Hatch) complete control over all company debts and assets.

When Hobart and Douglas learned what he'd done, they fired back with their own bankruptcy filing in Cheyenne, Wyoming. Referencing the company's physical location, the judge ruled in favor of Hobart and Douglas and agreed to replace Love with Hobart's own choice of receiver, a man named George Hulme.

In response, Hatch raised the stakes considerably by appealing directly to the U.S. attorney general, Benjamin Harris Brewster. But to his surprise, Brewster confirmed Hulme as the sole legitimate receiver. The decision likely reflected the far-reaching political influence of the Northern Pacific Railroad, which viewed Hobart as a "company man." Several weeks later, Hulme settled with the striking workmen at the National Hotel for $10,000 cash and free railroad passes.[3] As construction resumed, Hulme promptly "hired" Carroll Hobart as the onsite general manager of the now-defunct company, leasing all properties and assets to him at the cost of one dollar per year.

With the power of the mighty Northern Pacific, Hobart won the day over the infamous Wall Street tycoon Uncle Rufus Hatch. But this didn't change the fact that the Yellowstone Improvement Company now lay in bankruptcy.

* * *

Meanwhile, down in Cheyenne, the Wyoming territorial legislature took up a measure that would also render far-reaching effects on the park. The catalyst was a seemingly inconsequential event that had taken place one year earlier.

On Saint Patrick's Day, 1883, during a drunken fight among Hobart's workers, an Iowan named David Kennedy shot a man named Armstrong, who had tried to take away his gun during the holiday drink-fest. George Henderson was called to the scene to bandage up Armstrong and turn away the mob that was after Kennedy. He ordered Kennedy to donate his due wages to the injured man and to nurse him until Armstrong either died or recovered. Armstrong survived and both men left the park soon after.[4]

Although the matter was apparently resolved, Superintendent Conger reported the incident to Wyoming territorial governor William Hale, who not only ordered an investigation by U.S. Marshals but also directed the territorial legislature to take up the issue. On March 6, 1884, they did exactly that, passing a law that extended the territory's legal jurisdiction over the roughly 98 percent of Yellowstone National Park that lay within Wyoming's borders. The law established penalties for violating park regulations and provided funding for two judges and two constables to carry out enforcement alongside the park's existing assistants. For the first time in history, Yellowstone superintendents had the ability to threaten poachers and vandals with real consequences.[5]

Initially, Yellowstone's defenders applauded Wyoming's action. Park superintendents going back to Nathaniel Langford had requested legal jurisdiction and criminal penalties. Perhaps now Yellowstone's wildlife might be safe from poachers, campfires would be fully extinguished, and visitors would refrain from chipping away at geothermal formations for souvenirs or jamming debris into geysers in the hopes of watching it get launched into the air.

But while the law appeared to resolve one of Yellowstone's most vexing problems, in practice it created a whole new set of concerns. Wyoming-style frontier justice came steeped in a heavy dose of potential corruption. The law allowed judges to keep all court fees assessed, and witnesses for the prosecution (usually the constables themselves) received half of the fines imposed on offenders. Moreover, serving as a constable or justice of the peace required no experience or training whatsoever. As one might expect, this arrangement created powerful incentives to make arrests and render guilty verdicts regardless of the facts.[6]

* * *

Around July 4, 1884, the National Hotel reopened for business.[7] Elsewhere in the park, the Yellowstone Improvement Company's other businesses continued to limp along, facing increasing competition from small-scale independent enterprises that finally received formal ten-year leases of their own. These included George Marshall's lodge on the Firehole River and Uncle John Yancey's hotel/saloon establishment in Pleasant Valley. F. Jay Haynes also received leases for his photography studios in Mammoth and the Upper Geyser Basin, and Assistant Superintendent George Henderson's children, Walter and Helen, acquired a lease to begin construction of their Cottage Hotel in Mammoth.[8]

Conger, at least for the time being, continued serving as superintendent. During the spring and summer, he oversaw the construction of a new superintendent headquarters in Mammoth. The Norris Blockhouse, built for defensive purposes in the aftermath of the Nez Perce War, was too far from a water source and uncomfortably exposed to heavy winter winds. Conger also continued erecting five small cabins or "stations" for park assistants, adding new stations in the Norris Geyser Basin and on the shores of Lake Yellowstone in addition to those already built elsewhere in the park. In this task, Conger received aid from Lieutenant Kingsman, who provided funding and use of the Corps of Engineers' sawmill. And in spite of escalating tensions with Hobart, Conger also benefited from access to the Yellowstone Improvement Company's sawmill and scrap wood.

But despite these improved facilities and management's new legal authority, the relations between Conger, Henderson, and Hobart worsened. As Conger tried to stop Hobart from building bathhouses on the Mammoth Terrace, he received orders from Secretary Teller to remove squatters from the northeast corner of the park.[9] Regardless of the reason for this request, what really mattered was that Conger failed to act promptly. Though evidence suggests that Teller decided to remove Conger well before the 1884 summer season, the secretary used this moment as an excuse to fire him.[10]

On September 10, Richard Carpenter became the new superintendent of Yellowstone. Like Conger (and Henderson), Carpenter was a politically connected Iowa Republican, but this time, Hobart and Teller were convinced they finally had a "company man" on the payroll.

*   *   *

In one of Carpenter's first acts as superintendent, he ordered all squatters along the northern tier of the park to vacate immediately under threat of legal action. The order applied to those who had received verbal permission from Conger but held no formal lease, as well as those without any form of permission. After several arrests, Carpenter succeeded in clearing the area.

The achievement drew praise from park advocates. In *Forest and Stream* magazine, Grinnell expressed hope that Carpenter's tenure would lead to greater park protection.[11] But Carpenter had other, less honorable motives. The first clue was his decision to spend the winter of 1884–1885 as a houseguest of Carroll Hobart in Washington, D.C., indicating his close ties to the Yellowstone Improvement Company.

In February 1885, proponents of Jay Cooke's plan to build a new railroad line from Cinnabar to Cooke City sponsored a congressional bill to "segregate," or privatize, a portion of Yellowstone National Park for construction. The planned route cut across the northern tier of the park, from Gardiner along the Yellowstone and Lamar Rivers toward the northeast entrance, precisely where the former squatters' cabins had stood.

During his stay in D.C., Carpenter appeared to be working with Hobart to lobby Congress for passage of this bill. But he and Hobart had hatched a plan that went well beyond merely improving regional transportation.[12] Upon passage of the bill, Carpenter would telegraph his contact in Livingston, who would then use the new telephone line in Gardiner to alert fellow conspirators to rush into the newly opened lands and stake out private mining and homestead claims before anyone realized what had transpired. The parcels would then be sold to Jay Cooke for his new rail line or developed for private gain.

On Friday, February 20, Carpenter telegraphed his contact in Livingston that the deal was imminent. Unfortunately for him and his cronies, the telephone in Gardiner was inside the general store and offered only garbled reception. As a result, the "secret conversation" devolved into a shouting match of various code words in a public space. The first phrase, "Secure that horse at once!" wasn't too strange, but the man in Gardiner couldn't hear it. Therefore, the Livingston man switched to the backup phrase. But when he began yelling, "No wind in Livingston," into the phone, the local patrons loitering in the Gardiner store grew suspicious.

Early the next morning, when Carpenter's conspirators left Gardiner in haste for Yellowstone, they were followed by two dozen local residents curious to know what the fuss was about. In short order, everything became clear as Carpenter's men staked out claim posts and filed papers printed with such familiar names as C. Hobart and R. Carpenter.

But Carpenter had jumped the gun. The bill, which seemed like a sure thing in the House, failed to garner enough votes in the Senate. Regardless, the scheme was now exposed. Local newspapers, while generally in favor of a new Cooke City rail line, condemned his actions.

And then George Grinnell caught wind of the story.

In an article aptly titled "Remove the Superintendent," printed in the April 9 issue of *Forest and Stream*, Grinnell lambasted Carpenter for trying to profit from park privatization.

> In view of these facts the conclusion is inevitable that Superintendent Carpenter is not using his office for the purpose for which he was appointed, and we respectfully submit that he is thus not a fit person longer to hold this responsible position . . . He ought to be removed without delay.[13]

Since the national election in November 1884, which brought Democrat Grover Cleveland to the White House, Carpenter probably knew his tenure as Yellowstone superintendent would be limited. If only for political reasons, the new administration and new interior secretary, Lucius Q. C. Lamar, would want to replace him with their own man. But with the duplicitous events of February now national news, Carpenter's days as superintendent ended swiftly.

* * *

On July 1, 1885, Missouri Democrat and former colonel in the Union army, David Wear, replaced Carpenter. Handpicked by Senator Vest and supported by Grinnell and Sheridan, Wear stood ready to champion the park over moneyed interests. Working with Interior Secretary Lamar, Wear immediately fired the more ineffective and insubordinate assistants—including George Henderson—and replaced them with local mountaineers such as Yellowstone Jack Baronett and Ed Wilson. With legal jurisdiction and a trusted workforce, Wear was poised to fully enforce park rules for the first time in Yellowstone's history. And he did so with gusto.

The effect on local poaching was immediate. In one of the first apprehensions, Ed Wilson caught a party of hunters in possession of elk meat and beaver skins and hauled them in before a newly appointed justice. The hunters, who had operated with impunity for years, received fines ranging from seventy-five to one hundred dollars each. One even received a six-month jail sentence.[14] Such penalties sent a warning not just to local poachers but also to tourists, who could be charged with similarly hefty fines for leaving campfires unattended or damaging geyser cones.[15]

Wear prided himself on impartiality. When he caught a government scientist shooting a bison near Old Faithful, Wear arrested and fined the man even though he worked for Arnold Hague's Geological Survey. Even then, Wear was unsatisfied with the level of punishment and took additional steps to ensure the man lost his job as a federal employee.

Unsurprisingly, this kind of zeal made Wear plenty of enemies. Local residents, who had spent years helping themselves to park wildlife and timber without consequence, strongly resented him. Carroll Hobart held nothing but contempt for Wear. So did George Henderson, who did not leave the park after his firing but took on a new role as concessionaire.

That summer, Walter and Helen Henderson completed construction of the Cottage Hotel at Mammoth Hot Springs. Meanwhile, Jennie, another of Henderson's daughters, ran the Mammoth post office and the small general store attached to it. Henderson had always served as a park guide for tourists; now he did so as a private vendor.[16]

For Wear, this made an already awkward situation almost untenable. In fact, Wear became so paranoid that he arranged to have his mail sent to the post office in Gardiner instead of Mammoth, as he believed Henderson regularly opened his correspondence.[17] Wear's concerns were not unfounded; though he didn't know it at the time, Henderson's congressman brother, David Henderson of Iowa, was working hard to undermine him.

Still, Wear might still have succeeded as superintendent if not for a series of events beyond his control. They began, predictably, from his heavy-handed enforcement of park rules. But they escalated rapidly following an unexpected altercation between a justice of the peace and a prickly congressman on vacation.

* * *

On a late summer's day in 1885, Yellowstone received a party of eleven visitors that included congressman and former judge Lewis Payson of Illinois and *Chicago Tribune* editor (and former city mayor) Joseph Medill. Toward the end of their stay, Constable Joe Keeney arrested Payson for leaving a campfire smoldering. Despite Payson's claim of innocence and the support of numerous eyewitnesses, Justice Hall issued a guilty verdict, ordering a fine of sixty dollars and court costs of $12.80.

In response, Payson angrily declared the proceedings as nothing more than a "kangaroo court." Refusing to pay the fine, Payson stated his intention to appeal to the U.S. district court in Wyoming and offered a $1,000 bond.

Justice Hall realized he was in over his head. The justice, whose only previous work experience appears to be as a woodcutter, had grown accustomed to intimidating the tourists brought into his courtroom. Most never questioned his authority and quickly paid their fines so they could return home. But now a confident, legally trained congressman and former judge was challenging both Hall's ruling and his competence.

Sheepishly, Justice Hall called the defendant to his bench and asked him how to proceed. Did a judge have the authority to remit a fine or court fee once declared? Joseph Medill, sitting in on the proceedings, called Hall a "damned old Dogberry," a reference to the inept judge in Shakespeare's *Much Ado about Nothing*.[18] Though the insult likely went over his head, Hall learned from Payson that his ruling could be amended. He reduced the fine to ten dollars and the court costs to four dollars. But once again, Payson refused to pay. Confounded, Justice

Hall cut the fine to a single dollar and court costs to whatever the defendant thought fair. Payson still refused the fine but offered a small sum to help cover court costs, which ended the matter.

Or so it seemed to Justice Hall.

* * *

Payson's fellow traveler, Medill, decided to recount the affair in an editorial for the *Chicago Tribune*. After detailing the fiasco of Wyoming's frontier-style justice, Medill concluded that a national park deserved a set of national laws and federal jurisdiction. Embarrassed by the dismal portrayal of the Wyoming legal system in a national publication, Governor Hale called for a repeal of the law granting territorial jurisdiction over Yellowstone.

But well before this could happen, two other significant events came to pass. In the aftermath of the Carpenter-Hobart Yellowstone land scandal, on March 4, 1885, the U.S. House of Representatives appointed an investigative committee,[19] the Holman Select Committee, which arrived in Yellowstone about the same time as the Payson-Medill party.

Interestingly, the committee members reached the opposite conclusion to that proposed by Medill. Unaware of the potential for corruption, they found the use of territorial law in the park to be rather effective—so much so that they not only recommended that Yellowstone stay under territorial jurisdiction but that the entire park be handed over to Wyoming once it achieved statehood. Now there were two opposing sets of recommendations at play: one calling for Wyoming territorial law in Yellowstone to be replaced by federal jurisdiction, and the other calling for an end of the national park idea altogether.

In an attempt to get a clearer picture, Interior Secretary Lamar decided to launch his own independent investigation. On July 20, he dispatched secret agent William H. Phillips, a Supreme Court lawyer and close friend of George Grinnell, to conduct his own assessment. Arriving in the park on July 26 and staying until September 6, Phillips's stay overlapped with the visits of both the Payson-Medill party and the Holman Select Committee.

Phillips's report was comprehensive, covering all aspects of management.[20] Some of his harshest words were reserved for Hobart and the Yellowstone Improvement Company. Overall, Phillips found the company's new buildings to be of poor quality and not in accordance with their lease agreement. Time and again, he found structures lying beyond their legal allotments. At Mammoth, instead of remaining within the confines of its two leased acres, the company's National Hotel, numerous tents, and other structures—including a bathhouse, sawmill, storage sheds, and corrals—sprawled over some forty acres.[21] Elsewhere, Hobart's tents and buildings lay too close to Yellowstone's fragile features, were badly constructed, and did not comply with guest-occupancy requirements. In fact, almost all park leases were embroiled in confusion and dispute. F. Jay Haynes charged that the Henderson's Cottage Hotel stood on land belonging to his photography studio in Mammoth and that Hobart's new "shack hotel" occupied portions of his lease near Old Faithful.

Beyond issues of location and occupancy, Phillips also assessed the quality of visitor experiences. The National Hotel was enveloped in a foul odor emanating from its poorly designed sanitary system. In a letter appended to Phillips's report, a visiting physician wrote that the building used an old hot springs hole as a sinkhole for refuse; the "privy bowls" in the hotel's bathrooms were overflowing with human excrement; and behind the building, sewage spread across the open ground.[22]

As for park management, Phillips heavily criticized Wyoming's territorial jurisdiction over Yellowstone. As a federal lawyer, he argued that without congressional consent, the application of territorial law over federal land was illegal. He was particularly concerned about the potential for abuse of power. To wit, he included a copy of Medill's *Chicago Tribune* article that detailed the Payson arrest and so-called "trial." In the strongest possible terms, he recommended federal jurisdiction and a set of congressionally endorsed penalties for breaking park rules. He also recommended against the sale of liquor in the park and efforts to privatize portions to allow for a railroad right-of-way from Cinnabar to Cooke City.

On the positive side, Phillips praised the performance of Superintendent Wear, who he found to be ethical, trustworthy, and efficient.

His only recommendations were for an increase in Wear's budget and in the number of assistants under his command.

Phillips's official report and that of the Holman Select Committee would not be released to Congress until February 1886. But in fall 1885, drafts were more than enough for Secretary Lamar to take action on at least one issue: the problem of Carroll Hobart and the ever-struggling Yellowstone Improvement Company. On October 3, a new commercial entity emerged with the intention of taking over their leaseholds. As before, the new company was funded and essentially controlled by the Northern Pacific Railway. But by bringing in hotelier, lawyer, and philanthropist Charles Gibson of Saint Louis to front the venture, it appeared to be independent. Eventually named the Yellowstone Park Association, it initiated negotiations with the Interior Department in November in the hopes of signing a new lease agreement in the spring.

By December 1885, it was clear that new battle lines had been drawn. On one side, Senator Vest sponsored a bill providing federal legal jurisdiction over Yellowstone National Park. On the other side, Senator Samuel McMillan of Minnesota introduced a bill to privatize the northern section of the park for the railroad right-of-way. Vest succeeded in stopping McMillan's bill but, in the process, alienated potential railroad supporters for his own measure.[23] The interests of the Northern Pacific Railway and Yellowstone's defenders were diverging.

* * *

In February 1886, Congress formally received the two reports by Phillips and the Holman Select Committee. The picture painted by the two contradictory accounts suggested a need for significant and immediate change in Yellowstone. The national park experiment, it seemed, was starting to falter.

In March, as Congress took up its annual debate over appropriation bills for the next fiscal year, everything came to a head. Following the wishes of Governor Hale, on March 10, the Wyoming legislature repealed the 1884 law that had extended territorial jurisdiction over Yellowstone. However, without something to replace Wyoming law, Yellowstone was opened once more to a system of unenforceable rules.

Superintendent Wear lost the only legal tool he'd had to protect the park. Sensing weakness, Yellowstone's opponents pounced.

Meanwhile, during congressional budget debates, Yellowstone repeatedly wound up in the crosshairs. In the opening salvo, the Senate bill included the usual $40,000 for the park at Senator Vest's insistence. However, the House version slashed the budget to $20,000, with all funds earmarked for roads and bridges. Not a penny could be used for the park superintendent or his assistants.

In the House, it appeared that Representative Lewis Payson, still angry from his altercation with Justice Hall, had found common purpose with George Henderson's brother, Representative David Henderson. A coalition emerged of those beholden to the railroad lobby and those against the national park idea. If successful, the budget cut would not only end the Interior Department's management of Yellowstone but force its transformation into a state park controlled by Wyoming. Alternatively, it might trigger the replacement of Wear's administration with U.S. Army troops, per the 1883 Sundry Civil Act. Yellowstone's opponents welcomed either outcome, as they believed (as did Vest and Wear) that military control would result in essentially no management whatsoever. Many assumed that, without training or legal jurisdiction, the soldiers would be no more effective than Superintendent Conger's assistants.

Meanwhile, the Yellowstone Improvement Company passed quietly into oblivion as the new Yellowstone Park Association took over. This shift in management was significant but was dwarfed by the larger tide of change approaching. As word got out that, once again, there were no criminal punishments for violating park rules, those who had felt the sting of territorial law over the past year returned with a vengeance. Incidents of poaching, vandalism, and arson soared to new heights.

Back in Washington, Congress remained locked in stalemate. In an effort to ratchet up the intensity, Representative Henderson launched a vicious attack on Wear. In a classic political strategy, he falsely accused Wear of the very things that his own ally, Robert Carpenter, was guilty of doing: selling out park land for private gain, hiring inexperienced buffoons as assistants, and failing to protect Yellowstone against poachers and vandals. Many in Congress had difficulty distinguishing between the brief tenures of the past three superintendents, and Henderson's tactics stoked partisan passions regardless of the actual facts.

Yellowstone's defenders pushed back, attempting to set the record straight on Superintendent Wear, but to no avail. On August 4, 1886, as the final order of business before recessing for the fall, an exhausted Congress passed the version of the appropriations bill that cut all funding for Yellowstone's superintendent and assistants.

To be fair, Vest had put up a vigorous fight, but all his victories were defensive in nature. He stopped bills proposed by Representative Regan of Texas and Senator Plumb of Kansas that sought to dissolve Yellowstone by repealing the Yellowstone Act of 1872. He also blocked efforts to privatize portions of Yellowstone for railroads and halted attempts to transfer the park to Wyoming. But in the end, Vest lost the battle to fund Wear or any managers, much less instigate federal legal jurisdiction.

Meanwhile, as the summer wound down in Yellowstone, things were going from bad to worse. The repeal of Wyoming law in March wreaked havoc for Superintendent Wear, but the congressional vote on August 4 unleashed anarchy. Upon learning they would no longer be paid, most park assistants simply abandoned their posts and went home. As the park's managerial structure began to unravel, poachers and vandals descended anew.

Desperate and exhausted, on August 13, Superintendent Wear sent a telegram to Secretary Lamar calling for aid, noting that "since the action of Congress, lawlessness in park has rapidly increased." Four days later, on August 17, he sent another telegram in all capital letters that read: "THREE LARGE FIRES RAGING IN PARK BEYOND MY CONTROL."[24]

Help would arrive that same day. Shortly after the congressional vote on August 6, Secretary Lamar had contacted Secretary of War Endicott and invoked the 1883 Act, requesting U.S. military troops assume management of the park. Endicott sent the directive to General Sherman, who ordered Troop M of the First United States Cavalry under Captain Moses Harris to proceed at once from Fort Custer, Montana, to Yellowstone National Park.

The cavalry were on their way.

Showdown at Pelican Creek

13

(1886–1894)

ON THE FRIGID AFTERNOON OF MARCH 12, 1894, U.S. CAVALRY scout Felix Burgess and his young partner, Private Troike, stood quietly on the edge of a vast snowfield in the Pelican Valley of Yellowstone National Park.[1] Concealed within a stand of lodgepole pines, the two men felt the bite of late-winter wind as they peered toward a group of dark forms silhouetted against the white landscape: the carcasses of five recently killed bison.

A sixth figure moved between them, severing the great heads. Nodding in grim satisfaction, Burgess knew he had found the elusive target of his mission. The man before him was none other than the notorious poacher Edgar Howell.

With snowflakes sticking to his thick mustache and sun-weathered face, the old scout gingerly stamped his feet against the cold and assessed the situation. Howell's hunting rifle rested up against one of the carcasses. About fifteen feet away, the poacher crouched with his head down as he worked on another dead bison with his knife. Burgess measured the total distance between himself and Howell as roughly 400 yards.

Looking down at the newly issued .38 caliber army revolver in his hand, Burgess felt a knot growing in his stomach. Damn.

Without his rifle, the only way Burgess could get the drop on Howell was at close range. It would require a sprint into a powerful headwind and across an open snowfield while wearing heavy "snowshoes."[2] These so-called snowshoes (sometimes called "Norwegian snowshoes") were actually a pair of crude wooden cross-country skis, about ten feet in length, tapered up at the end and bound to Burgess's boots with leather toeholds. They were waxed or greased to allow for gliding downhill but also had strips of beaver fur attached to the bottom to prevent backsliding when climbing uphill. The wearer used a single wooden pole to propel forward, somewhat like a gondolier's oar. While the bulky skis kept people from sinking into hip-deep snow, they didn't allow for quick movement on uneven terrain.

For those 400 yards, Burgess would be exposed. If at any point during his run Howell looked up and saw him, it would be all over. Burgess might join the bison as one more carcass in the bloody snow.

As he considered this possibility, Burgess felt the beginnings of a familiar pain, a needlelike tingling creeping up from his right foot into his thigh. Though small in stature, Burgess was tough and battle-tested. Before replacing Ed Wilson as Yellowstone scout the previous year, Burgess had spent thirty years as a U.S. Cavalry scout in the Southwest. He fought in wars against the Apache and other tribal nations, where he gained skills as a tracker and hunter.[3] Now middle-aged, Burgess increasingly suffered the aftereffects of those battles. The pain in his leg was from an old injury sustained when he was captured by Indigenous warriors, who cut off several of his small toes and half severed the big toe on his right foot. The wound never fully healed and left his foot, and entire leg, vulnerable to recurring frostbite.[4]

Soon, the cold would make it excruciatingly painful just to walk, much less run. If he was going to act, the time was now.

* * *

In spring 1894, Yellowstone had been a national park for twenty-two years, but its future remained uncertain. For most of that time, it stood alone as the only national park of significant size. In 1875, Congress created a second park on tiny Mackinac Island in Lake Michigan but later transferred it to Michigan as a state park. New national parks in the Yellowstone mold did not emerge until 1890 with the creation of Yosemite, Sequoia, and General Grant (later renamed Kings Canyon) in California.

For the past eight years, the U.S. military had served as de facto park managers. No one had known what to expect when the army arrived, including the army. Though General Sheridan had long been interested in Yellowstone, army regulars were neither enthusiastic nor properly trained for the assignment.[5] But if Yellowstone's opponents hoped military management might lead to lax regulatory enforcement, they were mistaken. What they got instead was a series of commanders with Philetus Norris's energy and David Wear's strict commitment to duty, combined with the manpower of the U.S. War Department. As a result, Yellowstone's protection improved dramatically.

The first of these commanders, Captain Moses Harris, arrived on August 17, 1886, with fifty men of the U.S. First Cavalry. He formally took control of the park on August 20 for what everyone believed would be a temporary, months-long assignment. Assuming the title of acting superintendent, Harris quickly brought order to the chaos, stationing troops at major sites throughout the park and attempting to quell a series of raging wildfires likely set by arsonists in the waning days of Wear's tenure.

His second day on the job, Harris issued an updated set of park regulations and ordered his men to insist on absolute compliance using the only tools of enforcement at their disposal: confiscation and expulsion. New rules included bans on using firearms for any purpose, the sale of alcohol without a permit, and placing debris in geysers. Upon learning that his men would stay the winter, Harris constructed Camp Sheridan to billet the troops. He also hired a civilian scout to help lead winter poaching patrols—Yellowstone Jack Baronett in the first year, followed by Ed Wilson. Over the next year or so, the camp expanded to include amenities that ranged from a barracks, guardhouse, and stables to a headquarters, officers' quarters, and a hospital.

Tourists paid the uniformed soldiers more respect than the civilian managers they'd replaced, but the military still lacked legal mechanisms for penalizing violators of park rules. Frustrated, Captain Harris came to the same conclusion as all previous superintendents. In a letter to the interior secretary, Harris wrote:

> The enforcement of . . . rules and regulations will be difficult until some more effective penalty for their infringement

is provided than expulsion from the Park. The necessity of a form of government for the Park is becoming, year by year, more urgent, as the number of visitors to the Park increases. All sorts of worthless and disreputable characters are attracted here by the impunity afforded by the absence of law and courts of justice.[6]

Consequently, the soldiers resorted to extralegal practices. Vandals caught in the act (or by telltale names carved into geyser cones) were ordered to remove their handiwork. Under close supervision, and in full view of other tourists, violators scraped, scrubbed, or washed off the offensive damage until the trooper was satisfied. This public shaming may have caused a few potential vandals to rethink their actions, but it hardly solved the problem.

To combat hunting, soldiers stationed at park entrances applied tape and powder to visitors' firearms so they could not be used without breaking the seal. Those involved in illegal livestock grazing might be separated from their stock, each escorted to opposite sides of the park. But for poachers (also known as market hunters), once they'd been caught, there was little for enforcers to do but confiscate their equipment and expel them from park boundaries.

Although white poachers represented the primary threat to Yellowstone's bison and elk populations, Harris viewed subsistence hunting by Native Americans as a major problem—not just the killing of game but the occasional fire-setting as part of that process. Seeking to reinforce the ban on Indigenous people in and near the park, Harris wrote letters to federal Indian agents requesting they prohibit Native Americans from leaving their reservations.

Nor was he the only one with these concerns. In an 1889 editorial in *Forest and Stream* titled "Indian Marauders," George Grinnell supported Harris's efforts by repeating several widely held misconceptions about Indigenous peoples, depicting them as environmentally irresponsible and their use of fire as categorically destructive. He called the hunting parties "a serious danger menac[ing] the game and the forests of the park" and the forest fires "a far more serious injury . . . to drive the game from one place to another."[8] In time, ecologists would realize that Native American practices of lighting low-intensity fires actually benefitted wildlife by bolstering forage growth, maintaining meadows against encroaching shrubs and tree saplings, and reducing the chance of large-scale wildfires by limiting fuel loads during the dry season. Nonetheless, efforts to restrict or erase the presence of Indigenous people from Yellowstone would persist for decades.

Meanwhile, other legitimately harmful activities, including robberies, still occurred under military management. Harris's first annual report described a stagecoach holdup on July 4, 1887, in which thieves made off with twenty dollars and a unique 1811 Napoleonic coin taken from an Iowan lawyer named John Lacey. Less than two years later, Lacey would win election to the House of Representatives for the first of eight terms. In time, this Iowa Republican would join Democrat senator George Vest as one of Yellowstone's great congressional defenders, helping to establish federal penalties to enforce park regulations.

* * *

On June 1, 1889, after three years of service, Captain Harris was replaced by Captain Frazier Boutelle. During his term, Boutelle oversaw the construction of six "snow shoe cabins" for winter patrols, designated campgrounds, and blocked a proposal to build an elevator in the canyon near Yellowstone Falls. An avid angler, he also initiated the stocking of Yellowstone's rivers and lakes with brown trout, lake trout, and other invasive fish species, a practice that would create long-lasting ecological problems.

Serving for only eighteen months, Captain Boutelle's early dismissal may have been due to repeated clashes with Interior Secretary John Noble over the lack of resources, as well as with Eli Waters, general manager of the National Hotel. On more than one occasion, Boutelle tried to expel Waters for actions ranging from poaching to vandalism, including "soaping" geysers for VIP guests (putting detergent into the cones to trigger an eruption). Though fired from the hotel in 1889, the cantankerous Waters remained in the park for years, operating a forty-ton steamboat on Yellowstone Lake. Regardless of the reason, in February 1891, Captain George Anderson arrived to relieve Boutelle as acting superintendent.

Standing six feet two inches tall, the forty-two-year-old captain graduated fifth in his class at West Point, where he studied and later taught engineering. A lifelong bachelor, his army career included two tours of duty fighting the Apache in the Southwest, an inspection tour in Europe, and a road-building survey along the Colorado Front Range. As an accomplished, politically connected, sometimes brash figure, he also enjoyed the occasional nip of the flask, leading him to reestablish alcohol sales in park hotels. He claimed it helped visitors "adjust to the altitude."

Anderson's term marked a major turning point for Yellowstone. Congress never did (and never would) pass a law that made military control permanent, opting instead for annual renewal of the arrangement. Nonetheless, by 1891, most recognized that the army was there for the long haul. In fact, military units now managed all of the nation's parks, including those recently established in California. With this in mind, Congress approved funding to replace Camp Sheridan with a permanent military installation called Fort Yellowstone. Shortly after his arrival, Anderson received orders to erect stone headquarters, whose solid construction would be evidenced by their continued use into the twenty-first century.

Recall that the arrival of military stewardship in 1886 coincided with the rise of the Yellowstone Park Association (YPA). Headed by Charles Gibson, but still basically owned by the Northern Pacific, the new company had taken over the leases of the bankrupt Yellowstone Improvement Company. After purchasing Henderson's Cottage Hotel, Gibson began construction on a series of new hotels scheduled to open in the summer of 1891, including Lake Hotel, the Canyon Hotel, and the Fountain Hotel. Plans also called for electric lighting in the National Hotel in Mammoth and establishing telephone and telegraph lines connecting all hotels to park headquarters. It seemed the technological trappings of modern nineteenth-century civilization had finally arrived in Yellowstone.

As for park management, the most important change was the renewed vigor Anderson brought to the job. Such commitment was more necessary now than ever as the army's responsibilities expanded to include the newly created 1.2 million–acre Yellowstone Timberland

Reserve. Lying adjacent to Yellowstone Park, the reserve represented the first step in building the national forest system under the 1891 General Revision Act.

Meanwhile, like his predecessors, the captain continued to address the problems of vandalism and forest fires, but he paid special attention to poaching.[8] This last goal derived in no small part from the urgings of George Grinnell and his writings in *Forest and Stream*, including those expressing concern over the potential extinction of American bison.

* * *

From the beginning, Anderson made heavy use of winter patrols operating out of the "snowshoe cabins" in the park's backcountry.[9] Rather than use horses, the soldiers relied on the same crude cross-country skis used by scout Felix Burgess. The skis were introduced to the park in 1887 by famed Arctic explorer Lieutenant Frederick Schwatka, during his winter expedition through Yellowstone for *New York World* magazine.[10] But with temperatures falling to minus thirty-seven degrees Fahrenheit, Schwatka fell ill and got no further than Norris Basin before turning back. Not to be deterred, F. Jay Haynes, army scout Ed Wilson, and two others completed the journey on their own. Though they almost perished, the men managed to return to Mammoth with the first-ever winter photographs of the geyser basins and Yellowstone Falls. The following year, Wilson and his partners tested the skis for use in winter poaching patrols, leading to their widespread adoption.

In addition to the ski patrols, after 1891, the new telephone lines allowed soldiers stationed in various locations to keep track of those coming and going across park boundaries. Captain Anderson supplemented these efforts by cultivating a network of informants living just outside the park, ranging from U.S. Marshals to concerned citizens. Many of the latter were park tour guides or avid hunters also inspired to do their part by Grinnell's essays.[11]

With these strategies in place, in October 1893, Anderson accompanied a patrol in the Pelican Valley. Finding an abundance of bison droppings, he deduced that a small herd might be wintering nearby. Upon his return to headquarters, Anderson learned from informants in Cooke City that Ed Howell had in fact resumed his poaching in the same area. In early January 1894, the captain dispatched scout Felix Burgess to investigate.

Burgess soon found old tracks of "a man on skis drawing a toboggan," a hallmark of Howell's, known as one of the few men strong enough to travel in such a manner. Years earlier, the army tested this method for winter patrols but abandoned the toboggans as too heavy. Encouraged, Burgess continued the chase but was stopped when his axe broke. The axe was a necessary tool for winter survival, crucial for cutting firewood and building shelters. Its loss forced Burgess to return to headquarters.

Based on Burgess's report, Anderson sent a message to the Soda Butte Station, which guarded the northeastern entrance. Soldiers confirmed the presence of fresh tracks weaving over the hill behind the station toward Cooke City. Contacting his informants, Anderson learned that Howell had indeed recently appeared and was purchasing supplies for a return to the park.

* * *

In fact, Howell had been hunting undetected since September. Accompanied by his dog, a toboggan full of provisions, and a partner named Noble, Howell made camp near the confluence of Pelican and Astringent Creeks, several miles northeast of Yellowstone Lake. Getting there from Cooke City required a strenuous hike down Soda Butte Valley, across the Lamar River, and over Specimen Ridge, a nearly 9,000-foot-high barrier cutting diagonally across the park. According to Howell, a dispute led to Noble's departure, leaving Howell alone to complete his winter work.[12]

Howell's routine was well-practiced and extremely efficient. Having arranged buyers in advance, he spent the winter in search of bison. Once located, the killing required no special skill. With skis, Howell could easily approach his prey as they struggled and flailed in the deep snow. This allowed for point-blank shots, ensuring the slaughter of all bison in the herd.

In the 1890s, Yellowstone poachers enjoyed a steady market for bison trophies. Since the last great herd on the northern plains had been decimated in 1883, demand for bison skins and meat had risen dramatically. Heads represented the biggest prize, commanding prices upward of $500 in the United States and as much as $1,000 overseas.[13] Because they were too heavy to carry out of the park in the winter, Howell would sever the bison heads, wrap them in burlap, and hang them high in trees to protect them from predators. He would then return with pack animals in the spring to retrieve his bounty.

Given the 2 million–acre expanse of Yellowstone, it was fairly easy to avoid detection in the winter. Even if caught, penalties were so slight—eviction and confiscation of supplies—that they did little to outweigh the economic rewards of the offense. Such methods served Howell and other poachers well for decades. Moreover, as bison became scarcer, prices only went up, creating even greater incentives.

* * *

In March, believing Howell was back in the park, Anderson called on Burgess to make another try but this time "to come back with a whole axe and a whole prisoner, if possible."[14] As Anderson later explained, he also cautioned Burgess about the danger of confronting Howell directly. "I told him that I did not send him to his death . . . I did not want him to take risks or serious chances."[15]

Early in the morning of March 11, scout Burgess and Private Troike set out from the Yellowstone Lake Hotel. They made camp the first night a few miles west of Fern Lake, where Burgess had found tracks in January.[16] It isn't clear why the men were not better armed. They were equipped with full packs and must have known of Howell's reputation. But perhaps they had no intention of actually engaging with the poacher, wishing only to locate his camp and return with reinforcements.

In any event, by midmorning the next day, they rediscovered Howell's tracks, which led them to a grisly discovery: a cache of six bison heads wrapped in burlap and hanging from a tree. After several more miles, they found the poacher's camp, with a tepee and stash of supplies that suggested long-term use. As they searched the site, a series of gunshots shattered the silence. They hurried on and found a fresh set of tracks weaving through a nearby stand of timber. A mile or so later the trail crested, placing them on a small ridge overlooking a vast snowfield.

* * *

Now, as Burgess and Troike observed Howell from the pines, it was time for a decision. Glancing at his wide-eyed and unarmed companion, Burgess knew the task was his alone. So far, they were still undetected. Given the strength and direction of the wind, it was just possible that Howell would not hear Burgess approach.

His senses heightened, Burgess could detect every creak of the tall pines above him as they swayed against the winter wind. The thin crust on the snow crunched beneath his skis, and the smooth cold metal of the pistol felt like ice in his hand. A sudden throb of pain pulsed through his lame leg. Burgess knew it was now or never. This was going to hurt like hell.

Rechecking the load in his revolver, Burgess ordered Troike to stay hidden and wait for his signal. Then, with a deep breath, he bolted out onto the open snowfield.

For the first 200 yards, the scout made good time on his one-man charge, alternately skiing and running through the uneven terrain. Then suddenly, a ten-foot crevasse opened up before him. Unable to stop, Burgess attempted the jump, but the weight of his skis pulled him down. He fell into the gap, but the skins on his skis caught the snow on the far side, halting his backward slide. Once he scrambled clear of the ditch, he pushed onward, breathing hard. At thirty yards, he spotted Howell's rifle and shifted to position himself between the weapon and the poacher. Moments later, Burgess stood among the fallen animals and directly behind Howell.

Howell, now with his back toward the scout, continued to work on the dead bison. The howling wind made him oblivious to Burgess's presence. Even more unlikely was the silence of Howell's dog, a bobtailed mixed-breed shepherd, curled up away from the wind under the leg of another bison carcass. Burgess had only just noticed him. A single bark could have spelled his demise, but the shivering animal was too focused on trying to stay warm.

Visibly shaken from the exertion, Burgess straightened up, aimed his revolver at Howell, and in a loud voice ordered his surrender. The poacher jumped at the sound. He turned swiftly and rose to his feet, only to find himself looking into the barrel of the gun.

"That was the first [Howell] knew of anyone but him being any-where in that country," Burgess later explained. "He kind of stopped and stood stupid like and I told him to drop his knife." In response, Howell dropped the skinning knife, swore at his dog, and raised his hands. Burgess said later that Howell wanted to kill the dog for failing to warn him, but Burgess wouldn't allow it.[17]

"You would never have taken me if I had seen you first," said Howell.

"Why's that?" asked Burgess, with furrowed brow.

"Oh, I'd have got on my [snow] shoes and run away, of course."[18]

Casting a doubtful look at Howell, Burgess waved to Troike to ski down out of the trees. Together they marched their captive back to his camp. Given the late hour and the difficulty of moving the heavy bison heads, they decided to continue straight on to Yellowstone Lake.

The three-man party arrived at Lake Hotel well after dark. But before taking rest, Burgess telephoned Captain Anderson in Mammoth Hot Springs to inform him of Howell's capture. The captain received the message around 9:30 p.m. An eyewitness described him as "positively jubilant . . . He couldn't sit still he was so glad." Anderson ordered Burgess to bring Howell directly to headquarters the next morning. Before turning in, the captain arranged for a detachment of soldiers to meet Burgess and retrieve Howell's equipment and the bison remains.

* * *

If Captain Anderson seemed a bit overexuberant at Burgess's news, it was for good reason. Earlier that day, he had received an important visitor. Still exhausted from the long train ride from Chicago, Emerson Hough[19] sat across the desk from the captain and introduced himself as the western correspondent for *Forest and Stream* magazine. A tall man with sandy hair, tired eyes, and a quick wit, Hough explained that his editor, George Grinnell, had dispatched him to write a feature about a winter trek through the park that also highlighted the wild-life-poaching problem. For this assignment, Hough would be joined by park guide Elwood "Billy" Hofer and photographer F. Jay Haynes.

Captain Anderson could not have been more pleased. In fact, he had been expecting Hough for some time. The captain counted

Grinnell as a friend who shared his passion for protecting the park's remaining bison and elk herds. As he had done with Captains Harris and Boutelle, upon Anderson's appointment as park superintendent, Grinnell had reached out with offers of support and an invitation to join the prestigious Boone and Crockett Club. The two men had remained in frequent correspondence ever since.

Such actions were typical of Grinnell and reflected his commitment to the park. In the years since the U.S. Cavalry assumed management, Grinnell kept a close eye on what the change might mean for Yellowstone's wildlife. Generally, he was pleased by what he saw, but he remained painfully aware of the need for legal mechanisms. And the situation was growing desperate as Yellowstone's bison herd dwindled ever closer to extinction.

Congress was the only body with authority to offer legal protection. At least five times between 1883 and 1893, park supporters led by Grinnell and Senator George Vest sponsored bills to do just that, but none succeeded. Each time a bill passed the Senate, it would die in the House amid amendments to open up the northern portion of the park to railroad development.

Clearly, something more was needed to tip the balance in favor of Yellowstone's wildlife. Starting in the mid-1880s, Grinnell attempted to amplify the voice of *Forest and Stream* by forming civic organizations to boost public and political support for conservation.

In the February 11, 1886, issue, he announced a new organization called the Audubon Society. Dedicated to the protection of birds and their habitats, Grinnell called for birdwatchers across the country to form local and state-based clubs. Spurred by concerns over the decimation of passenger pigeons and potential loss of egrets, whose feathers frequently adorned ladies' hats, thousands heeded the call. One year later, Grinnell launched *Audubon Magazine*, providing a national voice for the movement.

Grinnell worked concurrently to establish a similar civic organization to protect big game. Central to this effort, it turns out, would be his introduction to a young Teddy Roosevelt. In 1885, Grinnell wrote a review of Roosevelt's book, *Hunting Trips of a Ranchman*, which documented the year Roosevelt spent in South Dakota after his mother and wife died on the same day. Already a New York State assemblyman, twenty-six-year-old Roosevelt was gearing up to launch his career on the national scale. Grinnell's review, however, was not entirely favorable, critiquing several assumptions that went against his own notions of ethical hunting. Not one to let criticism slide, Roosevelt met with Grinnell about the essay. After a lively discussion of their differences, Grinnell explained his concern over the eradication of big game, including Yellowstone's bison. The conversation forged a lifelong friendship and shared commitment to wildlife conservation.

In December of 1887, Roosevelt held a dinner party for guests with a special interest in sport hunting. That evening, he proposed forming an organization to protect wildlife and big game known as the Boone and Crockett Club. Formally established in January 1888 with Roosevelt as president, the club boasted a list of powerful members. Over time, these included Grinnell, General Sheridan, General Sherman, William Phillips, and Senator Vest. It also counted Representative John Lacey and geologist Arnold Hague among them, although neither was a hunter.

But even with these new organizations, in 1892, the wildlife situation became dire. Railroad lobbyists sponsored yet another privatization bill, and this time, to Grinnell's dismay, Senator Vest—the park's long-trusted ally in Congress—finally gave in. The exhausted Vest believed the only hope of achieving legal protections was to compromise: "The fact remains that no legislation can be had for the Park until the demands of these people are conceded," he confessed. "It is not a comfortable or pleasant reflection to a public man to make such an admission, but it is the truth."[20] He pledged to support the new bill in the Senate and be done with it.

Grinnell was initially shaken by the news but soon regained his resolve. In December, he published a four-page defense of Yellowstone against the new bill in *Forest and Stream* entitled "The Standing Menace," which offered ten point-by-point rationales for protecting the park and stopping the railroad scheme.

Pulling out all the stops, Grinnell and Roosevelt organized a special Boone and Crockett Club dinner at the exclusive Metropolitan Club in Washington, D.C. Hosted by Roosevelt, the guest list was a who's who of Washington power brokers, including Speaker of the

House Charles Crisp of Georgia, Secretary of War Stephen Elkins, and Interior Secretary John Noble. Before sitting down, Roosevelt introduced a resolution against the privatization bill and called passionately for a show of support among club members. But without Vest to lead the fight, the bill passed through the Senate. All that remained was a House vote, where passage was assured under the leadership of Representative Lewis Payson and those beholden to the railroad lobby.[21]

Just as it seemed the battle was lost, something unexpected happened. To ensure speedy passage of a bill in the House of Representatives, it was not uncommon for sponsors to request a vote under special rules known as "suspension," which disallowed opportunities for amendments, essentially fast-tracking it. A telegram from a railroad lobbyist to the Montana governor asked him to request just such a vote for the Yellowstone bill from the House Speaker. Given that the congressional session was almost over and time was short, it made sense to do so. But somehow, someone obtained a copy of the telegram and quietly sent it to the New York offices of *Forest and Stream*.

Grinnell opened the envelope with a smile. This was all the ammunition he needed.

Although there was nothing illegal or unethical about suspension votes in Congress, Grinnell deployed the full might of his literary skill to portray the move as undemocratic. He reprinted the telegram on the front page of *Forest and Stream* under the heading "Will Speaker Crisp Be Deceived?" The message was clear. The railroad lobby was about to "trick" the House Speaker into taking action that would reduce Yellowstone National Park into a "howling desert."[22]

Though his charges were exaggerated, Grinnell won the day. Speaker Crisp chose to avoid the political backlash of fast-tracking the vote, and the congressional session ended before any further action could be taken. His decision essentially killed the bill until the next session, when the entire process would have to begin anew.

As it turns out, there wouldn't be a next time. The 1892 effort would stand as the last serious attempt to push through a railway-privatization bill in Congress. By 1893, the political climate had changed. The Northern Pacific had completed an economic assessment of the mines in Cooke City and decided the mineral resources were neither as abundant nor profitable as they'd once perceived. Consequently, they lost interest. For the time being at least, Yellowstone was saved.

With this defensive victory in hand, Grinnell knew it was time to transition to offense while momentum was still on his side. The population of Yellowstone bison was down to approximately 200 animals. There was little time to waste.

Senator Vest and Representative Lacey began writing new legislation while Grinnell arranged for Hough's feature about the wildlife-poaching problem. Perhaps in Yellowstone itself, they could find the story that would turn the tide in Congress and maybe, just maybe, save from extinction one of America's national treasures.

* * *

By the evening of March 12, 1894, Grinnell's efforts seemed to be paying off. With the arrest of the "bison butcher" Edgar Howell that very day, the timing of Emerson Hough's arrival could not have been better.

Departing at dawn the next day from Fort Yellowstone, Hough and Haynes, along with guide Billy Hofer and a small detachment of soldiers, skied south on the Norris Road to meet scout Burgess and his captive. Before leaving, Hough sent a telegram to Grinnell, who printed it in the March 24, 1874, issue of *Forest and Stream*:

BUFFALO POACHERS IN THE YELLOWSTONE.
Fort Yellowstone, Wyo., March 17. – [*Special to Forest and Stream*] Capt. Scott, in charge of scouting party, reports from the Lake to Captain Anderson that Park Scout Burgess has captured Howell, the notorious Cooke City poacher with ten fresh buffalo skins, on Astringat [*sic*] Creek, near Pelican. The prisoner has been ordered brought in. This is the most important arrest ever made in the park. E. Hough.

The last line would become a self-fulfilling prophecy. In fact, this brief dispatch was just the opening salvo in what would soon become a powerful barrage of journalistic firepower aimed squarely at Congress.

In the late afternoon of the first day out from Mammoth, the *Forest and Stream* group arrived at Norris Station, where they met the northbound party of Scout Burgess, Private Troike, Edgar Howell, and two other soldiers. Both groups spent the night at the station, where Hough had his first chance to conduct interviews. The next morning, Hough returned with Burgess and his prisoner to Mammoth while Haynes and the others continued south to gather the bison remains and take additional photos.

Now armed with firsthand "breaking news," Hough sent a longer account of the capture to Grinnell, which ran in the March 31 issue of *Forest and Stream*. This was followed on May 5 with a full-blown multipart feature that included damning photographs of the slaughtered bison.

Hough presented Howell's capture as an epic struggle between good and evil. Scout Burgess was the wounded hero, willing to risk his life to bring an evildoer to justice and save from oblivion the last remnants of a noble species. In stark contrast, Hough painted Edgar Howell as the deceitful and greedy villain, whose ethical faults were reflected in his physical appearance: "Howell was, we found, a most picturesquely ragged, dirty and unkempt citizen," Hough wrote. "His beard had been scissored off. His hair hung low on his neck, curling up like a drake's tail . . . His carriage was slouchy, loose-jointed and stooping."[23] This unflattering description was paired with observations designed to emphasize Howell as a dangerous adversary. Not only was the poacher strong enough to pull a 182-pound toboggan behind skis but also tough enough to survive the Yellowstone winter with only the barest of supplies.

The focal point of the story, however, was the lack of a federal wildlife-protection law, as highlighted in the poacher's flippant attitude toward his arrest:

> "Yes," Howell said, in reply to our questions, "I'm going to take a little walk up to the Post, but I don't think I'll be there long.
>
> "About my plans? Well, I haven't arranged any plans yet for the future. I may go back into the Park again, later on, and I may not. No, I will not say who it was contracted to buy the heads off me . . ."[24]

In fact, while the hero of the story, scout Burgess, was having his few remaining frostbitten toes amputated by the army surgeon, Howell was relaxed and in good spirits, knowing he couldn't be imprisoned or fined. While dining at the Canyon Hotel, Hough noted that Howell "ate twenty-four pancakes for breakfast. He seemed to enjoy the square meals of captivity."

Moreover, the fact that the poacher "stood to make $2,000 and could only lose $26.75" (the cost of his confiscated supplies) meant the whole ordeal was only a minor financial setback in his otherwise lucrative enterprise. For the cavalrymen stationed at Fort Yellowstone, whose annual salary amounted to $200 per year, this had to rankle.

But although Edgar Howell's poaching personified all that was wrong in the management of Yellowstone, Hough saved his fiercest prose for the entity that both he and Grinnell saw as the root of the problem: Congress. "Nowhere can we find an ignorance and indifference on this subject equal to that which has so long existed in the halls of Congress," he wrote. "It is time the change should come." As the story concluded, Hough's voice rose to a crescendo:

> Let us remember, then, first, that Howell was killing [bison] cows and yearlings; second, that the few buffalo left are helpless when pursued in the snow; third, that for a crime of this sort Congress *provides no penalty!* As this is written the word comes that the Secretary of the Interior has ordered the release of Howell from custody. [H]e can now go into the Park again and kill more buffalo . . . Let us hope that by the time this shall be in print there will have been a new basis established by Congress, so that such villainy as this shall obtain punishment, prompt, adequate and just. Kill a Government mule and [see] what the U.S. Government will do to you. Yet a mule can be replaced. A buffalo cannot be replaced . . . But kill a Government buffalo, and what does the U.S. Government do? Nothing! Absolutely nothing! . . . Gentlemen of Congress can surely only need to have the matter called to their attention.[25]

And it worked.

Representative Lacey of Iowa introduced legislation to provide legal protections for Yellowstone's wildlife. The former victim of the 1887 stagecoach holdup, Lacey was well acquainted with the need for legal jurisdiction in the park. Now, as chairman of the House Committee on Public Lands, he could do something about it. Meanwhile, a reinvigorated Senator Vest introduced a companion bill in the Senate just as the story of Howell's capture appeared in newspapers across the country.

After sailing through the House and Senate, on May 7, 1894, approximately two months after Howell's capture, President Grover Cleveland signed the Yellowstone Game Protection Act into law.

* * *

When it was all over, Felix Burgess received honors from the Boone and Crockett Club and commendations from his superior officers for bravery. And just as Emerson Hough predicted, Edgar Howell was set free because his crime took place prior to the passage of the law. Nonetheless, Howell still found a way to become the first person charged under its authority. While sitting in a barber's chair at the National Hotel, soldiers arrested him for returning to the park after his expulsion. This time, Howell served one month in jail and paid a fifty-dollar fine.[26]

Ironically, Howell later basked in his notoriety, claiming he was responsible for saving the bison and passing the first game-protection law in Yellowstone. If not for him, he argued, the bison would have gone extinct. In a twist that brings the story full circle, the military superintendent of Yellowstone actually hired Howell three years later as a civilian scout to help track down a stagecoach robber. After this brief stint on the "other side" of the law, Howell disappeared, apparently moving to the Philippines to open a restaurant.[27]

* * *

Some say that the legacy of the 1894 act equals in importance the law that created Yellowstone National Park itself. A strong case can be made insofar as it played a key role in saving the last wild herd of American plains bison from potential extinction. Perhaps most significantly, it represented the first-ever national law protecting wildlife of any kind in the United States. Before this, the national government had little to say about wildlife. While the Constitution clearly establishes federal sovereignty over all land within the United States, it is silent about who controls the flora and fauna. Early Supreme Court decisions gave this power to the states. But the creation of the first-ever national park in an area where no states existed produced a legal limbo. The Yellowstone Game Protection Act resolved this ambiguity and created the space for new federal actions, including the creation of agencies like the U.S. Fish and Wildlife Service and laws like the Endangered Species Act.

Despite these powerful legacies, the act was far from perfect. It contained notable silences that, over time, created new problems. For example, the law said nothing about protecting predators. In fact, efforts to eradicate wolves, bears, and mountain lions increased after the passage of the 1894 law. Such actions wreaked havoc on the balance of food chains and led to overpopulation, habitat destruction, and disease outbreaks among Yellowstone's game species. Furthermore—and not surprisingly given the scientific understandings of the day—the law ignored the dangers of introducing invasive species, such as lake trout, into the park.

Although it did not address the issue of treaties directly, the Act also played a role in states' efforts to erase Native American hunting rights. The 1868 Treaties of Fort Laramie and Fort Bridger, for example, allowed continued subsistence hunting on "unoccupied" lands in the public domain. However, an 1896 Supreme Court ruling cited both the 1872 Yellowstone Act and 1894 Yellowstone Game Protection Act as negating treaty rights by transforming "unoccupied lands" into entities like national parks, where hunting was now prohibited.[29] Beyond Yellowstone, on other types of public lands like national forests, the court ruled that Wyoming's achievement of statehood in 1890 meant its control over wildlife superseded any Native American hunting rights established by treaty. Portions of this court decision would be reversed in 2019, but for the next century, efforts to remove Native

Americans from national parks expanded to include attacks on traditional hunting practices.

One other legacy of the act was the creation of Yellowstone's so-called "Zone of Death." Wyoming statehood necessitated a new federal district court that had jurisdiction over the portion of the park within state boundaries. Yellowstone is the only national park containing a federal courthouse, jail, and presiding magistrate judge, which allows for local adjudication of transgressions against the 1894 act and other crimes.

However, small portions of Yellowstone also lie within Idaho and Montana, thereby falling under those states' jurisdictions. But as these areas of the park have no legal residents, it is impossible to produce a jury for court proceedings. In recent years, some have surmised that this has created a geography of legal limbo: places inside the park where presumably one could commit a major crime but never be held accountable, as there is no way to conduct a criminal trial.[29] While no one has yet "gotten away with murder," the legal debate continues.

* * *

If the primary aim and effect of the 1894 Yellowstone Game Protection Act was to save the park's bison and elk from poachers seeking commercial gain, the larger question of who should own, sell, or otherwise profit from the park remained unanswered. Back in 1872, powerful economic and political forces came together to establish Yellowstone. Twenty-two years on, nature conservation emerged as a potent force of its own. But even as Grinnell, Vest, Lacey, and Roosevelt sought to tip the scales toward a conservation ethic in the face of a retreating railroad industry, others were busily staking a claim to the potential profits that might be had from park tourism.

A Park for the People?

(1895–1904)

ON APRIL 24, 1903, THREE MEN ON HORSEBACK LED A SMALL parade of soldiers and local dignitaries through the town of Gardiner, Montana. Amid the fanfare of a brass band and brightly decorated buildings, a cheering crowd of 3,000 lined the street, straining to see the man in the middle. Utterly recognizable with his bushy mustache, signature wire-rimmed glasses, and energetic disposition, the rider was none other than the twenty-sixth president of the United States, Theodore Roosevelt.

In the nine years since passage of the Yellowstone Game Protection Act, Roosevelt's political career had blasted off like a rocket. From his position as New York City police commissioner, he advanced to become the assistant secretary of the navy in 1897. Two years later, due in no small part to the fame gained from his Rough Riders escapade in Cuba, Roosevelt assumed the governorship of New York. And two years after that, he became President McKinley's vice presidential running mate for his reelection campaign.[1] Taking office in March 1901, Vice President Roosevelt served only six months before McKinley's assassination unexpectedly propelled him into the presidency itself.

Now, President Roosevelt was in the midst of a whirlwind eight-week tour of the American West. Traveling by rail in the president's personalized coach, the *Elysian*, Roosevelt planned to journey 14,000 miles across twenty-five states and deliver some 200 speeches. The trip included stops in Yosemite and the Grand Canyon, where the president would meet with John Muir and be inspired to declare the largest national monument in American history.[2] However, in Yellowstone, he looked forward to two weeks of rest and recreation, far from the prying throngs of political supporters and the press. Accompanied by acting superintendent Major John Pitcher, poet John Burroughs, park guide Billy Hofer, and a small military contingent, the president spent long days fishing, riding, and exploring.

Toward the end of his visit, Roosevelt was invited to give remarks at a ceremony dedicating a new gateway arch that would soon mark the northern entrance to Yellowstone. The Northern Pacific had finally completed its Yellowstone branch line into Gardiner, where workers were putting the finishing touches on a new depot. At last, train travelers could disembark at the park border rather than three miles away in Cinnabar. At the urging of army engineer Hiram Chittenden, an arch was included over the stage road to mark Yellowstone's entrance. Though neither the depot nor the arch were yet complete, the president's visit offered a chance for publicity too valuable to pass up.

Trotting his horse to the archway's stone foundations, Roosevelt dismounted and skipped up the steps to the platform. He smiled broadly and waved to the crowd before beginning.

It is a pleasure now to say a few words to you at the laying of the corner stone of the beautiful arch which is to mark the entrance to this Park. The Yellowstone Park is something absolutely unique in the world so far as I know. Nowhere else in any civilized country is there to be found such a tract of veritable wonderland made accessible to all visitors, where at the same time not only the scenery of the wilderness, but the wild creatures of the Park are scrupulously preserved . . . The creation and preservation of such a great national playground in the interests of our people as a whole is a credit to the nation . . . The scheme of its preservation is noteworthy in its essential democracy . . . the preservation of the scenery, of the forests, of the wilderness life and the wilderness game for the people as a whole instead of leaving the enjoyment thereof to be confined to the very rich . . .[3]

Throughout his presidency, Roosevelt would champion the national parks as tools for making nature accessible to all Americans regardless of wealth or status. This is what he meant when he spoke of Yellowstone's "essential democracy." To underscore the point, Roosevelt quoted from the 1872 act establishing Yellowstone as a place "for the benefit and enjoyment of the people." In time, those very words would be emblazoned atop the stone gateway, a structure that would later be commonly known as the "Roosevelt Arch."

However, in the summer of 1903, the same year Roosevelt delivered his speech, a glance at the tourists and hotels popping up in Yellowstone made one wonder just which "people" the park was actually designed to benefit.

* * *

Since taking over from the Yellowstone Improvement Company in 1886, the Yellowstone Park Association worked steadily to consolidate control over all major tourist concessions. Within five years, under the leadership of Charles Gibson, it largely succeeded. By 1891, the association bought out (and replaced) Marshall's hotel, Henderson's Cottage Hotel, and George Wakefield's stagecoach-transportation and tour business for Northern Pacific travelers. That same year, the association opened a series of new, albeit unfinished lodgings at Yellowstone Lake, the Grand Canyon of the Yellowstone, Norris Geyser Basin, and the Lower Geyser Basin.

Only a handful of operations remained independent, including Uncle John Yancey's hotel,[4] Eli Waters's tour-boat business, and F. Jay Haynes's photo shops and related enterprises, which allowed him to sell photographs and the famous *Haynes Guide Handbook of Yellowstone Park* in hotel gift shops.[5] Of these businesses, only William Wylie's ten-day tent-camping tours offered any sort of competition. Having operated in the park since 1883 on an annual permit basis, Wylie received a long-term lease in 1893. However, as he catered to middle-class tourists who could not afford hotels, he did not impinge on the association's core customer base, who tended to be wealthy enough to afford the railroad's all-inclusive tour packages.

The year 1891 also marked the arrival of a new contender for the park's tourism business. By the time of Roosevelt's speech in Gardiner twelve years later, this Gilded Age venture capitalist would assume monopoly control over nearly all of Yellowstone's concessions. In the process, he would bring the mighty Northern Pacific Railway to its knees, dictate national park policies, and do more than any other person to shape the architecture, tone, and aesthetic of visitor experiences in Yellowstone for the next one hundred years. He would also challenge the notion that the park was in fact intended "for the benefit and enjoyment of the people," unless those people could pay top dollar. Some called him the "robber baron of Yellowstone."[6] His name was Harry Child.

* * *

Born in 1857 to a wealthy family in San Francisco, Harry Child was small in stature. Standing five feet five inches tall, with thick eyebrows and hair parted down the center in the style of the day, Child was a born dealmaker with a quick wit and a knack for sniffing out economic opportunity.[7] Over time, he also developed a reputation for hardheadedness and a willingness to do whatever it took to succeed in business.

In his first commercial venture as a young man, with his family's backing, Child turned a hefty profit helping to establish the San Francisco Stock Exchange. Still in his twenties, he and an uncle then moved to Montana to invest in mining. There, Harry met local socialite Adelaide Dean, whom he married in 1883 at the age of twenty-six.

Four years later, Child served as general manager of the Gregory Silver Mine near Helena and lived in a stately house on Madison Avenue, just two doors down from the mansion of Samuel Hauser, member of the Washburn Expedition and territorial governor of Montana.[8] In the coming years, it seemed that Child made new fortunes at every turn, whether from banking, poultry farming, or real estate.

When he finally turned his attention to Yellowstone, there was no reason to expect the outcome would be any different.

* * *

It all began when Gibson and the Yellowstone Park Association purchased George Wakefield's stagecoach lease in 1890. As part of the deal, Gibson also bought the horses, coaches, and tack and kept on Wakefield and his partner, William Hoffman, as operators.

But the deal intersected with other political maneuvers. About the same time, Interior Secretary John Noble secretly decided to reassign the transportation contract to someone else, though he reassured Gibson that he would do no such thing. Gibson and Wakefield would soon learn the hard way about the importance of politics in government contracts.

Over the next several months, Noble justified his actions by blaming Wakefield for two unfortunate tourist incidents. The first occurred on a hot summer's day, when a stagecoach driver asked passengers to disembark on a steep road to ease the burden on the horses—a common practice at the time. As the guests hiked up the incline, an elderly former congressman named Guy Ray Pelton collapsed of a fatal heart attack.

The second incident occurred in early fall, when a group of visitors became temporarily stranded at a hotel in the Lower Geyser Basin due to lack of available coaches. The group included John Wanamaker, U.S. postmaster general, who issued a stern complaint to the interior secretary upon his return to Washington.[9] Though rare, such events were not unheard of and hardly a reason for executive intervention. Nonetheless, Noble used the opportunity to bring Wakefield to Washington for an investigation. But the meeting was just a formality.

As it turns out, Noble had already promised the lease to a Montana Republican named Silas Huntley. With years of experience running stage lines, Huntley had since retired to become a rancher and horse breeder. But most importantly, he maintained close personal and business ties with President Benjamin Harrison's son, Russell. In the end, this was all that really mattered. On March 30, 1891, just as the Grover Cleveland administration came in to replace the Harrison administration, Noble awarded the contract to Huntley on extremely generous terms, including an unheard-of clause that guaranteed profitability.[10]

All Huntley needed to do was raise approximately $70,000 to purchase Wakefield's old equipment, now owned by the Yellowstone Park Association. The price fell well below market value, but without the lease, the association was forced to sell. Unable to raise the necessary sum himself, Huntley looked to his brother-in-law, who, along with several other investors,[11] happily supplied the money. His brother-in-law's name? Harry Child.

The suspect nature of these events triggered a congressional investigation that resulted in a condemnation of Noble's actions for corruption.[12] Nonetheless, the transfer of the lease went forward and was finalized on April 17, 1892.

Though Huntley managed the operation, now called the Yellowstone Transportation Company, Child made all the financial decisions. This tactic—using extended family connections to quietly assume control over rival companies—would become a hallmark of Child's rise to power. The entrepreneur now had a foothold inside of Yellowstone National Park. As he eyed other park businesses, the only question was which would be the next to fall.

* * *

Child's next opportunity arose from the growing discontent between Charles Gibson and the Northern Pacific. As president of the Yellowstone Park Association, Gibson made all day-to-day management decisions. But the railroad held the purse strings. Since the Northern Pacific made most of its money on branch line fares from Livingston to Gardiner, it had less interest in park concessions. Time and again, railroad executives forced Gibson to lower prices for food and lodging and to extend the visitor season beyond what was profitable for the association in order to increase railroad profits. Constantly criticized for offering subpar service but unable to make necessary repairs and upgrades to meet customer demands, Gibson grew frustrated. In 1895, matters came to a head when he resigned and sued the Northern Pacific for breach of contract. In a settlement, Gibson agreed to sell his company shares back to the railroad, making the Northern Pacific once again the majority owner of the Yellowstone Park Association.

To avoid the charge of monopoly control, Northern Pacific executives employed a dizzying array of corporate maneuvers. In 1898, they formed a new shell corporation called the Northwest Improvement Company, which purchased all shares of the association from the railroad. Of course, all shareholders of the new company remained employed by or affiliated with the railroad.

To create a greater appearance of separation between the railroad and its park businesses, Northern Pacific executives searched for a new managing director, finally settling on Harry Child and his partners, Silas Huntley and Edmund Bach. After all, their Yellowstone Transportation Company produced steady profits. On April 4, 1901, the Northwest Improvement Company (which is to say, the Northern Pacific) sold all shares of the Yellowstone Park Association—one-third each—to Child, Huntley, and Bach. Shortly thereafter, Huntley and Bach elected Child as president of both the Yellowstone Park Association and the Yellowstone Transportation Company.

Interestingly, none of the three men had enough cash on hand to swing the deal. Consequently, the Northern Pacific—by way of the shell company—loaned them the money for the purchase. In time, the Northern Pacific would make so many loans to Child that the entrepreneur would accrue enormous debt, owing them over $1 million by 1915.[13] But oddly enough, this situation actually put the railway at Child's mercy rather than vice versa. The more the railroad lent him, the more dependent it became on his success to ensure repayment. This, in turn, created incentives for additional loans.

By 1901, all parties assumed the question of ownership over the Yellowstone Park Association was settled. But one year later, Huntley passed away and Bach became embroiled in a political scandal, forcing each of their respective one-third shares to revert back to the Northwest Improvement Company.[14] Though Child still served as president, Northwest Improvement now held two-thirds of the stock, making it the majority owner once again.

Unsatisfied with this arrangement, in 1905, the railroad approved new loans to Child that allowed him to become half owner. Two years later, another series of Northern Pacific loans gave Child complete control of the entire enterprise. By that point, Child had made his most profound and indelible mark on Yellowstone's landscape.

* * *

When Child took over the association in 1901, plans were already underway to construct a new hotel near Old Faithful in the Upper Geyser Basin. But the idea was not Child's.

The impetus sprang from F. Jay Haynes's ambitions to expand be-yond photography and into the transportation business. In 1898, Haynes and a partner established the Monida and Western Stage Company and secured a contract to drive visitors from the Union Pacific terminus in Monida, Montana, to Yellowstone Park via the western entrance. As part of this arrangement, Haynes proposed building a new hotel near Old Faithful to serve Union Pacific passengers in the same way that Yellowstone Association hotels served Northern Pacific patrons.[15]

Once alerted to Haynes's plans, Child moved quickly to snuff out the potential competition. Under the influence of the Northern Pacific, the Interior Department decided against Haynes's proposal, opting in-stead for a plan put forth by Child and the Yellowstone Park Associ-ation. Child intended to name his new hotel the Old Faithful Tavern.

The original plans called for a large formal structure built in the Queen Anne style, but Child soon abandoned this idea in favor of a series of nine "cottages," each containing fourteen to eighteen rooms. Built in the rustic style and anchored by a large "tavern" to serve as kitchen and dining room, the cottages included large verandas oriented to provide expansive views of the geyser basin.

In the early 1900s, the rustic architectural style was extremely popular among upper-class Americans. Emerging from the American Arts and Crafts movement of the late nineteenth century, rustic styling rejected the ornamentation of Victorian architecture in favor of simple clean lines, sturdy construction, and unique elements reflecting the ar-tisan's individualism. Its log and stone structures were set organically in the landscape, consistent with the Romantic ideal of connecting to nature. Interior designs stressed natural materials: exposed beams, sometimes with bark left on, and natural stained-wood floors and fur-niture. Significantly, *rustic* did not mean shoddy or worn elements; only high-quality materials would do, designed to provide all the comforts of a luxury holiday.

By the winter of 1902–1903, Child secured a $25,000 loan from the railroad to start cutting nearby lodgepole pine for timber. Workers took advantage of the snow-covered grounds, transporting wood and other materials to the building site by horse-drawn sleds.

Ultimately, the construction of this "tavern" at Old Faithful would represent one of Child's most significant legacies in Yellowstone. Central to its execution was a long-term partnership between the Child family and a quiet young architect named Robert Reamer.

* * *

Born in Oberlin, Ohio, in 1873, Reamer pursued a career as an architect from an early age.[16] After apprenticeships in Detroit and Chicago, he moved to San Diego in 1895 and established an architectural firm with partner Samuel Zimmer. A quiet and rather modest young man, Reamer tended to avoid self-promotion, preferring to let his finished work speak for itself. But such traits did not help a new firm win competitive bids. Reamer's lack of assertiveness—and therefore business contracts—created frustrations that may have exacerbated a lifelong struggle with alcohol.

Within four years, his business partnership dissolved. Reamer found work as a staff architect for Elisha Babcock, cofounder and general manager of the Hotel Del Coronado and the Coronado Beach Company on Coronado Island. Babcock's plans for the hotel included developing an adjacent resort community, which began as a "tent city" for wealthy vacationers and later evolved to include a golf course and a series of permanent buildings. Reamer designed or renovated many of these structures for Babcock, including the Music and Dance Pavilion, the Bay Bath House, and the Coronado Golf Club House. This last building included a set of expansive two-story verandas overlooking the rolling dunes of Coronado's golf course. Notably, these "rustic stylings" would catch the eye of one very important visitor to the Hotel Del Coronado and, in so doing, forever change Reamer's life.

* * *

Harry Child and his family vacationed annually in Southern California. On January 17, 1903, Harry and Adelaide arrived at the Hotel Del Coronado for a ten-day stay. While middle-class visitors might take the ferry across the bay from San Diego, the Childs traveled in a private train coach along the tracks lining the narrow Silver Strand beach that linked Coronado to the mainland, disembarking at the hotel's elegant front entrance.

Over the next few days, the couple strolled the well-manicured grounds. Harry spotted the new golf house and was taken by the architectural style. With Yellowstone ever on his mind, Harry asked Babcock about the architect responsible. In response, the hotelier spoke highly of young Reamer. Immediately, Child extended an offer to the twenty-nine-year-old to come to Yellowstone as the park's primary architect.

Reamer readily accepted and began preparations with his wife, Mabel, for an imminent departure to Wyoming. In fact, he left so abruptly that he failed to give notice to his former employers, causing Babcock to walk back his positive recommendation. In a follow-up letter to Child, he raised concerns about Reamer's professionalism and warned that Reamer might succumb to alcohol if not kept sufficiently busy.[17]

This may explain why Child put Reamer to work on so many projects in such a short time. Even on his train journey to Yellowstone, Reamer spent hours in his sleeper car drafting a new design for the Old Faithful Tavern. By the first week of February, he was on site in Mammoth with new plans that collapsed the multibuilding arrangement into a single large structure in the rustic style. In March, Child secured another $100,000 loan from the Northern Pacific for construction.[18]

Needing only final approval from Washington to begin work, Child and Reamer showed the plans to President Roosevelt during his 1903 Yellowstone visit and received an enthusiastic endorsement. As expected, in May, the Interior Department signed off without hesitation.

Reamer's first eighteen months in Yellowstone represented a remarkable period of creative productivity that secured his legacy not only in the park but in American architecture. He designed and constructed to completion no less than seven major projects in or near the park that spanned a range of styles. In addition to the Old Faithful Inn (completed in 1904), he designed the new Northern Pacific train depot in Gardiner; completed major renovations for the Lake Hotel; constructed the Thumb Lunch Station, the Yellowstone Transportation building, and the Yellowstone Hotel Company Commissary at Mammoth; and provided an addition to Henry Klamer's curio shop (later, Hamilton's) near Old Faithful.

Harry's wife, Adelaide (who went by Addie), also developed a friendship with Reamer that heavily influenced the interior design in many of his buildings. For the Old Faithful Inn, she chose the internal features—including stair railings, lighting, wall coverings, and mission-style furniture—to complement the rustic exterior. After Reamer's wife Mabel died from kidney disease in 1906, Harry and Addie essentially adopted Robert into their family. In 1909, they took him on a monthlong tour of Europe to see the architecture. And in 1911, Reamer married Louis Chase, niece of John Meldrum, the long-serving U.S. magistrate appointed to Yellowstone. Until his death in 1938, Reamer would play a role in the design of nearly every major construction project in the park.

* * *

In the summer of 1904, park tourists fell into four different categories according to how much they spent on Harry Child's concession businesses. On the lowest rung were the Sagebrushers. Present since the park's opening, these visitors were typically self-sufficient locals who provided their own transportation (usually horses and wagons), tents, and food.

The next rung up were the "Wylie Way" campers. These visitors may have arrived by train, but, rather than stay in Child's hotels, they purchased ten-day park tours offering food and accommodation via William Wylie's permanent tent camps. For in-park transportation, they contracted with small independent guides. Many tended to be teachers with summers off or middle-class people with enough resources for a train ticket but not the park's fancy hotels.

At the very top of the ladder perched the wealthy elite, those with enough leisure time and disposable income to afford several weeks, or even an entire summer, lounging in the park. These rare individuals spent liberally on Child's lodging and dining businesses but less on tours or train fare. Regardless, they were not plentiful enough to cover seasonal operating costs.

The group that mattered most to Child (and to the Northern Pacific)—and that made up his bread and butter—sat on the second rung from the top. They were still upper-class, to be sure, but usually looked for a shorter, five-to-six-day adventure rather than a season-long stay. The rapid turnover meant greater sales of train tickets, park tours, and souvenirs. Often European in origin but including a growing number of wealthy Americans, these customers were called Couponers because they purchased all-inclusive vacation packages directly from railroad companies. At each stop along the tour, these visitors clipped and presented a coupon for their prepaid hotel, food, or transportation service.

The typical packaged tour covered all the major sights in six days. Visitors traveled south from Mammoth to Norris Geyser Basin, then ventured counterclockwise to Old Faithful, Yellowstone Lake, and the Grand Canyon of the Yellowstone. A return back to Norris completed the circle, before retracing the route up to Mammoth for the trip home.

With the completion of the railroad's branch line and Harry Child's hotels, the trip was no longer as arduous, long, or expensive as it was in the 1870s. But in 1904, it still required ample time and money. Customers would board an early morning Northern Pacific train in Saint Paul or Duluth. Traveling first-class, they gazed upon the vast northern plains from luxurious lounge cars, wide-windowed excursion cars, or well-appointed dining cars and retired in the evening to Pullman sleeper coaches. The next morning, they reached Livingston, Montana, and transferred onto the Yellowstone branch line. Several hours later, guests arrived at the Reamer-designed depot in Gardiner. Disembarking onto a curved open-air platform, they stood beneath an elongated roof supported by thick log poles that retained their bark and branched out toward the top, giving the impression of living trees. Their itinerary would look something like this:

DAY ONE

Just outside the Gardiner depot, a line of bright-yellow Tally Ho stagecoaches awaited the travelers. These large coaches required six horses to operate and could hold over twenty people. Passing under the new stone gateway arch marking the entrance to Yellowstone, visitors soon arrived at the National Hotel, where porters unloaded the luggage and directed guests to their respective lobbies, one entrance for gentlemen and a separate one for the ladies. Originally constructed in 1883, the

National Hotel would not undergo its Robert Reamer rebuild until 1936 (when it became the Mammoth Hotel).

After checking in, visitors enjoyed a multi-course lunch in the hotel dining room before setting out to explore or tour Mammoth Hot Springs. In the evening, after-dinner entertainment included a black-tie gala with live orchestral music and dancing late into the night.

DAY TWO

The next morning, Couponers assembled on the National Hotel porch to find a string of smaller four-horse carriages that held eight passengers with one small bag each. They also received a seat assignment and linen covering to defend against the dust kicked up by the stages in front.

As visitors would quickly learn, long jarring hours in the stages with rough-and-tumble drivers formed a big part of the experience. The drivers, with names like Geyser Bob, Big Fred, and Society Red (who apparently never missed a dance), were often former cowboys, miners, or hunters known for their salty language, tall tales, and willingness to take risks to make up time.[19] Though service improved after Child took control in 1891, accidents triggered by spooked horses, mechanical breakdowns, and even drunk driving were not uncommon. At times, they could even be deadly. And despite the presence of U.S. Cavalry troops on patrol, stage holdups remained a real possibility (the largest, involving seventeen stage coaches, took place in 1908).[20]

Climbing the steep grade out of Mammoth, stages passed through the narrow gorge of the Golden Gate before topping out onto Swan Lake Flats and continuing on to Obsidian Cliff and Roaring Mountain. At Frying Pan Spring, drivers often spoke of birds drinking so much hot water that they laid hard-boiled eggs. About midday, visitors reached the lunch station in the Norris Geyser Basin. Served by the flamboyant Irishman Larry Mathews, guests dined at tables set under a canvas tent. As Rudyard Kipling recalled of his 1897 experience:

> Larry enveloped us all in the golden glamour of his speech
> ere we had descended and the tent with the rude trestle table
> became a palace, the rough fare delicacies of Delmonico's, and
> we, the abashed recipients of Larry's imperial bounty. It was

only later that I discovered that I had paid eight shillings for tinned beef, biscuits and beer, but on the other hand, Larry had said, "Will I go out and kill a buffalo?" And I felt that for me, and me alone, he would have done it.[21]

After lunch, visitors spent an hour or so exploring the geyser basin before traveling on to the Fountain Hotel near modern-day Madison Junction. Opened in 1891, the three-story structure with 350 rooms included electric lights, steam heating, and hot springs mineral baths. After dinner, guests could gather in the ballroom for another night of dancing or head out back to watch bears feeding on leftover food and trash tossed out to them by kitchen staff.

DAY THREE

Visitors took the relatively short eight-mile ride to the Upper Geyser Basin and Old Faithful, with some stopping to see Grand Prismatic Spring along the way. At Old Faithful Inn, they approached the building that has become one of the most iconic structures in the United States.

Walking through the massive front doors made a powerful impression. Built of native volcanic stone (rhyolite) and timber hewn from nearby lodgepole pine stands, the open lobby stretched four stories to the roof, highlighting the immense freestanding stone fireplace near the back. Around the perimeter of the cavernous lobby, twisting polished-wood railings and off-centered windows of various sizes and shapes gave the feeling of being in a forest with dappled sunlight filtering through the canopy. A staircase led to guest rooms and interior balconies dotted with sofas and writing desks, creating the sensation of being nestled in a tree house. At the highest point, a "crow's nest" could hold musicians, who filled the air with subtle classical melodies. The second floor offered passage to a partially covered exterior deck for observing the geyser basin. A searchlight mounted on the rooftop "widow's walk" allowed for special nighttime viewing of Old Faithful, wandering wildlife, or unwitting romantic couples pitching woo.

The inn, often called the largest log structure in the world (but without any supporting evidence), received a 100-room east-wing expansion by Reamer in 1913 and another 150-room west-wing expansion in 1928. In 1936, he completed the Bear Pit Lounge (moved to its current location in 1962). But the building's distinctiveness had less to do with immensity than with the outdoorsy feel of the interior space, which even today exudes the same treehouse-like sense of wonder.

DAY FOUR

The day began with a stagecoach ride to the West Thumb of Yellowstone Lake for lunch and a stroll near the hot springs. Afterward, visitors could choose to continue on by coach along the shoreline to Lake Hotel or board Eli Waters's steamer ship, the *Zillah*, instead. For tired tourists, the boat had its appeal, but it also required an additional fee. The crusty Waters tried to entice stage drivers by offering them a fifty-cent kickback for every tourist they sent to his boat, but eventually even this wasn't enough to keep Waters's business afloat.

At Lake Hotel, visitors found a completely different expression of Robert Reamer's talents. What began in 1891 as a flat-sided clapboard hotel of eighty rooms transformed after Reamer's 1903 redesign into a four-story, 210-room structure featuring a distinctive set of gables and a colonnade of fifty-foot-high Ionic columns. Painted a soft yellow with white highlights, the new lobby featured a grand piano and plush furniture. After Reamer's 1928 renovations, it included a special lounge with large windows offering sweeping vistas of the lake and mountains beyond. A far cry from rustic styling, the classical Lake Hotel made no effort to conform to its natural surroundings. Nonetheless, it became a favorite of those preferring to "spend the season" in Yellowstone.

DAY FIVE

After breakfast, Couponers traveled from Yellowstone Lake through the rolling meadows of Hayden Valley to the Canyon Hotel for their final night in the park.

Despite a short stop en route at the Mud Volcano, tourists arrived at the hotel with ample time for a tour of the Grand Canyon of the Yellowstone. Choices included an eight-mile tour by horseback along the rim or a scramble down into the canyon itself. The latter involved the guiding services of Uncle Tom Richardson, who built a series of

Jim Bridger, 1866.
(Courtesy of the National Park Service, Yellowstone National Park)

Nathaniel Pitt Langford,
undated. *(Courtesy of the Montana Historical Society Research Center)*

Dr. Ferdinand V. Hayden, 1870. *(Courtesy of the U.S. Geological Survey Photo Archives)*

Truman Everts, undated. *(Reproduced from Langford, 1905)*

Old Faithful Geyser, 1871, Hayden Second Yellowstone Survey, by William H. Jackson. *(Courtesy of the U.S. Geological Survey Denver Library Photographic Collection)*

Senator George Vest, undated. *(Courtesy of the National Park Service, Yellowstone National Park)*

Chief Joseph or Hin-mah-too-yah-lat-kekt, meaning Thunder Rolling Down the Mountain, undated. *(Courtesy of the National Portrait Gallery, #78.68)*

Philetus Norris, undated. *(Courtesy of the National Park Service, Yellowstone National Park)*

Emma Cowan,
undated. *(Courtesy of
the Montana Historical
Society Research Center)*

George Bird Grinnell,
editor of *Forest and Stream*,
cofounder of Boone and
Crockett Club, and founder
of Audubon Society, undated.
*(Courtesy of the National
Park Service, Yellowstone
National Park)*

Line of U.S. Cavalry in Lamar Valley, undated. *(Courtesy of the National Park Service, Yellowstone National Park)*

Tally Ho stagecoach at Mammoth Hotel, circa 1910. *(Courtesy of the National Park Service, Yellowstone National Park)*

Fishing catch at Yellowstone Lake by Lake Hotel employees, 1901. *(Courtesy of the National Park Service, Yellowstone National Park)*

Captured poacher Ed Howell (far right) being led back to Yellowstone headquarters, 1894, by F. Jay Haynes. *(Courtesy of the National Park Service, Yellowstone National Park)*

Bison heads recovered by military from poacher Ed Howell, 1894, by F. Jay Haynes. *(Courtesy of the National Park Service, Yellowstone National Park)*

President Theodore Roosevelt delivering his speech at the cornerstone laying ceremony for the north entrance archway, Yellowstone National Park, 1903. *(Courtesy of Archives and Special Collections, Mansfield Library, University of Montana)*

ABOVE: Robert Reamer at Canyon Hotel building site, 1910. *(Courtesy of the National Park Service, Yellowstone National Park)*

RIGHT: Yellowstone concessionaire Harry Child, 1920. *(Reproduced from Child, 2009)*

Old Faithful Inn showing rustic style, 1912, by F. Jay Haynes. *(Courtesy of the National Park Service, Yellowstone National Park)*

Lamar Buffalo Ranch, undated. *(Courtesy of the National Park Service, Yellowstone National Park)*

Three black bear cubs begging for food in Yellowstone, undated.
(Courtesy of the National Park Service, Yellowstone National Park)

Horace Albright with bears, undated. *(Courtesy of the National Park Service, Yellowstone National Park)*

Stephen Mather, first director of the National Park Service, undated. *(Courtesy of the National Park Service, Yellowstone National Park)*

U.S. AT WAR

Associated Press

WYOMING RANCHERS (center: WALLACE BEERY) DRIVE THEIR CATTLE ACROSS JACKSON HOLE
Harold Ickes stuck to his guns, too.

Wallace Beery and Jackson Hole ranchers at national monument protest, 1943, AP photo. *(Courtesy of* Time *magazine)*

Frank and John Craighead, pioneering wildlife scientists who studied Yellowstone's grizzlies, undated. *(Courtesy of the Craighead Institute)*

Holly McKinney with wayward tourists, concession employees, and journalists seeking safety on the boardwalk during the firestorm at Old Faithful, September 7, 1988, by Jeff Henry. *(Courtesy of Roche Jaune Pictures, Inc.)*

Crown fire in Yellowstone National Park, 1988, file photo. *(Courtesy of the Bozeman Daily Chronicle)*

Superintendent Bob Barbee, Mammoth Hot Springs, 1987. *(Courtesy of the National Park Service, Yellowstone National Park)*

U.S. Fish and Wildlife director Mollie Beattie (center), Yellowstone superintendent Mike Finley (second from right), and Interior Secretary Bruce Babbitt (far right) help to carry the first set of Canadian gray wolves to their holding pens in the Lamar Valley, January 1995, by Jim Peaco.
(Courtesy of the National Park Service, Yellowstone National Park)

A gray wolf in Yellowstone National Park, 2017, by Jacob W. Frank.
(Courtesy of the National Park Service)

Yellowstone bison arriving at Fort Peck Reservation, 2012, by Ted Wood. *(Courtesy of Ted Wood Photography)*

All Nations Tepee Village at Yellowstone National Park, northern entrance, 2022, by Jacob W. Frank. *(Courtesy of the National Park Service)*

stairways and trails down to the base of the Lower Falls in the late 1890s for this purpose.

In 1911, inspired by his trip to Europe with the Child family, Reamer produced another architectural marvel. By far his most ambitious project, Reamer's new Canyon Hotel would stretch 595 feet long and contained 430 guest rooms. It featured a 2,000-square-foot lounge that served not only as a lobby but also a ballroom, promenade, or theater. Unfortunately, as Reamer used the older structure's foundations, the building shifted down the hillside over time and was condemned by the Park Service in 1958.

DAY SIX

Couponers spent the entirety of the last day returning to Mammoth. To save time, stagecoach drivers took the Cutoff, an eleven-mile shortcut to Norris, where visitors lunched once more with Larry Mathews. Arriving back at the National Hotel, guests collected their belongings and partook of an early dinner. Afterward, the large Tally Ho coaches took them back to the Gardiner Depot in time for the evening train home.

For park workers, the seventh day was spent refreshing the rooms, cleaning the kitchens, and restocking supplies. The following day, another set of Couponers would arrive, and the cycle began anew.

* * *

By 1910, with the exception of F. Jay Haynes's enterprises, Harry Child was involved in every major hotel, transportation, and concession business in Yellowstone. What he didn't own outright he controlled indirectly through behind-the-scenes investments, as he did with William Wylie's tent-camping tour business (obtained in a hostile takeover),[22] Eli Waters's boating enterprise (now called the Yellowstone Boat Company), and Hamilton's General Stores (founded by a former employee to whom Child's son lent the startup capital). Over the next decade, Child would benefit even more as the railroads' "See America First" advertising campaign ramped up park visitation—and Child's profits—to record highs.

It is difficult to overstate Child's influence, which touched upon nearly every aspect of a visitor's experience in Yellowstone. Yet three legacies stand out, with effects reaching well beyond the borders of the park. The first and most tangible was the architectural vision he shared with Robert Reamer. Buildings such as the Old Faithful Inn not only became national treasures in their own right but established a distinctly American "parkitecture" style that influenced structures in national parks across the country.

A second major legacy concerns Child's monopoly over park concessions. Though not the first to attempt it, Child's control was the most complete and long-lasting in Yellowstone's early history. A member of his family held a stake in Yellowstone businesses from 1891 to the late 1960s. This way of soliciting and managing park business, for better or worse, continues to this day, throughout the national park system as a whole.

Finally, Child wielded significant influence on the presentation of Yellowstone as a resort designed for upper-class citizens. Again, he was hardly the first to do so; the Northern Pacific Railway and its allies had promoted such notions from the start. But Child's development of upscale hotels, restaurants, and touring services did much to advance the identity of Yellowstone as a leisure destination for the well-heeled, rather than a site for environmental protection or recreation for the masses.

Though it is true that middle-class tourists began to increase during these years, prompting Child's buyout of Wylie in 1905, such groups were tolerated rather than catered to. And in the case of Sagebrushers, not even that. In short, Roosevelt's "essential democracy" would not arrive in Yellowstone in any significant way until the first automobiles drove through the Roosevelt Arch in 1915.

Yet, even as Child's tourism empire expanded, elsewhere in the park, contraction and decline seemed the order of the day. This was especially true for Yellowstone's wildlife. Tourists often commented on the lack of wild animals seen, with the exception of garbage-eating bears. Just like the few remaining independent concessionaires forced to deal with the juggernaut of Harry Child, Yellowstone's wildlife soon found itself scrambling to maintain a foothold in the park.

Please Feed the Animals

(1902–1918)

ON FEBRUARY 14, 1902, THE ACTING SUPERINTENDENT OF Yellowstone, Major John Pitcher, wrote a letter to Interior Secretary Ethan Hitchcock.

> I have the honor to request authority to catch up all of the young buffalo that we have left, and to place them under fence at some convenient point where they can be carefully looked after and properly fed. We have already located twenty-two of these animals on the head of Pelican Creek, and there are probably a few more that we shall find a little later in the season. This herd is exceedingly wild and will probably never increase in size, and may possibly die out completely . . .
>
> The little herd that we have left in the park has been a matter of great interest to the public, and inquiries are constantly being made about it. But as far as I know not a buffalo has been seen by the tourists for a number of years.[1]

When the Yellowstone Game Protection Act passed in 1894, the park's bison population stood at approximately 200 animals. But over the next few years, despite the new legal protection and the rigorous anti-poaching campaigns, the number continued to dwindle.

In response, the secretary of the Smithsonian Institution, Professor Samuel Langley, proposed capturing Yellowstone's last herd in order to protect and expand it through a controlled breeding program. In 1895, Captain Anderson ordered guide Billy Hofer to construct a corral near Alum Creek for this purpose. But all efforts to capture the wild herd failed.

By the time Pitcher assumed the role of superintendent in 1901, the situation had grown worse. An energetic and inquisitive Texan with a thick handlebar mustache, forty-seven-year-old Pitcher had served in Yellowstone during the Nez Perce and Bannock Wars in 1877–1878. Eager to hit the ground running in his new position, Pitcher sent out scouts in January 1902 to tally the remaining bison. After several weeks of searching, they returned with disappointing news: Yellowstone's herd totaled approximately twenty-five head.[2]

The implications were clear. The iconic North American plains bison, numbering at one time in the tens of millions, now teetered on the brink of extinction in the United States.

* * *

Secretary Hitchcock responded to Pitcher's letter with a compromise. Rather than try to capture the entire herd, start a new one with bison purchased beyond park boundaries. This new captive herd would ensure the survival of bison in Yellowstone, even if the wild herd eventually died out. To maintain genetic continuity, Pitcher intended to capture a few young calves from Yellowstone's native herd to interbreed with those brought in from outside.

Congress agreed and provided funding to purchase the bison, construct an enclosure corral, and hire a game warden to oversee the program. Major Pitcher sprang to action, dashing off letters to all known sources of captive bison from Montana to Texas, while Secretary Hitchcock began the search for a new game warden.

Interestingly, these bison would not be the first ones imported to Yellowstone. Back in 1896, Eli Waters received permission to purchase four bison from the Charles Goodnight herd in Texas, keeping them caged on Dot Island in the middle of the lake as an attraction for his boat passengers. Waters's "zoo" also contained a number of elk. Notably, these animals remained separate from the park's wild herds and had nothing to do with the proposed breeding program.[3]

The stage was set for yet another powerful Yellowstone legacy. By adopting the captive breeding program, Yellowstone's managers were unwittingly taking the first steps toward something new in wildlife management. For the first time in American history, an intentional effort to save and restore an endangered species was underway.

* * *

Of course, decisions made by park managers had unintentionally altered wildlife ecology in Yellowstone since the beginning, more often than not exacerbating the very problems they hoped to resolve. The task was complicated by a dearth of scientific knowledge and dependence upon societal views of nature. In the nineteenth century, American society had a complex relationship with wild animals. While most people supported protecting game species like bison, elk, and deer, they were more than happy to eradicate predators or any creatures perceived as pests.

But deciding which was which wasn't always clear. Lacking an understanding of even the most basic ecological concepts, society often imposed human ethical standards on wildlife, labeling species as morally "good" or "bad," "innocent" or "bloodthirsty." Such ideas sprang from the erroneous notion that wild animals followed moral codes of conduct. Consequently, *Grimms' Fairy Tales* effectively demonized wolves in the eyes of many people. In contrast, early twentieth-century works by Ernest Thompson Seton and Jack London did the opposite, romanticizing wolves, mountain lions, and bears as misunderstood protagonists.

In the long run, both perspectives would prove enormously problematic for Yellowstone wildlife. But early in the century, the notion of predators as "evil" remained influential in the rural West and helped to justify the eradication efforts of early park managers. Declines in the bison population (and perceived but unverified declines in the elk population) were explained by overhunting. Ignoring the fact that bison and elk had thrived for millennia under the combined pressures of Indigenous hunting and natural predation, managers attempted to ban *all* hunting and eliminate *all* predators inside the park. While this slowed the primary culprits of population decline—tourists, concessionaires, and white poachers—managers also took the opportunity to reinforce bans of Native Americans from the park.

For predators, the new policies translated into a death sentence. The year after the Game Protection Act passed, Superintendent Anderson launched a campaign to eradicate coyotes from the park under the mistaken notion that Yellowstone's deer and pronghorn were under threat. In 1899, managers initiated a similar campaign against mountain lions and lynx, and, a year later, against wolves. In 1903, the park purchased a pack of lion hounds, leading to the killing of some sixty-five mountain lions over the next three years.[4]

* * *

In contrast, park managers deemed other species so desirable that they took great pains to usher them in. At the time of Yellowstone's founding—and extending back some 12,000 years—about 40 percent of the waters had no fish.[5] Although early Euro-American explorers documented the overabundance of cutthroat trout in Yellowstone Lake (Cornelius Hedges of the Washburn Expedition recorded catching over forty fish in a single afternoon), other waterbodies, including Shoshone Lake, Lewis Lake, and portions of the Firehole River, remained barren.[6]

Recall that in 1899, Superintendent Boutelle asked the U.S. Fish Commission to stock Yellowstone's lakes and rivers with non-native fish for sport fishing. As a result, commissioners introduced brown trout (a species native to the eastern U.S. and Canada) into the Firehole River, and lake trout (from the Great Lakes) into Lewis and Shoshone Lakes. Over the next few years, the park also received populations of Loch Leven and von Behr brown trout from Europe, along with rainbow trout, the only species native to the western United States (but not to Yellowstone). Some introduced species failed to establish themselves, including black bass, white fish, yellow perch, and salmon, which in hindsight was a good thing.[7]

In 1902, believing that the native black spotted and cutthroat trout in Yellowstone Lake were overabundant, Superintendent Pitcher ordered collection of their eggs to stock rivers and streams elsewhere in the park and throughout the United States and Europe. Collecting stations soon appeared in West Thumb for this purpose, and later at Trout Lake.[8] The combined practice of introducing non-native species while extracting native ones via egg gathering could only end badly for native ecosystems. Yet it continued unabated until the 1930s.[9]

The effects were not immediately detected. But before long, native fish stocks plummeted. Managers reacted not by changing their practices but by imposing size and catch limits on anglers—a six-inch size requirement in 1897, later raised to eight. In 1907, the park set a twenty-catch limit, and, after 1919, hotels could no longer catch trout in Yellowstone Lake to feed guests. Eventually, all native fish species in the park experienced significant population declines, and some, including the black spotted trout, disappeared altogether.[10]

Among the introduced species, two had particularly profound effects. Rainbow trout stood out not only for their ability to outcompete native cutthroats for food but also to interbreed with them.[11] The resultant hybrid form, which still exists today, accelerated the devastation of cutthroat populations.

A second species produced even greater and more enduring ecological damage. Living longer and growing much larger than Yellowstone's native trout, the voracious lake trout also fed on them for roughly 30 percent of their diet.[12] After their expansion into Yellowstone Lake—likely caused by a park visitor sometime in the 1980s—lake trout not only reduced and displaced cutthroat populations in the lake but also disrupted natural food chains. Since they are capable of living at greater depths, lake trout can avoid predation by eagles, ospreys, and bears, thus denying a food source to other species historically dependent on the native cutthroat.

* * *

Invasive species would ultimately impact Yellowstone's bison as well, but for now, the only planned introductions involved the purebred bison from outside the park. For the park's new gamekeeper, Secretary Hitchcock settled on Charles J. "Buffalo" Jones, a former buffalo hunter who gained notoriety during the bison extermination campaigns of the 1870s and '80s.

Jones, like Buffalo Bill Cody, later experienced a change of heart and began working to protect the species. Capturing stray bison calves, he built a small domestic herd in Kansas and began crossbreeding experiments with cattle. He hoped to produce what he called "cattalo," a commercially viable breed of beef cattle adapted to the harsh conditions of the Great Plains. Jones's efforts (and those of others with the same idea) largely failed, but in the process they helped to establish a legacy of domesticated cattle genes within American plains bison. A small percentage of these genes persist in virtually all North American commercial bison herds to this day. Only the wild herd in Yellowstone and a few other conservation herds retain genetic purity.

By the mid-1890s, Jones gave up on his "cattalo" scheme, sold his herd to pay off debts, and began a search for new economic opportunities. Twice, in 1896 and 1897, Jones tried and failed to secure the position of gamekeeper in Yellowstone. In 1899, he ramped up his self-promotion efforts by publishing a semi-autobiographical (and semi-fictitious) book about his life on the frontier.[13] In 1902, with congressional funding assured for a new bison program and Jones's reputation as a bison expert now confirmed—at least by his own book—Secretary Hitchcock, with George Grinnell's approval, finally offered him the job.

Jones's initial task involved building a corral to contain the new herd. He chose a site in Mammoth near Park Headquarters, which not only allowed him to keep a close eye on the animals but also provided viewing opportunities for park visitors.

The second step was to buy the new bison. Superintendent Pitcher's letters succeeded in locating eighteen purebred bison cows for sale from the Michel Pablo-Charles Allard herd in Montana's Flathead Valley. The Allard herd began with the purchase of thirteen stray bison from a Pend d'Oreille man named Samuel Walking Coyote in 1884.[14] (Ironically, Allard later enlarged his herd in 1893 with twenty-six bison from Jones's failed Kansas operation, a sign of their scarcity.) In addition to those from Allard, Jones acquired three bison bulls from Charles Goodnight's ranch in Texas, bringing the total head count to twenty-one.

So far, everything seemed to be going smoothly. But the third and final step required the capture of several young bison from the park's wild herd to ensure genetic continuity in the captive herd. To carry out this task, Pitcher placed Jones in charge of a group of army scouts. And at this point, things began to fall apart for Jones.

Despite his skill as a hunter (which he regularly employed to rid the park of mountain lions) and self-proclaimed expertise on bison conservation, Jones struck everyone in the park as gruff, contentious, and generally unlikeable. A teetotaler with a tendency toward bluntness, Jones drew the ire of the scouts under his charge, whom he frequently reported for laziness, drinking, or lack of discipline. In time, he earned the contempt not only of army regulars but also of park workers, tourists, and Superintendent Pitcher himself.

Beyond his brusque countenance, Jones also engaged in a number of practices that raised questions about his competence and decency. His tendency to "punish" black bears for stealing food by snaring them, tying them to a tree, and beating them with a switch shocked and angered tourists and concessionaries alike.[15] Then, in 1903, Jones wildly overstepped his bounds when he invited himself to join President Roosevelt's party. With the president clearly annoyed by Jones (and the hunting hounds Jones brought in tow), Superintendent Pitcher quickly stepped in and ordered the interloper to leave.

As complaints against the gamekeeper piled up, Jones countered by sending letters to the interior secretary criticizing Major Pitcher. The situation quickly grew untenable and, in September 1905, Jones offered his resignation.[16] Though Jones later claimed credit for "saving" Yellowstone's bison herd, his contributions had very little to do with the final outcome.

By 1907, realizing that the domesticated herd at Mammoth had outgrown the corral, managers moved them to a new location on Rose Creek in the Lamar River Valley, later known as the Lamar Buffalo Ranch.[17] That same year, Pitcher shut down Eli Waters's zoo on Dot Island, citing horrific living conditions for the animals. After setting loose the sickly bison and elk, Pitcher barred Waters from the park.

Over the next few years, supplemental feeding at the Lamar Ranch allowed the bison herd to expand rapidly. But all the while, Yellowstone's wild herd slowly and steadily rebounded on its own. It seems that finally bringing an end to poaching made all the difference. While the introduction of bison from outside the park undoubtedly contributed to the genetic diversity of the Yellowstone herd, in terms of sheer population growth, the breeding program was never needed.[18] In fact, in the long run, the program did much more harm than good.

* * *

Of course, bison were not the only species in need of saving. A major rationale for predator eradication had to do with the perceived threat to other game species. However, in contrast to Yellowstone's bison, which were in fact on the verge of extinction based on collected data, early superintendents knew very little about the populations of elk, deer, and pronghorn. But lack of hard numbers didn't stop them from viewing these animals through the same lens.

As early as 1899, Superintendent Boutelle grew anxious over the perceived loss of pronghorn that congregated each winter at the park entrance near Gardiner. At his urging, Montana and Wyoming issued bans on pronghorn hunting just beyond park borders. Then, after completion of the Roosevelt Arch in 1903, Superintendent Pitcher constructed a fence to keep pronghorn and other game from leaving. Of course, the animals were only crossing the park boundary to find food, so keeping them hemmed in meant providing the necessary forage. By planting and irrigating the fifty-acre field at the northern entrance, managers produced between 100 and 200 tons of alfalfa each year for the pronghorn, deer, and bighorn sheep in the area.[19]

These actions produced their intended effects and then some. In 1903, prior to fence construction and hay cultivation, park managers estimated a winter pronghorn population of approximately 1,000 head. By 1905, that number rose to 1,500.[20] But without any means of keeping the populations in check through hunting (now banned) or predators (now eradicated), managers created a new problem: overpopulation.

The same logic—and potential problem—carried over to elk management. But whereas Yellowstone's populations of mule deer, whitetailed deer, bighorn sheep, and moose had previously each numbered in the hundreds and pronghorn ranged in the low thousands, estimates for elk reached into the tens of thousands. Divided geographically into two herds—a northern herd centered on the Lamar Valley and a southern herd that wintered near Jackson Hole—the population stood several orders of magnitude higher than any other game species in the park.

Nonetheless, managers remained convinced that elk were at risk. This deeply held view likely emanated from influential accounts written in the 1870s, some authored by George Grinnell, which documented the relentless slaughter of elk by commercial hunters.[21] As those hunters had harvested only tongues and hides, carcasses were left to rot, offering grisly images reproduced in newspapers and magazines. Another rationale may have been confusion over the animals' seasonal migrations, which dramatically altered population counts depending on the time of year.

Regardless, park managers launched feeding programs for elk alongside those for bison and pronghorn. Hay grown for bison and cattle at the Lamar Ranch was made available to elk and other ungulates. In the winter of 1910–1911, elk numbers grew so much that the animals spilled out of the park onto adjacent private ranchlands, destroying crops and consuming forage meant for domestic livestock. In response, Montana and Wyoming extended game-preserve buffer zones next to the park boundary. But the elk population continued to grow.

By 1912, estimates of their numbers exceeded 50,000 head.[22] That same year, down in Jackson Hole, Congress established the National Elk Refuge to provide winter habitat for the southern herd. Given the extreme cold that first winter, refuge mangers decided to import hay to feed the elk. Then, despite a return to normal conditions the following winter, managers opted to feed them again. Supplemental feeding soon became standard practice and would continue for the next century.

To early managers, these practices appeared to be extremely successful. They wanted to increase the populations of some species and decrease others, and they did just that. But in the process, they also created a series of long-lasting ecological imbalances.

The combined effects of enforcing hunting bans, eradicating predators, and adopting wildlife feeding programs all set the stage for an overpopulation crisis. Although park managers regularly captured and sold Yellowstone wildlife specimens to zoos around the country, that number barely made a dent in population totals.

In ecological terms, the problem was one of positive feedback: the more food managers provided, the larger the elk population grew, further increasing the demand for food, and so on. There could only be one ending to this story: a population crash. Eventually, the number of elk would surpass habitat capacity regardless of supplemental feeding, leading to disease and starvation. And sure enough, a heavy winter in 1916–1917 caused the deaths of thousands of Yellowstone elk. Ironically, the event led to calls for even more supplemental feeding. In fact, it would be decades before scientifically driven wildlife management would arrive in the park.

* * *

Beyond all of these concerns, Superintendent Pitcher had one more major wildlife problem to grapple with during his tenure. It concerned the most complicated and misunderstood creature in the entire park: the Yellowstone bear.

Bears did not fit neatly into typical nineteenth-century classifications of animals as good or bad. They could, in fact, inhabit multiple roles at once: both frightening and cuddly, threatening and comforting, predator and scavenger. The same creature might be a violent consumer of red flesh, a skilled angler, and a quiet connoisseur of berries, pine nuts, and herbs of the forest. Such muddled perceptions gained influence through works like Ernest Thompson Seton's sentimental and heavily anthropomorphized life stories of wild animals, including Yellowstone bears. Understandings were further complicated with the 1902 emergence of the "Teddy Bear," a stuffed animal marketed in the wake of a famous hunting trip, during which President Roosevelt refused to shoot a bear that had been tied to a tree in order to ensure a successful "hunt."

Despite all of this confusion, in Yellowstone, it was still important to distinguish between the two species of bears that called the park home: the smaller, more numerous, and less aggressive (but still potentially dangerous) black bear, and the larger, more elusive (and much more dangerous) brown bear or grizzly.

Both species would show up at park hotels to feed on garbage. What began in the 1880s as a nightly gathering of bears rummaging through garbage pits transformed into a full-fledged tourist attraction by the next decade. Starting at the Fountain Hotel, concessionaires offered visitors the chance to see bears up close during so-called "feeding shows." Within a few years, all of the park hotels engaged in this after-dinner activity, with some even providing benches for guests and stages upon which bears could consume the evening's food waste.

These feedings may not have impacted bear populations in any significant way, but they did serve to erode the animals' natural fear of humans. While grizzlies generally appeared only during the evening shows, black bears started searching for human food at other times and places, breaking into storehouses, wagons, and, most worryingly, visitor campsites. Canvas tents were no match for a bear's powerful claws.

For Superintendent Pitcher, the bears presented a new and unexpected quandary. In 1902, he sent circulars to all hotels and camps warning guests to neither feed nor molest the bears. Nonetheless, later that summer, a bear injured a man from Michigan at one of the "shows," leading Pitcher to erect fences around all garbage-feeding sites and to modify the park's formal regulations. In the 1903 season, for the first time ever, Yellowstone's official rules included the mandate "Do not feed the bears."

But as the nightly garbage feedings evolved into a major attraction, hotel managers continued the practice. For many tourists, Yellowstone's no-feeding regulation appeared contradictory, especially considering the park's efforts to feed bison, elk, and other large game.

Once more, a new ecological problem was in the making. As bears became increasingly dependent on human food and more and more visitors demanded an opportunity to observe them, managers worried that stopping the shows would not only hurt park visitation but harm the bear population too. On the other hand, year after year, the number of visitors injured by bears rose steadily. Without a clear solution, the potential for crisis continued to build.

* * *

Several years later, in 1917, one of the most profound and persistent ecological problems caused by well-meaning park managers finally appeared. It stemmed not from the feeding of bears or elk, nor from the introduction of non-native fish. Rather, it emanated from the captive-bison breeding program.

On an early spring day, out on the Lamar Buffalo Ranch, several park employees walked down to check on the captive herd for the morning feeding. Moving through the crowded corrals, they were surprised to find two aborted bison calves lying dead on the frozen ground. Further inspection revealed the cause of death as brucellosis, an infectious and potentially deadly bovine disease that can cause abortions in bison and cattle.

In time, it would be confirmed that the disease originated in domestic cattle brought into Yellowstone to supply milk and beef to Harry Child's hotel restaurants.[23] Since 1907, these cattle had been kept together with the captive bison at Lamar Ranch for ease of management. But now, brucellosis had taken root in the bison herd. This discovery would eventually redefine bison conservation in Yellowstone National Park and set off a series of debates that would reverberate across the northern Rockies for the next century and beyond.

The Ranger

(1912–1919)

ON JUNE 28, 1919, WITH THE APPOINTMENT OF TWENTY-nine-year-old Horace Albright as superintendent, the National Park Service finally arrived in Yellowstone. After more than three decades of military stewardship, Albright's presence signaled a new era in park management. But this future of promise and possibility only came about after a series of crises brought Yellowstone dangerously close to the breaking point.

After Major Pitcher's departure in 1907, two issues arose that challenged some of the fundamental assumptions underlying the national park idea. The first was the arrival of the automobile. Since its initial (unofficial) appearance in the park in 1902, the newfangled contraptions had grown steadily in popularity across the country. Like the national bicycle craze of the 1890s, auto enthusiasts formed organizations to lobby for roadway access, roadbed improvements, and the expansion of the nation's road system. Meanwhile, Henry Ford's production-line innovations and savvy pricing strategies opened the way for middle-class car ownership.

In Yellowstone, the advent of cars threatened to upset the economic model that had dominated for decades. From the very beginning, the park depended on the railroad industry—not only for its congressional creation but for bringing in visitors, constructing hotels, and providing general services. All of it hinged on their continued political and financial investment. Clientele on packaged tours made the opulence of the

Old Faithful Inn and Lake Hotel possible. But if the bulk of tourists began arriving by car—coming and going at any time, camping anywhere they pleased—what might it do to the visitor experience, the concessionaire's profits, and the park itself? The official rules banned cars on the assumption they would spook horses and endanger guests, but auto clubs applied mounting pressure to let them in.

The second major issue occurred in 1914 with the outbreak of the Great War. The event amplified the military's discontent with its stewardship duties in the national parks, which did little to provide troops with the skills and training they needed for combat. Accordingly, the War Department made repeated requests of the Interior Department to take back responsibility for park management. But without congressional funding for staffing, the interior secretary had no interest in such a deal.

Over the next few years, the status quo held, but these pressing issues refused to go away. Alongside preexisting tensions over wildlife populations and visitor conflicts with bears, conditions in Yellowstone were ripe for fundamental change. Questions over who should manage the park led to larger debates over Yellowstone's purpose, including which members of society it was actually meant to serve.

Of course, change of such magnitude required a catalyst, an initial spark that might ignite the evolution. For Yellowstone, two such sparks would present themselves almost simultaneously, but in two very different and unlikely places: one from a retired businessman's unsatisfactory visit to Yosemite National Park, and the other from a quiet conversation on a college campus in Berkeley, California.[1]

* * *

In 1912, Horace Albright graduated with a degree in economics from the University of California, Berkeley. Lanky and bookish, Albright's plan to pursue a law degree was interrupted when one of his professors, William Colby, called the young graduate into his office. A member of the Sierra Club and well-connected in local politics, Colby maintained close ties to Franklin Lane, the former San Francisco city attorney, who now served as President Woodrow Wilson's secretary of the interior. In need of able staff members, Lane asked Colby to send him some vetted candidates. Confident that the young man before him possessed the necessary skills, Colby offered Albright a job on the spot to serve as one of Lane's assistants in Washington, D.C.

Albright was hesitant at first due to the great distance from his California home. But he ultimately accepted the offer and, in so doing, found the courage to finally call on a sharp-witted coed he had met at Berkeley named Grace Noble. Their first date launched a three-year written correspondence that would lead to a sixty-five-year marriage. But the next morning, with his head and heart swirling, Albright could only focus on the immediate future. Gazing out the window of a transcontinental train car, he wondered what might await him in the nation's capital.

Over the next three years, Albright spent his days as an assistant to Sectary Lane and his evenings taking law classes at Georgetown University. In 1914, he completed his law degree and in 1915, married Grace, who moved out to join him in Washington. That same year, Albright also started a new job, working for the recently appointed assistant secretary of national parks, Stephen Mather.

* * *

Mather made his fortune in the borax-soap business, where he coined the famous advertising slogan "20 Mule Team Borax." Standing over six feet tall with prematurely gray hair and striking blue eyes, Mather was a man of wealth, confidence, and energy. But he was also prone to bouts of anxiety and depression that could leave him incapacitated. While still in his mid-forties, the increasing recurrence of these episodes pushed him toward an early retirement.

No longer burdened by financial dealings, Mather gave more time to philanthropic pursuits. To soothe his frayed nerves, he turned to nature, becoming an enthusiastic visitor of national parks. He joined the Sierra Club in 1904 and began climbing mountains. A memorable encounter with John Muir in 1912 affirmed Mather's environmental convictions and led to his involvement in the campaign to save Yosemite's Hetch Hetchy Valley from dam construction.[2]

Sometime later, after a visit to Yosemite, Mather was so upset at the poor state of park accommodations that he wrote a scathing letter of complaint to Interior Secretary Lane. In response, Lane invited Mather—a fellow Berkeley alum—to come out to D.C. and run the fledgling system of national parks. Mather accepted the offer on the condition that he commit for only one year and take no salary. Upon his arrival in Washington, Lane appointed young Albright as Mather's new assistant.

The two men hit it off immediately. Like Mather, Albright was fascinated by the idea of environmental conservation, albeit for different reasons. Born and raised in the town of Bishop, California, on the dry eastern slopes of the Sierra Nevada, Albright watched as plans were made in 1905 to drain the water away from his beloved Owens Valley to the distant city of Los Angeles. In 1913, the City of Angels quite literally began to suck the life out of the arid eastern foothills, crippling the local agricultural economy. Albright saw firsthand the damage that unchecked development could do, not only to nature but to the families and communities that relied on the land for their well-being.

As a team, Albright and Mather complemented each other exceedingly well, though in a way that funneled most of the administrative work to the younger man. A charismatic, persuasive speaker, Mather focused on big-picture public relations. He worked tirelessly to convince potential donors, politicians, and other people of influence to support national parks. Albright, in contrast, excelled at bureaucratic and political machinations. He spent most of his time in meetings with politicians and administrative officials, grappling with the minutiae of behind-the-scenes policymaking. The blend of their distinctive skill sets produced a stream of impressive results that, in time, would alter the course of environmental conservation history in the United States.

* * *

When Mather first came to Washington, he had three major goals: to establish a National Park Service, increase park visitation, and expand the system. Like John Muir, Mather understood that in order for the system to survive, the parks needed friends.

Creating a new, dedicated federal agency would not only strengthen park protection but also improve visitor experiences. Mather believed these outcomes would lead to an increase in tourism, generating public support for creating even more parks. And if the system could become truly national in scope, the constituency for national parks would grow accordingly, incentivizing Congress to fund further improvements.

The idea of establishing a National Park Service stretched back at least to 1910, with a recommendation included in the Interior Department's annual report.[3] In 1912, President Taft declared support for the idea as well, but subsequent legislation died in Congress. Opposition came from logging, mining, and ranching interests; the USDA Forest Service (which viewed a new agency as a potential rival); and those concerned with fiscal expenditures. Nonetheless, the interior secretary established a special assistant position responsible for national parks, a role eventually filled by Stephen Mather.

Then, in 1915, the political landscape changed considerably. With the world at war and military leaders adamant that they be released from park-stewardship duties, Congress looked more favorably upon a National Park Service bill. To reinvigorate the campaign, Mather built a powerful coalition of supporters among leaders of industry, politics, and civic organizations.

Working with his old friend Robert Sterling Yard, former editor of *Century Magazine*, Mather produced the *National Parks Portfolio*, a color publication espousing the wonders of the national park system as part of the railroad industry's ongoing See America First campaign. Funded personally by Mather and the sponsorship of several railroad companies, the *National Parks Portfolio* was a masterpiece of marketing. Mather sent one to every member of Congress and distributed an additional 250,000 copies to the general public through the General Federation of Women's Clubs, the National Civic Association, and the Sierra Club—all free of charge.

As Representative William Kent of California and Senator Reed Smoot of Utah introduced a new National Park Service bill to Congress, Mather and Albright embarked on a cross-country tour. From Mesa Verde to Glacier and from Yellowstone to Yosemite, they assessed current park conditions and drew up a list of potential sites for new ones. In Colorado, they drove up to Estes Park for the opening ceremony of Rocky Mountain National Park, signed into law that January by President Wilson. And in San Francisco, they held a conference for all national park supervisors and concessionaires.

Later, Albright returned to D.C. to focus on the grinding work of pushing park-service legislation through Congress, while Mather stayed out West to continue his remarkably fruitful lobbying activities. In the course of one afternoon luncheon in San Francisco, Mather raised enough money to purchase outright the Tioga-entrance road into Yosemite. But he enjoyed even greater success from his so-called mountain parties, hiking and camping expeditions that offered a chance to strategize with influential park supporters, including George Lorimer of the *Saturday Evening Post* and Gilbert Grosvenor of the National Geographic Society. As a result, Grosvenor agreed to devote a special issue of *National Geographic* to the parks. Mather made certain the issue's publication would coincide with the congressional debate on the National Park Service bill.

* * *

Amid all of this activity, Mather also found time to address the goal of expanding visitor access. After meeting with Harry Child and other concessionaires in Yellowstone, Mather realized that despite the concerns of the railroad industry, automobiles represented the future of park tourism. By allowing greater numbers of people to visit the park, automobile access would help expand public support and provide additional revenue to help pay for the new Park Service agency. Consequently, Mather issued an order allowing motor vehicles into Yellowstone on a trial basis beginning August 1, 1915.

Given that park transportation and tour companies still relied exclusively on horse-drawn coaches, Mather imposed stringent regulations on auto use to reduce conflicts with horses. Car owners had to purchase a special permit and adhere to strict speed limits and rules of conduct. After that first season, Mather decided to convert all in-park services to automobiles starting in 1917, giving Harry Child time to replace his horses and carriages with a fleet of touring cars. Meanwhile, park managers moved to improve roads and close down outmoded camps and lunch-station facilities. As autos could travel farther and faster than horses, visitors no longer needed so many places to stop and rest between sights.

For concessionaires, the economic cost of this transition was enormous. Ironically, Harry Child, who owned the Yellowstone Transportation Company, could only afford such a large-scale purchase of automobiles by taking additional loans from the railroad companies. The railroads complied, as the increased visitation might benefit their hotel businesses, but in so doing, they also helped seal their own fate.

Realizing the potential hit to concessionaires' businesses, Mather took steps to revise park leases to incentivize investment and ensure profitable returns. He did so by offering long-term contracts under monopoly conditions, not only in Yellowstone but in all national parks. In this way, Harry Child found himself the sole leaseholder of all of Yellowstone's hotels and transportation services. In contrast, F. Jay Haynes was reduced to his photography businesses (opting out of an offer as a minority investor in automobile tourism). Meanwhile, A. W. Miles took control of all permanent camping businesses by combining the Wiley Camping Company and the Shaw and Power Camping Company under a single lease. At this time, Mather also authorized another new element in national park concessions: auto service stations.

Notably, Mather's changes did not rule out rail transport to Yellowstone. In fact, until 1919, most visitors continued to arrive by train, as Mather actively promoted the railroads' See America First campaign. But at the same time, he also encouraged travel by personal automobile, including promotion of the Park-to-Park Highway—an initiative that linked national parks via a common road system.

* * *

In summer 1916, as Washington, D.C., sweltered in heat and humidity, Mather and Albright watched their hard work pay off. The first victory involved park expansion. On July 8, President Wilson signed an executive order creating the Sieur de Monts National Monument, precursor to Acadia National Park in Maine, which would become the first national park in the eastern United States. Then, in early August, the president signed laws establishing Hawaii National Park and Lassen

Volcano National Park in Oregon.[4] But the crowning achievement that summer concerned the new Park Service agency bill.

In the final stages of congressional debate, the most robust opposition emerged from the Forest Service, which argued that it already managed public lands for conservation purposes and could just as easily take over the parks. Mather countered that the two differed in purpose: national forests allowed and, in fact, prioritized activities like logging, mining, and grazing, while national parks proposed a focus on nature preservation and visitor recreation. In the end, Mather's arguments won out, and on August 25, 1916, President Wilson signed the National Park Service Act into law.

* * *

The act not only created the National Park Service, it also defined the common purpose of the parks system as a whole. With words masterfully crafted by Frederick Law Olmsted Jr., the law mandated that national parks must "conserve the scenery and the natural and historic objects and the wildlife therein" and "provide for the enjoyment of the same in such manner and by such means as will leave them unimpaired for the enjoyment of future generations."

Much has been written about the apparent contradiction in the statement above. In hindsight at least, the idea of preserving nature in its "unimpaired form" while simultaneously promoting its "enjoyment" via human recreation seems an all but impossible task. Tensions between environmental protection and tourism lie at the core of the most persistent conflicts in Yellowstone—from wolf restoration to bison and bear management. Indeed, this paradox represents a powerful legacy of the Park Service Act. But in 1916, the idea that nature needed to be used in order to be saved lay at the heart of Mather's and Albright's strategy.

In Yellowstone, passage of the Park Service Act did not lead to an immediate change in management. Fearing economic losses from the closing of nearby military installations, local residents of Bozeman, Gardiner, and Livingston prodded Montana's congressional delegation to fight back. The politicians successfully blocked the Park Service funding in Congress long enough to force a skeleton crew of army troops back to manage Yellowstone for two more seasons. However, in 1919, funding was finally restored and the Park Service assumed full control.

Given the many years of military stewardship in the parks, it is not surprising that the army left a mark on the new agency. One explicit expression can be seen in the styling of Park Service uniforms, which to this day echo U.S. Cavalry attire from the 1910s. But the influence runs deeper. The first set of Park Service rangers included a number of recruits drawn from the soldiers and civilian scouts of Fort Yellowstone. These select few, who showed special interest in, and aptitude for, park duty, stayed on to form the core of Yellowstone's new ranger service, with Albright at the helm.

* * *

With the National Park Service now in place, Mather and Albright pressed on with their other goals. High on their list for 1917 were two bills slated for Congress. One would establish McKinley National Park in Alaska (later renamed Denali), and the other would expand Yellowstone to encompass the Grand Teton Range and other lands to the south and east.

The Yellowstone expansion bill derived from the western trip taken by Mather and Albright in 1915. During their visit to Yellowstone, the two decided to drive south to Shoshone Point for a first glimpse of the Tetons. What they saw in the far distance inspired a second trip down into Jackson Hole the following year for a full view of the mountains.

In July 1916, they drove out of Yellowstone's southern entrance to the Snake River Bridge along the eastern side of Jackson Lake. As the Teton Range slowly rose up on the horizon, the two men experienced for the first time the full expanse of this magnificent panorama. Awestruck, Mather and Albright heartily agreed that the area must be included as part of Yellowstone National Park. According to Albright, "It left us all speechless . . . I had never been more thrilled and excited. There was something about this awesome Rocky Mountain area, something about the jagged Tetons rising abruptly from this valley that struck a deep chord in my mind and spirit. All I could think of was, 'Now this is a national park!'"[5]

It was time to go to work.

* * *

The idea of an expanded Yellowstone National Park, insofar as it implies the goals of aligning the political boundaries with ecological ones, sounds much like the contemporary concept of the Greater Yellowstone Ecosystem. This concept, which gained prominence in the 1980s and 1990s, aimed to collectively manage a vast 19-to-22-million-acre area with Yellowstone at its core, encompassing the full habitat of the region's diverse flora and fauna.[6] But this idea, as it turns out, has a long history, stretching back at least as far as General Sheridan's 1882 War Department report, which called for expanding the park's boundaries to match the migratory range of bison and elk.[7]

Legislative efforts by Senator George Vest to implement Sheridan's vision in the 1880s failed to materialize. However, in 1891, an alternative strategy emerged with a special amendment in the General Revision Act, a law designed to revise and repeal several nineteenth-century land laws. Though not directly related to the act's primary purpose, the amendment, quietly promoted by George Grinnell and William Phillips, allowed presidents to create national timber reserves by executive order. As precursors to national forests, the reserves still allowed for logging, livestock grazing, and mining, but they also restricted homesteading, keeping the land under government management for the public good.

On March 30, President Benjamin Harrison invoked this new power for the first time to establish the Yellowstone Timberland Reserve. Significantly, the boundaries of the new 1.2 million–acre reserve matched precisely the southern and eastern Yellowstone expansions recommended by General Sheridan.

While many people, including Gifford Pinchot, worked for years promoting a system of national forests, the effort to expand Yellowstone National Park provided a critical turning point in this campaign. Not only did the Yellowstone ecosystem become the site of the nation's very first national forest reserve, but the process provided the legal means for the creation of an entire national forest *system*. In time, this system would comprise over 193 million acres nationwide, over twice the size of the national park system. Three presidents—Harrison, Cleveland, and Roosevelt—would use executive power to set aside nearly two-thirds of this land before ending the practice in 1907. In Yellowstone, this translated into roughly 6.5 million acres of protected forest lands, reorganized in 1908 into seven different national forests surrounding the Park.[8]

In 1912, another piece of the Greater Yellowstone puzzle was put into place when Congress formed the National Elk Refuge to protect the southern herd's winter feeding grounds. Beginning with 1,200 acres, the refuge would eventually grow to 24,700 acres and be managed by the U.S. Fish and Wildlife Service.

In sum, by the early 1900s, much of the ecosystem to the south and east of Yellowstone was protected as either national forest land or wildlife refuge. After 1905, the forests came under the supervision of the new U.S. Forest Service. Meanwhile, the grasslands and foothills stretching north and west from the town of Jackson remained as either private property (generally livestock operations or dude ranches), state-owned land, or public domain open for homesteading or grazing.

For Horace Albright, the new national forest and wildlife refuge designations were a start, but they were not nearly enough to ensure the protection of what he viewed as the crown jewel of the Greater Yellowstone region: the magnificent Grand Teton Range. The only meaningful solution was to include it within an expanded Yellowstone National Park.

* * *

At least initially, extending Yellowstone's borders seemed like it would be quick and easy. In October 1917, Interior Secretary Lane announced his support for the idea to local reporters in Montana and Wyoming. Then, in the December 1 issue of the *Saturday Evening Post*, Emerson Hough introduced the phrase "Greater Yellowstone" to a national audience in an article extolling the notion of park expansion.

Eager to bring more attention and tourism dollars to their state, Wyoming's governor and congressional delegation pledged their full support. So did cattle ranchers, once assured that their public-land grazing rights would be protected. Since the vast majority of the land in question was already set aside as forest reserves and much of the remainder lay in the public domain, the deal required no congressional funding for land purchases. Even the Forest Service, which stood to lose the most in terms of acreage, was firmly on board, as evidenced by a memorandum of support from chief forester Henry Graves.

Working closely with Albright and Mather, Wyoming representative Frank Mondell introduced a bill to Congress in April 1918. After a number of hearings, he submitted a revised version in December that called for extending the boundaries of Yellowstone National Park to include the Teton Range, Jackson Lake, and the series of lakes along the eastern foothills. It also encompassed the region to the southeast of the park known as the Thoroughfare, which contained the headwaters of the Yellowstone River and Two Ocean Pass.

In total, the bill expanded Yellowstone National Park by 38 percent, or 809,600 acres. Of these, 1,638 acres (0.2 percent) comprised state-owned lands, and 6,232 acres (0.8 percent) remained privately owned. Significantly, the bill allowed all existing livestock grazing to continue, and it fully protected the rights of private landowners within park boundaries.

In February 1919, the bill passed easily through the House of Representatives but was delayed by the Senate's full legislative calendar. The only way to bump it up for a vote during the current congressional session was through unanimous consent. But Idaho senator John Nugent refused to allow a vote, citing concerns over the potential loss of grazing rights if the land changed hands from the U.S. Forest Service to the National Park Service. Consequently, the bill was deferred to the next congressional session.

Thinking this was just a technical delay, everyone went home fully expecting to complete the business during the next session. Little did they know that with this deferral, the window of opportunity for establishing a Greater Yellowstone had in fact slammed shut.

Sometimes it is the small, barely noticed actions that can render the greatest effects; sometimes, they can even alter the course of history. Such was the case with the amendment quietly added to the General Revisions Act of 1891 that allowed for the creation of the national forest system. And such was the case in the Senate's deliberations in February 1919.

Ironically, Nugent's objection wasn't even based on the facts. Had the senator read the bill, he would have seen that it allowed for the continuation of existing grazing rights, and perhaps history would have been different. Instead, the stage was set for one of the great political battles of the era: a thirty-year fight that would kick off a war of ideas that rages on to this day.

* * *

Within months of the bill's deferral in the Senate, the first cracks began to appear in Yellowstone's pro-expansion coalition. It began with the local livestock industry. Cattlemen decided to pull their support, not because of any specific provisions but due to concerns over the park idea in general, which seemed unfavorable toward grazing. Stock growers were soon joined by a second group, Jackson Hole dude ranchers, who began to wonder if they would lose tourism business to monopolies run by park-based concessionaires.

A glance northward to Yellowstone National Park suggested such concerns were not unfounded. Although the 1916 National Park Service Act explicitly allowed grazing in all parks, Yellowstone remained an exception. Moreover, entrepreneurs like Harry Child maintained a firm monopolizing grip on Yellowstone's hotels and tour operations. What was to keep the same arrangements from extending south if the Yellowstone expansion bill passed?

Meanwhile, in preparation for the bill's expected passage, President Wilson signed an executive order setting aside all public land in the proposed expansion area from homesteading, logging, or mining. It also gave the Park Service veto power over any potential land uses. As most of this land consisted of national forests, it angered local Forest Service officials to no end. They had always been against the idea of giving so much national forest land to a rival agency, and this latest move was a bridge too far. Forest rangers began to spread word among ranchers and residents that Park Service control would bring an end to all economic activity on the land. In fact, during the interim, local rangers actually reduced the number of cattle allowed to graze in the expansion area, implying it was somehow linked to the Yellowstone bill.[9]

In May 1919, when Congress reconvened and Wyoming representative Frank Mondell reintroduced the Yellowstone expansion bill, he had no idea that the local political landscape had shifted so dramatically. And neither did Horace Albright.

* * *

In June, Albright assumed his new role as superintendent of Yellowstone. Though busy with the summer season, he happily accepted an invitation to speak about the expansion bill at a town hall–style meeting planned for August in Jackson. He assumed it would be an opportunity to extol the virtues of park expansion. He couldn't have been more wrong.

Instead of a friendly audience, Albright faced a room filled with angry, indignant locals, led by dude rancher and nationally known writer Struthers Burt. Educated and articulate, Burt was a formidable opponent. Albright found himself repeatedly criticized, accused, and shouted down by upset residents. Park expansion, they argued, was nothing more than a "land grab" by the federal government. "What a mistake!" Albright later recounted. "There was hardly a person in the meeting who favored the park. They let me know in no uncertain terms that they were vehemently opposed to hordes of tourists cluttering up their area."[10]

In the meantime, the Wyoming state legislature issued a unanimous statement to Congress declaring its opposition to the park expansion bill. In response, an embarrassed Congressman Mondell quickly retracted his bill from committee. In just a matter of months, from February to August 1919, the prospects of expanding Yellowstone National Park had gone from a "sure thing" to a political dud.

But just when the dream of a Greater Yellowstone appeared dead, the political landscape began to shift once more. The change emerged from a most unlikely source: the leading voice of the opposition.

High Noon in Jackson

(1923–1950)

ON JULY 13, 1926, HORACE ALBRIGHT SQUINTED THROUGH the windshield of his eight-passenger Lincoln touring car as the midmorning sun flickered between the pines.[1] Taking a deep breath, he pressed down on the accelerator and clenched the wheel. He leaned into the curves and flew over the bumps, all the while praying to avoid any errant elk or bison on the roadway. Though exhausted, Albright felt a twinge of nervousness at the prospect of his next task: welcoming a very important person at the Union Pacific train station. And he could not afford to be late.

Now thirty-six, Albright was in his seventh year as superintendent of Yellowstone and showed no signs of slowing down. In addition to that leadership role, Albright retained his position as assistant director of the entire National Park Service, making him responsible for all national parks in the western United States. This meant he not only managed day-to-day operations in Yellowstone but traveled frequently to Washington, D.C., and across the West, inspecting parks, approving major managerial decisions, and exploring potential additions to the system. Beyond that, Albright's boss, Stephen Mather, still suffered from intermittent bouts of depression that left him incapacitated. On such occasions, Albright quietly assumed responsibility for the entire system for weeks, even months, at a time.

Nonetheless, with his characteristic energy, Albright embraced the challenge of juggling a daily schedule brimming with deadlines and appointments. The previous evening, he addressed a group of Sierra Club members at a late-night campfire on Nez Perce Creek. This morning he had risen at 4:30 a.m. to share breakfast with his old college professor, William Colby, who was part of that group. Afterward, he rushed down to Old Faithful to meet the assistant secretary of agriculture about a proposed road from Cooke City to Red Lodge, Montana. And now, before the sun even reached midday, a groggy Albright raced along the road to his next engagement.[2]

But if Albright's exhaustion could be explained by his calendar, his nerves were a more complex matter. Since his early twenties, Albright regularly interacted with persons of great power, from senators to U.S. presidents, working to pass the laws that that not only created the Park Service but established new national parks across the country. Only three years earlier, he had given a personal tour of Yellowstone to President Warren Harding.

But the person Albright rushed to meet now wielded a unique kind of power. As the eldest son of arguably the wealthiest entrepreneur in history,[3] this individual was instrumental in the 1919 creation of Acadia National Park and had played key roles in protecting Mesa Verde, Yosemite, and Yellowstone. A committed supporter of the park idea, this person could operate beyond the limits of public office to render direct aid in times of need.

Pulling into the West Yellowstone station, Albright arrived just as the Union Pacific's Yellowstone Express chugged into view. With a squeal of its brakes, the train lurched to a final halt. Albright scanned the crowd of passengers on the platform. Moments later a short, bespectacled man emerged from a first-class coach, surrounded by a small entourage that included his wife and three young boys. Sighting Albright, the man's face lit into a warm smile.

The special visitor was John D. Rockefeller Jr. And on this day, Albright hoped he was the key to realizing the superintendent's long-held vision: the dream of a Greater Yellowstone.

* * *

During his tenure as superintendent, Albright was a catalyst for profound and long-lasting change in the park. One of the most dramatic examples concerned the growth of motorized tourism.

To better accommodate the needs of automobiles, Albright worked to improve Yellowstone's roads and constructed a series of gas stations and repair shops. He also introduced new midrange dining options, including cafeterias and lunch items sold in general stores. In an attempt to address drivers' tendencies to enter undeveloped areas (and promptly get stuck), Albright plotted out new car-friendly campgrounds. These not only reduced the need for park rangers to tow cars back to the roadway but also cut down on the environmental damage caused by unregulated camping.

Albright was also dedicated to developing the new national park ranger corps. He saw national parks as an opportunity for public education and believed rangers could do more than merely enforce the rules. They could also be guides and teachers. Park staff could offer nature walks, campfire talks, and wildlife auto-tours. In 1925, the Department of the Interior agreed and issued a memorandum equating education with recreation as part of the Park Service mandate. In one of his first official actions as superintendent, Albright appointed Milton Skinner to develop educational programs for Yellowstone. A few years later, Albright recruited Dorr Yeager from Yosemite to manage them.

At about the same time, Albright worked with Dr. Hermon Carey Bumpus of the American Association of Museums and architect Herbert Maier to design a series of roadside museums near the park's major sights.[4] Built in the rustic style, these characteristic log buildings set the standard for similar structures in other national parks. In Yellowstone, museums near Old Faithful and in Norris Geyer Basin focused on geothermal information. A third, in Madison Junction, offered park history, and a fourth museum near Fishing Bridge explained wildlife ecology around Yellowstone Lake.

Albright still quietly harbored ambitions of expanding Yellowstone National Park. But after the failure of congressional legislation in 1919 and the local backlash that came with it, he could no longer see a path forward.

Then, one day in 1923, hope unexpectedly arrived in the form of a letter. The sender was none other than Struthers Burt, once a leading opponent of the park expansion idea. But now, Burt was inviting Albright to a meeting in Jackson Hole to reconsider the matter. Hesitantly, Albright accepted, wondering what had led Burt to such a dramatic change of heart.

* * *

As it happened, after the park expansion bill was retracted back in 1919, local agricultural interests saw an opportunity to put the land to more productive uses. Between 1919 and 1921, the Wyoming state engineering office submitted a series of proposals to build irrigation dams on Jenny Lake, Leigh Lake, and others lining the Teton foothills.

The Forest Service consented to these plans. However, because of President Wilson's 1919 executive order, the National Park Service (meaning Albright) still held veto power over any proposed uses of land within the potential expansion area. When Albright rejected the dam proposals, arguing that dams were not consistent with national park standards, state engineers proposed projects farther east. Once again, the Forest Service consented, but Albright refused.

While Albright's actions antagonized farmers, the Forest Service, and Wyoming state officials, they had the unexpected effect of winning over local dude ranchers, whose main concern was preserving the wild and scenic character of the region. Albright's hard stance showed that the Park Service could be depended upon to defend natural areas against modern commercial development.[5]

All of this inspired Struthers Burt to organize a small gathering to discuss how the Jackson Hole valley might be saved from such forces. The meeting would be discreet, held at a cabin of a former East Coast socialite who had recently moved to Jackson Hole named Maud Noble.

* * *

On the evening of July 26, 1923, as the last rays of sun disappeared behind the Tetons, visitors began arriving at Noble's log cabin on the bank overlooking the Snake River. Noble greeted each guest, walked them inside to a seat near the fireplace, and offered a cup of tea. Led by Struthers Burt, the gathering included fellow dude rancher Horace Carncross, newspaperman Dick Winger, businessman Joe Jones, and rancher Jack Eynon, along with Albright and his assistant, Joe Joffe.[6]

Like her guests, Noble was passionate about the Jackson Hole landscape. Born into a wealthy Philadelphia family, she first visited the area in 1915. A single woman in her late forties, she spent the summer as a guest at Burt's Bar BC dude ranch and decided to stay on permanently. In 1916, she built a three-room cabin and began running a ferry business with her partner, Sydney Sandell. Because Noble also lived with him, the arrangement was quite scandalous for the time.[7] But true to her independent spirit, Noble never felt compelled to explain the nature of their relationship.

With everyone assembled, Burt laid out his vision for the valley— what he termed a "museum on the hoof" or later, simply, the "Jackson Hole Plan." Concerned with the threat of commercial development, not only in the mountains but also on the privately held land in the valley, Burt's plan called for a new form of conservation. In contrast to a national park, with all its restrictions, he preferred to allow residents to continue hunting, running cattle, and operating dude ranches, but in a landscape of unpaved roads, log-built structures, and native wildlife.[8]

Talk soon turned to how the vision might be realized. Could there be a way to purchase private land in the valley before it was bought by outsiders? Perhaps they could find a wealthy donor who could buy the land then transfer it to a conservation entity—possibly a federal agency—that could manage it as a "frontier landscape" or "recreational area"?

In Albright's mind, the National Park Service would be the perfect steward, even though the proposed "frontier" land uses did not align with current national park standards. Nonetheless, he remained silent, pleased that the group saw the Park Service as a potential partner.

As the flames diminished into glowing embers, the group finalized a plan of action. Dick Winger and Jack Eynon would travel to the East Coast in search of a donor willing to purchase private land for conservation purposes. Burt and Albright agreed to write letters of introduction and raised $2,000 for the trip. Weeks later, the two westerners returned from their journey empty-handed. The failed effort put the entire plan on hold. Albright, however, was not quite ready to give up.

Until the meeting at Noble's cabin, Albright had not considered the importance of the privately owned land to the Greater Yellowstone idea. This land contained not only sensitive winter habitat for elk and bison but also constituted the primary viewshed for the Teton Range. Filling it with unplanned development could jeopardize one of the most magnificent panoramas in North America.

But what if Albright took over the task of finding a wealthy donor? His boss, Stephen Mather, had worked with the Rockefeller family to purchase land that eventually became Acadia National Park in Maine. Perhaps Albright could do something similar in Jackson and, in the process, create a new kind of national park.

* * *

As luck would have it, later that same year, President Harding came to Yellowstone and requested a personalized tour. Here was an influential man indeed! By the end of the president's visit, Albright convinced him of the need to expand Yellowstone to encompass the Tetons and other areas to the south and east, including Jackson Hole. But it all became moot when, only one month later, President Harding died of a heart attack in a San Francisco hotel room.[9]

Though discouraged by the news, Albright didn't have long to wait for a second chance. In 1924, another important visitor arrived in the park. This man, referred to only as "Mr. Davison" to avoid attention, turned out to be John D. Rockefeller Jr., one of the wealthiest men in the world. Though Albright received orders from Mather to not pester Rockefeller with any financial requests, the trip allowed him to cultivate a friendship with the business magnate.[10]

The following year, the issue bubbled up once more. In response to growing disputes between the Forest Service and Park Service over land boundaries, President Coolidge appointed a "Coordinating Commission on National Parks and Forests." In Jackson Hole, the commission recommended turning all land in the proposed park expansion area back to the Forest Service except for roughly 100,000 acres surrounding the eastern side of the Teton Range. This land would become a new detached unit of Yellowstone National Park.

Soon, a bill to create the new Teton extension of Yellowstone appeared in Congress. During debate, Wyoming senator John Kendrick insisted that the Tetons be an independent national park rather than part of Yellowstone, and that it be called "Teton National Park *of Wyoming.*" However, realizing park expansion was still contentious in Wyoming, the senator asked to table it for another year.

Both Mather and Albright supported the new park bill, even though it represented only a small fraction of the area they wanted. However, with the legislative process on hold, Albright saw an opportunity to pursue a parallel, behind-the-scenes strategy. For the summer of 1926, it turned out that the Rockefellers planned a return to Yellowstone for a family vacation and asked Albright to organize a tour. If the right moment presented itself, Albright was ready to make the pitch for a rather audacious proposal: expanding Yellowstone National Park to encompass not only the Teton Range but the entirety of Jackson Hole itself.

* * *

Albright's tour for the Rockefellers began with a drive down to Jackson Lake, where they enjoyed a picnic at a spot known today as "lunch tree hill," located next to the modern-day Jackson Lake Lodge. From their shady vantage point, the party reveled in a panoramic view of the Tetons rising up across the lake. Standing against a sky of cobalt blue, the snow-encrusted peaks sparkled in the sun while a small group of moose grazed serenely in the foreground.

The next morning, the party continued south into Jackson Hole. But as they drove, they encountered a growing number of rundown buildings and other signs of ramshackle development: deserted buildings, empty billboards, abandoned gas stations. When they passed what looked to be a gaudy dancehall and saloon—and this during the era of prohibition—Abby Rockefeller could take no more. Turning to Albright, she implored if anything could be done "to prevent the desecration of this lovely country?"[11]

Albright replied that he could do nothing because most of what they had seen was on private land. And, he continued, it would likely get worse over time. As more people learned of the beauty of Jackson Hole, commercial development would only increase.

"Well, send me an estimate as to what it would take to buy the land and clear the junk out of this area," said Rockefeller. "And send me a map."[12]

Albright readily agreed. And with that, the party drove on to Struthers Burt's Bar BC Guest Ranch. The operation was both a working cattle ranch and a tourist destination. Rockefeller was intrigued to learn more about Burt's businesses and the valley itself. Burt wasted no time explaining the difficulties of agriculture and livestock production in Jackson Hole. With the long winters, high elevation, and rocky soils, conditions were not ideal. But the beautiful landscape of Jackson Hole? That was another matter entirely. It was perfectly suited for tourism as long as it could be preserved, possibly in the form of a national park.

With this plug for the Jackson Hole Plan, Burt waved goodbye to the Rockefeller party as it moved on to Henry Stewart's JY Dude Ranch for lunch. After enjoying the glorious view over Phelps Lake, they began the long drive back north, but Albright made one last stop. Pulling over beside an old wagon road, Albright led the Rockefellers on a short walk up a forested hill called Timbered Island to a place known as Hedrick's Point. Resting on fallen logs, the group was treated to a sublime view of not only the Tetons but the entire expanse of Jackson Hole.

As the slanting afternoon sun lit up the tranquil landscape, Albright laid out his grand vision: the dream of a Greater Yellowstone. With all the skill he could muster, Albright made the case for saving not only the Tetons (as per the bill in Congress) but the other mountainous areas south and east of Yellowstone (as per the original expansion plan), along with the remaining public and privately owned land in the valley.

When he was done, the Rockefellers said nothing as they turned to watch the last rays of sunlight disappear behind the jagged peaks. Worried that he'd overstepped his bounds, Albright escorted his guests back to the car in silence.[13]

* * *

Several months later, per Rockefeller's request, Albright arrived at the financier's cavernous New York City office with maps and cost estimates in hand. Clearing his throat, Albright proceeded to identify the privately owned parcels that might be purchased around Jackson Lake. They totaled about 14,000 acres at an estimated cost of nearly $400,000, a figure that Albright worried was asking too much.

Rockefeller's initial response seemed to confirm Albright's worst fears. Frowning at the maps and cost estimates, Rockefeller declared, "No, no, this isn't what I had in mind at all."[14]

Taken aback, Albright began to apologize that he must have misunderstood their discussion in Yellowstone in July. But then Rockefeller explained.

"You took us that afternoon to a hill where we looked out over the mountains and the whole valley . . . [Y]ou discussed an ideal project. I remember you used the word dream. *That's* the area for which I wanted you to get cost estimates. The family is only interested in an ideal project."

Albright protested, "Why, it might cost you as much as a million and a half or two million dollars to buy all that land."

"Well of course, you don't know yet what it would actually cost," replied Rockefeller. "But that is what I'm interested in. I'm only interested in the ideal proposition."[15]

Albright couldn't believe his ears. He had come to Rockefeller concerned about $400,000, and now he was leaving with orders to pursue a project costing potentially five times that much. He immediately sent word to Dick Winger to draft new maps and recalculate the figures.

Approximately one month later, Albright returned to New York with the updated information. Within days, Rockefeller gave approval to spend nearly $1.4 million to buy close to 115,000 acres. He ordered his assistant, Arthur Woods, to administer the project and made Albright lead consultant. In a letter to Woods, Rockefeller explained his purpose: "to buy the entire Jackson Hole Valley with a view to its being ultimately turned over to the Government for joint or partial operation by the Department of Parks and the Forestry Department."[16]

Keenly aware of the local political tensions, Albright recommended absolute secrecy, both to ensure land values didn't suddenly inflate due to Rockefeller's involvement and to avoid opposition over national park expansion. The best way forward was to establish a shell company to make the land purchases.

For help, Albright turned to an old college friend, Beverly Clendenin, a partner in a Salt Lake City law firm. In early 1927, they established the Snake River Land Company, incorporated in the state of Utah. For company president, they selected Vanderbilt Webb, a New York City attorney and associate of Arthur Woods. Clendenin's law partner, Harold Fabian, became vice president.

With these actions, Albright embarked on a potentially duplicitous path. On the public front, as Yellowstone superintendent and assistant director of the Park Service, Albright openly supported the Teton park bill working its way through Congress. But away from prying eyes, he oversaw a clandestine effort to create a Greater Yellowstone.

Albright had always excelled at working behind the scenes, but in this case, discretion meant engaging in various forms of deception. Secret land purchases were legal, of course, and not without precedent. Rockefeller had taken similar action to create Acadia National Park. But the intensity of opposition in Jackson and Wyoming raised the stakes considerably.

The obvious question was how long they could keep it all going. And what would happen if and when everything finally came to light?

* * *

After establishing the shell company, the next step was to hire a purchasing agent. They needed someone with local credentials but unassociated with Albright, Rockefeller, or pro–park expansion views. They settled on Robert Miller, president of Jackson State Bank, former supervisor of Teton National Forest, and a Jackson pioneer who had arrived in 1885. Most significantly, Miller was adamantly against Yellowstone's expansion and disliked Albright. No one would guess that selling land to Miller could benefit the National Park Service. But because of this, even more secrecy was required. Albright could not contact Miller to offer him the job, and Miller could never be told the truth about who owned the Snake River Land Company. Arranged through a third party, Miller took the position in June 1927 on a commission-based contract that offered a $15,000 bonus if he came in under budget.[17]

But within weeks, complications arose. To limit the amount of private land they would have to purchase, Rockefeller requested a presidential executive order that would close all remaining federal land in Jackson Hole to homesteading or mining claims. On July 7, 1927, President Coolidge agreed and signed the order.

Unfortunately, this executive order slammed like a trainwreck into ongoing negotiations to expand the National Elk Refuge, located just north of the town of Jackson. In April, President Coolidge had signed a similar order withdrawing lands adjacent to the refuge to prepare for a planned expansion. But that deal—struck between National Elk Commission chairman Charles Sheldon and the Wyoming congressional delegation—hinged on a promise that no additional land would be withdrawn from the public domain in Jackson Hole. The president's order on July 7 made Sheldon look like a liar to his Wyoming colleagues. Already, the first crack appeared in Albright's deception.

As Sheldon and other commission members complained to Washington, Albright and the Snake River Land Company realized they were in deep trouble. In October, they ordered Miller to stop making purchases while they decided on their next move. In December, company president Vanderbilt Webb met with Charles Sheldon and Wyoming political leaders to explain everything . . . almost. Webb described the land-purchase program but concealed Rockefeller's involvement and remained vague about the ultimate purpose, noting only that all land would be dedicated to "public use."

Amazingly, this argument worked and the president's order remained in place. But at what cost? Smoothing over the matter without coming clean only set up a future political fight, sowing seeds of distrust between the state of Wyoming on one side and Albright, Rockefeller, and the Park Service on the other.

* * *

In January 1929, Albright stepped down from his role as Yellowstone superintendent to succeed Stephen Mather as director of the National Park Service. Nonetheless, he remained closely involved in ongoing efforts to expand Yellowstone. In late winter, even as the land-purchasing scheme progressed, so too did the Teton bill in Congress. In February, President Coolidge signed the act establishing Grand Teton National

Park. And on March 1, he signed a law adjusting the border of Yellowstone National Park to better account for watershed boundaries in the northwestern and southeastern corners and along the park's eastern edge.[18]

For the vast majority of those involved, passage of these laws appeared to bring an end to the Greater Yellowstone debates. And they did so through compromise. Yes, Yellowstone expanded, but not nearly to the extent envisioned back in 1919. And the Tetons were now under Park Service protection, but as a separate, standalone park, rather than an extension of Yellowstone.

Only a handful of people knew the truth: in secret, efforts to expand Yellowstone were moving full steam ahead.

* * *

By the summer of 1929, most landowners willing to sell to the Snake River Land Company had done so. To convince those remaining, the company hired new purchasing agents and began pursuing alternative strategies. Working through the Department of the Interior, they pressured officials in the General Land Office to repossess homesteads that had not fulfilled their five-year investment contracts. Although the repossessions were technically legal, in practice, the Land Office rarely enforced the time limits. But doing so now would reduce the amount of private land Rockefeller needed to buy. At the same time, Park Service officials began approaching land owners living near the new Teton National Park, dropping hints that the new road system would make their lands inaccessible and lose value. Again, these actions were not illegal, but they raised troubling questions.

By spring 1930, the company owned between 25,000 and 30,000 acres of land in Jackson Hole. But the cloak of secrecy was breaking down. Rumors spread that Rockefeller was somehow involved. Hoping to remain one step ahead of the opposition, on April 6, the Snake River Land Company issued a press release that laid bare the entire plan, including the role of John Rockefeller Jr., the National Park Service, and their goal of transferring the land to the government as a national park.

With the truth finally out, Albright, Rockefeller, and their allies hoped to dissolve the Snake River Land Company and quickly transfer the land to the Park Service. But instead of resolving the issue, the news seemed to fan the flames of resentment. Instead of avoiding conflict, it ignited war.

* * *

In an attempt to alleviate further discord, Struthers Burt published two articles to explain the plan. In the *Jackson Hole Courier*, his essay laid out the economic logic to a local audience, namely that the future of Jackson Hole was in tourism rather than ranching, logging, or mining. The actions of the Snake River Land Company, therefore, ensured that local residents would benefit from this new economy.[19]

In his second piece, aimed at a national audience and published in *The Nation*, Burt appealed to Theodore Roosevelt's idea of parks as "essential democracy." By preserving beautiful places via federal control, the land became available for all citizens to enjoy, not just the wealthy few.[20] Unfortunately, neither argument was well-received.

For many people in Jackson Hole and throughout the rural West, Albright and Rockefeller's actions were anything but democratic or economically beneficial. Rather, they reflected the arrogance and privilege of eastern elites combined with the oppressive exertion of top-down federal power upon poor rural residents. In the context of the times, with the Great Depression unleashing its full force upon the vast majority of Americans, many found it difficult to see the conflict any other way.

Though westerners had long enjoyed the benefits of federal investment in things like railroads, highways, and military facilities, as well as tax subsidies in local agricultural and mining industries, many of them subscribed to notions of rugged individualism and resented "external" attempts to dictate how federal resources should be used. The actions of Albright, Rockefeller, and the Snake River Land Company seemed to exemplify such external control.

In short, even though the land-purchasing program was legal and potentially beneficial to local residents, its execution undermined its legitimacy. Local government officials saw only the loss of property taxes as private land became public. Former landowners felt betrayed, certain they had been tricked into accepting below-market prices, even though they may have received fair value for their property. And Wyoming politicians, who had originally opposed, then accepted, the creation of Grand Teton National Park in 1929, viewed the revelations as the worst sort of deception.

As a result, the opposition dug in for a long fight. When the editor of the *Jackson Hole Courier* decided to support the park expansion plan, opponents formed their own newspaper. Designed for the exclusive purpose of attacking and insulting the Park Service, *The Grand Teton* released its first issue in December 1931, quickly setting new standards for media wars in the rural West.

Then, in a turn reminiscent of more modern political scandals, a disgruntled Park Service employee broke into Albright's office and stole his correspondences with Rockefeller. Without hesitation, *The Grand Teton* began publishing Albright's personal letters to publicly humiliate him.

Meanwhile, Wyoming senator Robert Carey began calls for a "state park plan," in which all federal land in Wyoming, including Yellowstone and Grand Teton National Parks, all national forests, all wildlife refuges, and all land purchased by the Snake River Land Company would be turned over to the state to do with as it pleased.

In 1932, Franklin D. Roosevelt became president, signaling a return to conservation support in the White House. That same year, Leslie Miller won the election for Wyoming governor on a platform that included support for park expansion. Sensing it was now or never, Senator Carey scheduled senate hearings in Jackson Hole for August 1933.

While all of this was happening, Albright unexpectedly threw one more wrench into the works. In June, he announced his resignation from the National Park Service. For Yellowstone expansion advocates, the timing couldn't have been worse. The opposition jumped on the news as an informal admission of guilt. Why else would Albright step down, except to avoid the humiliation of being held accountable for his actions?

* * *

In fact, Albright had received an offer to serve as executive vice president of the American Potash Company back in November 1932. The company mined potash as a source of potassium fertilizer, and the new position offered double of Albright's Park Service salary. He actually accepted in February 1933 and was waiting for an ideal time to make his departure. Since becoming Park Service director in 1929, Albright had worked to transfer all historical monuments and battlefields to Park Service control. With FDR's election, Albright finally achieved this goal. And now, with the Yellowstone expansion effort close to a conclusion, he felt it was an opportune time to step down. In some ways, it was beneficial to remove one of the primary targets of the opposition. Albright continued to lend his support but would no longer be the public face of the National Park Service.

The senate hearings took place in Jackson from August 7 to 10, 1933. Despite Senator Carey's assertion that the investigation would reveal illegal action, by the end of the proceedings the Snake River Land Company was exonerated.

In response, the opposition folded. *The Grand Teton* newspaper closed its doors and Senator Carey offered a compromise bill in Congress to resolve the matter. The measure called for expanding Grand Teton National Park to include Rockefeller's property and Forest Service lands surrounding Jackson Lake. Compromises included guarantees for continued grazing rights and financial compensation to Teton County for lost property taxes due to the land transfers. The bill quickly passed in the Senate but died in the House due to conflict over the source of the funds paid to Teton County in lieu of taxes.

Over the next eight years, debates over park expansion periodically revived. Then, on November 27, 1942, Rockefeller sent a letter to Interior Secretary Harold Ickes demanding the federal government accept his gift of land or else he would dispose of it. The ultimatum triggered consideration of an entirely different strategy: to bypass Congress by invoking the Antiquities Act of 1906 to establish a national monument.

On March 15, 1943, FDR issued Executive Order 2578 to establish the Jackson Hole National Monument. The declaration totaled over 221,000 acres, including 32,117 acres from Rockefeller. The rest came from national forests and other public lands. In addition, roughly 1,400 acres of Wyoming State lands and 17,000 acres of private property ended up inside monument boundaries, but the designation did not impact these parcels in any way.

A national monument is not the same as a national park. Whereas the rules governing national parks are relatively standardized, monument land-use regulations vary greatly on a case-by-case basis. In this instance, monument status meant that the public lands within its borders were no longer open for logging, mining, or homesteading. However, public grazing and private property rights remained unchanged. Nonetheless, for opponents, FDR's declaration pushed the land battle into an entirely new phase.

* * *

On May 17, 1943, *Time* magazine ran a story under the headline "Gun Play":

> On a fair Wyoming morning last week, Hollywood's Wallace Beery rose up early at his ranch in the rugged Jackson Hole country, donned an old shirt, blue denim pants and cowboy boots. He put on his big black Stetson with the chin strap, grabbed his trusty six-shooter and climbed aboard his trusty white mare. In the fresh morning air he rode through the fertile valley to join a posse of ranchers.
>
> What made Rancher Beery and all his neighbors strap on their six-guns was a sudden executive order by Franklin Roosevelt, turning the entire Jackson Hole valley into a national monument . . . The ranchers opposed this [park] expansion because it would eliminate grazing land, and reduce county tax revenues. And they felt they had been tricked: national parks can be created only by Congressional action; monuments by mere executive order. Said Banker-Rancher Felix Buchenroth, "It may be a monument to [Interior Secretary] Ickes, but it's a tombstone to me."[21]

The event that *Time* and other news outlets reported on that day was, in fact, a publicity stunt, part of a media strategy orchestrated by wealthy seasonal resident and advertising executive Stanley Resor to garner sympathetic national attention to the anti-expansion cause.[22]

With reporters and photographers at the ready, this heavily armed group of horsemen pushed a herd of 550 cattle across the new monument as an act of defiance, daring federal authorities to stop them. Led by movie-star Wallace Beery, a popular leading man in western films of the day, organizers hoped to showcase rugged locals fighting back against abusive federal power.

Never mind that the monument declaration had no bearing on grazing rights, private property, or taxes paid on private land. Or that no federal officials ever appeared on the scene to "stop them." Or that Beery wasn't actually a rancher or even a full-time resident. He owned a Forest Service permit for a summer cabin on a half acre along the shore of Jackson Lake, but that was it. Apparently, he'd owned a milk cow at one time, but the animal had died.

Nonetheless, the event served its purpose: casting the national monument in the worst possible light. Nationally syndicated columnist Westbrook Pegler, a longtime critic of FDR, compared the declaration of the Jackson Hole National Monument to Hitler's invasion of Austria.[23] Wyoming senator Edward Robertson labeled the move "a foul, sneaking Pearl Harbor blow." Meanwhile, Teton County commissioners asked how the federal government could "reconcile taking away the homes of men who are now fighting to preserve their homeland."[24]

Of course, the charge of taking away homes and property was categorically false. In the context of the ongoing world war, such malicious accusations and comparisons seemed all the more severe. Amid the political firestorm, Wyoming governor Lester Hunt cast the entire issue in terms of states' rights. At the Western Governors' Conference in 1943, he declared, "I shall utilize all police authority at my disposal to exit from the proposed Jackson Hole National Monument any federal official who attempts to assume authority."[25] He never followed through on his threat, but he scored political points just the same.

In 1943, Wyoming congressman Frank Barrett introduced a bill to abolish the monument. In the Senate, Wyoming's Joseph O'Mahoney and Nevada's Pat McCarran cosponsored a bill to repeal the Antiquities Act of 1906. To gather testimony on both bills, the politicians scheduled what would be the third set of congressional hearings in Jackson Hole.

Tensions reached new heights when the assistant director of national parks, Conrad Wirth, called Congressman Barrett to make arrangements to attend the hearings and was told he might "get shot" if he showed himself in Jackson.[26] Despite intense debate, the hearings concluded without violence.

Back in Washington, Congress passed the bill abolishing the monument, which FDR promptly vetoed. Meanwhile, the State of Wyoming filed suit arguing that FDR's executive order represented a misuse of the Antiquities Act, but the case was thrown out of federal court.

In each of the next three years, Wyoming congressmen put forth bills to abolish the monument, rescind the president's authority under the Antiquities Act, and transfer all unappropriated federal lands to the states. But as before, all efforts failed. And, with the death of FDR in 1945 and the end of World War II, much of the anti-government feeling that had once fueled opposition to the Jackson Hole National Monument seemed to dissipate.

* * *

In 1949, realizing that the monument was unlikely to ever be abolished, Wyoming politicians agreed to meet with park supporters to discuss a compromise. On September 14, 1950, thirty-one years after the initial Yellowstone Park expansion bill was deferred in Congress, President Truman signed the law abolishing Jackson Hole National Monument and incorporating the land into Grand Teton National Park. The law included provisions for tax payments to Teton County for any lost private land, seasonal elk hunting (whereby hunters would be made temporary "rangers" by the Park Service), and the continuation of grazing leases. As imagined by Albright and Struthers Burt, the deal transformed Grand Teton into a new kind of national park.

But perhaps the most striking aspect was an agreement that "no further extension or establishment of national parks or monuments in Wyoming may be undertaken except by express authorization of the Congress." Never again could a president use the Antiquities Act to establish national monuments in Wyoming. With these words, the state containing the nation's first-ever national monument, Devil's Tower, became the first and only state to forever ban the practice.

* * *

Passage of the 1950 law did not mark an end to the Greater Yellow-stone story. Over the next fifty years, several new conservation areas would be introduced. In 1964, a rather large 585,000-acre chunk was included with passage of the 1964 Wilderness Act. The act not only established wilderness areas as a new category of federal conservation land but designated nine such areas across the nation, including the Teton Wilderness in national forest land located directly east of Grand Teton National Park.

Then, in 1972, Congress filled in another gap with the John D. Rockefeller Jr. Memorial Parkway. Consisting of 24,000 acres carved from the Teton National Forest, the parkway offered a national park "bridge" between Grand Teton and Yellowstone National Parks.

The final pieces were added some thirty years later. For decades, the Rockefeller family had kept the 3,300-acre JY Ranch as a family retreat. But in 1990, John's son Laurence donated 2,000 acres of the ranch to the Park Service. Later, in 2001 (at the age of ninety-one), he handed over the remaining 1,106 acres to serve as a nature center in Grand Teton.

* * *

The dream of a Greater Yellowstone—the vision shared by Horace Albright, John D. Rockefeller Jr., Struthers Burt, Maud Noble, and countless others stretching back to George Grinnell and General Sheridan—has today been realized, not as a single expanded Yellow-stone National Park but as a mosaic of different federal, state, and private lands comprising the Greater Yellowstone Ecosystem. With Yellowstone at its core, the area includes Grand Teton National Park, the National Elk Refuge, seven different national forests, and an assortment of other conservation areas. Together, these mountains, valleys, lakes, and rivers comprise the largest intact ecosystem in the continental United States. It remains one of the few places large enough and wild enough to accommodate large mammals, from wild bison, moose, and elk to grizzlies and gray wolves. The existence of Yellowstone as "America's Serengeti" could only be possible with pro-tection of this larger ecosystem.

But the story of *how* that vision was achieved through the decades-long battle for Jackson Hole left behind its own legacies, some of them not quite so benign. First and foremost is the profound ideological divide that came into sharp relief during the fight. Though anti-federal sentiment is nothing new in American history, the Jackson Hole conflict presented a congealing of ideas that formed the basis of modern public land conflicts. One can trace an ideological line running straight from Jackson Hole to the Sagebrush Rebellions of the 1940s and 1970s, to the County-Supremacy and Wise Use Movements of the 1990s, and to the armed takeover of the Malheur Wildlife Refuge in 2016. In this sense, public-private land conflict is also a legacy of the Greater Yellowstone story.

In the mid-1980s, at the age of ninety-five, Horace Albright wrote that one of the great "satisfactions" of his life was "seeing Grand Teton Park achieve its destiny."[27] Albright was proud to claim he had befriended many of his former adversaries in the Jackson Hole fight, especially as they came to appreciate the long-term economic and conservation benefits of park expansion. But long before this happened, one more major battle would be fought. This time the contest would not be over Yellowstone's landscape but the wildlife that called it home.

Part Four

YELLOWSTONE IN THE MODERN WORLD

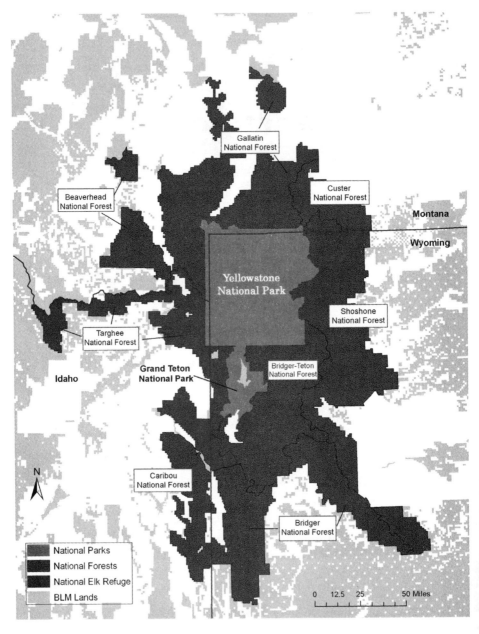

The Greater Yellowstone Ecosystem

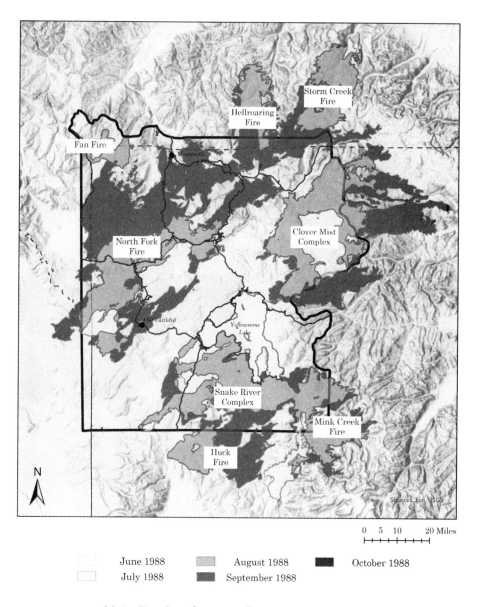

N

| | June 1988 | | August 1988 | | October 1988 |
| | July 1988 | | September 1988 | | |

0   5   10   20 Miles

Major Fire Complexes in Yellowstone, Summer 1988

Please Don't Feed the Animals

(1961–1983)

IN THE BITTER COLD OF AN EARLY DAWN IN JANUARY 1962, A group of heavily armed Yellowstone park rangers quietly fanned out along snow-filled paths in the Lamar Valley. Before them gathered a shadowed mass of figures numbering in the thousands: Yellowstone's great northern elk herd.

Using a series of prearranged temporary fences, the rangers carefully steered the elk into corrals containing piles of freshly cut hay. When the animals were locked inside, a ranger gave the signal. Suddenly, the air filled with the staccato pop and echo of rifle fire.

"We shot into the pile until they were all dead," one ranger remarked. "It was terrible."[1]

The rising sun illuminated a grisly scene. Amid the bloodstained snow, bulldozer-like vehicles stacked piles of elk carcasses onto the beds of idling trucks. Field-dressed, with heads and hooves removed, the rapidly freezing elk would be sent to Livingston for processing and distribution to Native American reservations and charities across Montana.[2] In the end, over 4,300 elk lay dead—not by poachers or recreational hunters; nor even by predators, disease, or starvation—but by the hands of those sworn to protect them.

Such actions were not new. Since 1935, the Park Service engaged in what it called "direct reduction" in order to keep the northern elk population within the limits of Yellowstone's rangeland capacity.[3] Typically this was done by private hunters on land outside the park during state-sanctioned hunts. Park Service kills only happened afterward and accounted for a smaller number of animals. However, those numbers increased after 1955, as mild winters meant fewer elk left the park during hunting season.[4]

Still, the event in 1962 was different. For the first time, rangers inside Yellowstone were responsible for almost all of the elk removed. Managers had hoped the Montana hunting season would reduce the elk herd of 10,000 down to 5,000, but, for a variety of reasons, it resulted in only 125 kills. Park officials "live trapped" and transferred another 310 elk to surrounding states, leaving some 4,565 for "direct reduction." That morning, rangers shot 4,309 animals.[5]

When news of the slaughter came to light, the public responded with anger and confusion. Hunters, locals, and state game commissioners wrote scathing letters, while Wyoming and Montana politicians called for congressional hearings. The bloody scene in the Lamar Valley seemed to contradict the many decades of effort spent protecting the great beasts. Campaigns to eradicate predators, provide winter feed, and stop poaching were meant to *increase* Yellowstone's game herds. Now, park managers were killing them. Did not the 1916 Park Service Act require national parks to *conserve* the wildlife?

What was going on in Yellowstone?

* * *

The "great slaughter" of 1962, and the controversy that followed, represented the culmination of a long evolution in thinking about wildlife in Yellowstone, a journey signposted with numerous warnings that old nineteenth-century assumptions about nature were pushing the park toward crisis.

One of the earliest signs appeared in 1916. This inaugural year of the National Park Service witnessed the first confirmed human killing by a bear in Yellowstone.[6] A grizzly entered the camp of a teamster and two laborers hauling hay and attacked one of the men. His companions chased off the animal and took the injured man to Fort Yellowstone, where he later died. They then returned to the camp and killed the bear with a baited charge of dynamite. Whether the bear was emboldened to approach as a result of becoming habituated to human food at hotel bear-feeding shows isn't known.

Later that year, another alarm sounded when early winter snows forced Yellowstone's northern elk herd down from the high country. Unable to find sufficient forage, the herd suffered a massive die-off from starvation. Thousands perished.[7]

Park managers responded to each of these episodes in ways that reflected the prevailing tendency to label species as "good" or "bad." In other words, kill the bear and feed the elk.

In 1919, during Horace Albright's first year as Yellowstone super-intendent, it happened again. A drought-laden summer followed by early October snows drove thousands of elk down from the high country and out of the park just as Montana's hunting season opened. The resultant "firing line" of hunters near Gardiner led to yet another scene of death and destruction. Animals stepped over the park boundary into a hailstorm of bullets. Any elk that somehow made it through the onslaught found themselves threatened or shot by ranchers defending their haystacks farther down the valley. Estimates suggested that over 10,000 elk were killed or maimed that winter.[8]

Shocked at the loss of this "desirable" game species and concerned that it might trigger an irreversible population decline, Albright and Mather bolstered the park's northern elk feeding program with a $30,000 uptick in federal funding.[9] Throughout Albright's ten years as superintendent (1919–1929) and subsequent four years as National Park Service director—and indeed, for the rest of his life—he fervently supported the park's wildlife feeding programs and remained skeptical of any effort to reduce them.

In terms of the 1916 National Park Service Act, with its dual mandate to "conserve the scenery and wildlife" while simultaneously providing for the "enjoyment of the same" to future generations, both Albright and Mather came down hard on the side of visitor enjoyment. But to their minds, the mission did not contain a contradiction. As underscored in the so-called "Lane Letter," a memo issued to translate the 1916 Act into more practical terms, Interior Secretary Lane declared that national parks should remain "absolutely unimpaired" while also serving as the "national playground."[10]

For Albright and Mather, *unimpaired* really meant stopping the commercial development of natural resources. Unlike national forests, national parks generally prohibited logging, mining, and hunting while welcoming development meant to enhance visitor experiences. Parks were intended to present an "ideal vision" of North America as a natural paradise, devoid of forest fires, human habitation (including Native Americans, unless brought in for tourist shows), and dangerous predators. Parks were a place to observe and possibly interact with bountiful herds of wild creatures in a way that invigorated the spirit and sense of national belonging.[11]

Consequently, Albright strongly supported eradicating predators, suppressing wildfires, enclosing wildlife for display, and, of course, providing them with supplemental food. Giving winter hay to elk and bison and providing hotel food waste to bears as part of nightly "feeding shows" was consistent with his vision because it ensured large, relatively docile herds of wildlife for visitor viewing.

* * *

This same sentiment carried over to the hand-feeding of bears, a practice that grew exceedingly popular with the rise of automobile tourism. Beginning in the 1920s, black bears began to stop traffic, blocking the roadway until passengers offered morsels of food. One of the most popular, a young bear nicknamed Jesse James, gained the attention of Albright himself for frequent "holdups" on the road to West Thumb.[12] But while park rangers recommended trapping and relocating the bear for traffic-safety reasons, Albright chose to highlight the delightful antics of this park celebrity, making sure that President Harding himself enjoyed an interaction during his 1923 visit.

Although park regulations going back to 1902 prohibited tourists from feeding bears, Albright was also aware that it was a major reason people came to Yellowstone. Informally, he encouraged the practice, allowing himself to be photographed doing so on numerous occasions. In fact, the cover of the park-rules brochure for 1922—which included a regulation *prohibiting* the feeding of bears—featured a photo of tourists doing just that.[13]

Unsurprisingly, as visitor numbers increased over the next two decades, so too did bear-related injuries. While the larger and more aggressive grizzlies tended to limit their presence to hotel feeding shows, black bears were drawn to campgrounds and roadsides, where they learned to beg for food. Of course, if people teased the animals by only pretending to have food or holding it up high in an effort to get them to stand on two legs, the bears would respond logically: climb up to get the food or try to knock it down. Humans typically came out on the losing end in such encounters, often with deep cuts and scratches.

In 1925, a single ranger station recorded eighty-eight injuries. In 1930, the superintendent's annual report estimated 100 to 300 injuries occurred each year, though only a fraction were ever reported.[14] Between 1931 and 1939, records document 527 injuries.[15] And bears also damaged property. In 1932, Yellowstone rangers reported 451 instances of bears tearing up campsites or breaking into cars and cabins in search of food.

Consequences for bears could be dire. Creatures labeled as repeat offenders might be trapped and relocated, but more typically, they were killed. As for tourists, it was merely an inconvenience. Those who lodged complaints with Superintendent Albright were usually ignored. Sometimes Albright would try to defuse the situation by reminding the injured party that bear scars made wonderful souvenirs. He was also particularly fond of telling a story about a woman losing her dress.[16] In any event, since the park rulebook clearly prohibited visitors from feeding wildlife, the Park Service faced little threat of a legal challenge from upset tourists.

By the mid-1920s, with the growing number of bear-related injuries and the elk overpopulation problem ever present, questions began to arise about Yellowstone's approach to wildlife management. Ironically, the Park Service efforts to increase wild game populations by eradicating predators and providing supplemental food had the opposite effect: overpopulation leading to episodes of mass starvation. Was there no way to maintain healthy game populations without triggering the problem of large-scale die-offs? The bear problem seemed equally perplexing. What if the promise of human food began to attract not just black bears to roadways and campgrounds but also grizzlies? What if visitor injuries transformed into fatalities?

Some began to wonder if the burgeoning science of ecology might have something to offer. Surprisingly, it was Albright himself who took some of the first steps to bring scientific management to Yellowstone.

During his tenure as superintendent, he would authorize the first eco-logical studies of the park's wildlife—and then spend much of the next four decades pushing back against their recommendations.

* * *

Early calls for an alternative approach to wildlife management came from some reputable sources, including President Theodore Roosevelt. In 1908, he argued to halt the killing of Yellowstone's mountain lions.[17] Five years later, he chimed in again, correctly warning that winter elk feeding was not "of the slightest use" given their hardiness and robust ability to reproduce.[18]

In 1915, the formation of the Ecological Society of America (ESA) added another voice to the growing chorus. That year, the University of California, Berkeley, established a program in wildlife biology and a museum of natural history led by biologist Joseph Grinnell. A distant cousin of George, Joseph was every bit as committed to conservation. His program produced a distinguished list of alumni that would influence Yellowstone's wildlife policy for years to come.

In 1921, the ESA issued a resolution against introducing non-native species into national parks, including the game fish brought to Yellowstone.[19] And, in 1925, Albright and Mather established a new education division in the Park Service, headquartered at Berkeley and focused on educational programming for park naturalists. Mather named Ansel Hall, one of Grinnell's early graduates, as the first direc-tor. That same year, ecologist Charles Adams of Syracuse University published research warning that overgrazing in national parks would lead to wildlife starvation. Whether influenced by Grinnell, Adams, or yet another elk-starvation event that may have occurred in the winter of 1927–1928,[20] Albright began to change course.

Back in 1923, Congress authorized culling Yellowstone's bison herd due to the perceived threat they posed in transmitting brucellosis to nearby cattle. In 1925, Albright agreed to an annual herd-reduction program since Yellowstone's bison seemed to be recovered but lacked value as a game animal for sport hunters (they tended to just stand there, yet were difficult to kill).[21] Though Albright sent individual bison to zoos and game preserves from time to time, the numbers were never enough to counter annual population growth. Intending to keep Yellowstone's herd at 1,000 head, rangers began killing any "surplus animals" and donated the meat to local tribes and the State of Montana.[22]

As for elk, in 1928, Albright arranged for Forest Service biologist William Rush to conduct the first scientific assessment of Yellowstone's northern range, the elk's primary grassland habitat. Three years later, after becoming National Park Service director, Albright ended "widespread" efforts to eradicate predators in all parks. Of course, by then, Yellowstone's wolves and mountain lions were largely eradicated anyway, with the last wolf killed in 1926. What's more, the new policy didn't apply to "pest species" like coyotes, which continued to face extermination.[23] And none of this applied to bears, which rangers never quite defined as predators and, regardless, continued to be fed by tourists and at hotel feeding shows.

However, Albright's most influential action in bringing science into Yellowstone was his decision to champion another of Joseph Grinnell's former students, a naturalist named George Melendez Wright.

* * *

Born in San Francisco in 1904 to a wealthy Salvadoran American family, Wright was orphaned as a small child and raised by an aunt. In childhood, he developed a lifelong fascination with the natural world. After completing his degree at Berkeley, Wright took a job at Yosemite National Park, where he witnessed the ecological harm caused by management decisions to eradicate predators and to feed big game. In 1928, he came into his inheritance and wrote a proposal for a scientific wildlife survey of all western national parks, notably offering to cover all expenses himself. Albright agreed, swayed by the financial arrangement as much as the opportunity to boost the park's naturalist program.[24] But more than anything else, Albright was swayed by Wright himself.

A bright, articulate, and well-mannered young man, Wright was not only a dedicated scientist but skilled in the art of influencing decisionmakers. He enthusiastically supported Albright's dream of a Greater Yellowstone, recognizing the need for park boundaries to encompass entire ecosystems. At the same time, he also applauded the Park Service mission to serve the public and embraced the challenge of managing natural systems within the context of human impacts. For Wright, the parks offered an opportunity to study resource management in "its most complex form."[25]

Assisted by colleagues from Berkeley, Ben Thompson and Joseph Dixon, Wright published the results of his study in 1933. Known as *Fauna No. 1* (intended as the first in of a series of surveys), it offered the first scientific report of natural resource management in the national parks. The recommendations suggested a wholesale reversal of ideas that had dominated the first fifty years of Yellowstone history.

They included adjusting park boundaries to incorporate the full year-round habitat of native species; establishing research areas, untouched by humans, to provide a baseline for future planning; ending wildlife feeding to allow each species to "carry on its struggle for existence unaided"; ceasing the killing of predators; reintroducing native species; and removing or limiting non-native ones. The end goal was the restoration of natural or "primitive" conditions.[26] In short, Wright changed the meaning of "unimpaired" in the Park Service mandate by redefining it in environmental terms.

To be fair, some recommendations still contained problematic assumptions. For example, what exactly constituted "natural" or "primitive" conditions? And once achieved, would such landscapes operate in a "natural balance"? In other words, would the land maintain itself forever if left untouched by humans?

In Yellowstone, Wright's findings included specific recommendations to end the practice of feeding wildlife. Moreover, Wright suggested that "the presentation of animal life of the parks . . . be wholly a natural one." In other words, Yellowstone's bear-feeding shows needed to go, zoo enclosures had to be shut down, and rules against hand-feeding needed to be enforced. To help transition bears away from human food, he suggested fencing around campgrounds and the development of "bear-proof" food and trash containers.

Other scientists supported Wright's conclusions. In 1932, William Rush's study of Yellowstone's northern rangelands found that they had deteriorated approximately 50 percent since 1914 from overgrazing.[27] Echoing *Fauna No.1*, Rush recommended a significant reduction of the elk population. Famed ecologists Adolph and Olaus Murie agreed.

Adolph had worked as a wildlife biologist for the National Park Service in Mount McKinley and Glacier, and now he studied predators in Yellowstone. Meanwhile, Olaus was a Bureau of Biological Survey scientist who had studied Yellowstone's southern elk herd in Jackson Hole since 1927. Both men supported herd reduction, not only to compensate for ending the artificial feeding programs but to adjust for the loss of winter habitat caused by urban development.

Interestingly, Albright stepped down as Park Service director the same year that Wright published *Fauna No. 1*. His replacement, Arno Cammerer, embraced Wright's recommendations as official national park policy and, in 1934, asked Wright to lead the new Park Service Wildlife Division. The following year, President Franklin D. Roosevelt appointed Wright as head of the National Resources Board.

In the winter of 1934–1935, Yellowstone managers carried out the very first "direct reduction" of the northern elk herd. Hunters on nearby lands outside of the national park killed 2,598 elk, while Park Service rangers acting inside the park accounted for 667.[28] The program repeated the following year and would continue for decades.

In 1936, however, tragedy struck. Sent to investigate potential sites for new international parks and wildlife refuges along the U.S.–Mexico border, Wright and Yellowstone supervisor Roger Toll died in an automobile collision on Highway 80 in New Mexico.[29] Wright was only thirty-one years old.

* * *

The loss of such an influential trailblazer was felt immediately. Under Wright's urging, twenty-seven wildlife biologists worked for the Park Service in 1936. Three years later, without Wright to advocate for the division, only nine remained.[30] In 1940, the interior secretary transferred the entire Wildlife Division to the Bureau of Biological Survey. Despite Director Cammerer's decision to adopt *Fauna No. 1* as official policy, implementation was slow. The rise of FDR's New Deal meant a focus on jobs and economic development. For the national parks, this translated into Civilian Conservation Corps projects emphasizing roads and campgrounds. And the onset of World War II meant budget reductions in all areas of government not directly related to the war effort.

Following Wright's recommendations, in 1937 Supervisor Edmund Rogers and Park Service chief biologist Victor Calahane ended the northern elk feeding program. Despite this move, the range failed to rejuvenate, and direct reductions continued.[31] As Teddy Roosevelt had predicted long ago, the elk's vigorous reproduction capabilities proved more than capable of compensating for loses claimed through hunting, culling, or starvation.

Other suggestions in *Fauna No. 1* went unheeded. Bison feeding at the Lamar Buffalo Ranch continued, as did efforts to exterminate predators (primarily coyotes), use pesticides, and import exotic fish species. Caging animals for tourist viewing also persisted and even expanded for a time. From 1935 to 1940, tourists could visit the "Antelope Creek Buffalo Pasture" near Tower Falls.[32]

As for Yellowstone's bears, in 1935, Superintendent Rogers closed the feeding show at Old Faithful Inn. However, knowing it would be controversial—especially to now-retired Park Director Albright, who still kept a close eye on Yellowstone—Rogers did not close the final show at Otter Creek near the Canyon Hotel until 1942, after the U.S. entered World War II and park visitation diminished. To be sure, roadside hand-feeding of bears continued, as did the practice of feeding them hotel food waste, only now it took place in Yellowstone's backcountry, away from the prying eyes of tourists.

* * *

Despite these changes, or perhaps because of them, yet another warning sign emerged that same summer. While new scientific ideas might be sound, changing past practices—especially when it involved undoing the learned behavior of bears—was never going to be easy. With visitation down due to the war, the number of bear-related visitor injuries predictably declined. But the frequency of property-damage incidents in campgrounds actually rose when adjusted for visitor numbers. As a result, Yellowstone rangers killed more "problem bears" that season (eighty-three) than in all of the last seven years combined.[33]

Then it happened. On August 23, 1942, at 1:45 a.m., a twenty-five-year-old nurse from Idaho named Martha Hansen left her cabin near Old Faithful to walk to the restroom. Attacked by a bear, most likely a grizzly, she was severely mauled and died four days later in the hospital in Mammoth Hot Springs.[34] It was the first visitor death by grizzly in twenty-six years.

The Park Service weighed a variety of responses, from reducing the bear population to fencing in campgrounds. But lacking accurate bear numbers and worried about the cost and visual impact that large fences might have on tourism, managers looked for other solutions.

In 1943, Olaus Murie agreed to study the problem and concluded that only about 10 percent of bear food came from human garbage. Murie argued that since bears could make do without it, all forms of artificial feeding should be stopped. This meant closing the backcountry bear-feeding dumps, ending roadside hand-feeding, and securing all human food and waste in bear-proof containers. He also suggested enclosing campgrounds with fences, at least until bears adapted to the new conditions.

In response, critics let their anguish be known. Writing in *The Backlog*, a camping magazine, Albright argued that the "traveling public" had a "right" to see wildlife when they vacationed in Yellowstone. Denying those rights by closing zoos and feeding shows would seriously harm the reputation of the National Park Service.[35] In the end, park managers gave in to critics, focusing instead on new visitor education programs and ramping up enforcement of the "no feeding rule." Nonetheless, backcountry trash feeding continued and roadside feeding by tourists actually increased, setting the stage for an escalation of bear-related conflicts.

* * *

As the postwar 1940s gave way to the 1950s, Yellowstone experienced an explosion of visitors. In keeping with other large-scale infrastructure projects of the time, like the Interstate Highway System, Park Service director Conrad Wirth proposed to Congress an ambitious plan to modernize visitor services. Harkening back to the priorities of the Mather-Albright era, the plan called for upgraded roads, expanded hotel amenities, and the development of modern visitor centers. With work scheduled for completion by the fiftieth anniversary of the National Park Service in 1966, the program was aptly named Mission 66.

In 1956, Director Wirth appointed Lon Garrison as the new

superintendent of Yellowstone. As the former head of the Park Service Steering Committee for Mission 66, his primary task was to lead the implementation of Mission 66 in the nation's flagship national park.

The new program entailed dramatic changes for Yellowstone. Departing from the rustic "parkitecture" aesthetics of previous decades, Mission 66 projects focused instead on efficiency. Historically, architects sought to integrate facilities within their natural surroundings. The new idea, based on modern urban zoning techniques, was to create all-inclusive "villages" in which visitors could find lodging, restaurants, parking lots, gift shops, gas stations, and all other services in one concentrated urban center. Clearly separating visitor zones from the rest of the park allowed major sights and natural areas to be left "unimpaired" (or less impaired, anyway).

Another major innovation of the program was the creation of visitor centers. For the very first time, in one place, tourists could find information on camping, lodging, and tours, as well as bathrooms, gift shops, and knowledgeable park staff. As a popular first stop for many travelers, the visitor centers soon became a staple of national parks throughout the country.

In Yellowstone, one of the first projects entailed the demolition of the old Canyon Hotel. Robert Reamer's massive one-mile-circumference building, while magnificent in many respects, had long suffered from foundational weaknesses. Efforts to replace it had been underway for two decades. Now, with the infusion of Mission 66 funding, workers quickly razed the building and commenced construction on its replacement in the new Canyon Village complex.

However, with all of this emphasis on visitor facilities, less attention (and even fewer resources) remained for scientific resource management. In 1955, Park Service chief biologist Victor Calahane resigned in protest, but nothing changed. Direct reductions of Yellowstone's bison and northern elk herd continued, while the bear problem only grew worse.

As visitor numbers increased from 62,000 in 1942 to over 1.3 million in 1955, so too did bear-related injuries. As before, offending bears were removed or killed, but otherwise, managers' response remained limited to visitor information campaigns and rule "enforcement" through verbal or written warnings. In 1957, rangers issued 908 written warnings along with 3,800 verbal warnings, but only two fines at five dollars each.[36]

In 1958, the cartoon company Hanna-Barbera capitalized on the apparent national pastime of feeding Yellowstone bears with a new character named Yogi. Based on the premise of a bear in Yellowstone (called "Jellystone" in the show), attempting to outwit "Mr. Ranger" to find human food via a "pic-a-nic basket," the TV series made Yogi Bear a superstar in the early 1960s.

Desperate to find new ways of reducing bear-visitor conflicts, the Park Service attempted to harness the power of this cartoon celebrity. Soon, Yellowstone information pamphlets featured Yogi, with his porkpie hat and Art Carney mannerisms, warning visitors to stay away from, and stop feeding, bears. But absent meaningful enforcement of park rules, bear-related injuries and conflicts continued to rise.

About the same time, frustrated Yellowstone naturalist David Condon tried another tactic. Without a sufficient budget to conduct his own research, Condon contacted John Craighead, a professor of wildlife biology at the University of Montana, about conducting a study of Yellowstone's bears. In 1959, they established a cooperative agreement between the Park Service; Craighead's Wildlife Research Unit at the University of Montana; and Craighead's brother, Frank, a biologist and military veteran with training in advanced telemetry and radar technology who now led the Environmental Research Institute. Over the next twelve years, scientific management in Yellowstone would enter a brand-new phase.

* * *

Concurrently, Yellowstone managers found themselves confronted with a new challenge. Led by state game commissioners in Wyoming and Montana, sport-hunting organizations pushed to allow recreational hunting in Yellowstone. Citing the precedent set in Grand Teton National Park and the increased need for direct reductions of Yellowstone's elk and bison, would it not be better to allow recreational hunters inside the park to accomplish the task?

Park director Wirth initially endorsed the idea but later recanted in the face of outrage from the National Parks Association and environmental groups.[37] Many, including Yellowstone superintendent Garrison, found direct reduction undesirable, but permitting recreational hunting contradicted a foundational principle of the national park system.

Moreover, the experience in Teton suggested that relying on private hunters for population control simply didn't work. Each year between 1951 and 1958, Grand Teton National Park made 1,200 elk permits available. However, only half were ever purchased. What's more, of those that did hunt, only 27 percent successfully killed an elk. The ratio of permits offered to elk killed was seven to one. This meant that Yellowstone would have to issue 35,000 permits in order to reduce the herd by 5,000 animals, and its hunt would compete with that in Grand Teton. Worse, during the hunt inside Grand Teton, rangers documented numerous instances of illegal killing of protected animals by unruly sportsmen, ranging from bears to moose.[38]

Nonetheless, the state game commissioners would not let the matter go. Although meat from direct-reduction activities provided a valuable resource for tribal nations and Montana charities, hunting advocates repeatedly labeled the Park Service action as a "wasteful slaughter." In contrast, they argued that killing elk by recreational hunters produced a respectable "harvest."

In June 1961, Garrison met with Wyoming and Montana officials to coordinate for the upcoming hunting season. Historically, state commissioners agreed to add late-season hunting periods if too few elk migrated out of the park in the fall. Late-season hunts, in December or January, benefitted everyone: they increased state revenue by allowing the sale of more hunting permits, provided more opportunities for hunters to succeed, and helped the park meet its elk-herd-reduction goals.

This time, however, the commissioners refused to cooperate. Unless they were allowed to hunt inside Yellowstone itself, they would not offer an extended winter season. With Montana's fall hunt accounting for only 125 elk and the winter fast approaching, state officials dug in their heels. By January 1962, only one option remained. Reluctantly, Yellowstone rangers prepared to do the killing themselves.

* * *

In the aftermath of the massive herd-reduction event, disgruntled hunting advocates labeled it a "slaughter" and fueled a media frenzy. Arguing that inept Yellowstone managers had decimated the elk population—and the regional hunting industry—state game officials demanded a count to confirm that, in fact, Yellowstone's northern elk herd still comprised roughly 5,000 head.

Superintendent Garrison agreed. Conducted by representatives from Montana Fish and Game, the Forest Service, three conservation organizations, and two Montana sports clubs, the census took place by helicopter in April. The final count showed over 5,700 elk remained. Yellowstone managers were exonerated.[39]

But for Wyoming politicians, this wasn't enough. A bill soon appeared in Congress that would allow recreational hunting in national parks and force the Park Service to jointly manage wildlife with adjacent states. Months later, Montana representative Arnold Olsen ordered hearings on the matter in Bozeman and published a scathing article in *Sports Afield* magazine entitled "Yellowstone's Great Elk Slaughter."[40] Ultimately, the bill failed, but the political brouhaha it stirred up led Interior Secretary Stewart Udall to convene a Blue Ribbon Committee to review the matter.

Comprised of the nation's leading experts on wildlife management, the five-member committee was chaired by A. Starker Leopold. A forty-eight-year-old professor from Berkeley, Leopold also happened to be a former student of Joseph Grinnell and the oldest son of legendary conservationist Aldo Leopold. The committee was charged with assessing the practice of direct reduction and the potential utility of recreational hunting inside national parks, but they also took the opportunity to address much larger issues.

Published in March 1963, the document, which came to be known as the *Leopold Report*, marked a major turning point in national park management. It strongly confirmed the use of direct reduction to protect Yellowstone's rangeland habitat in the absence of predators. And it soundly rejected the idea of allowing recreational hunting inside the park, viewing it as an imprecise and unreliable tool based on historical evidence.

Interestingly, many recommendations in the *Leopold Report* reflected those contained in George Wright's *Fauna No. 1*. Beyond the issue of elk management, the report also spoke to the need to stop predator-eradication programs, end the use of pesticides, reduce or eliminate non-native species, reintroduce lost native species, and consider the use of prescribed fire to restore natural landscapes.

The report then went on to define the primary management goal of national parks: to ensure "that the biotic associations within each park be maintained, or where necessary recreated, as nearly as possible in the condition that prevailed when the area was first visited by the white man. A national park should represent a vignette of primitive America."[41] While many leading scientists and environmental organizations applauded the *Leopold Report*, it contained two controversial ideas. The first concerned the phrase "primitive America" as a management goal. Like *Fauna No. 1*, this directive appeared to embrace the idea of nature as static—that there was, in fact, one "original condition" that, once achieved, would persist in some kind of natural balance. Such thinking not only ignored the inherent dynamism of environmental systems; it also disregarded the thousands of years Native Americans spent as stewards of the landscape.

A second point of contention had to do with the idea that management interventions be hidden from view. Since full environmental restoration was not possible in most cases, national parks should offer visitors a "reasonable illusion" of wildness. While this statement likely referred to ridding the parks of zoos and bear-feeding shows, it had the unexpected effect of clashing with new techniques in wildlife science: from the use of fences to mark off research areas to the use of ear tags and radio collars to track wildlife.

In time, Leopold attempted to correct both of these issues, recognizing that while healthy environmental systems are relatively stable, they are also dynamic and evolving. According to Leopold, had he known the report would be so widely read, he would have chosen his words much more carefully.[42] Nevertheless, in the 1960s, the *Leopold Report* convinced some Park Service officials to adopt a hands-off approach to management, avoiding any intervention that might disrupt the illusion of a "primitive scene" for tourists. In Yellowstone, this gave rise to a whole new series of debates over science and wildlife.

* * *

As with *Fauna No. 1*, the National Park Service soon adopted the *Leopold Report* as official policy. And like *Fauna No. 1*, implementation was mixed. After 1963, relations between Yellowstone managers and the game commissions in Wyoming and Montana improved. Direct reduction continued, but park officials began transporting elk to neighboring states during hunting season, where the disoriented beasts were quickly shot. Still, Wyoming politicians pushed to end direct reduction, arguing that it unfairly deprived hunters of increased bounty.

Then in 1967, Jack Anderson transferred from Grand Teton to become the superintendent of Yellowstone. Anderson brought with him Teton's park biologist, Glenn Cole, a rather introverted man with large glasses and a sincere devotion to environmental protection. Cole embraced a particular interpretation of the *Leopold Report*, which championed the hands-off approach called "natural regulation." He believed wildlife populations would, over time, naturally adjust to the carrying capacity of available habitat on their own, just as they had done for tens of thousands of years. But as modern urbanization had so radically reduced the amount of winter elk habitat outside the park, many questioned whether this approach could actually work.

Nonetheless, in March 1967, largely to satisfy Wyoming politicians, Interior Secretary Udall ordered Park Service director George Hartzog to end direct reduction in Yellowstone. In December, park officials issued their own statement confirming that "natural regulation" would guide management of the northern elk herd and bison. Culling would stop. Nature would now be free to take its course.[43]

Ironically, the *Leopold Report* actually called for the *continuation* of herd reductions in order to restore Yellowstone's rangeland habitat. It also advised that scientific data should provide the basis for all management decisions. In the case of the northern elk herd, the Park Service followed neither of these recommendations.

* * *

As for the bears, in keeping with the *Leopold Report*'s goal of reducing any visual sign of human manipulation, Anderson and Cole decided it was high time to end all feeding through strict regulatory enforcement. In the run-up to Yellowstone's centennial anniversary in 1972, Anderson hoped they could present to the public a park that finally allowed wildlife to thrive within a natural setting.

But these decisions soon conflicted with ongoing efforts to bring scientific management to Yellowstone. In 1967, the same year that

Anderson and Cole arrived, John and Frank Craighead delivered the draft report of their grizzly bear study to park officials. Their work pioneered numerous new techniques in ecological science. Pulling from Frank's military experience with radio telemetry, the brothers pioneered the first radio collars for tracking wildlife populations, developed methods and dosages needed to tranquilize large mammals for data collection, and made innovative use of tagging with tattoos and brightly colored streamers that enabled identification from significant distances. These innovations allowed, for the first time in history, accurate population counts of Yellowstone's grizzlies, including life cycle studies of individual bears and reliable measures of their territorial range.

However, the use of radio collars and brightly colored ear tags presented a conundrum for those attempting to present a "natural scene" for visitors. The recommendations in the Craigheads' report were even more controversial. Their research relied in large part on studying the grizzlies that frequented backcountry trash dumps. Aware that park officials wanted to close the dumps, the Craigheads advocated doing so slowly over a matter of years and, in the interim, providing the bears an alternative backcountry food source in the form of elk carcasses.

The Craigheads worried that if the trash dumps closed suddenly, bears would search for food in campgrounds, leading to more conflicts with visitors and, ultimately, more bear deaths at the hands of park rangers. The brothers warned that this might threaten the continued existence of grizzlies in Yellowstone.

Exacerbating these differences in viewpoint were differences in personality. The Craigheads represented the celebrity scientists of the day. Extroverted, tanned, and athletic from years of fieldwork, they had authored articles in *National Geographic* and starred in nature documentaries. Both brothers enjoyed ready access to media outlets. In contrast, Glenn Cole preferred to avoid the spotlight. He and his Yellowstone colleagues not only disagreed with the Craigheads' methods and conclusions but were unsettled by the brothers' tendency to share their views with the general public.

In the midst of these growing tensions, another warning sign flared up. In the summer of 1967, for the first time in park history, grizzly bears attacked and killed visitors in Glacier National Park. In two separate attacks on the very same night, grizzlies ripped young women from their sleeping bags and dragged them off to their deaths. Both occurred in camping areas located near old backcountry bear-feeding dumps. Later, these tragic events would be immortalized in Jack Olsen's book *Night of the Grizzlies.*

In an interview with the *Great Falls Tribune*, Frank Craighead responded to the tragic news by blaming the deaths on the Park Service policy of restricting bear-feeding programs in Glacier National Park.[44] Needless to say, managers in Yellowstone took notice.

* * *

In 1968, the Park Service brought in Starker Leopold to study the bear issue in Grand Teton and Yellowstone. His report, released in 1969, agreed with Yellowstone's plan to enforce roadside-feeding bans, use bear-proof trash bins in campgrounds, and stop feeding hotel food waste to bears. But it also agreed with the Craigheads' recommendation that Yellowstone's backcountry dumps be closed gradually by providing carrion food drops.

Later, Yellowstone managers issued their own policy statement. It agreed with all recommendations *except* for the provision of backcountry carrion drops. Believing a slow process would allow another generation of bears to learn dependency on human handouts, it called instead for a swift close of all backcountry feeding by 1972.

The summer of 1969, another mauling occurred in Yellowstone. This time, a little five-year-old girl was clamped in the jaws of a grizzly in the Fishing Bridge campground. Shaken and tossed aside, she suffered a punctured lung and broken rib, but she survived. Once more, the Craigheads blamed the event on Park Service policies, while Yellowstone officials denied responsibility.[45] The bear wasn't hungry, they claimed, but agitated. It was running away from a group of kids throwing rocks and bottles when it inadvertently ran into the little girl near the restroom. Nonetheless, within an hour the bear was hunted down and shot.[46]

Amid all of this acrimony, with their Yellowstone research permit ending in 1971, the Craigheads requested an extension for their grizzly bear study. Cole and other managers agreed as long as the brothers submitted all of their research for Park Service review before publication.

Unwilling to give up their academic freedom, the Craigheads refused, bringing their pioneering work in Yellowstone to a close.

* * *

Meanwhile, Yellowstone officials moved forward with their new bear-management plan. In 1969, for the first time in Yellowstone history, rangers strictly enforced the rule against roadside bear feeding. In the previous decade, rangers handed out roughly ten citations per year. That year, they issued eighty-nine.[47] The number of bear-related visitor injuries dropped like a rock. Within three years, hand-feeding all but vanished. In 1970, park managers moved ahead with closing the Rabbit Creek bear-feeding dump near Old Faithful. And in 1971, they closed down the last backcountry dump at Trout Creek, located five miles north of Fishing Bridge campground. In short, bear feeding was finally ending and visitor injuries were in decline. By all appearances, the new plan seemed to be working. Until it didn't.

In the summer of 1972, twenty-five-year-old Harry Walker and his childhood friend, Phillip "Crow" Bradberry, took a road trip from their home in Alabama to Colorado. Hitchhiking up to Livingston, Montana, the two caught a ride to Yellowstone with a young woman who worked at the Old Faithful Inn. The three companions spent the next few days exploring the geyser basin and hanging out in the evenings. Rather than stay in one of the campgrounds, they set up their tent on a hillside near the Grand Geyser.

Sometime after midnight on the third evening, as Harry and Crow walked back to the tent, their flashlight fell on a 400-pound grizzly digging into a bag of groceries they had left in camp. Seconds later, the bear lunged. Crow fell backward. As he rolled down the hill, he heard Harry scream, "Help me, Crow!"

Crow called back but heard nothing. Scrambling to his feet, Crow ran back to the Old Faithful Inn and burst through the doors yelling, "Bear! Has my friend!"

Rangers quickly organized a search party, but the disoriented Crow could not find his way back to the campsite. Early the next morning, searchers found Harry's lifeless body, mauled and partially devoured. Within a day, rangers tracked down and shot the grizzly, identified as a regular visitor to Yellowstone's backcountry garbage dump at Rabbit Creek prior to its closure.[48]

Harry's family sued the Park Service for half a million dollars, sparking a courtroom drama that put the controversy over scientific management in Yellowstone on full display.[49] Those taking the stand included Frank Craighead, who used the opportunity to not only blame the Park Service for closing the backcountry feeding dumps but also air his grievances over the agency's failure to embrace scientific research in general (including his own). Starker Leopold also testified, as did Superintendent Anderson and park biologist Cole. The trial ended in 1975, with the judge deciding that the ill-begotten influence of environmentalism had led the Park Service to pursue the misguided goal of restoring "natural conditions" at the expense of public safety. He awarded the Walker family damages of over $87,000. However, one year later, the decision was reversed on appeal in favor of the Park Service. The court argued that regardless of the potential impacts of bear-management decisions, the Park Service had the right to make them. Moreover, the fact remained that Walker had broken park rules by camping illegally and not securing food as instructed.

* * *

Overall, the 1972 season actually witnessed a decrease in bear injuries inside the park. This news offered some vindication to Yellowstone managers, suggesting that their dump-closing policies had succeeded. However, beyond park borders, data showed that in the two years after closing the last backcountry feeding dump, eighty-eight grizzlies were killed as the result of conflicts across the Greater Yellowstone Ecosystem. This finding appeared to support the Craigheads' contention that conflicts would increase with rapid dump closures.

So how could two parties look at the same data and draw opposite conclusions? Cole and his Yellowstone colleagues believed there were two distinct grizzly populations: one acclimated to trash that lived in the park; the other a wild population that lived outside it. Cole believed the "trash bears" would eventually be captured or shot anyway, leaving only the wild population to perpetuate itself and teach the next generation to hunt for natural food. However, he had no data to back up his proposition. The Craigheads, in contrast, had collected data that proved there was a single population in a single habitat stretching across the Greater Yellowstone Ecosystem. Thus, bears killed inside and outside the park all contributed to population decline. Between 1967 and 1972, a total of 229 grizzlies were killed in this region.[50] Given the slow rate of grizzly reproduction, this pace of killing could lead to their extinction.

In 1973, Congress passed the Endangered Species Act, triggering a series of studies to determine whether or not Yellowstone's grizzlies should be listed. That same year, the Department of the Interior established the Interagency Grizzly Bear Study Team to offer management guidance. Consisting of researchers from the Park Service, Forest Service, Fish and Wildlife Service, and state agencies, the Interagency Team confirmed that Yellowstone's grizzlies constituted a single population. In 1975, the bears were listed as a threatened species.

* * *

In the coming decade, the fraught evolution of ideas about Yellowstone wildlife would go on to inform conservation efforts nationwide. Along with applying the new scientific techniques pioneered by the Craighead brothers, Yellowstone was changing not only ecological science but the very way people understood and related to nature. With the United Nations' designation of the park as an International Biosphere Reserve in 1976 and as a World Heritage Site in 1978, Yellowstone's influence became truly global.

Meanwhile, park managers began implementing a new master plan. Adopted in 1972, the plan redefined Yellowstone's mission to maintain "natural ecosystems within the park in as near pristine conditions as possible for their inspirational, educational, cultural and scientific values for this and future generations."[51] This mandate finally allowed mangers to move closer to fulfilling the recommendations in both the *Leopold Report* and George Wright's *Fauna No.1*. In addition to eliminating non-native species, the mandate opened the door to restoring other elements in Yellowstone's ecosystem—elements long viewed in a negative light. They included predators, but also something that very few at the time understood in ecological terms: wildfire.

The Impossible Fire

(1988–1989)

AT 6:30 P.M. ON SEPTEMBER 7, 1988, *CBS EVENING NEWS* ANCHOR Dan Rather looked up from his desk and addressed the camera.

> Good evening. Part of our national heritage is under threat and on fire tonight. Wildfires [have] already burned more than 635,000 acres of Yellowstone Park. Tonight they menace the nation's most scenic sites. The so-called North Fork Fire closed in on the hotel and campgrounds of the legendary Old Faithful Geyser . . . Fires may be part of Nature's pattern, but Bob McNamara reports the stakes are high in this war against the wilderness flames.[1]

With furrowed brow and characteristic slurred speech, NBC's Tom Brokaw went a step further:

> Old Faithful at Yellowstone—one of America's most popular tourist attractions and our oldest national park—is under siege tonight. And there are a lot of angry people who believe that the National Park Service is responsible [unintelligible] the fires burn too freely for too long.[2]

That night, all three major television networks opened their evening news programs with the same ominous message, the apex of a national story that had been building since midsummer.

Footage featured massive walls of flame and billowing smoke that blocked out the sun, and in the aftermath, a landscape transformed. Places that were once green and lush were now blackened moonscapes of dead trees and barren soil. Over 1 million acres had already burned in the Yellowstone region. But most disturbing was the fact that the fires appeared poised for a final crescendo. Turning toward Old Faithful Inn, the firestorm now threatened the most iconic building in the nation's oldest and most famous national park.

For many viewers, the implication was clear: the demise of Yellowstone was nigh. A seemingly unstoppable force of heat, wind, and flame would reduce the park to ash. The massive scale of Yellowstone's conflagration was unprecedented in national park history.

But devastation was only half the story. The questions raised in Brokaw's newscast were echoed by a growing chorus of politicians, local residents, and tourists who wondered aloud if Park Service mismanagement was to blame.

As apocalyptic scenes filled the front pages of newspapers and flashed into living rooms across the nation, an anguished American public was left to wonder: How had it come to this?

* * *

Three months earlier and 2,000 miles away from those New York City studios, things looked dramatically different to park managers standing on the green, damp grounds of Yellowstone.

Fifty-two-year-old Superintendent Bob Barbee, a large, quick-witted, and good-natured man, now in his fifth season, met with his team of forest ecologists. The park had just experienced a particularly soggy May. Precipitation totals for the last two months topped out at 155 percent and 181 percent of normal, respectively.[3] In fact, the past five summers had been relatively wet and cool. All early signs suggested the trend would continue into the upcoming tourist season.

For Barbee and his team, this meant sticking with the park's fire policy: allowing naturally caused fires (triggered by lightning) to run their course as long as they posed no threat to visitors or sites of special value.

Reflecting the influence of the *Leopold Report*, Yellowstone's fire policy was premised on three major rationales. First, the vast majority of natural fires burned less than ten acres and typically died out on their own. Fighting them, therefore, was a needless expenditure of limited resources. Second, small fires actually helped to reduce the risk of larger blazes by limiting the amount of dead timber and dry underbrush on the landscape. Finally, scientists had documented the important ecological role fire played in the Rocky Mountain landscape. Most of the timber in Yellowstone consisted of lodgepole pine, a species that relied on fire to melt their resin-laced cones and release the seeds within. In other words, without fire, the forests could not regenerate.

In addition to allowing natural fires to burn, the policy also called for the intentional lighting of occasional "prescribed" fires to reduce fuel loads. Since 1972, park managers had treated over 34,000 acres in Yellowstone in this way.[4] Significantly, the policy also stated that all other human-caused fires must be fought as soon as they were detected.

Despite this sound scientific basis, managers administered the fire policy conservatively to ensure park and visitor safety. It was only applied in the absence of arid conditions and high winds, when there was little chance that fires would escalate. If fires did show signs of expansion, park officials were prepared to intervene at a moment's notice to put them out.

With the policy in place, Superintendent Barbee turned his attention to the long list of other managerial issues: from traffic congestion and renovation projects to making arrangements for VIP visits, including one planned in July for the vice president and recently named Republican presidential nominee, George H. W. Bush.

On a personal note, Barbee hoped the 1988 season would bring a much-needed reprieve. Upon his arrival in Yellowstone in 1983, Barbee found himself immediately embroiled in a dispute with Wyoming senator Alan Simpson and residents of Cody over the planned closure of the Fishing Bridge campground near Yellowstone Lake. Under terms of the grizzly-recovery plan ordered by the Endangered Species Act, the campground was to be replaced with facilities at nearby Grant Village to allow bears access to critical habitats. This change, along with the establishment of Bear Management Units—areas that restricted visitor access at certain times of the year—triggered protests from Cody business leaders who feared economic loss from decreased tourism. Though an extraordinarily patient man, Barbee found his emotional reserves tested over the issue. However, in May, after five years of debate, the Park Service finally settled the matter in favor of the bears, and Barbee looked forward to a summer season of relative tranquility.[5]

* * *

At the other end of the Park Service hierarchy, twenty-five-year-old Holly McKinney was beginning her very first summer as a Yellow-stone naturalist.[6] Originally from Georgia but fresh from a five-month stint as an environmental educator in the sun-drenched Florida Keys, McKinney spent the last weeks of May in a training program at park headquarters. Afterward, she transferred to her assigned area in the Old Faithful Geyser Basin, where she learned how to run the Visitor Information desk and lead educational programs.

Donning the freshly pressed forest-green uniform for the first time was the fulfillment of a childhood dream. To complete the ensemble, McKinney carefully positioned the iconic hat with brim set parallel to the ground. She was now part of one of the nation's most respected institutions. More than that, she was a member of the Yellowstone National Park family.

Another member of that family was Yellowstone's winter keeper, seasonal park ranger, freelance photographer, and author, Jeff Henry. Soft-spoken but rugged from years of working outdoors, Henry had spent the spring working for the Interagency Grizzly Bear Study Team on a survey of winter-killed carcasses in the Firehole Valley. During a short trip to Heart Lake in May, he noted the extraordinary slushi-ness of the snow cover. However, such conditions were not abnormal for that time of year and did not indicate that the upcoming summer weather patterns would be any different from years past.[7]

Like park employees all across Yellowstone, Henry had his hands full preparing for the rapidly approaching summer season. With a heave of his waterlogged snowshoes, he slogged his way through the deep slush and continued back to the trailhead.

* * *

In June, Yellowstone's summer season opened to little fanfare. As the number of visitors grew from a trickle to a steady stream, there was no reason to expect this summer to be any different from years past. But soon, a series of seemingly unremarkable events would trigger one of the most catastrophic episodes in the history of Yellowstone National Park.

First of all, it stopped raining.

Precipitation data for June showed a reversal of patterns from recent years, registering only 20 percent of normal. Though this change was notable, it was not yet cause for alarm. Recent weather history also indicated the rains would return in July. For five of the last six years, rainfall totals in July were more than twice the normal amount.[8]

Shortly thereafter, lightning from summer storms ignited several small fires in the region. Again, this was neither worrisome nor unexpected. Most of the fires consumed no more than a few acres before dying out of their own accord. Three of these tiny fires, however, persisted.

One had sparked to life on June 14 in the Custer National Forest, lying just north of Yellowstone National Park. In keeping with the convention of naming fires according to nearby landmarks, the Forest Service labeled this small blaze the Storm Creek Fire.[9]

Then on June 23 and 25, two additional lightning-caused fires popped up, this time inside park boundaries. The first, named the Shoshone Fire, emerged just north of Yellowstone's southern entrance near Shoshone Lake. The other, called the Fan Fire, burst forth in the far northwestern corner of the park near Gardiner, along the banks of Fan Creek. Park officials kept tabs on all three fires but did not view them as issues of concern.

* * *

For naturalist Holly McKinney, these small, faraway blazes were definitely not the focus of attention. Rather, June was filled with a whirlwind of fresh experiences. Early mornings might find her whizzing down the paved walkways of the geyser basin on her brown ten-speed Schwinn. With her Park Service hat held in place by her auburn ponytail, McKinney made the rounds visiting each of the major geysers as the sun began to rise. After measuring water levels and geothermal activity, she radioed reports to her fellow rangers at the Old Faithful Visitor Center. There, the data was used to calculate potential eruption times, which would be posted on visitor-information chalkboards.

This was McKinney's favorite assignment. On frosty mornings, the steam from geysers quickly turned into an icy layer that fogged her glasses and froze her hair as she pedaled over the rough blacktop paths. But these cool Yellowstone mornings typically blossomed into gloriously sunny afternoons. These were spent either out in the pine-scented forests surrounding Old Faithful, leading educational tours in the basin, or at the Visitor Center information desk fielding the never-ending stream of tourist questions. Yet, even when working indoors, time flew by.

Depending on her shift, evenings might find McKinney giving fireside talks or slideshows up at Madison Campground, or possibly taking midnight strolls with friends in the geyser basin. Sitting quietly on the boardwalks beneath star-filled skies, with each eruption, McKinney could hear the burbling give way to the gushing roar of the water, feel steam on her skin, and smell the slightly sulfurous aromas. Such experiences created powerful memories she would carry for the rest of her life.

Nothing during those first weeks of June suggested to McKinney, or any other park official, that disaster loomed. Superintendent Barbee and his leadership team still had every reason to believe rainy conditions would soon cancel out the dry days of June. As far as fire policy was concerned, he saw no reason to change.

* * *

As June gave way to July, the weather moved from bad to worse. Not only did the expected rainfall fail to materialize, but, instead, a succession of strong dry winds began pummeling the region.[10] As the moisture content in trees and shrubs dropped ever lower, the risk of catastrophic fire rose considerably. Little by little, the Yellowstone landscape was becoming ripe for ignition.

These conditions soon fueled the appearance of several new fires around the park. On the last day of June, a lightning strike ignited the

Red Fire, located just southeast of the Shoshone Fire.[11] Then, on July 5, the Lava Creek Fire appeared, only seven miles from park headquarters. In both cases, park officials allowed the fires to burn but monitored them closely.

However, this was only the beginning. Between July 9 and July 12, an array of new fires burst forth. Near Yellowstone's southern boundary, the Falls and Mink Fires emerged. And along the eastern boundary, new blazes included the Mist, the Clover, the Lovely, the Raven, the Shallow, the Fern, and the Sour. Ultimately, these eastern fires would join together into a single massive conflagration referred to as the Clover-Mist Complex.[12]

The sheer number of fires tested the limits of Yellowstone's policy. But after careful deliberation, Superintendent Barbee and the chief fire ecologist, Don Despain, once again decided to hold course. Their reluctance to deviate from the plan was based not only on recent weather patterns but also a blend of personal experience and historical data. Barbee was well-versed in fire ecology, having worked with natural fire planning since its inception in California during the late 1960s. But perhaps the greatest factor in Barbee's decision was the fire history of Yellowstone itself. The single largest fire in the entire history of the park (dating back to 1872) took place near Heart Lake in 1931 and totaled 18,000 acres.[13] The Park Service's modern firefighting capability was more than adequate to suppress fires of such magnitude.

So, while park managers kept a wary eye on the growing patchwork of small fires, they gave most of their attention to other tasks—including planning for the arrival of Vice President Bush—and prayed for rain.

* * *

On July 14, Yellowstone's chief ranger[14] Dan Sholly and two crew members were in a helicopter scouting a cabin in preparation for the vice president's visit. Unfortunately, the building lay directly in the path of the burgeoning Clover-Mist Complex. From their lofty vantage point, they watched as a sudden burst of dry wind transformed multiple scattered 200-to-300-acre fires into a massive 7,000-acre conflagration in a matter of minutes.[15] By the end of the day, the total area ablaze across the park surpassed 8,600 acres.[16]

In response, Barbee not only canceled the vice president's visit, but announced a change in Yellowstone's fire policy. From this day forward, no new naturally caused fires would be allowed to burn, and most of the existing fires would be vigorously fought.[17]

The strategy included a call for an interagency firefighting effort,[18] drawing personnel and resources from throughout the Park Service, Forest Service, Bureau of Land Management, National Guard, and U.S. Army. Barbee hoped this tactical change would mitigate the growing risk until the summer rains arrived.

* * *

But one week later, the rains still hadn't come. Despite the Park Service's best efforts, by July 21, the acreage burning throughout Yellowstone doubled to approximately 17,000 acres and prompted another change in policy. From now on, *every* fire in the park would be fought.[19]

However, the very next day, one of the most portentous twists in the 1988 fire season took place. The story has two versions. Both involve a group of firewood cutters working in the Targhee National Forest, just a few hundred yards from the Yellowstone border. In the first version, the men took a smoking break when one of them carelessly tossed a cigarette onto the dry grass. In the second version, a spark from one of the chainsaws was to blame. In both cases, the men didn't notice the flames until it was too late. Regardless of the fire's origins, all agree that careless human action caused what would become one of the most destructive blazes in Yellowstone history: the North Fork.[20]

A team of the most elite firefighters in the nation, called smoke jumpers, fought the fire from the moment it was detected. In addition, the Forest Service and Park Service dispatched hand crews, bulldozers, and slurry bombers, but to little avail.[21] Firsthand reports suggest that within hours of ignition, the firestorm evolved into an advancing wall of flame beyond any human control.

On July 23, Barbee ordered the first major evacuation in the history of Yellowstone National Park. With the rapid advance of the Shoshone Fire, park managers closed the Grant Village complex to all visitors and nonessential personnel.[22] Three days later, the fire jumped the South Entrance road and arrived at Grant Village with flames reaching 200 feet into the sky. And Jeff Henry was there to greet it.

By midsummer, Henry's seasonal winter-keeping duties transitioned into work as a seasonal park ranger. However, as the fires gained more attention, the park assigned Henry to use his photographic skills to document the 1988 fire season. Much like a war correspondent, this meant he constantly sought out the most dangerous sites. And although his primary task was to take photos, he tried to help out in other ways too. Consequently, on July 26, Henry found himself at the Grant Village service station, beneath a darkened sky filled with swirling ash. Firefighters rushed back and forth laying out hose line, clearing away brush, and wetting down rooftops. And in the distance, hidden by the gray smoke, the growing roar of an angry wall of flame rushed toward him like a rising tsunami.

In between snapping pictures, Henry, along with another man, aimed water hoses around the service station in hopes of preventing a gas explosion from the giant propane tanks behind the building. As he fought to hold his ground amid the wind and smoke, he looked up to see a massive airplane coming in low overhead—a slurry bomber. In an instant, it dropped a load of red flame retardant. With only seconds to react, he dove under the gas-pump shelter just in time to avoid getting slimed. Exhilarated by the near miss, Henry watched as the slurry staved off the fire, saving the propane tanks and preventing an explosion that might have killed him.[23]

When it was over, not a single major structure in Grant Village was lost thanks to the firefighters and volunteers on hand that day. Elsewhere in the park, however, the Summer of Fire raged on.

* * *

A few days later, national media began to take notice. While local and regional newspapers had covered the park fires for weeks, network television, including NBC and ABC, aired their first stories on July 25.[24] This development presented a brand-new challenge for Superintendent Barbee. What had once been a question of ecological science and resource management was now an issue of national political concern.

Given the high value that so many Americans placed on Yellowstone, reporters wondered how those entrusted with its care could ever have let such a debacle come to pass. Many settled on the Park Service's so-called "let it burn" policy as the likely culprit. This, in turn, raised questions about the competence of those who had adopted such a faulty policy. Superintendent Bob Barbee and Park Service director William Mott quickly found themselves at the center of a different kind of firestorm.

On July 27, Interior Secretary Donald Hodel arrived in Yellowstone to tour the damage and hold a press conference. Standing before a fleet of fire trucks in the Old Faithful parking lot, Hodel attempted to walk a middle line. On one hand he extolled the virtues of Yellowstone's natural fire policy, but on the other, he stressed that now, the Park Service and the Reagan administration were doing everything in their power to put the fires out.

To the casual observer—and most Americans—this was a befuddling message. The "we were for it before we were against it" approach was bound to confuse. Nonetheless, like a military parade, the show of firefighting force seemed to calm people's fears. Of course, *fighting* a fire is not the same as putting one out, a distinction lost among many in attendance that day, but one that would soon become apparent.

* * *

Those dispatched to fight Yellowstone's infernos quickly learned that conventional firefighting techniques were of little use. The combination of arid conditions, pummeling strong winds, and a centuries-old accumulation of dry trees and brush translated into wildfires of unprecedented proportions. For modern fire crews, the Yellowstone fires were something new.

This is not to say that massive wildfires had not happened before in American history: the huge 1845 blaze in Oregon, the Great Fires of 1871 in Michigan and Wisconsin, and the colossal 3 million–acre Big Blow Up of 1910 in the Pacific Northwest suggest otherwise. But each of these events came before the advent of modern firefighting techniques premised on suppression and control, strategies developed by the Forest Service and Park Service largely in response to 1910. In the decades since, American society simply hadn't witnessed fires of comparable size.

Known as "crown fires," the colossal Yellowstone blazes swallowed entire 150-foot-tall trees, with flames towering another 200 feet beyond that. The resulting smoke mushroomed out like nuclear explosions, reaching thousands of feet into the sky and becoming visible for miles. As the clouds drew near, they blotted out the sun, filling the air with hot wind, ash, and glowing embers.

The massive energy released by these infernos created its own weather system, instantly evaporating the moisture in nearby vegetation and sucking all oxygen toward itself in gusts of up to one hundred miles per hour. On top of this, the fires could move rapidly, easily covering five to ten miles in a day or, in some instances, within hours.

Conventional methods of fighting forest fires involved containing them until they died out for lack of fuel. This was done by creating fire breaks: clearing away trees, shrubs, grass, and anything flammable near the advancing perimeter of a fire. Breaks could be made by hand, using the combination axe-adze tool known as a Pulaski, or mechanically with chainsaws or bulldozers. When possible, crews made use of existing breaks like roadways and rivers. They might also set "backfires" in order to fight fire with fire. By igniting vegetation in front of an oncoming blaze, the backfire would be pulled toward the advancing flames along with all available oxygen. If successful, the backfire consumed the nearby fuel as it rushed toward the main blaze, creating a break in its wake.

For the past hundred years, these strategies generally proved successful. But in Yellowstone in 1988, they were of little use. The problem had to do in part with the fires' ability to constantly set new blazes. Known as "spot fires," they emerged when winds sent flaming embers out in front of the advancing fires. Spot fires can be countered if fire breaks are wide enough and the winds sufficiently mild. But in this case, the wind and flames were of such force that they could fling embers up to half a mile away. As a result, fires jumped over roads, rivers, and even the Grand Canyon of the Yellowstone with ease.

What firefighters could do—and *did* with tremendous success—was wage a defensive war to protect people and buildings. Creating breaks around visitor centers, administrative buildings, hotels, and so on, firefighters worked to limit the damage. They spent hours wetting rooftops, distributing flame-retardant foam, and scouting for spot fires. Despite the historical scale of the 1988 fires, crews could take great pride in the fact that inside Yellowstone National Park, not a single human life or major building was lost.[25]

Nonetheless, these nuances were often lost on the general public. For a generation raised on Smokey Bear, the idea that forest fires were categorically bad yet preventable remained a simple truth. The thought that fire might be necessary or that modern society could fail to control it sounded crazy.

As Superintendent Barbee recalled, "People kept saying why don't you just put the fires out? Well, why don't you just stop the hurricane? Or the tornado?[26] . . . We could have had the entire United States Army in here and it would not have made any difference."[27]

* * *

While the battle continued, Yellowstone's managers confronted another new challenge. At the highest level, Barbee faced enormous pressure from politicians in Wyoming and Montana to keep the park open. For decades, Yellowstone served as the major economic engine for tourism in both states. Park closure could mean the loss of millions of dollars.

For Barbee, visitor safety remained the top priority. However, given Yellowstone's 2 million–acre size, it was possible that fires burning thousands of acres in one part of the park would have little impact on the rest of it. Nonetheless, the unprecedented nature of the fires meant there were no guidelines. Just how *should* Park Service personnel manage the visitors and places that remained open in the context of an ever-growing threat?

For Holly McKinney, the strangeness of the situation expressed itself in a number of ways. Increasingly, she encountered visitors who were unaware of the danger. Assuming that "if the park was open, it must be safe," visitors took needless risks, actively seeking out the fires to take photographs or simply to experience events they had seen on TV.

McKinney had witnessed this behavior before. Visitors frequently ignored park rules as they approached elk, bison, or even bears to get that perfect photo. Sometimes they wandered off the boardwalks in the geyser basin for the same reason. Doing so might lead to serious injury and even death, but the danger currently posed by the Yellowstone fires was of another magnitude.

On one occasion, a family rushed in to the Old Faithful Visitor Center after driving their car over Craig Pass from Yellowstone Lake. Wide-eyed with excitement, they told McKinney of their journey through towering flames on either side of the road. Blinded by smoke, they had to drive with the front door open in order to follow the yellow highway lines. McKinney listened in disbelief as the family spoke like they had just been on a wild ride at a theme park. In reality, they had not only chanced a collision with another vehicle, firefighters, or animals on the roadway but faced the very real possibility of combustion and death if their car had been consumed by flames. For the first time, McKinney's confidence in the Park Service began to falter. If managers were missing this danger, what else was falling through the cracks?[28]

Ironically, at the same moment McKinney saw a need for more visitor education about the dangers of fire, park naturalists received an order limiting what they could say in response to visitor questions. In the Old Faithful Visitor Center, this meant refraining from discussing or even acknowledging the North Fork Fire.

To be fair, the order was likely an attempt to ensure consistent public messaging when things were in constant flux. But in practice, it made for some extremely awkward moments. As McKinney and her colleagues took visitors on guided hikes of the geyser basin, one couldn't miss the massive mushroom-shaped smoke plumes stretching across the sky. Unsurprisingly, curious tourists would pepper McKinney with questions: What had caused the fire? Were visitors safe in the park? Were the flames moving toward Old Faithful? What was the Park Service doing about it?

For environmental educators like McKinney, the recommended response of "I don't know" was unacceptable. Instead, she did her best to convey that the Park Service was aware of the fire, that visitors needn't worry, and that the focus of the tour was on the geysers.

While McKinney continued to hope that those in the upper tiers of park leadership would address the fires, she also took steps of her own to both warn and educate the visitors in her midst. Soon, the informational sandwich boards in the Visitor Center included the well-known surgeon general's warning: "Inhaling smoke is dangerous to your health."

* * *

As July became August, new blazes ignited while existing fires merged into ever-greater conflagrations. On August 2, the Clover-Mist Fire reached over 73,000 acres as it crossed into the Shoshone National Forest. By August 14, it expanded to 95,000 acres. Meanwhile, the North Fork Fire consumed almost 53,000 acres.[29]

A group of fire-ecology experts gathered in West Yellowstone to try to forecast weather patterns and fire behavior for the rest of the summer. Mockingly referred to as the "fire gods" by firefighters who felt the scientists lacked on-the-ground experience yet held enormous power over fire strategy, the experts pored over historical data and concluded that after one more large wind event in August, cooler and wetter conditions would return.[30] Unfortunately, their data only went back about one hundred years. Had they been able to look back 1,000 years, they would have seen that such massive fire events were actually a natural and recurring part of Yellowstone's history.

However, the worst was still to come.

On August 20, spurred on by continued high temperatures and cool, dry winds gusting upward of sixty miles per hour, the fires combined to burn 165,000 acres in a single day, an all-time record at Yellowstone.[31] Since June, the *total* acreage burned in the Greater Yellowstone area amounted to just over 370,000 acres. Yet in a single day, that number increased by almost 50 percent. They called it Black Saturday.

In the following days, the fires continued to expand. The North Fork Fire swept through Norris Geyser Basin and advanced on Canyon Village, causing another evacuation. In the south, fires forced a second evacuation of Flagg Ranch, while in the north, the Storm Creek blaze threatened Cooke City.[32] On August 23, Park Service director Mott announced that natural fire policies would be halted in all national parks.

By now, the fires had become the top news story in the nation. As reporters descended on Yellowstone, they found firefighters and park personnel stretched to the limit. Coordinating the movement of trucks, airplanes, helicopters, and firefighters from various federal agencies alongside thousands of state-agency personnel, National Guard reservists, and U.S. Army troops was a tremendously complex undertaking. On top of that, tourists kept showing up, expecting Park Service employees to conduct everyday duties.

It is perhaps not surprising that in the midst of such confusion, some significant missteps occurred. On August 30, ABC news reporter Brian Rooney delivered a doozy. Mistaking a tourist named Stanley Mott for Park Service director William Mott, Rooney conducted a nationally televised interview about the fires. "Well, I think [the fire] is one of the great wonders of Yellowstone," Stanley said. "I think everybody should get a chance to see this if possible."[33] It's not hard to imagine the groan emanating from Director Mott upon seeing this imposter deliver such a ludicrous message on national television.

But it would get worse. Media portrayals of the Park Service as irresponsible reached their climax in a front-page *Denver Post* article with the headline "Burn, Baby, Burn." Reporter Jim Carrier had conducted an interview with Yellowstone's chief fire ecologist, Don Despain, who uttered the phrase in response to seeing one of his research test plots burn, thereby allowing his experiments to proceed. However, taken out of context, the headline implied that the Park Service was pleased that the entirety of Yellowstone National Park might turn to ash.[34]

While there was, in fact, a good deal of responsible reporting (mostly in regional outlets), misinformation added fuel to the political flames. Cartoons presented Barbee as "Superintendent Barbee-que." Someone added a letter to the sign outside Cooke City so that it read "Cooked City." Barbee explained, "Somebody had to be the target. I kept waiting for Gaddafi or somebody to do something outrageous, but he didn't. So they all came to Yellowstone."[35] He concluded, "We were the only [news] game in town all summer long."[36]

Critics began calling for Barbee's and Mott's resignations. Meanwhile, public concerns heightened as the North Fork blaze turned toward Old Faithful. It appeared that everyone's worst fears were about to be broadcast in real time on the evening news.

* * *

For weeks, Holly McKinney had worked and slept in a smoky haze. Her transit house was not airtight. Some nights she would lurch awake with a choking gasp and jump out of bed to check the windows for advancing flames. But despite the lack of rest, her daily workload increased considerably. She now split her time between the visitor center at Old Faithful and the information desk at the camp set up for firefighters at Madison Campground.

At 8:00 p.m. on September 7, the West District ranger issued a statement that an evacuation of the Old Faithful area was not likely. However, by 10:30 p.m., he reversed himself, calling for a temporary closure of the inn and the evacuation of all visitors and nonessential Park Service personnel.

The next morning, his order changed again to a permanent closure and evacuation by 10:00 a.m. But unbeknownst to McKinney, and for reasons still not clear, day visitors were still being allowed to enter the park from the West Yellowstone gate.

McKinney got dressed and made her way to the visitor center, where she learned that she and the other naturalists were to forego their fire-retardant gear and dress in their usual Park Service green uniforms. They would perform normal duties—manning the front desk and leading educational programs—as if it were just another day. Surprised, McKinney complied, but all about her in the basin, slow-motion chaos seemed to be unfolding.

Closing the Old Faithful Inn required Park Service staff to knock on visitors' doors and ask them to leave. Soon, old yellow school buses arrived to evacuate employees from the hotel, gift shops, and restaurants. As they waited to load up, groups of young workers set up lawn chairs near (and even on top of) the buses. Some opened cans of beer and let out a raucous cheer every time an air tanker flew overhead. Meanwhile, firefighters cleared away flammable debris from buildings and saturated rooftops with water. In the parking lots, reporters from every major news organization huddled near their satellite-rigged vans, sipping coffee, prepping reports, and chatting expectantly.

McKinney's supervisor was nowhere to be seen. She was concerned that she and her colleagues were neither ordered nor allowed to wear the yellow Nomex flameproof clothing. Still, she dutifully manned the information desk as the morning turned to afternoon. Outside, the sky darkened as a dry breeze began to pick up.

For McKinney, the most surprising thing of all was the stream of new visitors that kept arriving at her desk. Wasn't there an evacuation underway? Who was letting cars into the park? Were these guests from the inn who simply refused to leave?

Phone calls to her supervisor went unanswered. Left on her own, McKinney realized she and the other naturalists needed to take matters into their own hands. Locking the visitor center, she huddled behind the building with her colleagues. McKinney knew that what they were about to do might cost them their jobs. But there was only one choice. They must close the basin and evacuate as many people as possible to safety.

Without delay, they fanned out, sending one runner to nearby campgrounds and another out to Observation Point. Deanna Dulen, the only naturalist with fire experience, went up to the main over-pass to turn away cars and keep watch for the firestorm. Meanwhile, McKinney and the others ran through the parking lots from car to car with a simple message: "Leave. Leave now. It's not safe here."

Most listened and evacuated. Others refused.

A little after 3:00 p.m., Old Faithful erupted right on cue. In the aftermath, as the steam faded and the waters simmered down, ash be-gan to fall from the sky.[37] In the distance, a dull rumbling emanated from black smoke plumes amassing behind the ridge. Deanna called in on the radio. She had lost all visibility on the road. Evacuation was no longer an option. It was time for phase two of their plan.

Gathering together everyone they could find—reporters, stray vis-itors, a middle-aged lady with a cat in a duffel bag, a pair of crying teenagers—McKinney and her companions moved to a safe point on the corner of the Old Faithful boardwalk. Located halfway between the geyser and the visitor center, surrounded by open space and bare earth, it seemed like the farthest point from flammable trees and buildings. If things got really bad, they would make a run for the river.

Here they would make their stand. Here they would watch and pray as 200-foot-tall flames crested the ridge and began a mad rush directly toward Old Faithful.

* * *

At that same moment, news programs began streaming their live broadcasts. Standing near the Old Faithful Inn, NBC's field correspondent Roger O'Neill delivered his report to anchor Tom Brokaw via live satellite. Struggling against gusts of smoky wind, O'Neill began:

> Tom, that North Fork Fire has been making a strong march toward Old Faithful since noon and it got considerably stronger in the last half hour. We now have fifty-to-sixty-mile-per-hour winds here and the fire is less than two blocks from the inn. There is one way out and the fire is on three sides.[38]

O'Neill went on to explain how 1,200 fire fighters had miraculously saved Cooke City and Silver Gate, two Montana towns, earlier in the day. Then, in a recorded segment, he reported on Old Faithful Inn:

> Six hundred guests were awakened by seven and asked to leave by 10:00 a.m. The evacuation was orderly and calm . . . Many wanted to take a last look at Old Faithful Geyser, the most famous symbol of Yellowstone. As the cars and buses left, the eighty-four-year-old inn stood alone. It is a magnificent structure. Once, the largest log hotel ever built. All of the wood beams of the original inn came from the forests of Yellowstone.

Returning to the live feed, Roger and Tom now spoke to each other on a split screen.

> Brokaw: Roger, to be absolutely fair about it to the Park Service . . . while they didn't fight the fire earlier they are doing almost everything they can at *this* hour I gather?

O'Neill: They are doing everything humanly possible. But I'm afraid not enough human manpower can control these fires, they are too big and the wind is much too strong.

Brokaw: And even with the [new] sprinkler system on top of Old Faithful—that is—to put it politely—a kind of a fire trap even though it is a magnificent hotel.

O'Neill: It is a fire trap. It is all wood. And they are putting foam on the backside of the inn now. It depends on the spot fires. And it depends on how hard the fire hits the inn. And it will be a short time before it does.

And that's where they left it. Of course, contrary to Brokaw's remarks, the Park Service had fought the North Fork Fire from the very beginning. But such distinctions were lost in the face of pending calamity. Instead of calming the fears of the public, the report offered little hope that the Old Faithful Inn would survive the night.

* * *

Back on the boardwalk, McKinney braced herself for the storm as she tried to comfort the thirty-some people gathered with her. Had she glanced up at just the right moment, she might have spotted a figure near the visitor center drop to one knee and snap a photo of the group before hastening toward the Old Faithful Inn.

Jeff Henry had arrived in the basin earlier that day on word that the North Fork Fire was heading toward Old Faithful.[39] Having spent the morning clearing flammable materials away from employee cabins, Henry now took up his camera and headed to the epicenter of firefighting activity: the defense of Old Faithful Inn.

The most iconic structure in the park, the inn was not only a historic treasure but, as Brokaw noted, extremely flammable. With three fire trucks deployed in the basin, firefighters stationed one of them directly behind the building to provide a constant spray of water on the roof against falling embers. They also readied the newly installed rooftop sprinkler system.

Climbing up to the "widow's walk," a high balcony at the very top of the inn, Henry found two fire spotters already in position. Using infrared scopes that allowed them to discern heat signatures, they tracked the oncoming blaze and radioed reports to fire crews on the ground. However, the intensity of the heat forced them to pull their eyes away from the scopes. With a flurry of expletives, the men put down their instruments and quickly pulled on their fireproof face masks and gloves.

The fire was coming fast. But you didn't need fancy infrared sensors or a pair of swearing firefighters to reach that conclusion. As the firestorm crested the ridge of the basin, Henry felt the radiant heat on his face, though it was still approximately one mile away.

Seconds later, he felt the punch of hurricane-strength winds, filled with swirling ash and red embers. Above him, a firebrand arced directly overhead in apparent slow motion. Henry watched as it landed near Observation Point and exploded into a brand-new fire, quickly engulfing the nearby trees.[40] As the flames reached the edge of Old Faithful Village, Henry sensed the danger of his position and decided to descend the stairs and exit through the main doors of the inn.

* * *

Down on the boardwalk, the situation was no less intense. The firestorm poured into the geyser basin like a tidal wave. McKinney turned toward the fire, but rather than feel heat on her face, she immediately sensed scalding hotness on the back of her neck and arms. Fearful of another blaze from behind, she turned quickly and realized she was experiencing the convection current. Heat from the towering storm cloud was collapsing on the other side of her and circling back, sucked toward the mammoth conflagration as it hungrily gathered all oxygen unto itself.

A powerful roar like jet engines filled the air as thick, spark-filled smoke swirled violently. In shock, McKinney realized she could no longer see her hand at the end of her arm. Dinner plate–sized firebrands darted by like missiles and seemed to explode all around her. At one point a massive fireball flew overhead, likely the same firebrand seen by Jeff Henry.

Huddling together on the boardwalk, the group gasped for breath and fought for composure against mounting fear that this could be the end. A couple of reporters used that moment to inform McKinney that they had to use the restroom and hurried off, never to return.[41]

An hour passed. Then another. Time crept by without any sense of measure. Between the deafening rumble, buffeting winds, and incessant sobbing of the teens, the strain was almost too much for McKinney. She felt responsible for the lives of those assembled and worried for her friends out battling the blaze. Deanna and two other colleagues never made it back to the meeting point.

Then, ever so slowly, the roaring subsided, the smoke began to lift, and the firestorm passed on from the geyser basin. They had survived.

As the sky cleared, Jeff Henry looked up from his own refuge point to see the silhouette of the Old Faithful Inn. Standing tall through remnant tendrils of black smoke, it reminded him of Herbert Mason's famous photograph of Saint Paul's Cathedral, intact above the smoke and devastation caused by the London Blitz on December 29, 1940. Just as the great cathedral gave the British hope in a time of need, the sight of the old inn intact brought a sense that perhaps Yellowstone might survive the Summer of Fire after all.[42]

* * *

Amazingly, the firestorm at Old Faithful took no human lives. Though nineteen employee cabins were lost, fire crews saved all major buildings. The mix of natural and human-made fire breaks provided by the parking lots and the basin itself played a key role in this outcome. But the most important factor was the heroic effort put forth by the firefighters.

Although the battle for Old Faithful was over, fires elsewhere showed no signs of slowing down. The North Fork Fire split into two branches. As the southern branch ran through Old Faithful, a northern arm now raced toward park headquarters. On September 9, fires in the Yellowstone region once again set new records, burning more acreage on a single day than even on Black Saturday.[43] Weather reports predicted that the next day would be even worse.

For Superintendent Barbee, this was the final straw. On September 10, with the fire closing in on Mammoth, he reluctantly ordered

Yellowstone National Park closed to all visitors for the first time in history. After ordering Mammoth evacuated, Barbee arranged for the buildings to be foamed and headed to West Yellowstone, where President Reagan had called for a cabinet-level meeting to decide next steps. For Barbee it felt like an admission of defeat. At least he knew it would be interpreted that way in the papers. But he also knew that Yellowstone's natural fire policy was not to blame. The Summer of Fire would have come anyway, regardless of any human action.

Then an even more remarkable thing happened.

In the early evening of September 10, humidity levels began to rise. In some parts of the park, raindrops started to fall. By the next morning, rain had turned to snow. To paraphrase one news account, in the end, what $120 million and 25,000 fire fighters could not do, nature achieved in a single day with a quarter inch of fresh powder.[44]

Of course, not all fires were immediately extinguished; most smoldered on for weeks. The North Fork and the Clover-Mist blazes burned another 10,000 and 20,000 acres respectively before dying out.[45] But for all intents and purposes, Yellowstone's Summer of Fire was over. The political debates, however, were just beginning.

* * *

In the final tally, 1.4 million acres burned in the Greater Yellowstone Ecosystem, with a little under 1 million of those acres inside the park. The Park Service organized task forces and Congress held hearings to find out why.

Overall, the findings reaffirmed the natural fire policy and absolved Superintendent Barbee and his staff of any wrongdoing. As Barbee had insisted all along, there was nothing they could have done to halt the North Fork or other major Yellowstone fires from running their course.

This is not to say that the Park Service walked away unchanged. The conditions under which natural fire practices could be applied were tightened considerably.[46] More importantly, the Park Service realized the need for proactive communication and better public education programs.

But the most influential outcome of Yellowstone's Summer of Fire had to be the national discussion it sparked about whether humans can or should control nature. Not only were the fires unstoppable, but the subsequent effects revealed their indispensable role in the regeneration of environmental systems. Within weeks, grasses and wildflowers began to pop up. Grazing elk and bison returned, picking their way through a newly greening landscape. By late September, the national narrative changed from a story of destruction to one of rebirth: Yellowstone as a phoenix rising from the ashes.

Articles in *National Geographic* and *Audubon* highlighted these transformations and, soon, tourists flocked back to see for themselves. Visitor numbers in October surged 40 percent over the same month a year before.[47] The following year, visitation hit a new all-time record of 2.7 million. Returning tourists found new informational material and displays on fire ecology, including roadside markers, classroom materials, and an exhibit in Grant Village telling the story of the 1988 fires.[48]

For the first time, an entire generation of Americans began to reevaluate Smokey Bear's simple but powerful message that wildfire should be, and could be, controlled. Smokey was right that humans are responsible for their actions in nature, including a commitment not to start forest fires. However, fire itself is not a moral thing, but a natural part of healthy ecosystems. And there are times when humans simply must adapt.

The Bad Wolf Returns

(1994–1997)

ON THE MORNING OF JANUARY 12, 1995, ROWS OF EXCITED elementary schoolchildren in colorful winter coats stood along the road between the Roosevelt Arch and the northern entrance station of Yellowstone National Park. Around them and flowing up the hillside, scattered groups of Park Service employees, television crews, and assorted spectators looked on in anticipation. Moments later, the crowd erupted into cheers and triumphant wolf howls as a caravan of Park Service patrol cars rolled into view escorting a large horse trailer: "Here they come! Here they come!"

Writer and founder of The Wolf Fund, thirty-six-year-old Renée Askins jumped up and down in jubilation and hugged her friend and fellow thirtysomething, Hank Fischer of the Defenders of Wildlife.[1] For Askins, Fischer, and many others assembled that morning, the event marked the culmination of a nearly twenty-year journey.

The trailer carried the first eight wolves destined for release in Yellowstone National Park. Crossing through the famous archway, the procession paused for a moment as Interior Secretary Bruce Babbitt said a few words to the press. "This is a day of redemption and a day of hope," he began. "It's a day when the limits of what is possible have been greatly expanded because we are showing our children that restoration is possible; that we can restore a community to its natural state."[2]

After another cheer from the crowd, the convoy continued into the park toward a series of acclimation pens in the Lamar Valley. Upon reaching their destination, Secretary Babbitt, Fish and Wildlife Service director Mollie Beattie, and Yellowstone supervisor Mike Finley carried the first crate along a snowy path to the nearest one-acre pen. A photograph commemorating the scene would soon grace the front pages of newspapers across the country.

After a seventy-year absence, the gray wolf had come home to Yellowstone.

* * *

In 1973, two years before Yellowstone's grizzly bears became listed as threatened, the U.S. Fish and Wildlife Service listed the northern Rocky Mountain gray wolf as endangered under the Endangered Species Act.[3] The law called for the protection and recovery of listed species within all or part of their historic range. For gray wolves, this eventually meant all of the lower forty-eight states except Minnesota, where a few packs still survived. However, the law only called for restoration in places where suitable habitat still existed.

For the northern Rocky Mountain gray wolf, whose historic range included Yellowstone, the designation made sense given that the last known wolves in the park were exterminated in 1926. But Yellowstone was also unique in that it offered one of the few remaining habitats still large enough and wild enough to accommodate potential restoration.

Of course, the idea of restoring wolves had been posed before. George Wright's reports of the 1930s called for predator reintroduction, as did Aldo Leopold in a 1944 article suggesting that Yellowstone was one of the last remaining places in which "gray wolves may be allowed to continue their existence."[4] Such notions were echoed later in the 1963 *Leopold Report* authored by Aldo's son, Starker, and again in Yellowstone's own 1972 Park Management Plan.

With the 1968 replacement of "direct reduction" practices with "natural regulation" for Yellowstone's elk, bison, and other wildlife species, it only made sense to restore predators to help manage population growth.[5] However, in practice, the idea lay dormant until the endangered species listing in 1973 brought renewed attention.

In 1975, the U.S. Fish and Wildlife Service took the first steps by establishing a Wolf Recovery Team to develop a plan for wolf restoration in Yellowstone. Consisting of federal-agency scientists, state game officials, university experts, and a representative from the Audubon Society, the Recovery Team also allowed interested members of the public to attend meetings.

Meanwhile, the Park Service moved forward on its own by inviting biologist John Weaver to conduct a study to determine whether or not any wolves still survived inside the park. If present, as some locals and tourists claimed, there would be no need for a reintroduction.

Weaver's volunteer research assistants included a recent graduate from Kalamazoo College named Renée Askins. With long brown hair parted down the middle and a quiet but articulate and determined voice, Askins began attending Recovery Team meetings in her off-hours. There she met Hank Fischer, newly employed by the Defenders of Wildlife and who also focused on the issue. Both would soon become key players in the wolf-reintroduction saga.

In 1978, Weaver completed his study. Concluding that no wolves remained in Yellowstone, he recommended reintroduction of the species. Two years later, the Fish and Wildlife Service released its initial wolf-recovery plan, but it was deemed inadequate for failing to actually address the reintroduction issue. Under the leadership of Wayne Brewster, the Fish and Wildlife Service restructured the Wolf Recovery Team, and in 1981, work began on a revised plan.

By the time of Bob Barbee's 1983 appointment to Yellowstone, aside from these studies, little actual progress had been made. According to Barbee, during his job interview with the assistant secretary of the interior, Ray Arnett, he was told "half-jokingly" that if he wanted the position, he needed to "not even flirt with the idea of bringing wolves back to Yellowstone, or you will find yourself a park planner in South Yemen."[6]

Yet, regardless of Barbee's views, the question was quickly swallowed up by other more urgent matters. Within days of his arrival in Yellowstone, Barbee faced the fight over grizzly bears and the planned removal of the Fishing Bridge campground. And once that matter settled, Barbee found himself plunged into the 1988 Summer of Fire.

But while wolf reintroduction remained a background issue for many Yellowstone officials, elsewhere, battle lines were being drawn.

* * *

The relationship between humans and wolves is complex. More so than elk, bison, and possibly even bears, the question of wolves has always carried deep social, cultural, and moral weight in Euro-American history. On one hand, few animals have been so demonized. The "bad wolf" popularized by *Grimms' Fairy Tales* has existed for hundreds of years, handed down from generation to generation. In this view, wolves are not only bloodthirsty but intentionally evil, producing in humans both fear and a moral duty to destroy them.

Consequently, while the common rationale for killing wolves in the American West had much to do with economic concerns—protecting ranchers' livestock and hunters' big game—lurking behind such arguments pulsed some powerful emotional elements. A 1920s Wyoming news story made the point. Announcing the death of an individual known as the Custer Wolf, the writer proclaimed that the "master criminal of the animal world . . . [had] at last been killed." "For nine years," the piece continued, "the Custer Wolf struck terror in the hearts of ranchers. Many credited the story that it was not merely a wolf, but a monstrosity of nature—half wolf and half mountain lion—possessing the cruelty of both and the craftiness of Satan himself."[7]

In stark contrast, wolves have simultaneously been venerated as symbols of wild nature. For millennia, Indigenous cultures have viewed wolves as beings imbued with special spiritual value. Ecologists know them as valuable keystone species, necessary for the functioning of heathy ecosystems. And for at least some forward-thinking environmental advocates, wolves' enduring survival—despite historical efforts to destroy them—gives the animals heightened meaning. From this perspective, wolves embody freedom, resilience—nature's ability to forge its own path beyond human control.

A minority perspective during most of U.S. history, by the early 1970s, this positive view of wolves began to gain greater currency in American society. This societal shift reflected a better understanding of ecology, changing environmental ethics, and, quite frankly, the fact that a declining number of people still made a living raising livestock on the open range.

For those still reliant on ranching, however, the idea of wolves as admirable or beneficial was hard to swallow. Many remained adamant that wolf restoration could only be detrimental to their livelihoods. As word spread of federal efforts to draft a wolf-recovery plan, deep economic and political divisions formed around the issue in the northern Rockies. Livestock growers in Idaho, Montana, and Wyoming shared their concerns with politicians and lobbying groups, like the Montana Wool Growers Association and the Wyoming Farm Bureau. Hence, while the Wolf Recovery Team held meetings to devise a new recovery plan, congressional representative Larry Craig of Idaho organized public hearings to air local concerns. Opponents charged that wolves posed significant threats to human safety and local economies. Not only would wolf restoration harm the livestock industry by killing cattle and sheep; it would also bring an end to logging and mining on public lands designated as part of critical wolf habitat.

In reality, as of 2023 at least, there has never been a scientifically confirmed human fatality caused by wild, non-rabid wolves in the lower forty-eight states. That said, attacks have happened. Since 1900, there have been six reported deaths in Canada and one in Alaska, which occurred in 2010. But while the possibility of a fatal attack remained extremely low, such fears helped attract support from those who did not share the ranchers' economic concerns. And soon, Congress stepped in.

Whether from a desire to weaken the Endangered Species Act as part of the Reagan Administration's anti-regulatory agenda, or simply to make the law better able to address concerns of local landowners, Congress passed an amendment in 1982 that created a new "experimental population" designation for endangered species reintroductions. Labeled as either "essential" or "nonessential," these experimental populations allowed for more flexible regulatory standards. Rather than protect every member of an endangered species in all circumstances, it allowed for exceptions if a species threatened the economic interests of private landowners. In such cases, an animal could be captured and removed or, if necessary, killed. Moreover, landowners could do the shooting themselves without fear of penalty as long as they had proof of an offence. The only caveat was that even when using this new designation, the final goal remained the same: full species recovery.

Notably, the "experimental" category only applied to reintroduced populations. Species that recovered through natural migration re-mained under a stricter set of ESA protections. In time, this distinction would play a major role in resolving the wolf question in Yellowstone.

* * *

In 1984, in an effort to gauge Park Service support for wolf reintroduc-tion, Hank Fischer met with Superintendent Barbee at park headquar-ters. Fischer was surprised to learn that Barbee was open to the idea. However, in Barbee's opinion, restoration would require significant public and political support, which currently did not exist. Barbee's superiors, including Assistant Interior Secretary Arnett, had stated in a recent congressional hearing that "there was going to be no intro-duction of the wolf into Yellowstone."[8] Moreover, politicians in Wyo-ming, Montana, and Idaho remained steadfast in their opposition. In a discussion with Senator Wallop of Wyoming, Barbee mentioned that there was growing interest in returning wolves to the park. The senator replied, "Do not say the 'W' word. Do not even think the 'W' word."[9]

Ever the pragmatist, Barbee suggested to Fischer that wolf reintro-duction was more about political and social values than anything else. For conservation organizations like Defenders of Wildlife, the focus should be on shaping public opinion. If successful, it might produce the needed political support.

Inspired by Barbee's advice, Fischer and his colleagues began work-ing on a new idea: bringing a natural history exhibit currently showing at the Science Museum of Minnesota to Yellowstone. The exhibit, en-titled *Wolves and Humans*, used interactive media technology to pres-ent the ecology of wolves, along with changing human attitudes over time.[10] With Barbee providing the venue and Renée Askins writing grants to cover the $25,000 loan fee, the exhibit opened in Yellowstone in June 1985 to immediate success. By the end of the summer, over 215,000 people viewed the exhibit. And while it did not advocate for wolf restoration per se, it did introduce many Americans to the issue.

That same year, President Reagan appointed his longtime friend, William Mott, as director of the National Park Service. As former chief of California state parks when Reagan was governor, Mott was a devoted conservationist, perhaps even more so than Reagan realized.

Now in his mid-seventies, Mott still exuded youthful energy and a contagious optimism. After meeting with Yellowstone managers, Mott quickly adopted wolf restoration as a personal priority, promising to devote resources to public education. Later, he even carried business cards that read, "With your support, we can bring wolves back to Yellowstone."[11]

After viewing the *Wolves and Humans* exhibit in Yellowstone, Mott met with Barbee, Fischer, Askins, and other environmental advocates to discuss wolf restoration. Mott advised that in addition to public outreach programs, conservation groups should address the opposition's economic concerns by developing a fund to compensate ranchers for livestock killed by wolves. Once again, Fischer took careful note.

In October, the Wolf Recovery Team completed their revised plan and sent it out for public review. It now included a call for wolf reintroduction in Yellowstone using the "experimental population" designation. The next step required approval from the Fish and Wildlife Service. But unlike William Mott, President Reagan's choice to lead the Fish and Wildlife Service, Frank Dunkle, was adamantly against the idea of bringing wolves back to Yellowstone. Nonetheless, after two additional rounds of public review, in August 1987, the agency finally signed off.

Typically, the next stage of an endangered species recovery plan involved completing an environmental impact statement (EIS). Established under the 1969 National Environmental Policy Act, an EIS requires federal agencies to assess the potential environmental, social, and economic impacts of any proposed federal project or management plan in order to anticipate potential problems. Only after an EIS is approved may the project proceed.

For the wolf-recovery plan, the agencies mandated to carry out the EIS included the U.S. Fish and Wildlife Service, National Park Service, and Forest Service, along with related state-level fish and game agencies. However, congressional delegations from Wyoming, Montana, and Idaho put pressure on the Reagan and Bush administrations to halt the process. In this situation, only congressional legislation could allow the EIS to proceed, which was unlikely to happen as long as politicians from the affected states opposed it.

But while the EIS remained in limbo, the wolves themselves did not. They were very much on the move.

* * *

By the mid-1980s, local ranchers reported a growing number of wolf sightings in northwestern Montana. At first, they appeared to be individuals wandering across the U.S. border from packs based in Canada. But by 1986, scientists confirmed a breeding pack of gray wolves had established itself in Glacier National Park.[12] It appeared that gray wolves were taking reintroduction into their own paws. But this natural restoration process also generated conflict.

As the number of wolves increased in Montana, so did the number of attacks on livestock. The epicenter for such activity, the town of Browning, suffered the highest losses of cattle and sheep. The Fish and Wildlife Service, working with the USDA Animal Damage Control Service—the agency in charge of eradicating "pest species" for farmers and ranchers and later renamed Wildlife Services—attempted to capture and relocate the problem wolves.[13] Unfortunately, neither agency was equipped with the necessary skills or tools for the job. Animal Damage Control excelled at killing, but capturing wild-born wolves was something else entirely.

Interestingly, the proposed wolf-recovery plan, though still without an EIS review, did allow for the killing of wolves that harmed livestock. Between 1986 and 1987, so many attacks took place in Montana that the agencies ended up taking out the entire seven-member wolf pack in Glacier National Park. In the final tally, four were shot dead and two relocated to captivity. The last one escaped for a time but was eventually killed by a rancher.[14]

While it may have seemed like a minor local issue, the events near Browning produced three lasting effects. First, they angered and alarmed those on both sides of the debate. While some wolf supporters criticized federal agencies for killing a legally protected species, ranchers claimed that the livestock attacks proved their point: if restored, wolves would seriously damage their livelihoods.

For the environmental groups directly involved in the wolf-recovery plan—groups like Defenders of Wildlife, the National Wildlife

Federation, and the Audubon Society—the events in Browning tested their resolve to break from other environmental organizations, like the Sierra Club, that protested the killing of wolves under any circumstances. Realizing that the lethal removal of wolves that attacked livestock was worth the cost of building local support for wolf restoration, they held their ground and defended the federal agencies that did the killing.

Going a step further, Hank Fischer decided it was time to act on Park Service director Mott's suggestion. In September 1987, in an effort to show good faith to the ranching families near Browning, Fischer raised $3,000 to compensate them for lost livestock (five cattle and nine sheep). By 1990, Defenders of Wildlife established a permanent $100,000 Wolf Compensation Trust that would continue to pay ranchers for wolf-killed livestock until 2010, when the federal government took over the program.[15]

Second, the Browning events convinced the Animal Damage Control Service to create a new wolf-specialist position. This person would respond to calls from ranchers reporting livestock attacks; determine whether or not wolves were to blame; and if so, capture and relocate or, if needed, exterminate said wolves. Carter Niemeyer, a big-shouldered former Iowa farm boy with extensive trapping experience, took the job. Soon, he would become the nation's leading wolf trapper/investigator.

The third and perhaps most important consequence of the Browning incident was the realization that wolves were coming back to the United States on their own, regardless of any recovery plan. If this continued, they would receive the highest level of protection under the Endangered Species Act, since the flexibility offered under the "experimental populations" category only applied to reintroduced populations. Ironically, for opponents of wolf restoration, these truths led to an uncomfortable and inescapable conclusion: if wolves were returning anyway, it was better to have it happen through human intervention.

It would take some time for this realization to sink in. In the meantime, and for the next four years, the conventional battle lines held firm.

* * *

In 1988, Representative Wayne Owens of Utah sponsored a bill authorizing the Park Service to conduct the EIS. The bill failed in the Senate but resulted in a compromise: a Park Service study on the implications of reintroducing gray wolves to Yellowstone. Published in four volumes in 1990 and 1992, *Wolves for Yellowstone? A Report to the U.S. Congress* concluded that wolves would render a positive impact on other wildlife species in the park, would benefit park visitors, and would not be detrimental to local ranchers or economies.[16]

But while these Park Service reports offered strong support for wolf restoration, they did not reach a large audience. In an effort to build broader public support, Renée Askins established The Wolf Fund in 1990, a single-issue nonprofit focused solely on restoring wolves to Yellowstone. Emphasizing public outreach and education, the group developed a newsletter, press packets, and a lecture series. They also launched a national media campaign, placing articles in outlets such as *Time* magazine and providing features for television news programs.[17]

In 1991, the tide finally turned. Realizing the advantages of a "nonessential experimental population" designation over natural restoration, several members of Wyoming's political delegation switched sides. Congress allowed the EIS to proceed, and, in November 1994, the Fish and Wildlife Service released the final recovery plan. Twenty-one years after their listing as an endangered species, and sixty-eight years after their extirpation, gray wolves would return to Yellowstone.

* * *

The final plan called for wolf restoration in three areas: northwest Montana, where it was naturally occurring, the Frank Church-River of No Return Wilderness in central Idaho, and Yellowstone National Park. Ed Bangs and Steve Fritts led the effort on behalf of the Fish and Wildlife Service, while Mike Phillips directed the program in Yellowstone. Now, they just needed some wolves.

On November 16, 1994, Animal Damage Control agent Carter Niemeyer and Fish and Wildlife Service biologists Val Asher and Alice Whitelaw filled two pickup trucks with trapping gear and drove north from Helena, Montana, to Alberta, Canada.[18] Their mission was to capture wolves from places similar to the release sites in the United

States, including from an area near Jasper National Park. For Yellowstone, they wanted to capture members of established packs or family groups in the hope of encouraging them to stay within park boundaries. For those going to Idaho, where there was more room to roam, they wanted individuals that might form new packs.

Upon arrival in Canada, however, Niemeyer and Asher found the arrangements in disarray. Perhaps due to the political volatility of the recovery plan, a U.S. federal agent had yet to secure local facilities for processing or storing captured wolves. On the plus side, contracts had been signed with local trappers to supply captured wolves and with local pilots to shuttle the American scientists into the backcountry. But U.S. personnel hadn't followed up in months, leaving frustrated locals to wonder if they had been manipulated.

Niemeyer experienced this frustration firsthand when he drove out to meet with one of the contracted trappers in his backwoods cabin outside of the town of Hinton, Alberta.[19] Initially met with suspicion by the man and his fellow trappers, Niemeyer learned they had interrupted their normal work to fulfill orders for live-trapped wolves to the U.S. government but had received no payment.

After offering Niemeyer copious amounts of homemade chokecherry wine, which he felt obliged to consume, they challenged him to an informal "wolf-skinning contest" against another trapper right there on the host's living room floor. It turns out the Canadian trappers had the bodies of two wolves killed that very day outside in their pickup. Recognizing this rite of passage for what it was, Niemeyer accepted. Groggy from too much wine, covered in blood from the skinning process, and surrounded by the unwelcome release of evacuated wolf bowels all over the carpet, Niemeyer ultimately emerged triumphant (miraculously, with all of his fingers still intact). After he won the respect and goodwill of the Canadian trappers, the program finally began to move forward.

As wolves were captured, they received physical exams, tags, and radio collars. Asher and Niemeyer then released them back into the wild. Then, U.S. agents would return at a later date to track the radio signals of these so-called "Judas wolves" back to their home packs and attempt to capture the lot.

To do so, bush pilots first roamed the area in search of radio signals.

Once located, they called in a helicopter with Niemeyer and his tranquilizer gun leaning out of the open door. Zooming in, he shot as many pack members as possible. After a hit, Asher and her colleagues moved in on foot or snowmobile to retrieve the wolf and haul it back to Hinton by pickup truck. At the collection center, local veterinarians and government biologists conducted physicals, took blood and tissue samples, tagged ears, and attached radio collars.

Then, quite suddenly, all activity stopped. On November 25, a lawsuit filed by the Wyoming Farm Bureau against the Fish and Wildlife Service halted the wolf-capture process pending a federal district court hearing in Cheyenne. But with the plaintiffs unable to prove that Wyoming ranchers would face "irreparable harm" from the wolf-restoration plan, the judge ruled in favor of the Fish and Wildlife Service. On January 3, 1995, the capturing process resumed.

On January 11, the first fourteen wolves were ready for shipment from Alberta to the United States. Along with Niemeyer and Asher, others on hand that day included Renée Askins, Alice Whitelaw, and Yellowstone winter keeper Jeff Henry, who was on assignment for the Defenders of Wildlife to record the capture operation through photos, including one of the wolves laid out and tranquilized for the long journey ahead.

Six of the animals would be sent to central Idaho and eight to Yellowstone National Park. After flying from Hinton to Edmonton, Alberta, and then on to Great Falls, Montana, they would travel by horse trailer to Yellowstone. The wolves were finally on their way.

* * *

When the first wolves arrived in Yellowstone, not everyone involved could be there in person. Back in September, Superintendent Barbee transferred from Yellowstone to become the Park Service regional director in Alaska. But as he watched the moment unfold on television along with millions of other Americans—from their triumphant arrival through the Roosevelt Arch to scenes of Secretary Babbitt and Fish and Wildlife director Mollie Beattie helping to carry the first crate up the snowy path—Barbee recalled, "I was there with them in spirit."[20]

Then, unexpectedly, everything came to a halt once more. News arrived that the Wyoming Farm Bureau had filed an emergency appeal against the federal court ruling in December. The Tenth Circuit Court of Appeals granted a forty-eight-hour stay while they reviewed the case. But this meant the wolves in Yellowstone had to remain locked inside their crates until a decision was rendered. To many observers, this tactic was nothing short of abusive to the already-stressed animals who had endured significant hardship during their long journey.

After his celebratory remarks earlier in the day, Secretary Babbitt hastily convened another press conference in the Mammoth Hot Springs Hotel. Speaking now in an entirely different tone, Babbitt expressed the concerns of many: "If we don't get those wolves out of those cages, they may turn into coffins."[21]

Fortunately, this did not come to pass. At approximately 7:00 p.m., the court threw out the appeal. Hours later, park officials opened the cages, and the wolves, for the first time, placed their paws onto the snow-covered grounds of Yellowstone National Park.

For the next two months, they would be fed elk carcasses tossed over the fence but would otherwise have little to no interaction with humans. Then finally, on March 21, 1995, park scientists opened the pens, and the wolves emerged as wild creatures. For the first time in over seventy years, the Yellowstone ecosystem included its top predator.

* * *

Wolf transfers from Canada continued for two more years. In the end, a total of seventy-six wolves were reintroduced, forty-one of them to Yellowstone.[22] According to the restoration plan, the criteria for delisting gray wolves (and therefore considering them fully restored) required the presence of ten breeding pairs in each of the three recovery zones (northern Montana, central Idaho, and Yellowstone) for three consecutive years. Later, the criteria were lowered to allow for a total of thirty breeding pairs *relatively distributed* over the same area and period. A breeding pair is defined as a male and female that produces at least two pups that survive a calendar year. The goal of thirty breeding pairs was first reached in 2000, and it reached the consecutive three-year mark in 2003. This made it possible to remove gray wolves in the northern Rockies from the endangered species list.

Delisting a species occurs for one of two reasons: the species has either recovered or become extinct. Delisting due to a successful recovery, however, does not bring an end to protection; it only means that state agencies take over management duties. State-sanctioned hunting of a formerly protected species may occur at this point, but only under an approved plan to ensure the population remains viable into the future.

Despite the apparent success of wolf restoration in Yellowstone, political fights over wolf delisting in subsequent years underscored just how contentious the issue continued to be. In 2008, the Fish and Wildlife Service removed gray wolves in the northern Rockies (including Yellowstone) from the endangered species list for the first time. This action required Idaho, Montana, and Wyoming to submit wolf-management plans for federal approval. But whereas the plans offered by Idaho and Montana appeared sound, Wyoming's did not. By categorizing wolves as a "pest species," Wyoming allowed wolves crossing over the Yellowstone National Park boundary to be shot on sight and without reporting it to government agencies. This arrangement made it impossible to ensure species survival. Consequently, the wolf was relisted that same year.

Then, in 2009, the Fish and Wildlife Service tried to delist wolves only in Montana and Idaho but not in Wyoming. Challenged in court as inconsistent with ESA-recovery-plan criteria, the decision was reversed and the wolves relisted in 2010. Congress then intervened in 2011 to reinstate the 2009 arrangement (delisted in Idaho and Montana but listed in Wyoming) by essentially amending the ESA law.[23]

But in 2012, the Fish and Wildlife Service agreed to delist gray wolves in Wyoming after the state promised to revise its wolf-management plan. However, the high number of wolves subsequently killed in the state (219) suggested Wyoming had no real intention of providing adequate protection. In 2014, a federal court ordered the wolves relisted in Wyoming once more. And on it went.

In 2017, a new round of court battles and congressional action led to yet another delisting of wolves in Wyoming. In 2020, the Fish and Wildlife Service delisted gray wolves in all of the lower forty-eight states. Then, in 2022, a federal court ruling reversed that decision, relisting all wolves in the lower forty-eight states except in the northern Rocky Mountain region—including Yellowstone—as a threatened species under the ESA.

This whiplash-inducing back-and-forth history illustrates the lingering divisions over the issue. On one side, ranchers worried about livestock losses, hunters concerned with a depletion of big game, and others generally opposed to federal regulatory interventions continually push against wolf restoration. On the other side, natural scientists, environmental advocates, the vast majority of park visitors, and those in related tourism industries (as well as two-thirds of U.S. citizens) view wolf restoration as a net positive.

All of which raises the question, after twenty-five years, what has been the impact of returning wolves to Yellowstone?

* * *

Few people are better positioned to answer this question than Doug Smith. Like many of Yellowstone's scientists, he is passionate, energetic, and extremely knowledgeable. Tall and silver-haired with a matching handlebar mustache and a kindly face tanned and weathered from years under the sun, Smith directed the Yellowstone Wolf Project from 1997 to 2023. During that time, on any given day, Smith might be found flying over the park in a Super Cub airplane, hanging out the side of a helicopter, or riding through the backcountry on horseback, all in an effort to manage, protect, and better understand the gray wolves in Yellowstone.

On the question of wolves' ecological impacts, Smith can say that the answers range from "as expected" to "surprising." As elk are by far the preferred food of wolves—accounting for over 90 percent of their diet—most scientists predicted that the park's wolf population would grow at the expense of Yellowstone's elk herd. And to some extent, this has happened.

At the time of wolf reintroduction, Yellowstone's northern elk herd population reached historically high levels—close to 20,000 head.[24]

Even with increases in winter hunting,[25] massive winter die-offs from lack of food continued to take place, with notable incidents in 1989 (after the 1988 fires) and again in 1997, but each time, the elk would bounce back.

Between 1995 and 2003, the wolf population in Yellowstone grew by about 10 percent per year, topping out at an estimated 160 individuals. During the same period, the winter elk herd dropped approximately 50 percent (from roughly 16,700 to 8,300 head).[26] However, after 2008, Yellowstone's wolf population also fell precipitously, leveling out at roughly eighty to one hundred animals in eight to ten packs as of 2020 (with approximately 500 wolves total in the Greater Yellowstone Ecosystem).[27] The decline was due in part to the on-again-off-again listing debates, which periodically allowed wolf hunting, along with episodes of disease and continued federal actions to lethally remove "problem" wolves.

The northern elk herd, in contrast, continued to drop until 2013, after which it also began to bounce back. As of 2019, the herd appeared to stabilize at around 5,800 head.[28] However, scientists are not convinced that the decline was due exclusively to wolf kills. In addition to the weather-related die-off in 1997, human hunting increased during this period. From 1976 to 1994, hunters averaged 1,014 elk per year, but from 1995 to 2004 they averaged 1,372. Elk have also been impacted by population increases of grizzlies and mountain lions and extended periods of draught related to climate change.

In short, as expected, wolves influenced elk populations, but their precise effect cannot be easily separated from other factors. Impacts by wolves on other aspects of Yellowstone's ecosystem, however, have been nothing short of surprising.

How can it be, for example, that the return of wolves could somehow alter Yellowstone's rivers and streams? Or that the presence of wolves would result in an increase in songbirds or amphibians? According to Smith, it is safe to say that no one saw these things coming.

Though still debated, the concept of the "trophic cascade" offers one of the best explanations of what has transpired. The term *trophic* refers to different levels in a food web—"producers" like plants and grasses that transform sunlight into edible energy; "primary consumers," like herbivores, that eat the plants; "secondary consumers," like carnivores, that eat the herbivores, and so on. The cascade suggests that introducing a new species at one end of the food web can have a domino-like effect across the entire system.

Hence, by reducing elk numbers, the wolves have indirectly allowed aspens, willows, cottonwoods, and other woody plants near riverbanks to rebound. This in turn has not only reduced stream-bank erosion but provided habitat for songbirds and many other species. The renewed presence of larger trees has also attracted beavers back to the park. Their dams have raised water tables and provided wetland habitats for additional species, some of which serve as food sources for eagles, ospreys, and even moose. The numbers tell the tale. According to Smith, when wolves first returned to Yellowstone in 1995, there was only one beaver colony inside the park. By 2021, there were nine.

Wolves may also have benefitted grizzlies by restricting elk browsing of the woody berry-laden plants typically consumed by bears and by providing elk kills that grizzlies can easily confiscate.[29] Wolves are also believed responsible for reductions in the park's coyote population, as coyotes likely filled the niche left vacant by wolf eradication in the 1920s. And fewer coyotes mean growth in pronghorn populations (a favorite prey of coyotes) as well as increases in "coyote competitors" like red fox, lynx, bobcats, pine martens, and wolverines.

But the cascade effects triggered by wolves result from more than their role in reducing elk numbers. Perhaps their most important influence is described through another concept: the "ecology of fear."

According to this idea, the mere presence of wolves on the landscape triggers a behavior change in elk. Instead of lingering long hours in one place to graze, often along rivers and stream banks, elk keep on the move, which reduces overgrazing. Moreover, during the winter months, when deep snows slow their movements, elk have learned it is safer to migrate to lower elevations outside of park boundaries to elude predators. Ironically, this also makes more elk available during hunting season.[30]

* * *

Given all the political acrimony around wolves, the most pressing questions concern their social and economic impacts. Have the worst fears of ranchers and hunters come to pass? Have wolves wreaked havoc on the livestock and hunter-tourism-based economies in the region?

The combined efforts of financial-compensation programs that pay ranchers for lost livestock and federal policies that allow for the lethal removal of "offending" wolves have made a difference. But ranchers remain concerned. Because compensation requires verification to ensure that the death wasn't caused by some other means, ranchers sometimes complain that it is too difficult to find carcasses in time to collect the needed evidence. Injured animals often do not qualify, and ranchers may feel cheated if they disagree with final decisions. Still, the programs are now administered by state agencies and supported by federal, state, and private funds. Moreover, they have expanded to compensate ranchers for kills by predators other than wolves. Ranchers in Wyoming received approximately $400,000 in 2016 and again in 2017. It dropped to $150,000 in 2018 due to a drop in documented attacks.[31]

In terms of livestock kills, in the first five years after restoration (1995–1999), wolves took an average of two cattle and twenty sheep per year. This was likely due to the unusually large elk population at the time, which was also unprepared for wolves, making them easy prey. Then, from 2000 to 2003, livestock kills increased to about twenty-seven cattle and seventy-nine sheep per year.[32] In Wyoming, after reaching a record high of 242 total livestock deaths in 2016, the number dropped considerably. Since 2018, deaths have remained fairly stable, ranging from about sixty-five to eighty-five total per year.[33]

To put this in context, in 2016, when wolves killed 242 total head of livestock, more than 37,500 sheep and lambs alone died in Wyoming from weather, disease, and other non-wolf-related causes.[34] Nationwide, in 2015, non-predator-related causes accounted for 98 percent of cattle deaths and 89 percent of calf deaths. Of deaths caused by predators, coyotes accounted for the highest percentage, and even domesticated dogs killed twice as many cattle as wolves.[35]

In sum, nationwide, wolf-killed livestock have accounted for less than 1 percent of annual losses.[36] Of course, individual ranchers who suffer greater losses find little comfort in such statistics. On the plus side, a nearby wolf pack that does not hunt livestock can potentially help protect ranchers by keeping out other wolves and reducing the coyote population. And to the extent they reduce elk-herd populations, wolves may also be providing additional forage for livestock that compete with wildlife on public lands during the summer months.

Such arguments, of course, only fuel the anger of hunting organizations who claim that wolves have significantly damaged the regional sport-hunting industry. It turns out that the data on this issue is also complicated.

As mentioned above, in the first ten years after wolf restoration, hunters actually *increased* their harvest of elk.[37] However, it is also true—as noted earlier—that Yellowstone's northern elk herd declined considerably from 1995 to 2013. As a result, in 2009, Montana halted the winter hunting season that had taken place near Gardiner since 1976. A complicating factor is that no one is yet certain how much of the elk population decline is due to wolves versus other factors. Statewide statistics show that the annual harvests of elk in both Montana and Wyoming have remained relatively steady, ranging between 20,000 and 30,000 per year since 2010 in Montana and roughly 22,000–24,000 per year in Wyoming. So is it possible that the impact of wolves has been overblown?

Ironically, wolves may actually benefit the hunting industry by helping to curb wildlife diseases. Elk represent the most common carriers of brucellosis and chronic wasting disease in the region. Since wolves tend to target sick individuals—and are immune to the effects of these diseases themselves—they may be helping to control the spread within the herds.[38]

Nonetheless, Wyoming estimates that elk killed by wolves equate to a loss of approximately $2.9 million per year to the local hunting industry when one includes indirect spending on hotels, restaurants, and other services.[39] But such numbers pale in comparison to the estimated economic benefits created by wolf restoration. In the Greater Yellowstone area, wolf tourism totaled more than $35.5 million in 2006.[40] In 2017, estimates of the annual economic contribution of wolves increased to over $65 million.[41] Of course, these figures do not placate most hunters in any way. And there remains a need for more rigorous and systematic research to confirm whether the economic gains of restoration in states like Wyoming and Montana outweigh the losses.

* * *

For Yellowstone scientists, the advent of wolf tourism is another un-expected outcome of restoration. Because all reintroduced wolves re-ceived radio collars and tags,[42] they offered researchers unprecedented opportunities to track their movements and study individual life cy-cles. Soon, park visitors joined in, giving rise to "wolf watchers": peo-ple armed with high-powered cameras, telescopes, and notepads that gather each day to follow the activities of various wolves and wolf packs in Yellowstone.

Interestingly, the wolf-watcher phenomenon led to the creation of celebrity wolves. This development harkens back to the stories of Ernest Thompson Seton and Jack London that detailed the lives of specific wolves and bears, imbuing them with human traits as they struggled with ethical dilemmas. While the data gathered by wolf watchers doesn't necessarily go that far, it has allowed documentation of the highs and lows faced by individual animals. On numerous occasions, entire books have been written, feeding the fanbase for biographies of celebrity wolves, including those authored by former Yellowstone nat-uralist Rick McIntyre.[43]

As Smith explains, the Park Service resists giving names to wolves precisely to avoid anthropomorphizing. Since they manage Yellow-stone's wolves based on population dynamics, it can become extremely complicated if a particularly famous wolf is shot for attacking live-stock or by a hunter (whether legally or not) as part of the overall wolf-management program. And of course, this is exactly what has transpired on more than one occasion.[44]

One cannot deny that the cumulative economic benefit of a celeb-rity wolf is orders of magnitude higher than the money accrued by the single hunter who might shoot it. Commentators have noted that such acts are equivalent to "killing the goose that lays the golden eggs." Yet the conflict continues.

Overall, in terms of economic impact, though more research is needed, available studies suggest that wolves generate more in re-gional employment and income than they take. And in terms of social perception, at the national scale anyway, the public holds a favorable opinion of wolf reintroduction in Yellowstone by a two-to-one margin.

Nonetheless, as the gains and losses are not distributed evenly, it's understandable why individual livestock producers or hunters might oppose restoration. Ecological questions remain about the precise impacts. For Doug Smith and his colleagues, the experiment continues.

* * *

Wolf restoration was, and remains, an extraordinary example of how Yellowstone once more forced us to rethink our relationship with the natural world. If the saga of Yellowstone bears challenged us to rediscover "wild nature" in something previously viewed as tame, the return of the wolves forced us to take the next step: find a way to accommodate and value something considered not only wild but also dangerous. Could we coexist in the landscape with something so long despised and even feared?

While these national discussions continue, the legacy of Yellowstone's wolf restoration is felt in efforts to reintroduce predators across the United States, from the red wolf in the Carolinas to the Mexican gray wolf and jaguar in the American Southwest to the Florida panther. Meanwhile, in the northern Rockies, the gray wolves refuse to stay still, spreading out and moving ever deeper into their historical range, into places like California, Colorado, and beyond.

Finally, of the many impacts of wolves on Yellowstone, both expected and unforeseen, it is noteworthy that most all of those predicted by park scientists came to pass, save one. This glaring exception had to do with the assumption that wolves would help reduce the population of all game species in the park. One species disproved the rule, one that represents yet another iconic Yellowstone resident: the plains bison.

Where the Buffalo Roam

(2000–2016)

THE EARTH RUMBLED WITH THE SOUND OF THUNDERING hooves. It was early on March 19, 2012, and inside the large corral of Yellowstone's wildlife-holding facility in Stephens Creek,[1] calls of "Yip! Yip!" echoed through the chilly air as park rangers on horseback cut left and right trying to round up sixty-three wild bison. After five to seven years of quarantine and over twenty years of political struggle, the iconic beasts were finally ready to leave Yellowstone National Park.

When the last bison stepped inside the trailer, the gate swung shut with a metallic clang. Plumes of warm breath shot out from the trailer's side like a steam locomotive. With the wave of a ranger's arm, the convoy headed out on a 500-mile journey to the far reaches of Northeast Montana. Their destination? The Fort Peck Reservation, home of the Nakota (Assiniboine) and Dakota Sioux nations.

The drive took ten hours, including detours to avoid roadblocks thrown up by disgruntled county sheriffs seeking to halt the transfer. But by nightfall, the convoy rolled into the town of Poplar, Montana. A few more miles of dirt road would take the bison to the 4,800-acre wildlife pasture that would serve as their new home on tribal land.

Out by the corrals set up to receive the bison, the rhythms of Native American drums and singing reverberated in the air. Tribal members gathered to dance and pray as flickering headlights signaled the approaching convoy. Among those present were Robbie Magnan, director of the Fort Peck Fish and Game Department, Jonathan Proctor of the Defenders of Wildlife, and Garrit Voggesser of the National Wildlife Federation. For fifty-eight-year-old Magnan, bundled in a thick coat with his ponytail snaking down from his ball cap, this day had been long in coming.[2] Working as a tribal game warden since 1989, Magnan began leading the effort to restore bison to Fort Peck in 1999. Despite the support of other tribal leaders, the National Park Service, and a number of environmental organizations, ultimately, the burden of standing up to every challenge had fallen on his shoulders. For two decades, in addition to his day-to-day resource-management duties, Magnan lobbied and wrote letters to state politicians, testified at legislative hearings, filed legal challenges, worked closely with the governor's office, served as spokesperson to the news media, and campaigned for financial support. Today was hard evidence that Magnan had withstood the tests.

Slowly, the trailer backed into position and the gate swung open. For a moment, nothing happened. The first bison stared back at the collected humans in apparent confusion.

Magnan leaned in and whispered, "It's okay. You're home now."

Suddenly, the bison leapt from the trailer, landing with a stumble onto the half-frozen prairie grass before running off at full speed. Immediately, the herd instinct kicked in and the others flowed out into the darkness in a steady stream. After their near-extermination some 130 years before, descendants of North America's only remnant, genetically pure wild bison herd finally returned to the Northern Plains.

* * *

Though the event took place nearly 500 miles away from the park, it marked a Yellowstone homecoming every bit as significant as the return of gray wolves seventeen years earlier. In this case, "coming home" meant allowing Yellowstone's wild bison to finally expand beyond park boundaries into portions of their historic range. Like the wolves, the reintroduction of bison to their original habitat carried substantial ecological, social, and cultural resonance. And, also like the wolves, the transfer was fraught with political and economic conflict.

But if bringing wolves *into* Yellowstone was both momentous and controversial, how could taking bison *out* of the park trigger similar responses? After all, bison are neither predators nor an invasive species. On the contrary, as the very first endangered species saved in U.S. history, Americans celebrate bison as a national symbol. They are featured on the U.S. nickel, the National Park Service emblem, and the logo for the Department of the Interior. Bison also serve as the state animal of Wyoming and the national mammal of the United States.

Nonetheless, bison differ from most other Yellowstone wildlife in one important respect: other than wolves, they are the only species *not* allowed to move freely across park borders. While bison remain largely protected inside the park, wandering beyond can mean certain death.

All of which raises the question: Why? Why should it matter so much where the buffalo—or rather, the bison—roam?

* * *

In 1902, the population of Yellowstone's herd, the last remaining wild herd in the nation, bottomed out at approximately twenty-five head. However, by the mid-1920s, it had grown to over 500. It seemed that the combined effects of ending poaching, eradicating predators, providing supplemental winter feed, and raising a new "captive herd" had succeeded in bringing the iconic species back from the brink of extinction in the United States.[3]

In fact, after 1923, there were so many bison that park managers began culling Yellowstone's herd to keep it from overgrazing the northern rangelands shared by elk. In the early years, Horace Albright insisted on keeping a bison herd big enough for annual "stampede" demonstrations for park visitors. But for most of the next forty years, direct-reduction efforts kept the bison population between 400 and 1,000 head. In 1952, the Park Service shut down the Lamar Buffalo Ranch, and the captive herd was free to blend into the park's remnant wild herd.[4]

Of course, park managers also subjected Yellowstone's elk to direct-reduction programs. But whereas the elk (and all other wildlife species) could cross park boundaries unmolested, managers did everything in their power to keep the bison from leaving. The primary rationale was driven by one overarching concern: the presence of brucellosis in the herd.

The disease was introduced into Yellowstone's captive herd in 1917 by domesticated cattle brought in to feed hotel guests. It can cause abortions in cows and poses a health risk to humans in the form of undulant fever. Consequently, it has long represented both an economic and public health risk. While the disease also leads to miscarriages in Yellowstone bison, such occurrences are infrequent and have had only a marginal impact on the population.

Brucellosis is caused by *Brucela abortus* bacteria, which reside in the lymphoid systems of cattle, bison, deer, moose, and elk.[5] It can remain dormant and difficult to detect until certain conditions, like a weakened immune system, allow it to grow. However, the highest potential for infection occurs during the calving process. Disease transference (whether to humans or to other animals) requires direct contact with birthing material (amniotic fluids, the fetus, or placenta) or the nursing milk of an infected cow. After bearing their first calf, some infected females shed the bacteria and become brucellosis-free. In others, the bacteria persists. Regardless, only infected, reproductively active females and their newborns can transmit the disease—males can become infected as calves but do not transmit the disease as adults. In the open air, the bacteria usually die within three to five days, hence it is exceedingly rare for transference between animals to happen under natural conditions. Transmission is more likely in situations where animals are crowded together in high-density settings (like corrals or human-run feeding grounds) and during specific times of the year (such as calving season in late winter or early spring).

In 1934, the USDA Animal and Plant Health Inspection Service (APHIS) began working to eradicate brucellosis in U.S. cattle herds, launching a formal national campaign in 1954. The program carried high stakes for the livestock industry. If a single cow was found to be infected, APHIS required the destruction of a rancher's entire herd. And if APHIS discovered cases in two different herds in the same state within a two-year period, the entire state would pay the price. APHIS would strip the offending state of its "brucellosis-free" status, thereby requiring all cattle to be quarantined before crossing state lines. With such significant economic ramifications, livestock growers near Yellowstone mobilized state politicians to ensure bison would not wander out of the park and potentially infect domestic cattle.

Given that Yellowstone is nearly surrounded by national forests, one might reasonably ask why it matters if bison cross from one form of federal land to another. After all, national forests are not private ranchlands. The answer is that ranchers can buy permits to graze private livestock on national forest lands during the summer months. For this reason, livestock growers argued that any movement of bison beyond the park presented a risk.

All of this added up to an uncompromising stance against bison leaving the park. But since Park Service managers already culled the population to prevent overgrazing, for much of the twentieth century, instances of bison crossing the borders were few and far between. Although Yellowstone managers found it unsettling to engage in the annual slaughter of a once-endangered, still-iconic species, the status quo held for over forty years. But it was just a matter of time before this unique arrangement would be tested.

* * *

The tipping point came in 1968, when Yellowstone adopted its natural-regulation approach to wildlife management. With culling no longer an option, but still without natural predators, bison and elk populations exploded. For both species, this meant that during winter months when food became scarce, their migration instincts kicked in. By the late 1970s and early 1980s, bison and elk increasingly moved out of the park en masse during harsh winters. For bison, this often meant movement into the National Elk Refuge in Jackson Hole (where supplemental feed was offered) or Montana, either across the northern or western borders.

Since Montana ranchers viewed Yellowstone bison as a major economic threat, tensions between the state and the Park Service quickly intensified. Initially, Yellowstone managers tried to keep the growing bison population inside the park by herding and hazing, but the genetic impulse to migrate was simply too strong. As Superintendent Bob Barbee explained in the 1980s, "Trying to herd a buffalo doesn't work. Buffalo are herded where they want to go."[6]

Hazing—chasing the animals back into the park by horseback or ATV—was never more than a temporary fix, and when these efforts failed, the killing resumed. In West Yellowstone, Montana game wardens built a capture facility where they engaged in the "lethal removal" of any bison that left the park. In 1985, Montana supplemented these culling programs with an annual state-licensed hunt. Any bison that crossed the northern border became fair game.

This uneasy situation continued for several years, until it came to a head in 1988 with Yellowstone's Summer of Fire. The one-two punch of wildfire-caused devastation to the northern range followed by an uncommonly severe winter pushed a record number of bison out of the park in search of food.

And the hunters were waiting.

As soon as the unwitting bison stepped over the boundary, the shooting began. Already habituated to crowds of tourists with pointing cameras, Yellowstone bison had little fear of hunters with guns. Just like the Yellowstone elk hunts in decades past, "hunting" these half-tame creatures did not require stalking nor anything resembling fair chase. It was shooting fish in a barrel. Once the bison realized the danger, usually after taking bullets from poorly aimed shots, pandemonium broke out. Frightened and injured animals ran or dragged themselves in every direction, desperately trying to escape the fusillade. In the end, hunters slaughtered 569 bison.

The resultant public outcry triggered a political response. Montana announced an end to its state-sanctioned bison hunt (officially ending in 1991) and agreed to work with the Park Service to develop an interagency bison-management plan that also included APHIS and the U.S. Forest Service. With all major state and federal players at the table, Yellowstone's managers hoped a solution was in the offing.

* * *

If Wyoming was the recalcitrant actor in Yellowstone's wolf-restoration effort, Montana played a similar role for bison.[7] To be fair, all three neighboring states—Idaho, Montana, and Wyoming—would take steps in the coming years to limit the ability of Yellowstone bison to move beyond park borders. Nonetheless, Montana soon distinguished itself by the lengths it was willing to go.

Over the next five years, the status quo remained intact. If any bison crossed into Montana, they were "lethally removed" by state officials. Montana's Director of Fish and Wildlife, K. L. Cool, summarized the state's position: "We're faced with a threat to our own livestock industry. The animal [bison] is not welcome in Montana."[8]

In 1995, the Montana State legislature passed legislation redefining bison as livestock and deeming the animals as posing "a significant potential to spread contagious disease to people and property."[9] The state then delivered an unexpected blow: it filed a lawsuit charging the Park Service with threatening Montana's brucellosis-free status by mismanaging the Yellowstone bison herd. As evidence, state lawyers cited a letter from APHIS threatening to downgrade Montana's brucellosis-free status due to the disease's presence in Yellowstone wildlife.

Later, it came to light that state officials possibly fabricated the threat. According to one account, the state veterinarian actually requested APHIS officials to issue the letter to justify the lawsuit. Since bison are considered wildlife by federal authorities, APHIS had no jurisdiction in the matter anyway and would have no say unless a breakout occurred in a livestock population.[10]

Regardless of these questionable maneuvers, a court-ordered settlement in late 1995 forced a compromise. In West Yellowstone, any bison moving across the park border would be caught and tested in a holding facility run by Montana state officials. Up to one hundred bison that tested negative for brucellosis would be allowed to graze on National Forest lands until April 1, then hazed back into the park. On the northern border, the Park Service built its own bison-holding facility. Any bison caught attempting to migrate north would be slaughtered regardless of infection status. Those that slipped through would be captured and killed by Montana state officials. Meat from the slaughtered animals would be given to Native American tribes since it is safe to eat, regardless of infection, as long as it is properly cooked. This arrangement, known as the Interim Bison Management Plan, would guide actions for the next five years.

* * *

To paraphrase writer Todd Wilkinson, most would agree that expecting wild animals to abide by invisible, politically drawn lines on a map is nonsensical.[11] But what if the rationale for keeping bison within park borders was also faulty? The controversy hinged on one extremely powerful assumption: that bison posed a significant risk of brucellosis transmission to cattle. For decades, this idea went unchallenged and served as the foundation for bison management in Yellowstone. But the history, science, and economics of the issue suggest there is more to the story.

First of all, it is true that bison can transfer brucellosis to domestic cattle under controlled conditions.[12] However, the risk of doing so in the wild is extremely small. In the 150-year history of Yellowstone National Park, there has never been a single incident of brucellosis transmission from wild bison to private livestock under natural conditions.[13] This is due in part to park rangers' and state officials' diligent efforts to keep the two species apart. But it has even more to do with basic ecology, timing, and conventional livestock growing practices.

The two species rarely come near each other during calving, which is the only time disease transfer tends to occur. Calving for both species typically takes place from late February through early April. Domestic cattle are on home pastures during this time so ranchers can keep tabs on the process and intervene if necessary. Bison, meanwhile, are either in the park or—post-1995—possibly on national forest or wildlife refuge lands. By the end of May, when cattle return to national forest grazing allotments, most bison have moved back into the park. But even if they remain on forest lands when cattle return, the risk of disease transfer is little to none since calving season is long over. Finally, even in the rare circumstance that bison and cattle might occupy the same patch of national forest land during calving, animals in the wild typically leave each other alone while giving birth, leaving the *Brucela abortus* bacteria time to die off.

Another factor determining the risk of disease transfer is how many bison are actually infectious. Opponents of conservation frequently say that roughly 40 to 60 percent of Yellowstone bison are infected with brucellosis. But this claim is somewhat misleading. Approximately half do test seropositive for brucellosis, but that is not the same as being infectious. It only means they have been exposed, the same way humans who have taken the measles or chicken pox vaccine will test seropositive for exposure to those illnesses. Moreover, since males cannot transmit the disease, the actual number of infectious bison in Yellowstone is roughly 10 to 15 percent of the female population.[14]

A second point concerns economics. Bison advocates have argued that the annual amount spent on hazing, capture, testing, vaccination, and slaughter programs far exceeds the profits generated from livestock production in lands adjacent to Yellowstone National Park.[15] Consequently, some argue it would be far cheaper for American taxpayers to simply send ranchers a check each year for any lost income and let the bison roam.

The most common counterargument is that the stakes go well beyond the financial well-being of any regional group of ranchers, since the entire state of Montana could suffer if infections are found in more than one herd. But in 2010, APHIS changed its rules so that livestock growers no longer had to destroy an entire herd if one cow was found sick. Nor would a state lose its disease-free status if multiple herds were found to test positive. In other words, it appeared that the worst fears of those opposed to free-roaming bison had been addressed.

But perhaps the most poignant issue in this entire debate is the fact that other species of wildlife also carry brucellosis and present a risk to livestock. One particular species has done so on numerous occasions and constitutes 99 percent of the transmission risk to cattle.[16] Given that the risk of disease is the primary rationale for the entire bison conflict, surely the state of Montana would demand that this offending species be subject to slaughter if any individuals attempted to cross the park border. However, this is not the case. In truth, the primary source of brucellosis transfer to cattle in the Greater Yellowstone Ecosystem comes from a species that not only moves freely across park boundaries but is rarely mentioned in discussions of the disease: elk.

Cue the sound of scratching needle across vinyl record.

Elk are not only allowed to intermingle with cattle on national forest lands but can even enter private pastures during calving season. Moreover, wildlife agencies have spent significant amounts of taxpayer money to inadvertently create conditions in which brucellosis and other diseases, like chronic wasting disease, can possibly grow and spread through the regional elk population. They do so by continuing the century-old practice of artificially feeding elk in winter feeding grounds.

The largest of these grounds is on the National Elk Refuge just north of Jackson, which draws both elk and bison, but there are also over twenty smaller winter feeding grounds run by the state of Wyoming around the Greater Yellowstone Ecosystem. These places bring elk close together in high-density groups during times that can correspond with calving season, creating breeding grounds not just for young elk but, potentially, for disease.

Livestock producers rightly argue that the winter feeding keeps the elk away from private pastures. But it also creates the problems associated with overpopulation. Lawsuits by environmental groups led to an agreement in 2019 to reduce and potentially end regular supplemental winter feeding on the National Elk Refuge.[17] But the practice persists elsewhere.

For a brief time in the 1980s and early 1990s, APHIS declared Montana, Wyoming, and Idaho as brucellosis free, but the disease reappeared in 2002. It turns out that elk were responsible for the new outbreak.[18]

Such revelations bring the stated rationale for state-level opposition to bison conservation into question. If brucellosis transmission really is the primary reason for a zero-tolerance stance against Yellowstone bison crossing park boundaries, then why do nothing about elk? The short answer, again, is most likely economics. Elk are the most popular game animal in the regional hunting industry. Although, in recent years, Montana officials have asked Wyoming to curtail its winter elk-feeding operations, the bottom line is that Montana has shown it is willing to accept a wildlife species that harbors brucellosis and actively spreads it to livestock while taking an absolutist stance toward bison, a species that has never transmitted brucellosis to cattle in the wild.

Considering the cultural and historical importance of bison to Native Americans, some observers view the Montana state legislature's continued opposition as a reflection of harmful attitudes toward Indigenous peoples. Given the historical, economic, and scientific evidence regarding brucellosis, one wonders if there isn't some truth to such claims.

* * *

While the 1995 Interim Bison Management Plan bought time for the major federal and state players to develop a more permanent solution, other stakeholders in the bison debate continued working on a number of alternatives. One of these groups, the Greater Yellowstone Coalition, formed in 1983 by local environmental advocates, sought to promote ecosystem management in the region. The bison controversy, which cried out for a geographic solution based on something other than park borders, seemed perfectly suited to such an approach.

A few years later in 1991, Native American tribal nations created the Intertribal Bison Cooperative.[19] This organization sought to restore wild bison to tribal lands in the United States and Canada, recognizing them as an ecological, cultural, and economic resource. Instead of killing Yellowstone bison that wandered across the park border, why not transport them to places where they would be welcomed?

Beyond stopping wasteful slaughter, Yellowstone bison held particular interest for the plains tribes due to the animals' genetic purity. Several Indigenous nations, including the Nakota (Assiniboine) and A'aninin (Gros Ventre) nations at the Fort Belknap Reservation and the Blackfeet nation, already had some bison on their lands by the late 1970s.[20] Purchased from private ranchers, the small herds generated revenue through occasional commercial hunts and breeding. But these animals, like the vast majority of the roughly 500,000 bison living in North America in 2022, typically contained a small percentage of cattle genes: a remnant of failed turn-of-the-nineteenth-century efforts to produce the elusive hybrid "cattalo" by Charles J. "Buffalo" Jones and others. Since those efforts corresponded with the low point in national bison numbers, they produced an evolutionary bottleneck, allowing cattle genes to persist in the species for the next 130 years.

The major exception to this rule is found in the bison of Yellowstone—the only continually free-ranging and genetically pure herd of wild buffalo in the United States. As such, they are extremely important not only for their genetics but for cultural reasons. Native American plains tribes view the Yellowstone bison as direct descendants of the ancestral buffalo that are woven into the origin stories and histories of several nations. The Yellowstone bison are spiritual relatives, a significant part of tribal identities. As Assiniboine religious leader Larry Wetsit noted, "the bison's return represents a renewed celebration of who we are as a people."[21]

In 1997, the National Wildlife Federation entered into a partnership with the Intertribal Bison Cooperative, the first agreement of its kind between a national environmental NGO and a tribal group, to help make the transfer of Yellowstone bison to Indigenous lands a reality.[22]

But that same year, another major die-off occurred when harsh winter conditions forced record numbers of bison across the park boundary. When it was over, two-thirds of the Yellowstone herd lay dead by either starvation or slaughter. Once more, the killing led to public criticism, but this time it also led to the formation of a new environmental organization. Native American activist Rosalie Little Thunder and non-native environmentalist Mike Mease joined forces to create the Buffalo Field Campaign. By bringing public attention to the buffalo killing, they hoped to change minds and, eventually, policy.

In 1999, in a bid to influence the formal and ongoing interagency effort to develop a permanent bison plan, the Greater Yellowstone Coalition released its alternative proposal: the Citizen Management Plan to Save Yellowstone Bison. The document proposed using adjacent national forest lands as bison habitat, allowing hunting to control population numbers, and relocating "excess" bison to tribal lands, where they could be quarantined until deemed disease-free.[23] As a public-outreach effort, the plan succeeded in garnering support from tens of thousands of park visitors, but whether it would influence the final plan remained unknown.

* * *

At the Fort Peck Reservation in northeastern Montana, tribal leaders continued their own work to bring bison back to their lands. In 1999, Robbie Magnan assumed leadership of this effort, and in 2001, the tribes purchased one hundred bison from their sister reservation at Fort Belknap. Though not genetically pure, these bison generated income for the tribe through public hunts, while also providing a source of lean meat for tribal consumption and for cultural ceremonies.

The next step was to develop what Magnan referred to as a cultural herd, comprised of Yellowstone bison. Working with the Intertribal Bison Cooperative, the Park Service, and partners from the National Wildlife Federation and Defenders of Wildlife, Magnan developed facilities at Fort Peck Reservation to receive, care for, and manage bison that were otherwise under threat of slaughter. As he explained, "Since the beginning of time, the buffalo have taken care of us. Now it's time that we take care of them."[24]

* * *

In 2000, the final Interagency Bison Management Plan was released. It called for maintaining a population of 3,000 bison in Yellowstone. If bison migrated out of the park to the north or west, they would be captured and tested for brucellosis. If they tested negative, individuals would be vaccinated and returned to the park, up to the number equaling a total population of 3,000. If they tested positive, or if the park number already stood at 3,000 or higher, individuals would be sent to slaughter.

Notably, the plan called for vaccinating all bison that tested negative (and ultimately inoculating the entire herd), but absent an effective vaccine, this never became a viable solution. A mandated vaccine does exist for cattle, which is roughly 60 to 65 percent effective. But the efficacy of the cattle vaccine in bison is roughly 15 percent or less. Results are similarly dismal for elk. Moreover, even if all Yellowstone bison suddenly became brucellosis-free tomorrow, as long as the disease enjoys safe harbor in the regional elk population, the risk of transmission from elk to cattle, and from elk to bison, persists.

Still, no one was satisfied with the 2000 plan, and the search for alternatives carried on. In 2005, Montana reinstituted its state-sanctioned hunt but this time included members from tribal nations based on the restoration of treaty-based hunting rights first established back in the 1850s and '60s.

While the hunts helped reduce the need for slaughter inside the park, they also brought new tensions. Montana required that the hunts adopt a concentrated "firing line" format to ensure no bison escaped. But this forced Native Americans seeking to exercise their traditional hunting rights to engage in a process that many found deplorable. As James Holt, Nez Perce tribal member and executive director of the Buffalo Field Campaign, explained, the state's decision to organize the hunts this way disrespected the sacred tribal relationship with bison. By viewing the hunt as a mere management tool, it ignored the historical and cultural importance of bison in Native American society. Although tribal nations generally welcomed the reinstatement of treaty-based hunting rights, the conditions under which the hunts took place underscored the need to allow wild bison more space to roam.[25]

Meanwhile, in a notable break with the Montana state legislature, newly elected Montana governor Brian Schweitzer supported efforts by the Montana Department of Fish, Wildlife and Parks and APHIS to develop a formal process for designating brucellosis-free status to Yellowstone bison. If bison could achieve this designation, it could potentially allow them to move beyond park borders without consequence. Between 2005 and 2012, they ran a pilot quarantine study that involved repeated testing of bison over multiple years, including through an entire pregnancy cycle for females.

In response, Robbie Magnan applied to receive some of these bison "graduating" from the program on behalf of the Fort Peck Reservation, where he was constructing a 4,800-acre pasture with special wildlife fencing. He also moved forward with plans to build a state-of-the-art quarantine facility that would allow the designation of brucellosis-free bison on site, saving the lives of countless more Yellowstone bison and making Fort Peck a hub for disseminating them to tribal lands across the nation.

Despite these advances, the winter of 2007–2008 witnessed another record number of bison killed, this time over 1,200 through a combination of hunting, slaughter, and starvation. The event demonstrated yet again the urgency of finding a conservation solution.

* * *

Over the next few years, progress accelerated significantly. In 2008, the U.S. Department of the Interior pledged to restore wild bison to their "ecological and cultural role on appropriate landscapes within the species' historical range."[26] The DOI's bison-conservation initiative sought to achieve this goal by developing partnerships with "States, Native American tribes, landowners, agricultural interests, conservationists and others."

In 2010, the National Park Service reaffirmed support for this idea. In its *Call to Action* report, the agency announced the goal of restoring "three wild bison populations across the central and western United States in collaboration with tribes, private landowners, and other public land management agencies."[27]

To Magnan, all of this was welcome news as he waited to hear the fate of Fort Peck's application to receive some of the Yellowstone bison. When they were deemed "brucellosis free" by the 2010 APHIS pilot quarantine program, the animals were allowed to move beyond the park bounds for the first time. But their destination wasn't Fort Peck.

Although several tribal nations and one Wyoming state park had requested some of the bison, state officials sent them instead to media magnate Ted Turner and his Flying D Ranch. Located just northwest of Yellowstone in Gallatin Gateway, Montana, the Flying D was the largest privately owned commercial bison ranch in the United States. State officials argued that Turner was best prepared to manage the animals, but tribal leaders, including Magnan—given the long and troubled history of federal-tribal relations in the United States—felt there may have been other unspoken reasons for the decision.

Harry Child, the wealthy industrialist who held monopoly control over Yellowstone's hotels and concessions for so long, had once owned the Flying D Ranch. And ironically, the ranch may also have been the source of the infected cattle that initially gave brucellosis to Yellowstone's captive bison herd back in 1917.

Be that as it may, the delay in sending bison to Fort Peck was only temporary. In 2011, a second group of bison in the APHIS pilot quarantine program completed their testing. And in March of 2012, Montana finally agreed to send wild Yellowstone bison to tribal lands for the first time.

* * *

The morning after the bison arrived in Fort Peck, Magnan and other tribal leaders learned of legal action taken by bison opponents. A federal court ordered a stay on the transfer of bison from Yellowstone the day before, but of course, it had arrived too late. The best the ruling could do was place a hold on the secondary transfer of some twenty-five bison from Fort Peck Reservation to Fort Belknap Reservation in north-central Montana. Since the brucellosis argument no longer carried weight, arguments now centered on the potential damage bison would cause if they escaped tribal pastures and began eating grass meant for domestic cows. The ensuing legal battle went all the way to the Montana supreme court, which struck it down in 2013. The Montana state legislature responded with new bills designed to stop the movement of Yellowstone bison to the tribes, but these eventually failed as well, opening the way for intertribal bison distributions to proceed.

In 2012, Yellowstone National Park signed an agreement with the Intertribal Bison Council to partner on providing surplus Yellowstone bison to Native American tribes. And in 2016, Yellowstone bison gained the right to graze in national forest lands adjacent to the park border without consequence, essentially widening their seasonal habitat.

In slow, patchwork fashion, Yellowstone bison are beginning to reinhabit portions of their historic range on the Great Plains. Through the Park Service's Bison Conservation Transfer Program, Yellowstone managers agreed to share quarantine duties with Fort Peck, whereby after one to two years of testing by APHIS, the third and final year of testing can take place on the reservation. By 2020, Fort Peck had shared Yellowstone bison with eighteen different tribal nations in ten states. In early 2022, park managers launched a plan to incorporate this practice as part of a new long-term Yellowstone bison management strategy.[28]

At the same time, state politicians in Montana continued to challenge efforts to legalize free-roaming bison. Between 2009 and 2017, they proposed twenty-nine bills, the vast majority of which sought to block the movement of Yellowstone bison into Montana or to tribal lands.[29] Time and again, Robbie Magnan, Jonathan Proctor, and their allies found themselves traveling to Helena to testify in legislative hearings or to mount legal defenses in court. Most bills during this period died in committee or received vetoes from the governor. However, since 2020, the state has adopted new strategies, including efforts to block conservation groups like American Prairie from using federal grazing permits to allow wild bison to further expand their range.[30]

* * *

The arrival of wild Yellowstone bison to Fort Peck marked a new era in bison conservation in the United States. For the first time in park history, Native American tribes acted not just as Park Service partners or consultants but as formally recognized leaders in protecting Yellowstone wildlife. As John Proctor remarked, the transfer of wild bison to Fort Peck would never have happened without the vision and decades of commitment by Robbie Magnan and other tribal leaders. In this way, Indigenous people are helping to move the needle on one of the park's oldest wildlife conservation efforts.

While Yellowstone buffalo play a particularly important role in the history and culture of the plains tribes, they are also an iconic species for all of American society. Once more, the story of Yellowstone is the story of the United States itself. The influence of the park ripples across the nation as Yellowstone bison become the seed for new herds on tribal and conservation lands across the Great Plains and beyond.

Legacies

(2016–2022)

THE STORY OF YELLOWSTONE BEGAN WITH A SINGULAR GEOG-
raphy that gave rise to a landscape filled with fantastical geothermal
features and a distinctive array of wildlife. For at least 11,000 years,
Indigenous peoples knew it as a homeland filled with essential mineral
resources, opportunities for hunting and gathering, and sites with medicinal and spiritual value. In the nineteenth century, the high altitude
and long winters kept Euro-American settlers and explorers at bay and,
in so doing, provided a refuge for wildlife hunted to extinction elsewhere. In time, these unique qualities, combined with their perceived
economic and political value, would help usher something new into the
world: the first-ever national park.

Ever since, we've continually debated just what that designation means. What should Yellowstone—and national parks more
generally—actually stand for? The protection of unique landscapes?
Of wildlife? Of human history and cultures? The promotion of recreational tourism and national heritage? If all of the above, how might
we balance everything out? How should nature be valued or managed
in such contexts, and for whose benefit?

Yellowstone's history contains various, ongoing attempts to answer
these questions. In the process, these negotiations have shaped the way
Americans understand and relate to nature. Between the 2016 centennial celebration of the national park system and Yellowstone's 150th
anniversary in 2022, a new series of events brought these discussions

once more to the national stage. Together, they shone a bright light on some of Yellowstone's most enduring living legacies.

* * *

In early 2020, few people anticipated the catastrophic upheaval the COVID-19 pandemic would unleash upon the world. But in the aftermath, even fewer were aware of Yellowstone's surprising role in enabling the science that helped us get through it.

Scientific study has been part of Yellowstone's history since the 1870 expeditions, but its application in park management took decades to evolve. Part of the delay was waiting for the ecological science to develop and then, once it was available, convincing the powers that be to actually adopt it. It took time to shift the dominant idea of nature as a commodity into something wild that deserved protection. Even after, there were decisions that took decades to correct—like the attempts to kill all predators, stamp out every wildfire, and introduce invasive fish species for sport.

On the other hand, park managers successfully pioneered the nation's first endangered species recovery program with wild bison. Then, in fits and starts, they ended artificial feeding, stopped predator eradication, and instigated the first-ever reintroduction of gray wolves in the United States. In the aftermath of the 1988 Summer of Fire, the national reckoning ushered in new public understandings of wildfire's rejuvenating ecological role. Each of these events were controversial at the time. But they were also essential in helping to reshape the way American society conceptualized the natural world. In this sense, Yellowstone has been a stage upon which one can observe the evolution of scientific knowledge over time.

Nowhere is this truer than the park's role in the COVID-19 pandemic. It began in 1964, when microbiology professor Thomas Brock from the University of Wisconsin visited Yellowstone for the first time and happened to catch a ranger-led tour of the park's hot springs. His curiosity was stoked by the bright colors in the pools, which the ranger identified as blue-green algae. Brock wondered if there could there be other forms of life capable of surviving such extreme conditions, where water temperatures might surpass the boiling point. Over the next few years, he returned to Yellowstone to research this question and eventually discovered a bacteria called *Thermus aquaticus* in the park's Mushroom Pool. This finding, along with Brock's other work, fundamentally changed scientific assumptions about the conditions under which organisms could exist and even thrive on Earth.[1]

Then, in the late 1980s, biochemist Kary Mullis was developing a new process to replicate DNA molecules. He needed an enzyme that could withstand extreme temperatures and found the perfect candidate (called Taq polymerase) in Yellowstone's *Thermus aquaticus* bacteria. The DNA-replication process, known as polymerase chain reaction (or PCR), not only earned Mullis a Nobel Prize in 1993 but also opened the door to modern DNA analysis. It became used in everything from genetic sequencing to crime investigations, from tracing family heritage to providing new medical treatments. In time, the PCR process also made possible the gold-standard test for COVID-19.

In a strange and unexpected way, Yellowstone helped provide tools to manage and contain the virus until the time arrived when we could travel, convene, and interact as members of a shared society once more.

* * *

As well as serving as a laboratory for generating knowledge, Yellowstone has evolved into a classroom for educating the public. The park's original forms of information sharing—the tall tales stagecoach drivers told to visitors in the 1880s and '90s—gave way to Horace Albright's trailside museums and park-naturalist programs of the 1920s and '30s. The innovation of modern visitor centers in the 1950s and '60s was another step forward, eventually leading to the 1990s publication of *Yellowstone Science*. This freely available journal shares the findings of research conducted in the park, including topics in archeology, geology, wildlife ecology, and various other disciplines.

Arguably, the most important topic in environmental education in recent decades has been climate change. The scale of impact is vast, affecting not only every aspect of conservation in Yellowstone but, in fact, all aspects of life in the United States and the world. As the climate warms, it directly influences precipitation and temperature patterns. Dry areas become drier—as record-setting droughts in the American

West and Europe attest—and wet places wetter, as warm air over the oceans holds more moisture and energy, leading to more frequent and intense hurricanes (and even snowstorms).[2]

In Yellowstone, the effects of climate change are tangible in the seasons. As summers become hotter and longer, and winters milder and shorter, the result can be catastrophic for the park's winter snowpack. Yellowstone snowmelt feeds the headwaters of two of the continent's largest waterways, the Missouri/Mississippi and Snake/Columbia Rivers. Typically, winter snows melt gradually over the summer months and help to maintain year-round water flow downstream. However, if the snowpack melts too quickly, it not only causes water shortages in late summer but can lead to massive flooding in the short term.

This is what happened in June 2022, smack dab in the middle of Yellowstone's 150th-anniversary celebrations. A torrent of flooding forced Superintendent Cam Sholly to order the evacuation and closure of the park for only the third time in Yellowstone's history (the first due to the 1988 fires and the second due to the COVID-19 pandemic in spring 2020). The cause was a summer storm that brought two to three inches of rainfall, combined with warming temperatures that further melted another five and a half inches of snow cover. The resultant runoff washed out roads in and around Yellowstone, stranding 10,000 tourists and cutting off power to the park.[3]

Climate change in Yellowstone also determines whether its vegetation flourishes or declines, with the loss of food sources rippling throughout the entire ecosystem. For example, the reduced production of whitebark pine nuts in recent years is one factor impairing the viability of Yellowstone's grizzly bear populations. While wild animals may be able to migrate in search of cooler climates, there is no guarantee they will find appropriate food when they arrive. Forests and vegetation can also migrate, albeit much more slowly, over generations. Regardless, specialist species—like pikas, which are uniquely adapted to high-elevation alpine environments—have nowhere else to go as the climate warms. In the end, only generalists, like coyotes or wolves, may persist due to their ability to thrive in a wide range of environmental conditions.

Of course, Yellowstone has experienced the staggering effects of a warming climate before. At the end of the last ice age some 12,000 years ago, climate change melted the half-mile-thick ice cap lying atop the Yellowstone Plateau as it ushered in the Holocene epoch. But those changes occurred over thousands of years. Climate change today is happening over a matter of decades, corresponding with the rise of modern industrial society and its dependence on fossil fuels.

The fact that political and economic decision-making could actually do something to slow or possibly even reverse this process makes the educational legacy of Yellowstone all the more relevant. Visitors can see and experience tangible expressions of climatic changes on the landscape and be exposed to the scientifically proven causes of this phenomenon. They can also witness potential solutions: Yellowstone's park-greening programs offer pragmatic examples of more sustainable living through initiatives that reduce waste, energy usage, and carbon footprints in visitor services.

* * *

The centennial of the national park system in 2016 brought renewed focus to the Park Service's long struggle to fulfill its hundred-year-old dual mandate: to balance nature preservation with the promotion of recreational tourism. In Yellowstone, the centenary also coincided with a new annual attendance record. With over 4.25 million visitors, it seemed that at least in Yellowstone, the scale was tilting toward tourism.

The rapid growth in visitation (nearly 50 percent higher than ten years earlier) presented a clear conundrum for Yellowstone managers.[4] On one hand, the increase, driven in part by a sharp rise in international tourism, created overcrowding, overuse, and maintenance backlogs.[5] On the other hand, visitor studies showed that American tourists tended to represent a particular segment of society. Relatively absent were young people and members of racial and ethnic minorities.[6] International visitors certainly added to diversity, but not in a domestic sense. As a national institution, Yellowstone is intended for all members of society—a "park for the people," according to the 1872 act. Moreover, on a pragmatic level, if parks are to remain relevant into the next century, it is important that they "have friends" among future generations and across the widest possible swath of American society. Consequently, park managers found themselves in the untenable position of having both too many visitors and not enough.

In response, the Obama administration introduced the "Every Kid in a Park" initiative in 2015. The program provided a free national park pass to every fourth grader in the United States for use by the child and their family. It became one of the few federal programs to receive support from each of the next two presidential administrations. Maintenance budgets also got a boost, and several parks, not including Yellowstone, experimented with new online reservation systems to better manage visitor numbers.

Nonetheless, the century-old question of "Yellowstone for whom?" remained. In the park's earliest days, it stood at the center of efforts to forcibly remove Native Americans from their ancestral homelands. Later, it informed tensions between the so-called Sagebrushers, camping out in their wagons, and the Couponers, arriving in first-class train cars for all-inclusive park tours. In the early 1900s, it framed the dichotomy between Harry Child's vision of exclusive hotels and Teddy Roosevelt's democratic ideal. Over one hundred years later, the question has yet to be resolved. Even with a free park pass, unless one happens to live nearby, a visit to Yellowstone still involves a significant investment of time and money, something that lies beyond the reach of many American households.

Providing tourist services also requires commercial development. Recall that at its core, the political will that moved Congress to establish Yellowstone National Park stemmed not from an environmental ethic but from economic interests, including those of the Northern Pacific Railroad. Those incentives persist today in the monopolization of park hotels and concessions.

For over eighty years, Harry Child and his heirs, with financial backing from railroad companies, maintained control of Yellowstone's hotels, restaurants, and transportation services. In 1966, the contracts passed to a corporate conglomerate with ties to the Wyoming mining industry known as General Host. Then, in 1979, they were acquired by TW Services, a corporate enterprise at one time linked to TWA Airlines and renamed Xanterra in 2002. For the past forty-three years, this company has run concessions at Yellowstone and several other national parks, including Glacier and the Grand Canyon. In 2013, Xanterra received a new twenty-year lease in Yellowstone.

Another historic park monopoly, Hamilton's General Stores, lasted even longer. Established by Child's protégé and business partner Charles Hamilton in 1915, this business expanded to include Yellowstone's first gas stations in the 1920s and nineteen Haynes Photo Shops in 1967. In 2002, after eighty-seven years, Hamilton's General Stores and related businesses were bought out by the Delaware North Corporation, which, as of 2024, still held the contracts.

Yellowstone's monopoly-focused concession contracts set a precedent for the entire national park system. Whether or not the lack of free-market competition has been beneficial for the park or its visitors is an open question. Long-running debates over winter snowmobile access and recent upticks in visitor-wildlife injuries suggest that the challenge of fulfilling the agency's dual mandate continues.

* * *

On June 9, 2022, as part of Yellowstone's 150th-anniversary celebrations, the Park Service announced they were changing the name of Mount Doane, a peak lying just east of Yellowstone Lake, to First Peoples Mountain.[7] Nineteenth-century cartographers had named the peak for Lieutenant Gustavus Doane, a key member of the 1870 Washburn Expedition. But recall that Doane also led a military attack that same year against a Piegan Blackfeet encampment in Montana, resulting in the deaths of 173 women, children, and elderly tribal members. The event was known as the Marias Massacre. Doane later boasted of his role in the attack as he sought military promotion. Given this troubling history, in 2017, a group of Native American leaders from the Rocky Mountain Tribal Council requested that the name of the mountain be changed. Following a unanimous vote by the fifteen-person U.S. Board on Geographic Names, the request was approved.[8]

The decision was one among a series of recent steps toward repairing the relationship between park and tribal nations. Yellowstone managers set the damaging precedent of banning and removing Native Americans from national parks in the nineteenth century. Now, they sought to acknowledge and possibly reestablish an Indigenous presence. Such efforts followed the collaborative development of Yellowstone's Bison Conservation Transfer Program between the Park Service and various tribal partners, as well as recognition by federal and Montana state authorities of treaty-based hunting rights that have allowed for annual (albeit controversial) bison hunts outside of park boundaries.

For the park's sesquicentennial in 2022, Yellowstone also inaugurated a series of new visitor programs, events, and education centers designed to celebrate Native American ties to the park, both historical and contemporary. Through installations like the Yellowstone Tribal Heritage Center and the All Nations Tepee Village in Madison Junction, Native American artists, scholars, and presenters engaged with visitors to share Indigenous stories, artwork, and perspectives on Yellowstone. These efforts were joined by programs such as the Tribal Internship Program and events like the Shoshone-Bannock Tribal Gathering in Old Faithful. Together, these programs signal the potential for a new direction in park management, one that actively embraces the more than 11,000-year history of Indigenous peoples who knew, and continue to know, Yellowstone as a homeland.

* * *

Without question, Yellowstone's legacies are complex: at times celebratory, at times troubling. They reflect broad social, cultural, and environmental values that speak directly to the constant evolution of American society. Together they underscore Yellowstone's unique role in U.S. history: as a place imbued with iconic significance that also serves as a touchstone for our relationship with nature and with one another.

At the same time, Yellowstone's first 150 years as a national park—or 11,000 years as a homeland, or 2.1 million years as a unique geologic landscape—is also just the beginning of an ever-unfolding story. Just as American society continues to grow and change, so too will this special place called Yellowstone.

Acknowledgments

Years ago, I wrote a book about the U.S. public land system, covering everything from national parks and forests, to refuges, rivers, and trails. It seemed at every turn, I kept running into Yellowstone as a place of enormous influence. Trained as a geographer, I've long been interested in sense of place: how different place meanings evolve over time to impact individuals and society writ large. I began to wonder if Yellowstone didn't serve as a fundamental "place" in U.S. history, shaping how we have come to think about nature, our relationship to it, and by extension, to each other.

For the past eight years, I've had the privilege of learning everything I can about Yellowstone National Park. I am extremely grateful to the many generous people who have helped me along the way. First, I must thank Kevin O'Connor for seeing the potential of this project, but equally for his professionalism, contagious energy and unending optimism. One couldn't ask for a better agent. For similar reasons, I am extremely grateful to my editor, Dan Smetanka, who made this project possible. In addition, I owe a great deal to Tajja Isen for her insightful feedback and tremendous editorial skills. I am also indebted to Yukiko Tominaga, Laura Berry, Barrett Briske, Lena Moses-Schmitt, Rachel Fershleiser, Megan Fishmann, Dan López, Wah-Ming Chang, and Miriam Vance.

At Yellowstone, I had the honor of spending time with legendary Yellowstone winter keeper Jeff Henry, former park historian Lee Whittlesey, former wolf project director Doug Smith, former bison project leader Rick Wallen, former NPS agency spokesperson

357

at Yellowstone, Joan Anzelmo, ecologist and climate scientist Mike Tercek, and Yellowstone archivist, Ann Foster. Beyond the park, others that gave generously of their time included wolf expert, Val Asher, park naturalist and educator, Holly McKinney (now at Grand Teton), Jonathan Proctor from the Defenders of Wildlife, and Garrett Voggesser from the National Wildlife Federation. I must also thank April Craighead, Ted Wood, Nolan Wilson, and the staff at the Montana Historical Society, the University of Montana's Mansfield Library, and Yellowstone's Heritage and Research Center. From the Assiniboine and Sioux nations at Fort Peck Reservation, I am deeply indebted to Jonny BearCub, Helen Bighorn, Robbie Magnan (Director of the Fort Peck Fish and Game Department) and all members of the tribal council.

At Gettysburg College, I owe thanks to Katrina Kohn, Sam Donnelly, Kevin Aughinbaugh, Jack Luedekke, Natalie Kisak, Jack Joiner, Alyssa Papantonakis, and Molly Hoffman. Professors Rud Platt and Andrew Wilson assisted with the maps. I am also grateful for research support during my term as the Thompson Chair of Environmental Studies.

Finally, I must thank my life-long friend Shawn Arstein, both for the encouragement and reading every word of the early drafts. The book is dedicated to my parents but would not have been possible without the support of my family, Robin, Orrin, Nolan, and Olivia (and Savannie).

Notes

Epigraph

1. Throughout the book, unless otherwise noted, I attempt to include names for Indigenous nations and individuals in their original language before reverting to more well-known anglicized forms.

Preface

1. Lee H. Whittlesey, *Yellowstone Place Names, Second Edition* (Gardiner, MT: Wonderland Publishing, 2006), 268-269. Aubrey L. Haines, *The Yellowstone Story, Revised edition, vol. 1* (Boulder: University Press of Colorado, 1996), 4.

1. The Day the Earth Screamed

1. These pageants took place up through the early 1970s as documented in the Yellowstone Cub publications; see Jackie Jerla, "Here She Comes: Miss Yellowstone National Park," *In the Shadow of the Arch* (blog), Yellowstone National Park, June 25, 2012, www.nps.gov/yell/blogs/here -she-comes-miss-yellowstone-national-park.htm.
2. Not kidding.
3. Associated Press, "Scars Linger from Killer Montana Quake of '59," *Deseret News*, August 16, 2009, quoted in Larry Morris, *The 1959 Yellowstone Earthquake* (Charleston, SC: History Press, 2016), 32.
4. The main sources for the account of the tragedy that befell the families camping in the Madison River Canyon include Larry Morris's *The 1959 Yellowstone Earthquake* as well as first-person accounts by Irene Bennett Dunn, *Out of the Night: A Story of Tragedy and Hope from a Survivor of the 1959 Montana-Yellowstone Earthquake* (Sandpoint, ID: Plaudit Press, 1998), and Anita Painter Thon, *Shaken in the Night: A Survivor's Story from the Yellowstone Earthquake of 1959* (North Charleston, SC: CreateSpace Independent Publishing Platform, 2014). Other personal accounts include archived recorded interviews with survivors taken by the U.S. Forest Service and multiple newspaper accounts.
5. Italics mine. Gustavus C. Doane, *Report of Lieutenant Gustavus C. Doane Upon the So-called Yellowstone Expedition of 1870 to the Secretary of War*, 41st Cong., 3d Sess., Exec. Doc. 51 (Washington, D.C.: GPO, 1870).

6. Ferdinand V. Hayden, *Preliminary Report of the United States Geological Survey of Montana, and Portions of Adjacent Territories: Being a Fifth Annual Report of Progress* (Washington, D.C.: GPO, 1872), 82.

7. Robert B. Smith and Lee J. Siegel, *Windows into the Earth: The Geologic Story of Yellowstone and Grand Teton National Parks* (London: Oxford University Press, 2000), 19.

8. Ibid., 21.

9. USDA Forest Service interview with Mildred "Tootie" Green, April 2001, available at www.youtube.com/watch?v=T8U5HSIWOFQ. See also Mary Pickett, "Waking to Disaster," *Billings Gazette*, August 16, 2009, and Morris, *1959 Yellowstone Earthquake*, 16–19.

10. Smith and Siegel, *Windows*, 21.

11. This depends on how one measures size and power. The claim is based on how much erupted material (called *tephera*) a volcano releases during an eruption. Scientists estimate Yellowstone released approximately 600 cubic miles of tephera during its first super-eruption. A larger eruption likely took place about 28 million years ago in the La Garita Caldera in the San Juan Mountains of southwestern Colorado (with an estimated 1,200 cubic miles of tephera), but La Garita is no longer considered active. The only other active volcano comparable to Yellowstone is Lake Toba, Sumatra. Toba last erupted about 75,000 years ago, emitting an estimated 670 cubic miles of tephera. However, some scientists believe the Yellowstone estimate is too conservative and could actually have been up to three times larger, resulting in 1,800 cubic miles of debris. If true, this would make Yellowstone's eruption the largest known to science. But if you prefer to measure your volcanoes in terms of height, then the largest active volcano in the world is Mauna Loa in Hawaii. It is also the tallest mountain in the world when accounting for its full mass, which extends not only to the seafloor but down into the earth's crust, due to its massive weight. When all of this is taken into account, Mauna Loa is estimated to be over 56,000 feet, almost twice the size of Mount Everest. See "Yellowstone Volcano Observatory," USGS, accessed January 31, 2024, volcanoes.usgs.gov /observatories/yvo/index.html.

12. The Pleistocene lasted from about 2.58 million years ago to 11,700 years ago. Our current geologic epoch, the Holocene, begins at this point with the end of the Last Glacial Period (or Last Ice Age) and corresponds to the current interglacial warming period in which human civilizations began to grow and develop across the globe. Some argue that today we have entered another new geologic epoch, the Anthropocene, in which humans for the first time are reshaping the earth system in more fundamental ways, such as through global climate change.

13. Smith and Siegel, *Windows*, 50.

14. Ibid., 88.

15. Morris, *1959 Yellowstone Earthquake*, 137.

2. Homeland

1.   Douglas MacDonald, *Before Yellowstone: Native American Archeology in the National Park* (Seattle: University of Washington Press, 2018), 76.
2.   As a foundation for these events, I rely on Peter Nabokov and Lawrence Loendorf, *Restoring a Presence: American Indians and Yellowstone National Park* (Norman: University of Oklahoma Press, 2002) and MacDonald, *Before Yellowstone.*
3.   MacDonald, *Before Yellowstone*, 51, 57. See also Lorena Bercerra Valdivia, Michael Waters, Thomas Stafford Jr., and Thomas Higham, "Reassessing the Chronology of the Archeological Site of Anzick," *PNAS* 115, no. 27 (2018): 7000–7003. The latter study dates the radiocarbon age of the remains and artifacts to 10,915 years ago, plus or minus fifty years, and the calibrated age between 12,695 and 12,905 years ago.
4.   Morten Rasmussen et al., "The Genome of a Late Pleistocene Human from a Clovis Burial Site in Western Montana," *Nature* 506 (February 2014): 225–29.
5.   MacDonald, *Before Yellowstone*, 48 and 60.
6.   Shane Doyle, "Commemorating Yellowstone's 150th Birthday with the Parks 'First Family,'" *National Park Conservation Association*, March 1, 2022.
7.   Interestingly, the Clovis period also corresponds with the mass extinction of most of these "ice age species": mastodons, mammoths, saber-tooth tigers, etc. But while Clovis hunter-gatherers may have contributed to this loss, most scientists believe the human population was never large enough to render such a profound ecological effect across the continent. The more likely culprit was the changing climate.
8.   Douglas MacDonald, "Archeological Significance of Yellowstone Lake," *Yellowstone Science* 26, no.1 (2018): 53–62.
9.   Nabokov and Loendorf, *Restoring a Presence*, 49–53.
10. MacDonald, *Before Yellowstone*, 204. Material artifacts associated with the adoption of the bow and arrow by many Indigenous peoples after AD 500 provide better evidence of ties to specific modern tribal nations. But for artifacts found prior to this time, it is much more difficult. Moreover, archeological studies in Yellowstone National Park remain in their infancy. Although 1,850 archeological sites have been identified, according to the National Park Service, as of 2024, less than 3 percent of the park area had been inventoried. Future finds may lend additional insight into such questions. See "Archeology," Yellowstone National Park, National Park Service, last updated January 16, 2024, www.nps.gov/yell/learn/history culture/archeology.htm.
11. Quoted in Nabokov and Loendorf, *Restoring a Presence*, 42–44.
12. MacDonald, *Before Yellowstone*, 204. As mentioned earlier, throughout the book, unless otherwise noted, I attempt to identify Indigenous nations and individuals in their native language before reverting to more well-known anglicized versions.

3. First Sight

1. Ronald M. Anglin and Larry E. Morris, *The Mystery of John Colter: The Man Who Discovered Yellowstone* (Lanham, MD: Rowman & Littlefield, 2014).

2. Ibid., 100–101.

3. Thomas James, *Three Years Among the Indians and Mexicans* (Waterloo, Il: Office of the War Eagle, 1846), 23. James also provides an account of Colter's famous run and other adventures in the northern Rockies, quoted in Haines, *Yellowstone Story*, 1: 37.

4. John Bradbury, *Travels into the Interior of America in the years 1809, 1810 and 1811* (London: Smith & Galway, 1817).

5. William H. Goetzmann, *Exploration and Empire: The Explorer and the Scientist in the Winning of the American West* (New York: Alfred A. Knopf, 1966), 16, quoted in George Black, *Empire of Shadows: The Epic Story of Yellowstone* (New York: St. Martin's Griffin, 2012), 20.

6. Clarence E. Carter, ed., "The Territories of Louisiana-Missouri, 1803–1806," in *The Territorial Papers of the United States*, vol. 13 (Washington, D.C.: GPO, 1948), 243, quoted in Haines, *Yellowstone Story*, 1: 5–6.

7. General Wilkinson was in fact a traitor and a spy working for the Spanish Crown. In league with Aaron Burr, it is thought that Wilkinson and Burr hoped to create their own independent nation in the American West. Wilkinson then turned against Burr, leading to the former vice president's arrest for treason. See Andro Linklater, *An Artist in Treason: The Extraordinary Double Life of General James Wilkinson* (New York: Walker, 2009).

8. Carter, "Territories of Louisiana-Missouri," 243. Wilkinson also dispatched Zebulon Pike on his westward expedition without first seeking permission from President Jefferson, though it was approved retroactively.

9. William Clark, "Miscellaneous Memoranda," in *Original Journals of the Lewis and Clark Expedition, 1804–1806*, vol. 6, ed. Reuben Gold Thwaites (New York: Arno Press, 1904), 266–67, cited in Black, *Empire of Shadows*, 21. It is possible that Clark was referring to a river other than the Yellowstone since he locates this finding on a branch of the "Rochejhone."

10. Paul Allen, ed., *History of the Expedition under the Command of Captains Lewis and Clark*, vol. 2 (Philadelphia: Bradford and Inskeep, 1814), cited in Haines, *Yellowstone Story*, 1: 35–38.

4. Building the Myth

1. Ashley was appointed to the post in 1820, the same year that Missouri achieved statehood.

2. Glass actually hired on with Ashley in 1823. See Robert M. Utley, *A Life Wild and Perilous: Mountain Men and the Paths to the Pacific* (New York: Henry Holt, 1997), 48.

3. Given Bridger's birthdate on March 4, 1804, he was probably still seventeen

years old when he signed on but eighteen years old at the time of departure from Saint Louis in April 1822.

4. The United States signed a treaty with Britain in December 1814 ending the War of 1812. However, the Senate did not ratify the treaty until February 1815. Meanwhile, in January 1815, unaware of these events, American troops fought and won the Battle of New Orleans.

5. Just as Major Stephen Long never ascended his namesake mountain on Colorado's Front Range, Zebulon Pike never climbed the famous Colorado peak named for him.

6. One other unexpected legacy of the Astorian expedition occurred on the overland return journey to Saint Louis, when they discovered South Pass. This relatively direct and accessible route over the Continental Divide laid the groundwork for the Oregon Trail.

7. The arrowhead was removed by Dr. Marcus Whitman, an early missionary to Oregon who passed through the annual rendezvous on the Green River in 1835. The surgical event was witnessed and recorded by another missionary named Samuel Parker. See Samuel Parker, *Journal of an Exploring Tour Beyond the Rocky Mountains*, 4th ed. (Ithaca: Andrus, Woodruff & Gauntlet, 1844), 72, cited in Utley, *Life Wild*, 162–63.

8. Potts's identity as author was discovered in the 1940s by Yellowstone National Park historian Aubrey Haines. He recounts the tale in his book, *Yellowstone Story*, 1: 41–42. The full set of Potts's letters can be found in National Park Service, "Early Yellowstone and Western Experiences," *Yellowstone Nature Notes*, 21, no. 5 (September–October 1947): 49–56.

9. A good example of early company reports are those penned by Alexander Ross, a Scottish-born Canadian employee of the Hudson Bay Company who wrote of Yellowstone's geysers as witnessed by British and French trappers in 1818 and 1824. Cited in Haines, *Yellowstone Story*, 1: 38.

10. Osborne Russell, *Journal of a Trapper*, ed. Aubrey L. Haines (Portland: Oregon Historical Society, 1955), 46.

11. The earliest biographical account of Jim Bridger is the obituary written by his friend, Major General Grenville M. Dodge, *Biographical Sketch of Jim Bridger: Mountaineer, Trapper and Guide* (New York: Unz and Company, 1905). It is included in the biography by J. Cecil Atler, *James Bridger: Trapper, Frontiersman, Scout and Guide, A Historical Narrative* (Columbus, OH: Long's College Book, 1951), 497-525. Also see Stanley Vestal, *Jim Bridger: Mountain Man* (Lincoln: University of Nebraska Press, 1970), first published in 1936 by Morrow (New York).

12. This was also the time that some believe Bridger was involved in the Hugh Glass incident. Made famous in the Oscar-winning film *The Revenant*, based on Michael Punke's book *The Revenant: A Novel of Revenge* (New York: Carroll and Graf, 2002), the story suggests that during the Ashley Expedition, Bridger and another trapper named John Fitzgerald abandoned Glass in the wilderness after he suffered an attack from a grizzly.

Glass miraculously survived and returned to seek revenge on Fitzgerald but ultimately forgave Bridger. However, there is little evidence to support Bridger's participation in these events. For a detailed analysis, see Jerry Enzler, "Tracking Jim Bridger: Finding the Trail of Old Gabe," *Rocky Mountain Fur Trade Journal* 5 (2011): 1–19.

13. Vestal, *Jim Bridger*, 64. Others claim that Etienne Provost may have been the first Euro-American to see the Great Salt Lake that same year. See Utley, *Life Wild*, 72.

14. Dodge, *Biographical Sketch*, in Atler, *James Bridger*, 522.

15. Bridger married his first wife, Cora Insala, in 1835. The daughter of a Salish chief, Cora died in 1845 giving birth to their third child, Josephine. Bridger then married a Ute woman in 1848 who died the following year, again in childbirth. And finally, in 1850, he married Little Fawn, who passed away in 1857 while giving birth to their second child, William.

16. William S. Brackett, "Bonneville and Bridger," *Montana Historical Society Contributions* 3 (1900): 182, citied in Utley, *Life Wild*, 173.

17. Eugene Fitch Ware, *The Indian War of 1864* (Topeka, KS: Crane, 1911), 283-285. Also cited in Aubrey L. Haines, *Yellowstone National Park: Its Exploration and Establishment* (Washington, D.C.: National Park Service, 1974), 19.

18. Ware, *Indian War*, 284.

19. In 1842, Fremont's first expedition mapped the route as far as South Pass. His second expedition in 1843, again guided by Kit Carson, continued on to the Pacific coast.

20. The annexation of Texas included land that later became Oklahoma and parts of Kansas. The Oregon Compromise ceded modern-day Oregon, Washington, and Idaho to the United States. The U.S. gained most of modern-day Arizona, New Mexico, Colorado, Utah, Nevada, and California in the Treaty of Guadalupe Hidalgo, which ended the war with Mexico.

21. John W. Gunnison, *The Mormons, or Latter-Day Saints in the valley of the Great Salt Lake* (Philadelphia: Lippincott, Grambo, 1852), 151, cited in Haines, *Yellowstone National Park*, 24.

22. Haines, *Yellowstone National Park*, 22.

23. Hiram M. Chittenden and Alfred T. Richardson, eds., *Life, Letters and Travels of Father Pierre-Jean DeSmet, S.J., 1801-1873* (New York: Francis Harper, 1905), 660–62, cited in ibid., 23–24.

24. Eugene S. Topping, *The Chronicles of the Yellowstone: An Accurate and Comprehensive History* (Saint Paul, MN: Pioneer Press, 1883), 16, cited in Haines, *Yellowstone National Park*, 19.

5. Standing on the Edge

1. Ferdinand V. Hayden, *Preliminary Report of the United States Geological Survey of Montana, and Portions of Adjacent Territories; Being a Fifth Annual*

Report of Progress (Washington, D.C.: GPO, 1872), 7, cited in Mike Foster, *Strange Genius: The Life of Ferdinand Vandeveer Hayden* (Niwot, CO: Roberts Rhinehart, 1994), 74.

2.   Foster, *Strange Genius*, 60–61.
3.   Joseph Leidy to Hayden, January 17, 1858, cited in ibid., 75.
4.   See William F. Raynolds, *Report on the Exploration of the Yellowstone and Country Drained by That River*, 40th Cong., 2d Sess., S. Exec. Doc. 77 (July 17, 1868).
5.   Foster, *Strange Genius*, 83–84.
6.   Hayden to Spencer Baird, October 13 and November 24, 1859 (RG 57.2.3 Correspondences, National Archives), cited in Foster, *Strange Genius*, 85.
7.   Raynolds to Humphreys, October 4, 1860 (William Franklin Raynolds Papers, Beinecke Library, Yale University), cited in Foster, *Strange Genius*, 86.
8.   Raynolds, *Report*, 85.
9.   Ibid., 86.
10. Ibid., 91.
11. Ibid., 92.
12. Ibid., 99. Burnt Hole refers to an area in the Madison River Valley that had undergone a forest fire. See Aubrey L. Haines, *The Yellowstone Story: A History of Our First National Park*, vol. 1, rev. ed. (Boulder: University Press of Colorado, 1996), 89n7.
13. Raynolds, *Report*, 92.

6. Chasing Glory

1.   An Act to Provide for the Protection of Overland Emigrants to California, Oregon, and Washington Territory, 12 Stat. 333 (1862), cited in Helen McCann White, "Minnesota, Montana, and Manifest Destiny," *Minnesota History* 38 (June 1962): 56.
2.   Idaho Territory would be established the following year, in 1863.
3.   McCann White, "Minnesota, Montana," 57. Fisk's work in the 1850s for William Noble's Fort Ridgely and South Pass Wagon Road project (a trail never completed, but intended to link Minnesota to California), along with his time as a secretary for the Dakota Land Company, was enough apparently to qualify him for the job. See also Helen McCann White, "Captain Fisk Goes to Washington," *Minnesota History* 38 (March 1963): 217.
4.   McCann White, "Minnesota, Montana," 58.
5.   Ibid., 58.
6.   Western mining camps operated under their own grassroots legal code and elected "judges" to rule on disputes over mining claims and other matters.
7.   Walter W. De Lacy, "A Trip to the South Snake River in 1863," *Contributions to the Historical Society of Montana*, vol. 1 (Helena, MT: Rocky Mountain Publishing, 1876), 128, quoted in Aubrey L. Haines, *The Yellowstone*

Story: A History of Our First National Park, vol. 1, rev. ed. (Boulder: University Press of Colorado, 1996), 64.

8. For a thorough accounting of the various excursions by prospectors during this period, including treks made by George Phelps, John Davis, George Huston, and A. Bart Henderson, among others, see Haines, *Yellowstone Story*, 1: 60–83.

9. In 1862, Bannack fell within the jurisdiction of the massive Territory of Dakota, which encompassed all of modern-day North and South Dakota, much of Montana and Wyoming, and a small portion of Nebraska.

10. See Paul Taylor, *The Most Complete Political Machine Ever Known: The North's Union Leagues in the American Civil War* (Kent, OH: Kent State University Press, 2018).

11. Langford was extremely proud of the "work" of these vigilantes, even writing a book in his later years that glorified their exploits. See Nathaniel Pitt Langford, *Vigilante Days and Ways* (Boston: J. G. Cupples, 1890).

12. Railroad companies were expected to sell the land within approximately five years, using the proceeds to cover construction costs.

13. Haines, *Yellowstone Story*, 1: 73–74.

14. Langford to Hauser, March 25, 1865, Montana Historical Society Archives. The letter is dated 1864. Some commentators have suggested that the date is an error. However, Langford may have penned the letter in December of that year after receiving word of his charter from the Territorial Legislature or in anticipation of these events. In his memoirs, Langford claims he first met Bridger in 1866, but this is most likely an error.

15. Nathaniel Pitt Langford, *The Discovery of Yellowstone Park: Journal of the Washburn Expedition to the Yellowstone and Firehole Rivers in the Year 1870* (Lincoln: University of Nebraska Press, 1972), xxix, originally printed by the author in 1905 as *Diary of the Washburn Expedition to the Yellowstone and Firehole Rivers in the Year 1870*.

16. Francis X. Kuppens, "On the Origin of the Yellowstone National Park," reprinted from *The Woodstock Letters* (1897) in *The Jesuit Bulletin* 41, no. 4 (October 1962): 6, quoted in Haines, *Yellowstone Story*, 1: 90.

17. Cornelius Hedges, "An Account of a Trip to Fort Benton in October, 1865, with Acting Governor Thomas F. Meagher to Treat with the Blackfeet Indians," *Rocky Mountain Magazine* 1, no. 3 (November 1900): 155.

18. Black, *Empire of Shadows*, 174.

19. According to some accounts, a tipsy Meagher flipped over the rails of a riverboat and drowned in the Missouri River at Fort Benton. But others contend that foul play was afoot and the incident was nothing less than murder. Meagher's body was never found despite Langford's offer of a $1,000 reward. For a detailed biography of Meagher, see Timothy Egan, *The Immortal Irishman: The Irish Revolutionary Who Became an American Hero* (New York: Houghton Mifflin Harcourt, 2016).

20. Haines, *Yellowstone Story*, 1: 91.

21. "Expedition to the Yellowstone," *Helena Weekly Herald*, July 29, 1869,

quoted in Aubrey L. Haines, *Yellowstone National Park: Its Exploration and Establishment* (Washington, D.C.: National Park Service, 1974), 46. Coulter's Hell is a confusing misnomer. Although it is an actual place located near Cody, Wyoming, many commentators, even today, confuse it with Yellowstone's geyser basins. The "Mysterious Mounds" refer to the Mammoth Hot Springs terraces.

22. One casualty of this violence was Langford's friend, Malcolm Clarke, who was killed in a dispute with extended family members. Langford stayed behind in part to conduct the funeral for his friend.

23. David E. Folsom, *The Folsom-Cook Expedition of the Upper-Yellowstone in the Year 1869* (St. Paul: H.L. Collins, 1894), 10.

24. Ibid., 16.

25. Ibid., 20.

26. Haines, *Yellowstone National Park*, 103.

27. The "superficial expedition" became the Washburn Expedition of 1870. However, the "larger engineer-led expedition" was not the Hayden Survey of 1871, as most would expect, but the Barlow Expedition, which transpired concurrently with Hayden's trip. Phillip H. Sheridan, *Personal Memoirs of Phillip Henry Sheridan, General, United States Army: New and Enlarged Edition,* 1 (New York: D. Appleton, 1904), 550, quoted in George Black, *Empire of Shadows: The Epic Story of Yellowstone* (New York: St. Martin's, 2012), 277.

7. Thirty-Seven Days

1. The account of Truman Everts's adventure derives primarily from his firsthand publication, "Thirty-Seven Days of Peril," *Scribner's Monthly* 3 (November 1871), 1–17. I also rely on the commentary and additional documentation provided in Truman Everts, *Lost in the Yellowstone: "Thirty-Seven Days of Peril" and a Handwritten Account of Being Lost,* ed. Lee H. Whittlesey (Salt Lake City: University of Utah Press, 2015). See also Nathaniel Pitt Langford, *The Discovery of Yellowstone Park: Journal of the Washburn Expedition to the Yellowstone and Firehole Rivers in the Year 1870* (Lincoln: University of Nebraska Press, 1972); Gustavus Doane, "Report of Lieutenant Gustavus C. Doane upon the So-Called Yellowstone Expedition of 1870," 41st Cong., 3d Sess., S. Exec. Doc. 51, 1873; and Cornelius Hedges, "Yellowstone Lake," *Helena Daily Herald,* November 9, 1870. Secondary sources are many, including Aubrey L. Haines, *The Yellowstone Story: A History of Our First National Park,* vol. 1, rev. ed. (Boulder: University Press of Colorado, 1996), and George Black, *Empire of Shadows: The Epic Story of Yellowstone* (New York: St. Martin's, 2012).

2. Everts, like Langford, was appointed to the post by President Lincoln. However, with the rise of the Johnson administration, he lost his job. By summer 1870, he remained unemployed.

3. David E. Folsom, *The Folsom-Cook Expedition of the Upper-Yellowstone in the Year 1869* (St. Paul: H.L. Collins, 1894).

4. Some accounts suggest President Johnson actually ordered Langford removed from the tax-collector position in 1868 in anticipation of appointing him to the governorship. So the Senate's reconfirmation of Langford in that role may also have been an act of defiance against the president. See Black, *Empire of Shadows*, 216-27.

5. Haines, *Yellowstone Story*, 1: 105.

6. *Consumption* is a nineteenth-century term for *tuberculosis*.

7. Kim Allen Scott, *Yellowstone Denied: The Life of Gustavus Cheyney Doane* (Norman, OK: University of Oklahoma Press, 2007).

8. Langford, *Discovery of Yellowstone*, 51.

9. One of these, Mount Doane, was changed to First Peoples Mountain in 2022 at the request of regional tribal leaders.

10. Haines, *Yellowstone Story*, 1: 317.

11. Everts, "Thirty-Seven Days," 10.

12. Everts, *Lost in the Yellowstone*, 20.

13. "Arrival of Warren C. Gillette, of the Yellowstone Expedition," *Helena Herald*, October 3, 1870, quoted in Haines, *Yellowstone Story*, 1: 130.

14. Warren Gillette never married and died a bachelor in 1912.

15. Theodore Garrish, *Life in the World's Wonderland* (Bidleford, ME: N.P., 1887), 238. This statement derives from an interview conducted with Baronett in 1886. Quoted in Haines, *Yellowstone Story*, 1: 132.

16. Nathaniel P. Langford, "The Wonders of Yellowstone," *Scribner's Monthly* 2 (May–June 1871): 113–28.

17. Truman C. Everts, "Thirty-Seven Days of Peril," *Scribner's Monthly* 3 (November 1871): 1–17.

18. Ibid., 17.

8. Final Discovery

1. E. P. Oberholtzer, *Jay Cooke, Financier of the Civil War*, vol. 2 (Philadelphia: George W. Jacob, 1907), 235–36, quoted in Aubrey L. Haines, *The Yellowstone Story: A History of Our First National Park*, vol. 1, rev. ed. (Boulder: University Press of Colorado, 1996), 137.

2. In 1880, he would eventually move to Hyattsville, Maryland, on the outskirts of Washington, D.C.; marry a fourteen-year-old girl; and take a low-ranking bureaucratic position with the U.S. Postal Service. Aubrey L. Haines, *Yellowstone National Park: Its Exploration and Establishment* (Washington, D.C.: National Park Service, 1974), 102.

3. For details on Langford's claims, most made years after the fact, see Haines, *Yellowstone Story*, 1: 138–40.

4. Hayden to George Allen, March 17, 1871, quoted in Marlene Deahl Merrill, ed., *Yellowstone and the Great West: Journals, Letters, and Images*

from the 1871 Hayden Expedition (Lincoln: University of Nebraska Press, 2003), 28.

5. Mike Foster points to a letter received by Hayden on December 28 from his friend Anton Schönborn, replying to Hayden's earlier request to serve as chief topographer on a journey to explore some "new country." Foster hints that this "new country" is Yellowstone, but it is never stated explicitly. Mike Foster, *Strange Genius: The Life of Ferdinand Vandeveer Hayden* (Niwot, CO: Roberts Rhinehart, 1994), 203–4.

6. This budget represented an increase of $15,000 over the previous year, including a $1,000 salary increase for Hayden himself (now set at $4,000 annually).

7. Mike Foster argues that as early as 1868, Hayden recognized the value of incorporating photographs and other visual imagery into his written geological reports so that they might appeal to a wider audience. Hayden's *Sun Pictures of the Rocky Mountain Scenery*, published in 1870 by Julien Bein and sponsored by the Union Pacific Railroad, serves as an example. Foster, *Strange Genius*, 197–98.

8. In Haines's first history of Yellowstone, published in 1974 (*Yellowstone National Park*, 101–2), the author notes that Hayden may have known about Barlow well before his arrival at Fort Ellis. But in Haines's later history of the park, published in 1996, he states that Hayden didn't learn about Barlow until his arrival at Fort Ellis in early July. See *Yellowstone Story*, 1: 142.

9. Other names in use at the time include Soda Mountain, Sulphur Springs, Great Springs, and Mysterious Mounds. See Haines, *Yellowstone Story*, 1: 144 and 349n128.

10. Ibid.

11. Ferdinand V. Hayden, *Preliminary Report of the United States Geological Survey of Montana, and Portions of Adjacent Territories; Being a Fifth Annual Report of Progress* (Washington, D.C.: GPO, 1872), 66.

12. Ibid., 66–67.

13. Baronett asked Everts more than once but received the same response each time. Haines, *Yellowstone National Park*, 139.

14. Hayden, *Preliminary Report*, 80–81.

15. Ibid., 83–84.

16. Ibid., 84.

17. Ibid., 112.

18. Ibid., 115.

19. Ibid., 125.

20. Ibid., 121.

21. Kim Allen Scott, *Yellowstone Denied: The Life of Gustavus Cheyney Doane* (Norman: University of Oklahoma Press, 2007), 83.

22. Letter in Record Group 57, National Archives, Washington, D.C., *Records of the Department of Interior*, Geological Survey, letters received by F. V. Hayden, 1871, cited in Haines, *Yellowstone Story*, 1: 155.

9. The World's First National Park

1. Cong. Globe, 42d Cong., 2d Sess. (December 18, 1871), 158.
2. Wallace Stegner, "The Best Idea We Ever Had," in *Marking the Sparrow's Fall: The Making of the American West*, ed. Page Stegner (New York: Henry Holt, 1998), 137.
3. Randall K. Wilson, *America's Public Lands: From Yellowstone to Smokey Bear and Beyond*, 2nd ed. (Lanham, MD: Rowman & Littlefield, 2020), 327n5.
4. Congress established Yosemite National Park in 1890. That same year, California returned Yosemite Valley to federal control. The valley was added to the park in 1906.
5. Hiram Chittenden, *The Yellowstone National Park* (Cincinnati, OH: Stewart and Kidd, 1895).
6. Nathaniel Pitt Langford, *Diary of the Washburn Expedition to the Yellowstone and Firehole Rivers in the Year 1870* (printed by the author, 1905).
7. Haines deserves credit for bringing this observation to light. See Aubrey L. Haines, *The Yellowstone Story: A History of Our First National Park*, vol. 1, rev. ed. (Boulder: University Press of Colorado, 1996), 173. A more recent investigation is found in Paul Schullery and Lee Whittlesey, *Myth and History in the Creation of Yellowstone National Park* (Lincoln: University of Nebraska Press, 2003).
8. Ibid.
9. David Folsom, *The Folsom-Cook Expedition of the Upper-Yellowstone in the Year 1869* (St. Paul: H.L. Collins, 1894).
10. Kuppens notes that Cornelius Hedges was present as a member of Meagher's party. Francis X. Kuppens, "On the Origins of the Yellowstone National Park," reprinted from *The Woodstock Letters* (1897) in *The Jesuit Bulletin* 41, no. 4 (October 1962): 7, cited in Haines, *Yellowstone Story*, 1: 90.
11. Letter from Hayden to Secretary of the Interior Carl Schurz, February 21, 1879, 45th Cong., 2d Sess., H.R. Exec. Doc. 75.
12. Letter from Clagett to the Minnesota Historical Society in 1894. Reprinted in Langford, *Diary*, xliv–xlviii.
13. Haines, *Yellowstone Story*, 1: 166–67.
14. Ibid.
15. House report, reprinted in Ferdinand V. Hayden, *Preliminary Report of the United States Geological Survey of Montana and Portions of Adjacent Territories; Being a Fifth Annual Report of Progress* (Washington, D.C.: GPO, 1872), 164.
16. Ibid., 164.
17. Ibid.
18. Cong. Globe, 42d Cong., 2d Sess. (January 23, 1872), 520.
19. House report, reprinted in Hayden, *Preliminary Report*, 164. For more on this argument, see Alfred Runte, *National Parks: The American Experience*, 4th ed. (Lanham, MD: Rowman & Littlefield, 2010), 43–55.
20. Cong. Globe, 42d Cong., 2d Sess. (January 23, 1872), 697,

21. Cong. Globe, 42d Cong., 2d Sess. (February 27, 1872), 1243.
22. Ferdinand V. Hayden, "Wonders of the West II: More About the Yellowstone," *Scribner's Monthly* 3 (February 1872): 396.
23. Yellowstone National Park Act of 1872.
24. Nathaniel P. Langford, *Report of the Superintendent of the Yellowstone National Park for the Year 1872*, 42d Cong., 3d Sess., S. Exec. Doc. 35 (Washington, D.C.: GPO, 1873), 4–5.
25. Windham T. W. Dunraven, *The Great Divide* (London: Chatto and Windus, 1876).
26. William E. Strong, *A Trip to the Yellowstone National Park in July, August and September, 1875* (Washington, D.C.: GPO, 1876).
27. William Ludlow, *Report of a Reconnaissance from Carroll, Montana Territory, on the Upper Missouri to the Yellowstone National Park, and Return, Made in the Summer of 1875* (Washington, D.C.: GPO, 1876).
28. Editorial, *Bozeman Avant Courier*, August 20, 1875, cited in Haines, *Yellowstone Story*, 1: 204.

10. The Nez Perce War

1. The details for this story derive heavily from a number of primary and secondary sources. The major primary source is Emma Carpenter Cowan's *Reminiscence* (SC 576, Montana Historical Society Archives, 1902). I also rely on Frank Carpenter, *The Wonders of Geyser Land* (1878), reissued by Heister Dean Guie and Lucullus Virgil McWhorter as *Adventures in Geyser Land* (Caldwell, ID: Caxton Printers, 1935). Secondary accounts include Elliott West, *The Last Indian War: The Nez Perce Story* (Oxford: Oxford University Press, 2009) and Aubrey L. Haines, *The Yellowstone Story: A History of Our First National Park*, vol. 1, rev. ed. (Boulder: University Press of Colorado, 1996). Additional information on Native Americans in Yellowstone and the national parks more generally derives from Peter Nabokov and Lawrence Loendorf, *Restoring a Presence: American Indians and Yellowstone National Park* (Norman: University of Oklahoma Press, 2004); Philip Burnham, *Indian Country, God's Country: Native Americans and the National Parks* (Washington, D.C.: Island Press, 2000), Robert Keller and Michael Turek, *American Indians and National Parks* (Tucson: University of Arizona Press, 1998); and Mark Spence, *Dispossessing the Wilderness: Indian Removal and the Making of the National Parks* (New York: Oxford University Press, 1999).
2. Lee Whittlesey, *Gateway to Yellowstone: The Raucous Town of Cinnabar on the Montana Frontier* (Helena, MT: Two Dot, 2015).
3. Historian Aubrey Haines observes that according to military records, this encounter took place no later than August 17, when it is recorded that General Sherman left the park. Emma's account puts the meeting at August 23, but she was writing twenty-five years after the fact. See U.S. War

Department, *Reports of Inspection Made in the Summer of 1877 by Generals P. H. Sheridan and W. T. Sherman of Country North of the Union Pacific Railroad* (Washington, D.C.: GPO, 1878), 81–82. Also cited in West, *Last Indian War*, 212 and 219.

4. Cowan, *Reminiscence*, 166.

5. Ibid.

6. The term Nez Perce comes from early French fur traders and means "pierced nose." Despite the fact that the Nez Perce did not typically adorn themselves with nose piercings, the term was later picked up and used by English-speaking trappers and settlers. The actual name of the Nez Perce is Nimíipuu, meaning "the people." For this chapter, I use the term Nez Perce as it remains the most commonly used term and continues to be used by the Nez Perce Tribe as well.

7. This account of the Nez Perce War draws heavily from West, *Last Indian War*; Jerome H. Greene, *Nez Perce Summer 1877: The U.S. Army and the Ne-Me-Pu Crisis* (Helena: Montana Historical Society, 2000) and Bruce Hampton, *Children of Grace: The Nez Perce War of 1877* (New York: Holt, 1994).

8. See Dave Ballard, "Bird Canyon: First Fight of the Nez Perce Flight," *Wild West*, February 2001: 30-37.

9. Cowan, *Reminiscence*, 166.

10. Ibid., 167.

11. Ibid., 170–71.

12. Ibid.

13. Some accounts note that this man was not a deserter but had been honorably discharged.

14. *Helena Daily Independent*, extra edition, September 6, 1877.

15. This explanation comes from Elliott West, *The Last Indian War*, 220

16. Lucullus V. McWhorter, *Yellow Wolf: His Own Story* (Caldwell, ID: Caxton Printers, 1940).

17. Clarks Fork is a tributary of the Yellowstone River. Not to be confused with Clark Fork River, which flows into the Columbia.

18. The best work on the Nez Perce route through Yellowstone is Lee Whittlesey, "The Nez Perce in Yellowstone in 1877: A Comparison of Attempts to Deduce Their Route," *Montana: The Magazine of Western History* 57, no. 1 (Spring 2007): 48–55, and William L. Lang, "Where Did the Nez Perce Go?" *Montana: The Magazine of Western History* 40, no. 1 (Winter 1990): 14–29.

19. Accounts differ on this point. Elliott West says it likely happened while still in Yellowstone, forcing the Nez Perce to choose the Clarks Fork route. Other sources say they met the Crow only after the Nez Perce reached the Clarks Fork and began traveling north.

20. Estimates vary from 40 to 400.

21. There is no way to confirm if Chief Joseph actually uttered the words as

written or if they were embellished or even invented by the army translator himself. Historians note the rising popularity of romantic rhetoric in
describing Native Americans during this period. The army translator submitted the speech for publication in the nation's newspapers the following
day.

22. *Bozeman Avant Courier*, September 13, 1877.
23. *Bozeman Avant Courier*, September 20, 1877.
24. *Helena Daily Independent*, August 29, 1877.
25. Philetus W. Norris, *Report Upon the Yellowstone National Park, to the Secre-
    tary of the Interior, for the Year 1877* (Washington, D.C.: GPO, 1877), 842.
26. Kyle V. Walpole, "'Bivouac of the Dead': The Battle of Bennett Butte,
    Miles' Fight on the Clark's Fork Reexamined," *Annals of Wyoming* 71, no.
    1 (Winter 1999): 17–40. See also Nabokov and Loendorf, *Restoring a Pres-
    ence*, 234.
27. See Spence, *Dispossessing the Wilderness*.
28. Occasionally, a small number of individuals received permission to stay
    in national parks until they passed away or chose to move. In some cases,
    there was also an employment requirement with the NPS. This was the
    case for Indigenous people in Yosemite largely because they did not have
    a reservation option. For more on the Shenandoah case, see Darwin
    Lambert, *The Undying Past of Shenandoah National Park* (Lanham, MD:
    Roberts Rinehart, 1989), and Sue Eisenfeld, *Shenandoah: A Story of Con-
    servation and Betrayal* (Lincoln: University of Nebraska Press, 2015).

11. Selling Yellowstone

1. "A Road to Yellowstone Park," *New York Times*, January 15, 1882, 1. The
   announcement was also later picked up by regional news publications, including the *Bozeman Avant Courier*.
2. "Another 'Faber-Pusher' after Col. Norris," *Bozeman Avant Courier*, September 9, 1880, cited in Aubrey L. Haines, *The Yellowstone Story: A History
   of Our First National Park*, vol. 1, rev. ed. (Boulder: University Press of
   Colorado, 1996), 250.
3. "The Yellowstone Park—Its Management," *Bozeman Avant Courier*, September 30, 1880, cited in Haines, *Yellowstone Story*, 1: 250.
4. The blockhouse was razed in 1909, but the foundations can still be detected
   today.
5. Known as the Berthold Party.
6. "Wasting Public Money: Startling Deficiency in the Postal Department,"
   New York Times, December 11, 1879, 1.
7. Haines, *Yellowstone Story*, 1: 258.
8. Norris to Secretary Shurz, October 20, 1880, National Archives, Record
   Group 48 (Microcopy 62), cited in Richard Bartlett, *Yellowstone: A Wilderness Besieged* (Tucson: University of Arizona Press, 1985), 228.

9. See Allison to President Arthur, February 1, 1882, cited in Bartlett, *Yellowstone*, 236. Contrary to some accounts, Patrick Conger was not the brother of Michigan senator Omar Conger, nor the brother of Iowa congressman, Edwin H. Conger.

10. Lee Whittlesey, "The First National Park Interpreter: G. L. Henderson in Yellowstone, 1882–1902," *Montana: The Magazine of Western History* 46, no. 1 (Spring 1996): 28.

11. Patrick Conger, *Annual Report of the Superintendent of Yellowstone National Park* (Washington, D.C.: GPO, 1882).

12. Bartlett, *Yellowstone*, 126–27.

13. Ibid.

14. H. Duane Hampton, *How the U.S. Cavalry Saved Our National Parks* (Bloomington: Indiana University Press, 1971), 53-54. See also Mark Daniel Barringer, *Selling Yellowstone: Capitalism and the Construction of Nature* (Lawrence: University Press of Kansas, 2002), 24-25.

15. Bartlett, *Yellowstone*, 127.

16. Conger to Secretary Teller, November 6, 1882, National Archives, Record Group 48, cited in Bartlett, *Yellowstone*, 137–38.

17. Haines, *Yellowstone Story*, 1: 263

18. Ibid.

19. Lieutenant General Philip H. Sheridan, *Report of an Exploration of Parts of Wyoming, Idaho and Montana in August and September 1882* (Washington, D.C.: GPO, 1882), 17.

20. Ibid., 18.

21. Michael Punke, *Last Stand: George Bird Grinnell, the Battle to Save the Buffalo, and the Birth of the New West* (New York: Smithsonian Books, 2007), 117.

22. Cong. Rec., 47th Cong., 2d Sess., S71, cited in Bartlett, *Yellowstone*, 140.

23. "A Last Refuge," *Forest and Stream*, December 14, 1882, 381–82.

24. Bartlett, *Yellowstone*, 144.

25. George Grinnell, "The Park Grab," *Forest and Stream*, January 4, 1883, 441.

26. A full copy of the bill was printed as "The Senate Bill," *Forest and Stream*, January 11, 1883, 462. See also Haines, *Yellowstone Story*, 1: 268.

27. George Grinnell, "The Park Monopolists Checked," *Forest and Stream*, January 11, 1883, 461. Grinnell quotes a story from the *Bozeman Avant Courier* (January 7, 1883) as evidence of the wild game contract.

28. George Grinnell, "The People's Park," *Forest and Stream*, January 18, 1883, 481.

29. Ibid. A full copy of Secretary Teller's memo was reproduced in the January 18 issue of *Forest and Stream*.

30. Bartlett, *Yellowstone*, 145.

31. Haines, *Yellowstone Story*, 1: 272.

32. Ibid., 274.

33. Ibid., 277.

34. Haines offers several detailed first-hand accounts from early guests. See ibid., 274–91.

35. L. B. Carey to Halton Frank, first assistant postmaster general, February 2, 1884, National Archives, Department of the Interior, citied in Hampton, *U.S. Cavalry*, 66.

36. Ibid., 65.

37. Bartlett, *Yellowstone*, 142–43. See also Joseph Iddings, "Memorial to Arnold Hague," *Bulletin of the Geological Society of America* 29 (March 1918): 35–48.

38. See Lee Whittlesey, *Gateway to Yellowstone: The Raucous Town of Cinnabar on the Montana Frontier* (Guilford, CT: Two Dot, 2015).

39. Haines, *Yellowstone Story*, 1: 282.

40. Ibid., 297.

12. Sending in the Cavalry

1. Richard Bartlett, *Yellowstone: A Wilderness Besieged* (Tucson: University of Arizona Press, 1985), 148.

2. Details of the conflict are drawn from Bartlett, *Yellowstone*, 147–49.

3. Aubrey L. Haines, *The Yellowstone Story: A History of Our First National Park*, vol. 1, rev. ed. (Boulder: University Press of Colorado, 1996), 310.

4. Ibid., 271.

5. H. Duane Hampton, *How the U.S. Cavalry Saved Our National Parks* (Bloomington: Indiana University Press, 1971), 68.

6. Hampton, *U.S. Cavalry*, 72–73, and Haines, *Yellowstone Story*, 1: 321–23.

7. Bartlett, *Yellowstone*, 149.

8. Ibid., 117–18, 154. See also Kiki Leigh Rydell and Mary Shivers Culpin, *Managing the "Matchless Wonders": A History of Administrative Development in Yellowstone National Park, 1872–1965* (Yellowstone National Park, WY: NPS, Yellowstone Center for Resources, 2006), 25.

9. Hobart to Secretary Teller, July 11, 1884, cited in Rydell and Culpin, *"Matchless Wonders"*, 26.

10. Senators Wilson and Allison to Teller, July 3, 1884, cited in Bartlett, *Yellowstone*, 243.

11. George Grinnell, "Last Season in the Park," *Forest and Stream*, January 8, 1885, 461.

12. Details of this scam draw from the account in Haines, *Yellowstone Story*, 1: 315–16.

13. George Grinnell, "Remove the Superintendent," *Forest and Stream*, April 9, 1885, 201. Grinnell's argument continues with additional detail in *Forest and Stream*, April 23, 1885, 245.

14. Ibid.

15. Bartlett, *Yellowstone*, 246.

16. See Lee Whittlesey, "The First National Park Interpreter: G. L. Henderson

in Yellowstone, 1882–1902," *Montana: The Magazine of Western History* 46, no. 1 (Spring 1996): 26–41.

17. Bartlett, *Yellowstone*, 248.

18. This exchange is detailed in Michael Punke, *Last Stand: George Bird Grinnell, the Battle to Save the Buffalo, and the Birth of the New West* (New York: Smithsonian Books, 2007), 169, who cites the *Livingston Enterprise*, August 15, 1885; August 22, 1885, 2; and August 29, 1885, 3, on the Dogberry comment.

19. Hampton, *U.S. Cavalry*, 71. The committee also examined Native American education issues.

20. See "Letter W. H. Phillips on the Yellowstone Park," 49th Cong., 1st Sess., S. Exec. Doc. 51.

21. Bartlett, *Yellowstone*, 150.

22. Ibid.

23. Hampton, *U.S. Cavalry*, 75.

24. David Wear telegrams to Muldrow, August 13 and August 17, cited in Bartlett, *Yellowstone*, 249.

13. Showdown at Pelican Creek

1. For this story, major sources include the accounts by Emerson Hough, "Forest and Stream's Yellowstone Park Game Exploration," *Forest and Stream*, May 5, 1894, 377–79, and George Anderson, "Protection of Yellowstone National Park," in *Hunting in Many Lands* (New York: Field and Stream Publishing, 1895). Secondary sources include H. Duane Hampton, *How the U.S. Cavalry Saved Our National Parks* (Bloomington: Indian University Press, 1971), 113-29, and Aubrey L. Haines, *The Yellowstone Story: A History of Our First National Park*, vol. 2, rev. ed. (Boulder: University Press of Colorado, 1996), 60–65. Note that Hough and Haines differ as to whether Troike is listed as an army sergeant or a private. I follow Hough on this point.

2. The webbed version of snowshoes were considered too bulky and prone to clogging up with snow. The best account of the use of Norwegian snowshoes in Yellowstone is in Paul Schullery, *Yellowstone's Ski Pioneers: Peril and Heroism on the Winter Trail* (Worland, WY: High Plains Publishing, 1995).

3. Frederick Remington, "Policing the Yellowstone," in *Pony Tracks* (New York: Harper, 1898), 174–92.

4. Ibid.

5. Thomas Rust, *Watching over Yellowstone: The US Army's Experience in America's First National Park, 1886–1918* (Lawrence: University Press of Kansas, 2020).

6. Letter/report from Moses Harris to secretary of the interior, October 4, 1886, YNP Archives, cited in Hampton, *U.S. Cavalry*, 87. The report was

also printed as a government document: S. Exec. Doc. 40, 49th Cong., 2d Sess. (SN 2448), 1–5.

7. George Grinnell, "Indian Marauders," *Forest and Stream*, April 4, 1889, 209. In a later essay, Grinnell softened his rhetoric, saying he recognized Native Americans had rights but that such actions threatened the general welfare. He went on to suggest that it would be cheaper for the federal government to supply Indigenous peoples with "unlimited beef" than allow for subsistence hunting and burning to continue.

8. George Anderson, *Report of the Superintendent of Yellowstone National Park* (Washington, D.C.: GPO, 1894), 9–10. Also described in Anderson, "Protection of Yellowstone," 401.

9. They included Soda Butte Station near the northeast entrance, Snake River to the south, Riverside on the Madison, and Norris Station in the park's center. During the winter, there was an additional station in Hayden Valley. In the summer, additional stations were established in the Upper Geyser Basin, West Thumb, and near the Grand Canyon of the Yellowstone. See Anderson, "Protection of Yellowstone," 401.

10. Haines, *Yellowstone Story*, 2: 8–11.

11. As examples, Michael Punke identifies U.S. marshal William McDermott in Butte, Montana, and John Krachy, state game warden of Wyoming, based on letters sent from McDermott and Krachy to Superintendent Anderson, located in YNP Archives. See Michael Punke, *Last Stand: George Bird Grinnell, the Battle to Save the Buffalo, and the Birth of the New West* (New York: Smithsonian Books, 2007), 194.

12. Howell claimed that Noble exited the park through Jackson Hole. George Anderson and Emerson Hough both questioned this story, believing Noble probably left to deliver bison skins to buyers. See Hough, "Yellowstone Park Game Exploration," 378.

13. This figure comes from Captain Anderson's letter to the interior secretary, May 24, 1894, YNP Archives, Letters Sent, 58, cited in Punke, *Last Stand*, 198. The $1,000 figure is for a purported sale in London and is repeated by Anderson in his memoirs. See Anderson, "Protection of Yellowstone," 400.

14. Hough, "Yellowstone Park Game Exploration," 377

15. Anderson, "Protection of Yellowstone," 398.

16. Emerson Hough, "The Capture of Howell," *Forest and Stream*, March 31, 1894, 270.

17. Hough, "Yellowstone Park Game Exploration," 378.

18. Ibid.

19. Pronounced as "Huff," according to Paul Schullery, *Old Yellowstone Days* (Albuquerque: New Mexico Press, 2010), 136.

20. Punke, *Last Stand*, 187.

21. Ibid., 191.

22. George Grinnell, "Will Speaker Crisp Be Deceived?" *Forest and Stream*, February 23, 1893, 155.

23. Hough, "Yellowstone Park Game Exploration," 378.
24. Ibid.
25. Ibid.
26. Schullery, *Yellowstone's Ski Pioneers*, 110.
27. Ibid., 115. See also Haines, *Yellowstone Story*, 2: 205–7.
28. See Justice Edward White's majority opinion and Justice Henry Brown's dissent of *Ward v. Race Horse*, 163, U.S. 504 (1896), available at supreme. justia.com/cases/federal/us/163/504/case.html.
29. Brian Kalt, "The Perfect Crime," *Georgetown Law Journal* 93, no. 2 (2005): 675–88.

14. A Park for the People?

1. Ironically, the decision by Republican Party leaders to nominate Roosevelt for the vice presidency was intended to end his political career rather than advance it. The VP position was symbolic and held no significant power. The attempt to put Roosevelt "out to pasture" was in response to his unwelcome role in spurring war with Spain, including his decision to resign his position with the navy to form the Rough Riders in 1898. McKinley's assassination, of course, changed everything. See Edmund Morris's masterful biography, *The Rise of Theodore Roosevelt* (New York: Coward, McCann & Geoghegan, 1979).
2. The declaration of Grand Canyon National Monument in 1908 was the largest such declaration in terms of land area up to that point in American history.
3. The text of Roosevelt's speech is drawn from "The Corner Stone Was Laid," *Gardiner Wonderland*, April 30, 1903, cited verbatim in Lee H. Whittlesey and Paul Schullery, "The Roosevelt Arch: A Centennial History of an American Icon," *Yellowstone Science* 11, no. 3 (Summer 2003): 2-24.
4. John Yancey would continue to operate his hotel until his death on May 7, 1903, at age seventy-seven. His nephew continued the business until the building burned down in 1906.
5. Haynes gained the right to sell his wares in hotel gift shops in 1899. Some of the smaller operators of note include Ole Anderson, who held a permit to sell "encrusted articles from the springs to tourists," which he had been doing unofficially since 1883. In addition, George Henderson's daughter, Jennie Henderson Dewing, gained permission to sell items on the side in the post office during her term as postmistress, and the acting army medical officer received authorization to conduct a private practice within park boundaries as a service to guests and park employees.
6. Richard Bartlett, *Yellowstone: A Wilderness Besieged* (Tucson: University of Arizona Press, 1985), 175. Quote is by former YNP superintendent Edmund G. Rogers.
7. Harry W. Child II, *Montana Pioneers: The Huntley, Child and Dean Families*

(self-pub., 2009). A copy is available in the YNP Research Library. This account of Harry Child also draws from Mark Barringer, *Selling Yellowstone: Capitalism and the Construction of Nature* (Lawrence: University Press of Kansas, 2002), 34-83.

8. Barringer, *Selling Yellowstone*, 36.
9. Ibid., 31–32.
10. Bartlett, *Yellowstone*, 158–60.
11. In addition to Child, other investors included Edmund Bach, the brother of Child's other brother-in-law.
12. Bartlett, *Yellowstone*, 160.
13. Aubrey L. Haines, *The Yellowstone Story: A History of Our First National Park*, vol. 2, rev. ed. (Boulder: University Press of Colorado, 1996), 53.
14. Barringer, *Selling Yellowstone*, 39.
15. Haines, *Yellowstone Story*, 2: 119.
16. Background information derives from Ruth Quinn, *Weaver of Dreams: The Life and Architecture of Robert C. Reamer* (Gardiner, MT: Leslie and Ruth Quinn Publishers, 2004); Karen Wildung Reinhart, "Old Faithful Inn: Centennial of a Beloved Landmark," *Yellowstone Science* 12 no. 2 (Spring 2004): 5–22; and Ruth Quinn, "Overcoming Obscurity: The Yellowstone Architecture of Robert C. Reamer," *Yellowstone Science* 12 no. 2 (Spring 2004): 23–40.
17. Quinn, *Weaver of Dreams*, 7, 29, and 172.
18. Northern Pacific Railway Company, "Report of the Executive Committee," March 26, 1903, president's files, NPRR, Minnesota Historical Center, cited in Quinn, *Weaver of Dreams*, 8.
19. Haines, *Yellowstone Story*, 2: 107.
20. Ibid., 149–52.
21. Rudyard Kipling, *From Sea to Sea* (Garden City, NY: Doubleday, 1920), 100. Cited in Haines, *Yellowstone Story*, 2: 110.
22. Child kept the name of Wylie's business (the "Wylie Way") in order to keep his own involvement hidden and thereby avoid charges of monopoly control. Child's investment group forced Wylie to sell by manipulating his creditors and suppliers. For additional cover, Child registered the new corporation in West Virginia rather than Montana or Wyoming. See Barringer, *Selling Yellowstone*, 49–50.

15. Please Feed the Animals

1. John Pritchard to Ethan Hitchcock, February 14, 1902, Army-Era Records, Letters Sent 1887–1906, YNP Archives.
2. Mary Meagher, *The Bison of Yellowstone National Park* (Washington, D.C.: National Park Service, Scientific Monograph Number One, 1973), 21.
3. Aubrey L. Haines, *The Yellowstone Story: A History of Our First National Park*, vol. 2, rev. ed. (Boulder: University Press of Colorado, 1996), 70–71.

4. Haines, *Yellowstone Story*, 2: 81.
5. Yellowstone National Park, *Yellowstone Resources and Issues Handbook: 2018* (Yellowstone National Park, WY: GPO, 2018), 264–65.
6. Ibid.
7. Ibid., 91–92.
8. Haines, *Yellowstone Story*, 2: 93.
9. The practice of collecting and disseminating native cutthroat trout eggs continued until the 1950s. Yellowstone National Park, *Handbook*, 265.
10. Haines, *Yellowstone Story*, 2: 91. Haines refers to R.J. Fromm's 1939 study "An Open History of Fish and Fish Planting in Yellowstone National Park" (YNP Archives, 1939), which states that black spotted trout had disappeared from their native range in the Upper Madison River.
11. Yellowstone National Park, *Handbook*, 275.
12. Ibid., 276–77.
13. Charles Jesse Jones and Henry Inman, *Buffalo Jones: Forty Years of Adventure* (Topeka: Crane, 1899), cited in Paul Schullery, "Buffalo Jones and the Bison Herd in Yellowstone: Another Look," *Montana: The Magazine of Western History* 26, no. 3 (Summer 1976): 40–51.
14. Michael Punke, *Last Stand: George Bird Grinnell, the Battle to Save the Buffalo, and the Birth of the New West* (New York: Smithsonian Books, 2007), 220.
15. Ibid., 223.
16. Haines, *Yellowstone Story*, 2: 74.
17. Ibid., 75.
18. See Schullerly, "Buffalo Jones," 51.
19. Haines, *Yellowstone Story*, 2: 83.
20. Ibid., 84.
21. See Paul Schullery, "Yellowstone's Ecological Holocaust," *Montana: The Magazine of Western History* 47, no. 3 (Autumn 1997): 16–33.
22. Haines, *Yellowstone Story*, 2: 78.
23. Mary Meagher and Margaret E. Meyer, "On the Origin of Brucellosis in Bison of Yellowstone National Park: A Review," *Conservation Biology* 8, no. 3 (September 1994): 645–53.

16. The Ranger

1. The events covered in this chapter draw primarily from Horace Albright and Marian Albright Schenck, *Creating the National Park Service: The Missing Years* (Norman: University of Oklahoma Press, 1999), and Horace Albright's published memoir, *The Birth of the National Park Service: The Founding Years 1913–33* (New York: Howe Brothers, 1985).
2. Franklin Lane championed the dam project while serving as San Francisco city attorney and, later, as interior secretary. The dam was approved in 1913, but it is unclear if it ever became a point of contention between Lane and Mather. While many feared the dam in Yosemite would set a

precedent for weakening national park protections, it is ironic that Lane appointed the man most responsible for strengthening park protection in the years to come.

3. Robert MacFarland, head of the American Civic Association, apparently led an early campaign to create a park bureau within the Interior Department. See Aubrey L. Haines, *The Yellowstone Story: A History of Our First National Park*, vol. 2, rev. ed. (Boulder: University Press of Colorado, 1996), 284.

4. In 1961, Hawaii National Park split into two distinct parks: Haleakala National Park on the island of Maui and Hawaii National Park on the Big Island.

5. Horace M. Albright and Marian Albright Schenck, *Creating the National Park Service: The Missing Years* (Norman: University of Oklahoma Press, 1999), 139.

6. Robert Keiter, "The Greater Yellowstone Ecosystem Revisited," *University of Colorado Law Review* 91 (Winter 2020): 1–182.

7. Aubrey L. Haines, *The Yellowstone Story: A History of Our First National Park*, vol. 1, rev. ed. (Boulder: University Press of Colorado, 1996), 267–68.

8. After numerous mergers and reorganizations, the seven national forests included the Absaroka, Beartooth, Bonneville, Shoshone, Targhee, Teton, and Wyoming. After additional modifications, today the surrounding national forests are known as the Custer-Gallatin, Shoshone, Bridger-Teton, and Caribou-Targhee.

9. Robert W. Righter, *Crucible for Conservation: The Struggle for Grand Teton National Park* (Moose, WY: Grand Teton Association, 2008), 29.

10. Horace Albright, *The Birth of the National Park Service: The Founding Years 1913–33* (New York: Howe Brothers, 1985), 98. See also Righter, *Crucible for Conservation*, 31.

17. High Noon in Jackson

1. This chapter draws from interviews with Horace Albright conducted by his daughter, Marian Albright Schenck, and published as "One Day on Timbered Island: How the Rockefellers' Visit to Yellowstone Led to Grand Teton National Park," *Montana: The Magazine of Western History* 57, no. 2 (Summer 2007): 22–39, 93–94. I also rely on Horace Albright and Marian Albright Schenck, *Creating the National Park Service: The Missing Years* (Norman: University of Oklahoma Press, 1999), and Horace Albright's published memoir, *The Birth of the National Park Service: The Founding Years 1913–33* (New York: Howe Brothers, 1985). The major secondary source is the excellent book by Robert W. Righter, *Crucible for Conservation: The Struggle for Grand Teton National Park* (Moose, WY: Grand Teton Association, 2008), first published in 1982.

2. Horace Albright diary, July 13, 1926, Schenck Collection, quoted in Schenck, "Timbered Island," 25.

3. Kat Eshner, "John D. Rockefeller Was the Richest Man to Ever Live. Period," *Smithsonian*, January 10, 2017, www.smithsonianmag.com/smart -news/john-d-rockefeller-richest-person-ever-live-priod-180961705/.

4. See the highly readable account of Yellowstone's museum development in John Clayton, *Wonderlandscape: Yellowstone National Park and the Evolution of an American Cultural Icon* (New York: Pegasus Books, 2017), 96–114.

5. Righter, *Crucible for Conservation*, 32–34.

6. Ibid.

7. In fact, Sandell apparently had a wife elsewhere. See Samantha Ford, "Maud Noble Cabin," Jackson Hole Historical Society, accessed January 28, 2024, jacksonholehistory.org/page/21/?attachment_id.

8. Struthers Burt, "The Jackson Hole Plan," *Outdoor America* IX, no. 6 (November–December 1944): 4–7, 16.

9. Howard Markel, "The 'Strange' Death of Warren G. Harding," PBS, August 2, 2015, www.pbs.org/newshour/health/strange-death-warren -harding.

10. Schenck, "Timbered Island," 24.

11. Horace M. Albright, "Reminiscence" (unpublished manuscript, 1972), Schenck Collection, 6, quoted in Schenck, "Timbered Island," 28–29.

12. Albright, *National Park Service*, 164.

13. According to Righter, *Crucible for Conservation*, 46–47, Rockefeller probably already knew about the Jackson Hole Plan, as one of his associates met with Struthers Burt in New York City in December 1925 and again in March 1926 to discuss the idea of purchasing land for conservation purposes. Still, the summer tour with Albright seemed to be the catalyst for taking action.

14. This statement and the dialogue that follows derive from Albright's account recorded by Robert Cahn in Albright, *National Park Service*, 166.

15. Ibid.

16. John D. Rockefeller Jr. to Arthur Woods, February 16, 1927, Rockefeller Archives, New York, quoted in Righter, *Crucible for Conservation*, 48.

17. Ibid., 51.

18. Aubrey L. Haines, *The Yellowstone Story: A History of Our First National Park*, vol. 2, rev. ed. (Boulder: University Press of Colorado, 1996), 328.

19. Struthers Burt, *Jackson Hole Courier*, June 5, 1930, cited in Righter, *Crucible for Conservation*, 67.

20. Struthers Burt, "The Battle for Jackson Hole," *The Nation*, March 3, 1926, 225–27.

21. "Gun Play," *Time*, May 17, 1943, 21.

22. Righter, *Crucible for Conservation*, 114–15.

23. Westbrook Pegler, "Roosevelt-Ickes Grab Resembles Hitler Seizure," *El Paso Herald-Post*, May 1943.

24. Righter, *Crucible for Conservation*, 110–11.

25. *Jackson Hole Courier*, April 15, 1943, cited in ibid., 113. According to

Righter, the quote was printed on the papers' masthead from April 15 through August 16, 1943.

26. "Interview with Conrad Wirth," Ed Edwin, June 21, 1966, 10–12, Oral History Collection, Columbia University, cited in ibid., 118.

27. Albright, *National Park Service*, 332.

18. Please Don't Feed the Animals

1. Quoted in Jordan Fisher Smith, *Engineering Eden: A Violent Death, a Federal Trial, and the Struggle to Restore Nature in Our National Parks* (New York: Crown, 2016), 92.

2. Ibid.

3. Richard Sellars, *Preserving Nature in the National Parks: A History* (New Haven, CT: Yale University Press, 1997), 114–15.

4. Douglas Houston, *The Northern Yellowstone Elk: Ecology and Management* (New York: McGraw Hill, 1982), 17.

5. Robert Howe, "Addendum to Final Reduction Report 1961–1962, Northern Yellowstone Elk Herd," Yellowstone National Park, May 17, 1962, iv.

6. A visitor's disappearance in 1900 may also have been due to a bear attack, but as the body was never found, there is no evidence to confirm. See Aubrey L. Haines, *The Yellowstone Story: A History of Our First National Park*, vol. 2, rev. ed. (Boulder: University Press of Colorado, 1996), 86–87, 117–19.

7. Ibid., 79.

8. Smith, *Engineering Eden*, 94. Questions remain about the accuracy of early Yellowstone elk population estimates.

9. R. Gerald Wright, *Wildlife Research and Management in the National Parks* (Urbana: University of Illinois Press, 1992), 70. Also see Wendy Zirngibl, "Elk in the Greater Yellowstone Ecosystem" (master's thesis, Montana State University, 2006), 47.

10. Lane to Mather, May 13, 1918, cited in Sellars, *Preserving Nature*, 90.

11. Sellars, *Preserving Nature*, 88.

12. Alice Wondrak Biel, *Do (Not) Feed the Bears: The Fitful History of Wildlife and Tourists in Yellowstone* (Lawrence: University Press of Kansas, 2006), 22.

13. US Department of the Interior, "Yellowstone National Park," 1922, Box K-2, YNP Archives, cited in Biel, *Do (Not) Feed*, 4, 23.

14. Biel, *Do (Not) Feed*, 26.

15. Smith, *Engineering Eden*, 37–38.

16. Horace Albright, "The Lady Who Lost Her Dress," in *Yellowstone Bear Tales*, ed. Paul Schullery (Boulder, CO: Roberts Rinehart, 1991), 102–3.

17. Theodore Roosevelt to Lieutenant General S. B. M. Young, January 22, 1908, YNP Archives, quoted in Haines, *Yellowstone Story*, 2: 82.

18. Theodore Roosevelt, "Three Capital Books of the Wilderness," *The Outlook*, November 30, 1912, 712–15.

19. Smith, *Engineering Eden*, 54–55.

20. Wright, *Wildlife Research*, 72.

21. James Pritchard, *Preserving Yellowstone's Natural Conditions: Science and the Perception of Nature* (Lincoln: University of Nebraska Press, 1999), 178.

22. Sellars, *Preserving Nature*, 75–77.

23. Ibid., 113.

24. Albright to NPS director, November 8, 1928, YNP Archives, cited in Sellars, *Preserving Nature*, 87.

25. Smith, *Engineering Eden*, 60.

26. George Wright, Joseph Dixon, Ben Thompson, *Fauna of the National Parks of the United States* (Washington, D.C.: GPO, 1933).

27. William Rush, *Northern Yellowstone Elk Study* (Helena: Montana Fish and Game Commission, 1932).

28. Sellars, *Preserving Nature*, 115.

29. Richard Sellars, "Celebrating George Wright: A Retrospective on the 20th Anniversary of the GWS," *George Wright Forum* 17, no. 4 (2000): 46–50.

30. Ibid., 48–49.

31. Wright, *Wildlife Research*, 70.

32. Sellars, *Preserving Nature*, 118.

33. Biel, *Do (Not) Feed*, 41–42.

34. D. Bremer, "Individual Bear Injury Report," Yellowstone National Park, August 23, 1942.

35. Horace Albright, "New Orders for National Park Bears," *The Backlog: A Bulletin of the Camp Fire Club of America* 22, no. 1 (April 1945): 11, quoted in Biel, *Do (Not) Feed*, 50–51.

36. Biel, *Do (Not) Feed*, 65.

37. Conrad Wirth, "Wildlife Conservation and Management in the National Parks and Monuments," *Billings Gazette*, September 14, 1961, National Archives, RG 79.161, quoted in Sellars, *Preserving Nature*, 199.

38. Lemuel Garrison, Memorandum to District Managers, "Comments on Attached Report by E. J. Skibby," with attachment "Big Game Hunting in National Parks" and memoranda, 1960, YNP Archives, cited in Zirngibl, "Elk," 126–28.

39. "Northern Yellowstone Elk Herd Helicopter Census," April 2–4, 1962, YNP Archives.

40. Arnold Olsen, "Yellowstone's Great Elk Slaughter," *Sports Afield* 148 (October 1962): 40–41, 87–88.

41. Advisory Board on Wildlife Management, "Wildlife Management in the National Parks" (Washington, D.C.: WMI, 1962), 3.

42. Paul Schullery, *Searching for Yellowstone: Ecology and Wonder in the Last Wilderness* (Boston: Houghton Mifflin, 1997), 168–69.

43. Sellars, *Preserving Nature*, 247.

44. See Biel, *Do (Not) Feed*, 94.

45. Ibid., 95.

46. Ibid.
47. Ibid., 96.
48. Lee Whittlesey, *Death in Yellowstone: Accidents and Foolhardiness in the First National Park*, 2nd ed. (Lanham, MD: Roberts Rinehart, 2014), 44–49.
49. The best account of the trial and the larger issues surrounding it is Smith, *Engineering Eden*.
50. Biel, *Do (Not) Feed*, 107.
51. Ibid.

19. The Impossible Fire

1. Dan Rather, *CBS Evening News*, September 7, 1988.
2. Tom Brokaw, *NBC News*, September 7, 1988.
3. Hal K. Rothman, *Blazing Heritage: A History of Wildland Fire in the National Parks* (New York: Oxford University Press, 2007), 158.
4. Rothman, *Blazing Heritage*, 159.
5. Michael Yochim, *Protecting Yellowstone: Science and the Politics of National Park Management* (Albuquerque: University of New Mexico Press, 2013), 40.
6. Holly McKinney's account of these events is drawn from a personal interview conducted on December, 7, 2017, in Grand Teton National Park, Wyoming.
7. Henry, personal interview, December 9, 2017, Paradise Valley, Montana.
8. Rothman, *Blazing Heritage*, 160.
9. Throughout this chapter, specific starting dates for named fires in and around Yellowstone are drawn from Yellowstone National Park press releases and Jeff Henry, *The Year Yellowstone Burned: A Twenty-Five Year Perspective* (Lanham, MD: Taylor Trade Publishing, 2015).
10. The monthly rainfall data for June reached only 79 percent of normal.
11. Eventually the Shoshone Fire and Red Fire would come together to threaten the Grant Village campground and visitor's complex.
12. Covering some 400,000 acres, it became one of the two largest fires in the Yellowstone region during the summer of 1988. See Henry, *Year Yellowstone Burned*, 37.
13. Rothman, *Blazing Heritage*, 160.
14. Not to be confused with Yellowstone's superintendent, who was the final authority at the park, the chief ranger's primary duty was law enforcement.
15. In a controversial move, Sholly decided to land and try to save the cabin from the oncoming flames. He took two crew members with him, even though they only had two emergency fire shelters for three people. The shelters were essentially small foil-like tents made for one person and designed to reflect the intense heat as a person lay on the ground and the fire rushed over the top. Caught in advancing flames and forced to deploy the shelters, Sholly and crew member Kristen Cowan shared one while the third crew member, John Dunfee, took the other. The three survived the

firestorm and saved the cabin, but the wisdom of Sholly's decision remains controversial. See Henry, *Year Yellowstone Burned*, 45–46.

16. Rothman, *Blazing Heritage*, 160.
17. Henry, *Year Yellowstone Burned*, 41, 45.
18. Rothman, *Blazing Heritage*, 160.
19. Ibid.
20. Henry, *Year Yellowstone Burned*, 65.
21. Ibid., 66.
22. Ibid., 65. Grant Village would be reopened after the fire passed through, only to be closed a second time on August 20, known as Black Saturday.
23. This story comes from Henry, personal interview, December 9, 2017.
24. CBS followed on August 22. See Dan Whipple, "Yellowstone Ablaze: The Fires of 1988," Wyoming Historical Society, June 27, 2015, www.wyohistory.org/encyclopedia/yellowstone-ablaze-fires-1988. National newspapers, including the *Los Angeles Times*, began coverage of fires across the western United States on July 18, though *The New York Times* and *The Washington Post* would not begin giving serious front-page coverage until September 11 and September 8, respectively.
25. Two human casualties were recorded due to the fires, but these occurred outside the boundaries of Yellowstone National Park. Rothman, *Blazing Heritage*, 163.
26. Bob Barbee interview, "Summer of Fire," Retro Report, *New York Times*, September 2, 2013, www.nytimes.com/video/us/100000002411859/summer-of-fire.html. Quote also found in Rocky Barker, *Scorched Earth: How the Fires of Yellowstone Changed America* (Washington, D.C.: Island Press, 2005), 209.
27. Associated Press, "Yellowstone Fires Grow," *Livingston Enterprise*, August 23, 1988, quoted in Barker, *Scorched Earth*, 209.
28. McKinney, personal interview, December 6, 2017.
29. Rothman, *Blazing Heritage*, 162.
30. Henry, *Year Yellowstone Burned*, 86.
31. Rothman, *Blazing Heritage*, 162.
32. Henry, *Year Yellowstone Burned*, 169.
33. Stanley Mott, interview by Brian Rooney, *ABC Nightly News with Peter Jennings*, August 30, 1988.
34. Jim Carrier, "Burn, Baby, Burn," *Denver Post*, August, 28, 1988, 13A.
35. Barbee interview, "Summer of Fire."
36. Rothman, *Blazing Heritage*, 164–65.
37. Barker, *Scorched Earth*, 5.
38. Roger O'Neill, *NBC News with Tom Brokaw*, September 7, 1988. The subsequent dialogue is drawn from transcripts of the same telecast.
39. Henry, *Year Yellowstone Burned*, 224–26.
40. Ibid., 227. Eyewitness Rocky Barker also made note of a large firebrand or burning log sailing overhead; see Barker, *Scorched Earth*, 217.
41. McKinney, personal interview, December 6, 2017. Rocky Barker

corroborates this event, as he was one of the reporters who ducked out; see Barker, *Scorched Earth*, 215.

42. Henry, *Year Yellowstone Burned*, 240.
43. Ibid., 243.
44. "Summer of Fire," Retro Report, *New York Times*, September 2, 2013, www.nytimes.com/video/us/100000002411859/summer-of-fire.html.
45. Henry, *Year Yellowstone Burned*, 272.
46. Federal managers had to guarantee that prescribed fires would never get out of control before lighting them. One can imagine the hesitancy that might accompany the decision to use prescribed fire under such conditions. See Rothman, *Blazing Heritage*, 182, and Yochim, *Protecting Yellowstone*, 71–72. However, in the mid-1990s, the use of prescribed fire increased under a new rationale having less to do with ecology and more with reducing the risks to firefighters.
47. Mary Ann Franke, *Yellowstone in the Afterglow: Lessons from the Fires* (Mammoth Hot Springs, WY: National Park Service, 2000), 40–42.
48. Yochim, *Protecting Yellowstone*, 70.

20. The Bad Wolf Returns

1. Renée Askins, *Shadow Mountain: A Memoir of Wolves, a Woman, and the Wild* (New York: Doubleday, 2004), 195.
2. Quotation in Hank Fischer, *Wolf Wars: The Remarkable Inside Story of the Restoration of Wolves to Yellowstone* (Guilford, CT: Globe Pequot Press, 1995), 161–62.
3. Erin Ward, *The Gray Wolf Under the Endangered Species Act (ESA): A Case Study in Listing and Delisting Challenges*, R46184, Congressional Research Service (January 27, 2020): 8.
4. Aldo Leopold, "Review of *The Wolves of North America* by S. F. Young and E. A. Goldman, 1944," *Journal of Forestry* 42 (1944): 928–29.
5. Doug Houston, *The Northern Yellowstone Elk: Ecology and Management* (New York: Macmillan, 1982).
6. Bob Barbee, "Barbee Retrospective: Yellowstone Wolf Reintroduction," *Yellowstone Science* 13, no. 1 (Winter 2005): 5.
7. Dixon Merritt, "World's Greatest Animal Criminal Dead", USDA Press Release (January 17, 1921), 1-4. An abridged version apparently ran in several local papers, including in the *Dillon Examiner*, as cited in Fischer, *Wolf Wars*, 18.
8. Fischer, *Wolf Wars*, 67.
9. Ibid., 68.
10. The exhibit was funded by the National Endowment for the Humanities.
11. Fischer, *Wolf Wars*, 68.
12. Ibid., 100.
13. Typically they would be relocated to zoos or captive-wildlife centers.
14. This was unconfirmed but was the most likely outcome according to those

involved. See Carter Niemeyer, *Wolfer: A Memoir* (Boise, ID: Bottlefly Press, 2012), 160.

15. "Wolf Compensation Trust," Defenders of Wildlife, accessed January 30, 2024, defenders.org/sites/default/files/publications/full_list_of_payments_in_the_northern_rockies_and_southwest.pdf.

16. Douglas W. Smith and Gary Ferguson, *Decade of the Wolf: Returning the Wild to Yellowstone* (Guilford, CT: Lyons Press, 2012), 25. See also Michael Yochim, *Protecting Yellowstone: Science and the Politics of National Park Management* (Albuquerque: University of New Mexico Press, 2013), 123.

17. Askins, *Shadow Mountain*, 127.

18. This account relies heavily on a personal interview with Val Asher, October 8, 2018, in Bozeman, Montana.

19. Niemeyer offers the full account of this entertaining tale in his memoir, *Wolfer*.

20. Bob Barbee, "Barbee Retrospective," 5.

21. Fischer, *Wolf Wars*, 162–63.

22. Douglas Smith et al., "Wolf Restoration in Yellowstone: Reintroduction to Recovery," *Yellowstone Science* 24, no. 1 (2016): 4.

23. Ward, *The Gray Wolf Under the Endangered Species Act*, 17.

24. Douglas W. Smith, Daniel R. Stahler, and Daniel R. MacNulty, eds., *Yellowstone Wolves: Science and Discovery in the World's First National Park* (Chicago: University of Chicago Press, 2020), chap. 15, loc. 5431 of 10504, Kindle.

25. Montana instigated a second winter hunting season for elk in 1976.

26. Douglas Smith et al., *Yellowstone Science* 13 no. 1 (2005): 23.

27. Smith et al., "Wolf Restoration," 7. According to the Park Service, as of December 2021, an estimated ninety-five wolves in eight packs inhabited Yellowstone. See "Gray Wolf," Yellowstone National Park, National Park Service, last updated April 25, 2023, nps.gov/yell/learn/nature/wolves.htm.

28. "Elk on the Northern Range," Yellowstone National Park, National Park Service, December 14, 2023, www.nps.gov/yell/learn/nature/elk.htm.

29. Grizzlies and black bears are fierce predators but are generally too slow to capture elk, deer, moose, pronghorn, or bighorn sheep. Wolves, in contrast, can hunt down all of these species.

30. Daniel MacNulty et al., "The Challenge of Understanding Northern Yellowstone Elk Dynamics after Wolf Reintroduction," *Yellowstone Science* 24, no. 1 (2016): 26.

31. Wyoming Fish and Game Dept. et al., *Wyoming Gray Wolf Monitoring and Management 2020 Annual Report* (Cheyenne: Wyoming Game and Fish Department, 2019), 23.

32. P.J. White et al., "Yellowstone After Wolves: Environmental Impact Statement Predictions and Ten-Year Appraisals," *Yellowstone Science* 13 no. 1 (2005): 37

33. Wyoming Fish and Game Dept. et al., *Wyoming Gray Wolf*, 19.

34. National Agricultural Statistics Service, Mountain Regional Field Office, *Wyoming Sheep and Lamb Loss Report*, USDA, 2016.
35. USDA, *Death Loss in U.S. Cattle and Calves Due to Predator and Non-Predator Causes, 2015* (Fort Collins, CO: USDA, 2017).
36. White et al., "Yellowstone After Wolves," 38.
37. White et al., "Yellowstone After Wolves," 37.
38. Margaret A. Wild, N. Thompson Hobbs, Mark S. Graham and Michael W. Miller, "The Role of Predation in Disease Control: A Comparison of Selective and Nonselective Removal on Prion Disease Dynamics in Deer," *Journal of Wildlife Disease* 47, no. 1 (2011): 78-93.
39. Aaron Bott, "Keeping Wolves at the Door: The Economic Benefits (and Struggles) of Wolves in Yellowstone," *Good Nature Travel*, December 12, 2019, www.nathab.com/blog/economic-benefits-of-wolves-in-yellowstone/.
40. John Duffield, Chris Neher, and David Patterson, *Wolves and People in Yellowstone: Impacts on the Regional Economy* (Bozeman, MT: Yellowstone Park Foundation, 2006); and John Duffield, Chris Neher, and David Patterson, "Wolf Recovery in Yellowstone Park: Visitor Attitudes, Expenditures, and Economic Impacts," *Yellowstone Science* 16, no. 1 (2008): 20–25.
41. Smith et al., *Yellowstone Wolves*, loc. 6763–69 of 10504, Kindle.
42. Currently, about 25 to 30 percent of Yellowstone wolves have radio collars.
43. For an example of his many works, see Rick McIntyre, *The Rise of Wolf 8: Witnessing the Triumph of Yellowstone's Underdog* (Vancouver, B.C.: Greystone Books, 2019).
44. See, for example, Thomas McNamee, *The Killing of Wolf Number Ten: The True Story* (Westport, CT: Prospecta Press, 2014).

21. Where the Buffalo Roam

1. The Stephens Creek facility is located near Gardiner, Montana.
2. The account of restoring Yellowstone bison to Fort Peck is based in part on personal interviews with Robert Magnan, Jonny BearCub, and Helen Bighorn conducted in Wolf Point, Montana, on October 12, 2018. Interviews were also conducted with Jonathan Proctor, in Denver, Colorado, on April 17, 2017, and Rick Wallen, in Gardiner, Montana, on October 10, 2018. As always, any factual errors expressed are my own.
3. But as noted in chapter 15, poaching was the primary cause of the bison population decline. In hindsight, it turned out that predator eradication, supplemental feeding, and the development of a captive herd were not necessary.
4. Mary Meagher, *The Bison of Yellowstone National Park, Scientific Monograph 1* (Washington DC: National Park Service, 1973). See also P. J. White, Rick Wallen, and David Hallac, eds., *Yellowstone Bison: Conserving an American Icon in Modern Society* (Yellowstone National Park: Yellowstone Association, 2015), 48.

5. The discussion of *Brucela abortus* draws from White, Wallen, and Hallac, *Yellowstone Bison*, 19–43.

6. Associated Press, "Montana to Allow Shooting of Bison," *New York Times*, November 20, 1989, 12.

7. Clearly, not all members of Wyoming's legislature were against wolf restoration, but for years, a majority of state-level politicians led the opposition. The same was true in Montana regarding Yellowstone bison. A majority of Montana state politicians fought against allowing free-roaming bison outside the park. However, some were supportive, including governors Schweitzer and Bullock, both of whom advocated for bison conservation on tribal lands.

8. Associated Press, "Montana to Allow," 12.

9. Joe Kolman, "Bison Management," Montana Legislative Services Division, 2013; Helen Thigpen, "Jurisdiction over Wild Bison from Yellowstone National Park," Montana Legislative Services Division, 2013.

10. Jean Lavigne, "Where the Buffalo Roam: Boundaries and the Politics of Scale in the Yellowstone Region," *GeoJournal* 58 (2004): 288.

11. Todd Wilkinson, "The Killing Fields Await Yellowstone Bison Once Again," *Mountain Journal* (December 15, 2017).

12. According to APHIS, disease transfer was achieved by researchers at Texas A&M University under controlled conditions in the early 1990s. See "Brucellosis and Yellowstone Bison," APHIS, USDA, accessed January 30, 2024, www.aphis.usda.gov/animal_health/animal_dis_spec/cattle /downloads/cattle-bison.pdf.

13. National Academy of Sciences, Engineering, and Medicine, *Revisiting Brucellosis in the Greater Yellowstone Area* (Washington, D.C.: National Academies, 2020).

14. White, Wallen, and Hallac, *Yellowstone Bison*, 24. See also J. C. Rhyan et al., "Pathogenesis and Epidemiology of Brucellosis in Yellowstone Bison: Serologic and Culture Results from Adult Females and Their Progeny," *Journal of Wildlife Diseases* 45, no. 3 (July 2009): 729–39.

15. Greater Yellowstone Coalition to MacWilliams Cosgrove Smith Media Consultants, January 5, 1998, 3–4, cited in Lavigne, "Where the Buffalo Roam," 290.

16. B. Schumaker et al., *A Risk Analysis of* Brucella abortus *Transmission Among Bison, Elk, and Cattle in the Northern Greater Yellowstone Area* (Davis: University of California, Davis, 2010), cited in White, Wallen, and Hallac, *Yellowstone Bison*, 26.

17. U.S. Fish and Wildlife Service, *Bison and Elk Management Step-Down Plan, National Elk Refuge, Grand Teton National Park, Wyoming* (Lakewood, CO: DOI, USFWS, NPS, 2019).

18. White, Wallen, and Hallac, *Yellowstone Bison*, 23.

19. The Intertribal Bison Cooperative was initially called the Intertribal Bison Council.

20. Hila Shamon et al., "The Potential of Bison Restoration as an Ecological Approach to Future Tribal Food Sovereignty on the Northern Great Plains," *Frontiers in Ecology and Evolution* 10 (January 28, 2022), www.frontiersin.org/articles/10.3389/fevo.2022.826282/full.

21. Daniel Glick, "Bison Homecoming," *National Wildlife Magazine*, September 19, 2012.

22. Garrit Voggesser, "When History Matters: The National Wildlife Federation's Conservation Partnerships with Tribes," *Western Historical Quarterly* (Autumn 2009): 349–57.

23. Lavinge, "Where the Buffalo Roam," 289.

24. Magnan, personal interview, October 12, 2018.

25. James Holt, "Yellowstone Buffalo Hunt: A Native Perspective," Buffalo Field Campaign, May 31, 2018, YouTube video, www.youtube.com/watch?v=9GfoDhk6WGY.

26. Department of the Interior, *DOI Bison Report: Looking Forward, Natural Resource Report NPS/NRSS/BRMD/NRR—2014/821* (Fort Collins, CO: National Park Service, 2014), 1.

27. National Park Service, *Call to Action* (Washington, D.C.: DOI, 2010).

28. Brett French, "Yellowstone Looks at New Bison Plan, Less Focus on Slaughter," *AP News*, January, 29, 2022, apnews.com/article/business-health-travel-environment-montana-02700b3c128c573d316be7b2b6e5033e.

29. Kolman, "Bison Management"; Thigpen, "Jurisdiction over Wild Bison."

30. Darrell Ehrlick, "Montana Gov. Gianforte, AG Knudsen Try to Stop American Prairie's Bison through Political Pressure," *Great Falls Tribune*, December 6, 2021.

22. Legacies

1. Marybeth Shea, "Discovering Life in Yellowstone Where Nobody Thought It Could Exist," National Park Service, Parks in Science History Series, last updated November 8, 2018, nps.gov/articles/thermophile-yell.htm.

2. A. R. Crimmins et al., *Fifth National Climate Assessment* (Washington, D.C.: U.S. Global Change Research Program, 2023).

3. Jim Robbins, Thomas Fuller, and Christine Chung, "Flood Disaster at Yellowstone Is Just the Start," *New York Times*, June 16, 2022, A1.

4. Julie Turkewitz, "National Parks Struggle with a Mounting Crisis: Too Many Visitors," *New York Times*, September 27, 2017.

5. NPT Staff, "National Parks a Magnet for International Visitors," *National Parks Traveler*, November 3, 2016; *Seattle Times* staff, "More Chinese Tourists Visiting Yellowstone National Park Area," *The Seattle Times*, November 8, 2015. The Chinese government began to develop their own system of national parks on the Tibetan Plateau, based in part on the Yellowstone model. See Associated Press, "Yellowstone Park to be the Blueprint for

Chinese Network of National Parks," *South China Morning Post*, November 11, 2019.

6. National Park Service, *Yellowstone National Park Visitor Use Study: Summer 2016* (Washington, D.C.: USDOI, 2017).

7. Morgan Warthin, "Yellowstone's Mount Doane Name Changes to First Peoples Mountain; Action Taken to Remove Offensive Name from America's First National Park," press release, Yellowstone National Park, June 9, 2022.

8. Nate Hegyi, "Native Americans Propose Change to Yellowstone Landmark Names," National Public Radio, September 9, 2018, www.npr.org /2018/09/09/641330248/native-americans-propose-change-to-yellowstone -landmark-names.

Index

© Sara Cawley

RANDALL K. WILSON, PhD, is a professor of environmental studies at Gettysburg College, where he teaches courses on environmental history, policy, natural resource management, and the geography of the American West. He is a former Fulbright fellow, and his book *America's Public Lands: From Yellowstone to Smokey Bear and Beyond* was named an Outstanding Academic Title from *Choice Reviews* and won the John Brinkerhoff Jackson Prize from the American Association of Geographers.